Vaiṣṇavism:

Contemporary Scholars Discuss
the Gauḍīya Tradition

Vaiṣṇavism:

Contemporary Scholars Discuss the Gauḍīya Tradition

Steven J. Rosen, editor

MOTILAL BANARSIDASS PUBLISHERS
PRIVATE LIMITED • DELHI

First Indian Edition: Delhi, 1994
First FOLK Books Edition: 1992

ISBN: 81-208-1235-7

Also available at:

MOTILAL BANARSIDASS

41 U.A. Bungalow Road, Jawahar Nagar, Delhi 110 007
120 Royapettah High Road, Mylapore, Madras 600 004
16 St. Mark's Road, Bangalore 560 001
Ashok Rajpath, Patna 800 004
Chowk, Varanasi 221 001

PRINTED IN INDIA

BY JAINENDRA PRAKASH JAIN AT SHRI JAINENDRA PRESS,
A-45 NARAINA, PHASE I, NEW DELHI 110 028
AND PUBLISHEDBY NARENDRA PRAKASH JAIN FOR
MOTILAL BANARSIDASS PUBLISHERS PVT. LTD.,
JAWAHAR NAGAR, DELHI 110 007

Table of Contents

Preface — *i*
Foreword / *Edward C. Dimock, Jr.* / *vii*
Introduction / **1**
Gauḍīya Vaiṣṇavism / *A.N. Chatterjee* / **7**
The Vedic Literature / *Michael Witzel* / **19**
The Rāmāyaṇa / *H. Daniel Smith* / **27**
Mahābhārata / *Alf Hiltebeitel* / **49**
Bhāgavata-purāṇa / *Clifford Hospital* / **61**
Kṛṣṇa in the Performing Arts / *John Stratton Hawley* / **77**
Bhakti Poetry / *Richard Davis* / **89**
Biographies of Śrī Caitanya / *Tony Stewart* / **101**
Saṁpradāya of Śrī Caitanya / *William Deadwyler* / **127**
Sahajiyā Tradition / *Robert Sailley* / **141**
Gauḍīya Vaiṣṇavism in the Modern World / *Charles Brooks* / **149**
The Bengal of Śrī Caitanya Mahāprabhu / *Richard Eaton* / **167**
Śrī Caitanya's Pilgrimage to the South / *David Kinsley* / **179**
Śrī Caitanya's Tour of Vraja / *Alan Entwistle* / **189**
The Glories of Rādhā-kuṇḍa / *Mohan Gautam* / **199**

Jagannātha Purī / *Frédérique Marglin* / **207**
Vaiṣṇavism and Christianity / *Klaus Klostermaier* / **219**
Sādhana Bhakti / *Joseph O'Connell* / **229**
Personalism vs. Impersonalism / *O.B.L. Kapoor* / **239**
Acintya Bhedābheda / *Shrivatsa Goswami* / **249**
Sonic Theology / *Guy Beck* / **261**
Mysticism, Madness and Ecstasy / *June McDaniel* / **283**
Rasa Theology / *Gerald Carney* / **295**
Kṛṣṇa-līlā / *David Haberman* / **305**
Rādhā: Beloved of Vraja / *Eric Huberman* / **327**
Index / **347**

Preface

The religious path known as Vaiṣṇavism can be described as devotion to Kṛṣṇa, Rāma, Viṣṇu, or any of his divine incarnations. It is seen by its adherents as a type of monotheism in which worship of a personal God is the focus. In sheer numbers, it prevails as the leading religious system over Śaivism, Śāktism, and the many other paths commonly associated with Hindu *dharma*.

There are ancient scriptural texts that form the basis of this religion: the Vedas, the Purāṇas, the Mahābhārata (including the Bhagavad-gītā), the Rāmāyaṇa, and the writings of the great *ācāryas*. Some of these texts date back to at least the second century B.C., with an oral tradition that goes back to antiquity. Vaiṣṇavism is known as *sanātana dharma*, or "the eternal function of the soul," and it is also referred to as *bhakti-yoga*, or "the devotional path through which one can link with the supreme." The religion of Vaiṣṇavism is expressed in various ways throughout the Indian subcontinent.

One such expression is *Gauḍīya* Vaiṣṇavism. This is a form of the religion that began in sixteenth-century Bengal with the great *avatāra*/saint Śrī Caitanya Mahāprabhu, but which participates in the much older form of the tradition. It is called *gauḍīya* because Śrī Caitanya proclaimed his mission in the region that was then known as Gauḍadeśa. This extended throughout the southern side of the Himalayan Mountains and the northern part of the Vindhyā Hills, which is called Āryāvarta, or the land of the Āryans. This portion of India is divided into five parts or provinces: Sārasvata (Kashmir and the Punjab), Kānyakubja (Uttar Pradesh, including the modern city of Lucknow), Madhya-gauḍa (Madhya Pradesh), Maithila (Bihar and part of Bengal), and Utkala (a portion of Bengal and all of Orissa).

The celebrated ancient capital of Gauḍadeśa, or Gauḍa, was situated in what is now the modern district of Maldah. The seat of the Sena dynasty, this capital was eventually transferred to the ninth or central island on the western side of the Ganges at Navadvīpa, which is now known as Māyāpura (although at that time it was called Gauḍapura). Caitanya Mahāprabhu appeared in that area, and so Gauḍīya Vaiṣṇavism naturally took on that nomenclature to commemorate the event.

There are scholars, however, who argue that since the term "Gauḍīya" refers only to Bengal or Gauḍadeśa, it is not appropriate for the religious tradition. The ideological aspect of Gauḍīya Vaiṣṇavism, they say, extends beyond the designated parameters of Gauḍadeśa, and so they prefer to call the tradition "Caitanya Vaiṣṇavism" or "Caitanyaite Vaiṣṇavism," which is apparently more accurate in the sense that the religion is based on the inspiration and teaching of Śrī Caitanya—not on a geographical location.

Addressing this objection, there is a scholarly contingent who have pointed out that there is a material Gauḍa (the land in and around Bengal) and a spiritual one—Gauḍa maṇḍala—which is the "sacred space" of the same area. This conception is reinforced by the etymology of the word "Gauḍīya," for the primary noun, *guḍa* (anglicized as *gur*), which literally refers to molasses, or sweetness, can be extended to the adjective *gauḍa*, the name of the country associated with Gauḍīya Vaiṣṇavism. This is a grammatical, poetic, and even spiritual derivation, since Gauḍīya Vaiṣṇavism is viewed by its practitioners as the culmination of a long spiritual evolution, like the proverbial icing on the cake. Adherents consider Gauḍīya Vaiṣṇavism the cap on the Vaiṣṇava tradition—it adds the necessary "sweetness" to an already delicious recipe. The secret ingredient, say the Gauḍīyas, is Śrī Rādhā, for it is her sweet devotion to Kṛṣṇa that embodies the essence of Gauḍīya Vaiṣṇavism. Her *madhu-sneha*, or honey-like love, was not fully revealed before the time of Śrī Caitanya Mahāprabhu.

Rabindranath Tagore and others have written about the profusion with which sugarcane grows in Bengal, and that the sweetness of that region overflows into many aspects of everyday life, not least in the indigenous religion. Such writers are quick to point out that Gauḍīya Vaiṣṇavism, unlike other forms of Vaiṣṇavism, emphasizes *mādhurya*, or the sweet love of God, as opposed to *aiśvarya*, or God's majesty. Consequently, the title "Gauḍīya" has deeper implications than one might at first suspect. Ordinary or conventional understanding (*sāmānya*) of terms such as Gauḍīya tells only one side of the story; but the tradition gives another perspective, one that is infused with a spiritual sensibility (*pāramārthika*).

A real Gauḍīya Vaiṣṇava, then, is not one who merely lives *in* Gauḍa but one who lives *for* gauḍa: one who lives for the sweetness associated with the love and worship of Rādhā and Kṛṣṇa. A Gauḍīya Vaiṣṇava is one who is absorbed in Rādhā-Kṛṣṇa and in Caitanya Mahāprabhu. This is eloquently expressed by Kṛṣṇadāsa Kavirāja Gosvāmī in his *Caitanya-caritāmṛta* (*Ādi-līlā*, 1.19):

ei tina ṭhākura gauḍīyāke kariyāchena ātmasāt
e tinera caraṇa vandoṅ, tine mora nātha

"The three deities of Vṛndāvana [Śrī-Śrī Rādhā-Madana-mohana, Śrī-Śrī Rādhā-Govinda, and Śrī-Śrī Rādhā-Gopīnātha] have absorbed the heart and soul of the Gauḍīya Vaiṣṇavas [followers of Śrī Caitanya]. I worship their lotus feet, for they are the lords of my heart." According to this verse, a Gauḍīya Vaiṣṇava is one who is *ātmasāt*—"surrendered to" or "absorbed in"—the three primary forms of Kṛṣṇa, which are now situated in Vraja and Jaipura.

Conceptually, these deities embody *sambandha*, *abhidheya*, and *prayojana*, which refer, respectively, to one's relationship with the Lord, activities that enhance that relationship, and the perfection of that relationship. One who becomes absorbed in these activities is a Gauḍīya Vaiṣṇava.

Madana-mohana was established by Sanātana Gosvāmī and he is thus the principal teacher of *sambandha-jñāna*; Rūpa Gosvāmī established the Govinda deity and so he is the *ācārya* of *abhidheya-jñāna*; Madhu Paṇḍita established the worship of the Gopīnātha deity, but he shares his position as *prayojana ācārya* with Raghunātha dāsa Gosvāmī, who is the teacher par excellence of the ultimate mystery: the love of Rādhā-Kṛṣṇa.

Gauḍīya Vaiṣṇavas perceive the culminating objective of esoteric Vedic hymns—and of all religion—as devotional service to Kṛṣṇa as Madana-mohana, Govinda, and Gopīnātha. Madana-mohana is glorified as that feature of God that is so indescribably beautiful that he even charms Cupid, the god of love; Govinda is the Lord as the pleaser of the senses, and in this conception he even brings pleasure to the docile cows, who graze peacefully in his creation; and Gopīnātha gives insight into his internal *līlā* as the lord of the *gopīs*, the cowherd girls who are his greatest devotees.

According to the Gauḍīya Vaiṣṇavas, these three conceptions of the deity help the spiritual aspirant progress from the material conception of life to the spiritual pursuit—and finally to the perfection of *rasa*, or one's relationship with God. This is the goal of Gauḍīya Vaiṣṇavism, and its achievement coincides with the realization of Caitanya Mahāprabhu as the essence of these three deities combined. Mahāprabhu is seen as a saint, as an *avatāra*, and as the source of all *avatāras*. To Gauḍīya Vaiṣṇavas, he is the combined essence of Rādhā and Kṛṣṇa. Thus, his place in Vaiṣṇava history is unique.

This uniqueness has been noted by outsiders as well, and while they do not often articulate the exact position of the Gauḍīyas, they do convey a sense of what Caitanya Mahāprabhu means for the Indian subcontinent. For example, Christian theologian John Moffitt expressed his view of Śrī Caitanya in *Journey to Gorakhpur: An Encounter with Christ Beyond Christianity* (1972:129, 135-36):

> If I were asked to choose one man in Indian religious history who best represents the pure spirit of devotional self-giving, I would choose the Vaishnavite saint Chaitanya, whose full name in religion was Krishna Chaitanya, or "Krishna Consciousness." Of all the saints in recorded history, East or West, he seems to me the supreme example of a soul carried away on a tide of ecstatic love of God. This extraordinary man, who belongs to the rich period beginning with the end of the fourteenth century, represents the culmination of the devotional schools that grew up around Krishna. . . .
>
> When he debated with philosophers, Chaitanya could be as scholarly as the great teachers, or *acharyas,* of old—Shankara, Ramanuja, and Madhva. . . .In his teaching of the path of devotion to the general public, however, he continued to stress utter devotion to the Lord. This devotion was to be developed through hearing and singing the name and glories of Krishna, meditating on his form and attributes and his life on earth, worshiping him in his temples, resigning oneself to his will, trying to do only what would please him, serving his devotees, and showing kindness to all beings.
>
> Chaitanya aroused in his followers a flood of passionate love of God. As a result, a wave of religious fervor swept over Bengal and Orissa. Yet despite the emotionalism his teachings brought about, he himself was extremely strict. He closely watched the morals of those who were around him, sternly reproving any form of self-indulgence. . . .Though literally worshiped by thousands as Krishna himself, he led a simple and even austere life.
>
> Chaitanya delighted intensely in nature. It is said that, like St.

> Francis of Assisi, he had a miraculous power over wild beasts. His life in the holy town of Puri is the story of a man in a state of almost continuous spiritual intoxication. Illuminating discourses, deep contemplation, moods of loving communion with God, were daily occurrences.

Śrī Caitanya, with his deep, emotional love for Kṛṣṇa, revitalized the Brahma-Mādhva *saṁpradāya*, the ancient Vaiṣṇava lineage with which he was aligned. He gave the sweet joy of love to a ready and waiting theistic tradition. This tradition was primed by the great *ācāryas*, who taught their followers to prepare the Lord's plate with awe and reverence, to add the spices of disciplined life, the herbs of scriptural knowledge, and the condiments of devotion. But Mahāprabhu's contribution was the sweet love of *mādhurya-rasa*. It is this that makes one a true *rasika bhakta*, a devotional connoisseur. And this brings us straight back to our gastronomic metaphor: the guḍa (*gur*) conception. When *gur* is moist and syrupy it is used like jam—spread on breads, confections, and cereals. The sweet nectar of Śrī Caitanya's love for Rādhā and Kṛṣṇa and the process he set in place for developing that love was spread on the Brahma-Mādhva line like the most tasty jam, giving the bread of Vaiṣṇavism a new flavor indeed. Through Śrī Caitanya, Gauḍīya Vaiṣṇavism gave "heart" to a seemingly "heady" religious tradition. And it is the heart—more than any other part of the spiritual anatomy—to which Gauḍīya Vaiṣṇavism speaks.

Foreword

*Edward C. Dimock, Jr.**

This is an unusual and significant book in many ways. Its primary purpose is to elucidate the depth and complexity of the form of religious devotionalism that is old but still powerful in India, and with not a little strength in this country and in Europe as well: it is that form of the worship of Kṛṣṇa as himself the full divine being rather than as an *avatāra* or manifestation of Viṣṇu. This view took its modern and most effective shape under the influence of the revivalist Caitanya, who lived in Bengal between 1486 and 1533 of the present era.

Not least interesting is the very fact that such a book as this, not by any means an introduction, can be written. A quarter of a century ago, there were two or three books in English on the subject (by Melville Kennedy and the great scholar S.K. De, for example), a few in Bengali, and a few translations of varying purpose and success, to be had. Today, you will find on library shelves not only books by most if not all the writers represented in the present book, but hundreds more in a wide variety of languages. Some of these books are devotional in nature, for the popularity of the religious attitudes propounded has grown greatly both within and without India. Many of them are also objective scholarship, for scholars who have nothing to do with the devotionalism of the movement have found its study rewarding. This will be readily seen: the scholars represented in this book each approach the matter from an idiosyncratic point of view, and collectively manage only a hint of its complexity.

---

* Edward C. Dimock, Jr. is Distinguished Service Professor in the Department of South Asian Languages and Civilizations at the University of Chicago and Chairman of the American Institute of Indian Studies.

Eaton's enlightening remarks, for example, give us with unusual clarity a picture of the Islamic environment in which Caitanya's movement grew; Hiltebeitel takes on the often asked but rarely answered question as to whether the various Kṛṣṇas mentioned throughout the texts are one or many; Stewart finds in the biographical texts of Caitanya still larger questions of the nature of religious biography; Marglin's information about the temple environment in Purī are both perceptive and humanizing. Each of the others could be singled out as well. Several scholars want to address the relationship between religious and esthetic experience, which is one of the most important contributions that Rūpa Gosvāmī and the other theologians of the movement made. And as a suggestion as to the breadth of the stimulus, there is room for speculation as to the extent to which the doctrine of *acintya bhedābheda*, i.e. "simultaneous difference and non-difference, which is beyond cognition," posits a tolerance for ambiguity to which the closest parallel in western thought seems to be quantum theory.

Each of the contributors has thus added in a very special way a bit of color; the result is a pointillist painting in which the effect is both what it seems and not what it seems. It is, as I said, not a book for a beginner in the study of Vaiṣṇavism, though that beginner will find from place to place in the conversations hints as to how to turn back to the beginning. One could do a lot worse than to turn back to one of Kinsley's books, for instance.

Steven Rosen, the editor, has done the contributors a great favor, for by choosing the interview format he has not only taken much of their labor on himself but has managed to keep a conversational style and thus a moderately unassuming prose moving well. He has brought together an overview of a highly technical subject as interpreted by acknowledged experts in the field, thus informing further the already informed and, it is to be hoped, stimulating the uninformed to inform themselves of a highly rewarding system of thought and instructive slice of religious history.

As Mr. Rosen has pointed out in his introductory statement, Norvin Hein has mentioned with his usual acumen the creative tensions that fortunately exist between belief and the history of belief, and the reader will find some of that tension in these pages. But just as one can easily (and many do) debate eternally the status of the passages in *Isaiah* 7 and 9 that foretell the coming of Christ as proof or accident or interpolation, so one can argue about passages in the Vedas and Purāṇas that do or do not foretell the coming of Caitanya and its significance. Prediction and antiquity both of course lend validity to any position, and it is not difficult to understand that such discussions are sometimes heated.

This book fortunately has more light than heat, though there will be questions as to the interpretation of terms: "Veda" means something quite specific to the Indic scholar, and something a little broader to the devotee; "Yavana" simply means "Greek" (Ionian) to the philologist, and in many interpretations carries with it little despective weight (similarly the term *mleccha* early and often refers merely to those barbarians who do not speak Sanskrit, and more specific connotations do not appear until later); and *hindu*, a term used in the *Caitanya-caritāmṛta*, seems merely to separate from more normal society a group of people from another culture, rather than to denote a particular religious system.

But all these matters and a great many more are discussed in the book, and discussed with far more authority than I possess and wit than I can muster. This is a good book. I have learned a lot from it, and I am glad that Steven Rosen decided to do it. It makes me want the fuller studies, and I think it will have that effect on you too.

Introduction

I first came into contact with Gauḍīya Vaiṣṇavism in 1972, when I met devotees of the International Society for Krishna Consciousness (ISKCON), and specifically when I met their spiritual master and the society's founder, His Divine Grace A.C. Bhaktivedanta Swami Prabhupāda. Soon thereafter, Śrīla Prabhupāda became my teacher and through him I came to see the richness of the tradition. I have been deeply interested, academically and as a practitioner, ever since. The storehouse of Vaiṣṇava literature is something of which I cannot get enough, and my practice of Gauḍīya Vaiṣṇavism continues to be a central part of my life.

Interest in both scholarship and devotion has led me to compile this book. Generally, these two approaches sit on opposite sides of the fence. Adherents can be doctrinaire, clinging to established formulas and exercising little consideration for the findings of contemporary scholars. These findings, however, can be useful in the lives of practitioners by confirming their faith. Archaeological and historical research has indeed shed light on the tradition, as, for example, in the findings at Dvārakā and in the textual analysis of the scriptures. Even when such research points away from traditional conclusions, it prompts in the believer a deeper reflection upon his or her faith. Consequently, I decided to interview *scholars*—people who have dedicated much time and energy to researching the tradition of Gauḍīya Vaiṣṇavism and yet who are removed enough to give a balanced, clinical assessment. However, it should be noted that just as the practitioner may at times miss the forest for the trees, as they say, the academic is beleaguered by a similar disadvantage—without adhering to a tradition and experiencing it emotionally, there are areas of it that cannot be penetrated, areas that remain outside the domain of intellectual analysis.

In *Vaiṣṇavism: Contemporary Scholars Discuss the Gauḍīya Tradition*, the reader will find a merging of interests, exploring perspectives from both sides of the fence. I have tried to represent the orthodox practitioner, the "insider's" point of view, while the academics being interviewed represent the realm of "outside" scholarship. The line between practitioner and scholar is not as distinct as one might at first suspect. At the American Academy of Religion Conference of 1982, McGill University's Katherine Young spoke of "insiders" and "outsiders" as dated concepts. Today, she said, insiders often approach their tradition by drawing upon historical and philosophical studies, and they use the language of modern academic disciplines. Outsiders, for their part, examine the tradition with all the vehemence of a convert, often living in Vraja, studying Bengali, Sanskrit, and related languages. The conclusion is clear: it takes devotion and discipline to be a scholar, and learning and proficiency are required to be a steady devotee.

My fascination for both devotion and scholarship impels me to believe that devotees and scholars can learn from each other, and encourage each other to achieve the goals of their respective endeavors. As Norvin Hein has written in his foreword to my *Six Gosvāmīs of Vṛndāvana*:

> Ultimately, the contenders need each other. We even dare to say that scholars need the orthodox and do well to give thoughtful attention to their work. They need the histories and clear statements of approved doctrine that sectarian literati produce. For the scholarly historians of religious movements they are indispensable definers of the identity of the groups whose history the scholars trace. The writings of the learned orthodox comprise the usual starting point of scholars. The orthodox are the persons most attentive to a scholar's work, a major readership for his writings and, as such, often, they are his bread and butter. They are for him a natural community of professional conversation, emotionally supportive to him however uneasy his citizenship at times may be. . . .Likewise the contributions of scholars are needed even by traditionalistic sects to which they are most irritating. The irksome scholar is, at the same time, a giver of new life. Sects survive social exigencies and continue their existence through successive overturns in culture only if they are able to review their histories and discover new meanings that are relevant to the problems of the

> new age. Sects that can solve only the problems of the past and can apply only the solutions of the past, become fossil religions. Happy is the faith that has scholars of its own, but even the criticism of external scholarship has often produced the regeneration in a faith. Scholar and priest are a bickering pair but they illustrate the biblical proverb that friend sharpens friend as iron sharpens iron. In restive but effective combination, they lead religious movements down paths of vigorous life, prospering each other and the faiths that can accommodate both.

Vaiṣṇavism: Contemporary Scholars Discuss the Gauḍīya Tradition is a series of informal interviews with some of the most important people in Hindu studies and South Asian religions. Scholars from institutions of learning such as Yale, Harvard, and the Sorbonne, have given their time and knowledge to make the transcribed conversations enlivening, educational, and academically useful. The book provides a forum for scholars of the tradition to discuss what is most interesting to them, their current research, and the application of their findings. This should be useful to practitioners and should not be ignored by them.

The book is divided into three sections. The first part deals with the literature and the historical development of the Gauḍīya tradition. The second part is concerned with the pilgrimage sites connected with Śrī Caitanya Mahāprabhu and his associates, and delineates Śrī Caitanya's life in relation to the sacred places he visited. The third addresses the theology and practice of the tradition. More than one of the interviewed scholars have stated that they could foresee using this work as a textbook for their courses in Religious Studies, Hinduism, Southeast Asia, and Eastern Philosophy, because it presents an overview of this complex tradition.

Each chapter has a theme, and I attempt to make the discussion interesting for students and laymen by asking questions that highlight the subject and its more intriguing aspects. Each interviewee answers my questions with thoughtful and often enlightening perspectives. Although I have conducted scores of hours of interviews, what you find in this book is the essence of all of those conversations.

The book opens with an overview—the social implications of the Gauḍīya tradition—by **A.N. Chatterjee** (Delhi University). This conversation sets the groundwork for the book by defining Vaiṣṇavism and exploring related issues.

Michael Witzel (Harvard University) discusses the Vedic roots of the Gauḍīya tradition. This chapter elucidates the Indian scriptural tradition in general and shows the much-debated links to modern-day Vaiṣṇavism.

H. Daniel Smith (Syracuse University) discusses the *Rāmāyaṇa* and explains its ramifications for the Vaiṣṇava movement.

The *Mahābhārata,* including the *Gītā,* is the subject of my discussion with **Alf Hiltebeitel** (George Washington University), who explains its importance for the Gauḍīya lineage.

Clifford Hospital (Queens Theological School, Canada) elaborates upon the *Bhāgavata Purāṇa* and the philosophical underpinnings of the Vaiṣṇava *saṁpradāya.*

John Stratton Hawley (Barnard College, Columbia University) tells us about Kṛṣṇa in the performing arts, showing how Gauḍīya practices developed around dramatic performances.

Bhakti poetry is discussed by **Richard Davis** (Yale University), who shows the similarity between Kṛṣṇa poetry and that of the Śākta tradition.

Tony K. Stewart (North Carolina State University), discusses Caitanya Mahāprabhu's biographies and other important Gauḍīya texts of the sixteenth and seventeenth centuries.

William Deadwyler (Temple University, ISKCON) explores the debate regarding Śrī Caitanya's lineage. Is the Gauḍīya *sampradāya* a new sect, or can it legitimately be aligned with the Brahma-Mādhva-*saṁpradāya*?

The Sahajiyā tradition is sensitively dealt with by **Robert Sailley** (Sorbonne), who explains controversial aspects of the Gauḍīya movement and later heterodox traditions.

Chuck Brooks (New York University) discusses Gauḍīya Vaiṣṇavism in the modern world, and analyzes it in its contemporary context. In discussing modern Vaiṣṇavism, Dr. Brooks naturally includes ISKCON, viewing the institution with a critical eye and scholarly distance. This ends Part One.

Part Two begins with a discussion of Bengal in the time of Śrī Caitanya. **Richard Eaton** (University of Arizona) examines the Muslim government of medieval Bengal in the light of Arabic and Persian source materials, showing the administration's influence on Gauḍīya Vaiṣṇavism.

A survey of Śrī Caitanya's tour of South India by **David Kinsley** (McMaster University, Ontario) explains the implications of Mahāprabhu's travels and analyzes the places associated with his journey.

A conversation with **Alan Entwistle** (University of Washington) about Śrī Caitanya's tour of Vraja includes an elaborate description of the holy places connected with Kṛṣṇa *līlā.*

M.K. Gautam (University of Leiden, the Netherlands) discusses his research in Rādhā-kuṇḍa, explaining its sacred status for Gauḍīya Vaiṣṇavas.

Jagannātha Purī is discussed with **Frédérique Marglin** (Smith College), who explains the roots of the Vaiṣṇava involvement with the Jagannātha deity. Her explanation of Ratha-yātrā finishes this section with eloquence and style.

Part Three opens with a discussion of Vaiṣṇavism and Christianity with **Klaus Klostermaier** (University of Manitoba, Canada), in which he explores Gauḍīya Vaiṣṇavism in the light of Western religious ideals.

Joseph T. O'Connell (St. Michael's College, University of Toronto) discusses the practice of Vaiṣṇava *sādhana,* both in terms of formal ritual and on the level of spontaneous mysticism.

O.B.L. Kapoor (University of Allahabad) deals with the traditional philosophical debate about the nature of the absolute—is God impersonal or personal? Dr. Kapoor explains the Gauḍīya perspective.

Shrivatsa Goswami (Śrī Chaitanya Prema Saṅsthāna, Vṛndāvana) elaborately outlines *acintya-bhedābheda* and Mahāprabhu's contribution to Indian philosophy, showing its multi-faceted implications.

Guy Beck (Louisiana State University) examines *mantra* meditation and the chants, prayers, and songs that are distinctive to Gauḍīya practices.

Mysticism and "divine madness" are discussed with **June McDaniel** (University of Charleston, South Carolina), as she explains the emotional and ecstatic content of the tradition.

Rasa theology is fully explained by **Gerald Carney** (Hampden-Sydney College, Virginia) with examples from classical Indian aesthetics and the writings of the Gosvāmīs.

Aṣṭa-kālīya-līlā, the eight-hour day of Rādhā and Kṛṣṇa, is explored by **David Haberman** (Williams College). His recounting of pilgrimage experiences enables one to understand how the divine *līlā* can be seen in everyday life.

The last section is reserved for Śrīmātī Rādhārāṇī, because Śrī Rādhā is considered the ultimate worshipable deity by Gauḍīya Vaiṣṇavas. **Eric Huberman** (Columbia University) thoroughly explains her ontological position and her importance for the tradition.

While this book presupposes a basic knowledge of Indian religion, and especially Vaiṣṇavism, I have tried to arrange the chapters in such a way that a layman can grasp the contents. Still, some of the conversations are at times technical and a bit rigorous for those unacquainted with the tradition. But one who swims through this ocean will learn much about Indian religion and, more specifically, the nectarean waves of Kṛṣṇa *bhakti.* Thus, I feel the book will be useful to students of Hinduism and to scholars of various disciplines.

While many of the chapters are short (this book is hardly exhaustive), I have purposely constructed the interviews to treat each major area of Gauḍīya Vaiṣṇavism, although, naturally, some of the interviews overlap. They are meant to entice the reader to further explore the tradition and its literature. Such an exploration has enriched my life and can work the same miracle, I am certain, for my readers. Although my own initial exposure to Gauḍīya Vaiṣṇavism was through ISKCON, the scholars I have interviewed have no affiliation with that organization. The only exception is William Deadwyler, who maintains a leading position in the movement.*

I have conducted the interviews more as "conversations," for as I became more experienced, I found that scholars often preferred a give-and-take discussion by encouraging me to express my own ideas. This openness and informal format led to more fruitful exposition. In editing, I have tried to retain the conversational tone of the original dialogue, purposely avoiding stylistic homogenization.

I hope the readers will appreciate, as I do, the effort taken by these distinguished scholars, who have shared their research to make this book a reality. More importantly, I hope you will appreciate the profundity and beauty of the Gauḍīya Vaiṣṇava tradition, which their scholarly research has helped to reveal. Such research was initially sparked by Edward C. Dimock, Jr., the doyen of Bengali Vaiṣṇava studies in the West, who, as Wendy Doniger wrote in her Foreword to the 1989 Edition of *The Place of the Hidden Moon*, "has been an inspiration to an entire generation of Indologists." *Vaiṣṇavism: Contemporary Scholars Discuss the Gauḍīya Tradition*, then, is an outgrowth of his initial endeavor, which opened up a field that many have since explored. Some of the scholars in this book, for example, have personally studied under Professor Dimock, and the others, if from afar, have also benefited from his now legendary work. In this sense, he has made the present volume possible. For this, and for his gracious Foreword, we are deeply grateful.

—Steven J. Rosen,
New York, 1992

* Guy Beck was, at one time, affiliated with the Sanskrit Department of the Bhaktivedanta Book Trust, and Eric Hubermen was a long-time associate of the movement.

Gauḍīya Vaiṣṇavism

A.N. Chatterjee

Amarnath Chatterjee has been teaching history in Shaheed Bhagat Singh College (University of Delhi) for more than a decade. His special field is Caitanyaite Vaiṣṇavism, its historicity and theology, a subject on which he has written extensively, contributing to numerous academic journals. After travelling throughout Bengal and Orissa, conducting research and lecturing at noted institutions of learning, he wrote Sri Krishna Chaitanya: An Historical Study of Gaudiya Vaishnavism *(New Delhi, Associated Publishing Company, 1986), which was well-received by scholars and laymen. Dr. Chatterjee is presently working on a massive historical study, in Bengali, tentatively titled,* Śrī Caitanya-O-Madhya Yuge Vaiṣṇava Saṁskṛti.

SR: I understand that the word "Hindu" is a misnomer. There is no such word in the original Vedic texts. It was introduced by Persians, perhaps in the twelfth or thirteenth century, to describe the people who lived near the Indus River, who held a vast array of religious beliefs. Consequently, one is hard-pressed for a singular definition of Hinduism. So, my first question would be this: How would *you* define Hinduism, and how does it relate to Vaiṣṇavism?

Dr. Chatterjee: This is quite a complicated question. As you suggest, Hinduism baffles all attempts at a clear-cut definition. Still, we shall try. Let me begin by amending some of your ideas. I can say that according to reliable sources the term "Hinduism" was introduced by the Arabs in the eighth century A.D. while referring to those who followed the prevailing religion of India, that is, primarily, the worship of Viṣṇu and Śiva. All forms of Hinduism are essentially based on the teachings of the *Vedas*—scriptures that contain eternal truths regarding the nature of Ultimate Reality. Although, by "Hinduism," we do not exactly mean a set of abstract philosophical theories or a host of religious dogmas, one might venture to say a few words about some of its cardinal principles: the non-duality of Godhead, the divinity of the soul, the unity of existence, and the harmony of religions.

SR: Well, people will explain these things in various ways. It is still quite vague. By your definition, though, Vaiṣṇavism, or the worship of Viṣṇu, or Kṛṣṇa, is, in a sense, another type of Hinduism—and it usually *is* identified in that way. But, then again, so is *any* religion that originates in India. According to the tradition itself, however, Vaiṣṇavism constitutes *sanātana dharma,* or the original, eternal religion of the soul. All other forms of Vedic religion must culminate in Vaiṣṇava *dharma.* This is the idea. *Karma-kāṇḍa. jñāna-kāṇḍa*—it should all lead to the ultimate path, which is *bhakti-mārga.* And this is the worship of God with love and devotion. Now, when one reaches that level, there are various forms of Vaiṣṇavism, various approaches. You have Rāmānuja's system, Madhva's system, and, ultimately, you have Caitanya's system. So let us proceed by asking a related question: Where does a study of Vaiṣṇavism begin? If we accept the Gauḍīya premise that it sort of culminates in Caitanya Mahāprabhu and his religion of *bhakti,* divine love, should we begin with a study of his life and teachings?

Dr. Chatterjee: Well, it would be more advantageous to go to the beginning, to make a study of ancient Indian history. Historians usually report that the theological ideas that developed in India from 200 B.C. to 400 A.D. were quite revolutionary. This is the period during which the theistic approach was emphasized. With the growth of the concept of the Absolute or the Universal Soul in the philosophy of the Upaniṣads, there also developed, at this time, the idea of the trinity of gods, that is, Brahmā, Viṣṇu, and Śiva, or Maheśvara. While Brahmā was considered the creator, Viṣṇu was considered the supreme preserver, and Maheśvara was considered the ultimate destroyer. This arrangement worked in harmony with the universal conception of creation, preservation and destruction. Of these three manifestations of the absolute, Viṣṇu and Śiva gained an immense following and consequently the Vaiṣṇavas and the Śaivites came to be the two main sects of what we now know of as Hinduism.

Historians say that with the development of Vaiṣṇavism in ancient India, a gradual shift occurred in Hinduism itself. From the domain of rituals, emphasis was getting directed toward "*bhakti*," that is, toward establishing a personal relationship with a personal God. In this way, monotheistic ideas came to prominence in Hinduism, along with devotion (*bhakti*) and divine grace (*prasāda*). This, of course, is the historical unveiling of something that is, in fact, an eternal principle. And if one studies Vedic texts, one can see evidence of these things from the earliest periods. But one should be willing to study with an open mind.

SR: Yes. If we go to the later "Vedic" texts, especially the Purāṇas, we can get a more holistic perspective. It may be said that practitioners are not critical or objective—but sometimes scholars are not critical or objective either. If we want to truly understand Gauḍīya or Caitanyaite Vaiṣṇavism, we must approach our study of the tradition with a certain degree of deference—proper respect. Otherwise, we will not be able to see the forest for the trees, as they say. Now, in addition to this, we need to be objective. To properly study any religious tradition, I think, one must secure an appropriate balance of devotion and scholarship. Too much devotion will bias us in one way, and the cold academic approach will bias us in another. The best devotees have also been scholars, like Jīva Gosvāmī, for example. And the best scholars, if they really want to penetrate the tradition, will also have to be devotees, at least to some extent.

So I agree with you—I would say that we should critically examine the Vedic literature, and the tradition as it sees itself, to see what light, if any, it sheds on Gauḍīya Vaiṣṇavism. Hermeneutics, or the study of philosophical interpretation, is important, too, especially since early Vedic texts can be interpreted in a number of ways. This leads to the conception of *guru*, since, for a disciple, it will be the *guru's* interpretation, or the interpretation of the *saṁpradāya*, that determines just how a disciple reads a given text. . .

Dr. Chatterjee: Yes. All of these things are important, and they all have their place in determining absolute reality. Ultimately, though, everything is traced to the Vedic texts; but, as you say, it all depends upon how one interprets them. For example, Caitanya's descent (*avatāra*) is predicted throughout the scriptures. But not everyone will accept this.

SR: Still, Mahāprabhu's descent *is* alluded to in the Mahābhārata; the Śvetāśvatara Upaniṣad; the Muṇḍaka Upaniṣad; the Kṛṣṇa-yāmala; the Brahma-yāmala; the Ananta-saṁhitā; the Tantras; the Purāṇas. It's in so many sections of the Vedic texts—certainly it's there in the *smṛti.* The *Bhāgavatam,* for example, is a prime source of inspiration for the Gauḍīya Vaiṣṇava, and Mahāprabhu's whole method of worship can be adduced from this scripture. The *Bhāgavatam* endorses Kṛṣṇa as the highest God—the supreme—and it gives the whole rationale behind his love dalliances with the *gopīs,* the cowherd maidens. A life of devotion to Kṛṣṇa, which was promoted by Śrī Caitanya, finds its original substantiation in the *Bhāgavatam.* So to see the importance of Mahāprabhu and for the verification of his teachings, one needs to have a thorough overview of the original texts upon which his movement is based.

Dr. Chatterjee: Definitely. This is a significant point. Especially the prediction in *Bhāgavata Purāṇa,* or *Śrīmad Bhāgavatam,* about Śrī Caitanya. This is a central text for Gauḍīya Vaiṣṇavas. But the later literature is equally important—there is a great deal of biographical material on the life of Śrī Caitanya Mahāprabhu and his associates. Some scholars like to say that the material is only of a hagiographical nature, but there is a great deal of corroboration—historically verifiable. There are so many texts. Caitanya's contemporaries were aware of his *specialness,* shall we say, and they consequently were quite careful when documenting his activities for future generations. The main biographies were Murāri Gupta's diary; the two lengthy works by Kavi Karṇapūra; Vṛndāvana dāsa's *Caitanya-bhāgavata;* Kṛṣṇadāsa's *Caitanya-caritāmṛta;* Locanadāsa's *Caitanya-maṅgala*—these were considered the most important biographies of Śrī Caitanya. So these works give us a wealth of information, not only about Caitanya's life and doctrine, but also about Bengali culture in general and about spirituality in particular.

In addition to these, there were many other works—Govindadāsa's diary and Svarūpa Dāmodara's, although this latter one is no longer extant; Jayānanda's *Caitanya-maṅgala;* Prabodhānanda Sarasvatī's work; Īśvara dāsa's *Caitanya-bhāgavata;* and Mādhava's *Caitanya-vilāsa.* So there is so much literature. And then there is the second and third generation work. After the Six Gosvāmīs. You have, of course, the mammoth *Bhakti-ratnākara,* which is a veritable storehouse of information. It is really endless. An historian would really have his hands full. [laughter] The details are there. Little is left to the imagination. . .

SR: As an historian, which of these biographies do you think is most important? I'm not necessarily talking about philosophy, now. Which one do you think gives us the clearest historical picture of Caitanya and his movement? Which is the most reliable from a strictly empirical point of view?

Dr. Chatterjee: Well, we would have to look for those authors who were first-hand witnesses. Who was actually there? Among the biographers, Murāri was Caitanya's old friend from Navadvīpa—one of his closest friends. So the early episodes of Caitanya's life, as recounted by Murāri Gupta, are considered quite reliable. Kavi Karṇapūra, when he was only a child, had the good fortune to meet Caitanya, and Karṇapūra's biographical accounts are quite thorough, dealing with Caitanya's entire lifespan. Prabodhānanda met Caitanya in South India, soon after Caitanya had taken *sannyāsa,* so he also gives a first-hand account. Svarūpa Dāmodara and Raghunātha Dāsa, too, are considered reliable, since they kept diaries while they were in the master's presence, and Vṛndāvana dāsa and Kṛṣṇadāsa Kavirāja both base their works on these diaries, at least in part. Vṛndāvana dāsa also consulted Nityānanda, one of Caitanya's closest associates. So, you can say that there is much to gain from all of these accounts, and, when taken as a whole, they give quite an illuminating picture of Caitanya Mahāprabhu's life and times. The comparatively recent study, by the late B.B. Majumdar, deserves mention. In his exhaustive *Caitanya Cariter Upādān,* he considers all of these early biographies at length. He creates a synthesis which is very useful, especially for a scholarly study. . .

SR: Unfortunately, that work only exists in Bengali, and English readers are thus denied access to it. To my knowledge, the only English edition of a full-length biographical account is Kṛṣṇadāsa Kavirāja's *Caitanya-caritāmṛta.* This has been translated, with explanatory notes, by Śrīla A.C. Bhaktivedanta Swami Prabhupāda. Seventeen volumes! It is a wonderful study. . .

Dr. Chatterjee: Yes. It was a fantastic contribution. Very thorough, although it accentuates the devotional point of view. There are other English works, not quite at that standard, but they are also useful. O.B.L. Kapoor's study is quite good. Debnarayan Acharyya—his work is also good. And the work of Bhakti Pradip Tirtha Swami, Sambidananda, and Sannyal—these are good English studies. There are many scholars now—more and more studies are coming out. People are becoming increasingly aware of Caitanyaite Vaiṣṇavism and its potential contribution to society.

SR: Why? Why are they becoming aware of the movement? This interests me. How did people first find out about the movement, and how does it continue to grow? To what do you attribute the growth of the Caitanya movement?

Dr. Chatterjee: Do you mean initially or today?

SR: Both. Let's start with the initial proliferation of the movement and then we can discuss why it is spreading so rapidly today.

Dr. Chatterjee: Okay. First of all, I would say that there were six factors that contributed to the initial growth and longevity of Caitanya's movement in India, and I explain these at length in my book on Śrī Caitanya's life. Briefly, the six factors can be expressed in this way: (1) The beginnings of the movement were initiated by Caitanya himself in Bengal, Orissa, and South India; (2) There was subsequent growth in Bengal under the leadership of some of Caitanya's closest followers, such as Nityānanda and Advaita; (3) There were important leaders in Bengal in the post-Chaitanya period, like Jāhnavā, the wife of Nityānanda, her son Vīrabhadra, and then Narottama dāsa Ṭhākura; (4) The movement developed in Orissa after Caitanya—Śyāmānanda and his disciple Rasikānanda did much to propagate the movement there; (5) By such zealous missionary activity, the movement spread to various other pockets of northern India; (6) And then there was the initial impact of the movement in Assam and in the south. So this is how the movement spread—initially. And the voluminous literary work of the Gosvāmīs should not be overlooked, either. This was important. Five of the Six Gosvāmīs were prolific writers—Raghunātha Bhaṭṭa did not write. But those who did explained the whole Caitanyaite doctrine in complex Sanskrit terminology, and this led to its eventual widespread social acceptance, especially among the brahminical class.

Now there has been a class of teachers that have periodically revived the confidential Gauḍīya Vaiṣṇava teachings throughout history. After Jīva Gosvāmī, the last and the most scholarly of the initial Six Gosvāmīs, Narottama, Śrīnivāsa and Śyāmānanda were the big preachers. There were others. Then Viśvanātha Cakravartī. Then Baladeva Vidyābhūṣaṇa.

In modern times, the Śrī Gauḍīya Maṭha—Kedāranātha Bhaktivinoda Ṭhākura and Bhaktisiddhānta Sarasvatī—did much to spread Gauḍīya Vaiṣṇavism. And, of course, Bhaktivedanta Swami brought it to the Western world when he formed the International Society for Krishna Consciousness, and now the age-old, distinguished line of Gauḍīya Vaiṣṇavism is practiced throughout the world. But you know this story better than I. . .

SR: But what is the magic? Why the attraction? I mean, there are other traditions that are more familiar, or, let us say, they offer something practical. It is not just a matter of abstract philosophy. Why does Eastern mysticism, even today, attract people from all walks of life? I can understand what attracts people to Mother Teresa—she *feeds* people. It's pragmatic—it's something anyone can relate to. Do Vaiṣṇavas. . .

Dr. Chatterjee: Oh, yes, of course, you know as well as I that Vaiṣṇavas are not merely given to "abstract philosophy." Practical application is a big part of the tradition: *prasādam* distribution. Tons of sacred vegetarian foodstuffs have been distributed. You know, in Saptagrāma, for example, Nityānanda Prabhu initiated one Dibākāra Datta, a rich local jeweler, giving him the religious name of "Uddhāraṇa Datta." Perhaps you've heard of him. Much of the initial growth of the movement was financed by this person. He financed the building of temples and, under the guidance of his *guru*, he distributed free food to the poor during a famine. At Trishbigha he constructed public kitchens for serving food to the poor during the outbreak of several famines. Oh, yes. The Gauḍīyas have a strong sense of ethics. They distribute sacred vegetarian food. In this way, they help people practically, by feeding them, and spiritually, by giving food that has first been offered in sacrifice.

But, you see, the greatest allurement that they have is a fundamentally complete philosophical system. This is what attracts people. Their sacred literature is quite vast, and it doesn't ask for dogmatic followers. Rather, all questions are answered, using a profound system of *nyāya*, or logic. Caitanya Mahāprabhu's system of inconceivable distinction and non-distinction is a very mature philosophical system, incorporating much of classical Indian philosophy, and synthesizing that which is best from all prior Vaiṣṇava schools.

It should also be known that Caitanya was a revolutionary. His impact on medieval Indian society was profound for this reason as well. He defied the norms of both the Hindus and the Muslims. He reacted against social conservatism. Isn't this always alluring? [laughter] Especially when you have a strong philosophical basis. He rebelled against the existing caste system. You see, originally, the system was not rigid, nor was it solely based on one's birth. The most important considerations were one's mental make-up, or his *guṇa,* and one's aptitude for certain kinds of work, one's *karma.* This is mentioned by Lord Kṛṣṇa in *Gītā* (4.13). Later, brahmins changed the focus for their own interests. So Caitanya Mahāprabhu was trying to gradually change it back. Not totally, but enough to provoke thought. He succeeded in getting many people to think. This, of course, is a step in the right direction.

SR: But didn't he fully uphold the Varṇāśrama system? His followers were strict. Haridāsa, who was known as a Muslim, would not enter the Jagannātha temple. Even Sanātana Gosvāmī did not enter, since, due to his association with Muslim personalities, he was considered not of the proper caste. Besides, some people say that Mahāprabhu would not even take his meals in the home of a non-brahmin. Of course, there *are* examples to the contrary.

Dr. Chatterjee: Yes. And so I would not say that Caitanya upheld the Varṇāśrama system as such. Although himself a brahmin, he had no respect for the idea of the superiority of his caste. I have discussed this point in my book and I am sure that if you go over the sections on "ethics" and "Caitanya's reaction against Social Conservatism," you will remember my views in this regard. After studying all of the relevant texts, I conclude that his feeling about the prevailing Varṇāśrama system was that it was counter-productive, at least for attaining the grace of Lord Kṛṣṇa.

Kṛṣṇadāsa Kavirāja, author of *Caitanya-caritāmṛta,* wrote in chapter twenty-two of his *Madhya-līlā* that the Varṇāśrama system is inefficient for higher attainments. And these are Caitanya's own words. Rāmānanda Rāya, too, frowns on the efficacy of the Varṇāśrama system. Caitanya and his followers were respectful, but, in the same way that Gandhi would try about 400 years later, he and his followers tried to gradually change the consciousness of the people. He started a non-violent civil disobedience movement—the first one India had ever seen. Some of the prevailing ideas about Varṇāśrama were among the most important changes that Caitanya had hoped to make.

And, by the way, it is not true that Mahāprabhu did not take his food in the company of non-brahmins. In Purī, he once refused an invitation from a group of brahmins because he had doubts about their spiritual attainments. He clearly said that he only accepts invitations from those who perform *japam*—chanting Kṛṣṇa's name on the rosary—for at least 100,000 times a day. In other words, he preferred to associate with devout Vaiṣṇavas only, irrespective of their caste status. You see, he was trying to teach that the real issue is spirituality—universal, nonsectarian spirituality. And all other concerns, however righteous they may be, are only secondary or subservient. This was his teaching.

SR: While we are on the subject of Mahāprabhu's teaching, what would you say is the main distinguishing factor in his philosophy? What distinguishes it from other schools of thought, particularly the other Vaiṣṇava schools?

Dr. Chatterjee: Oh, this is a huge question! [laughter] To briefly summarize: There are basically two distinguishing factors that separate the Gauḍīya school from other Vaiṣṇava schools. Firstly, you have the doctrine of *acintya-bhedābheda*—"The inconceivable difference and non-difference between God and His energies." This was, according to the Gauḍīyas, the original Vedic doctrine. After being distorted by Buddha and then Ādi Śaṅkarācārya, it was reinstated, at least partially, by Rāmānuja, who taught *viśiṣṭādvaita*—"qualified monism." Śaṅkara had claimed oneness, that the living entity—God's energy—was one with God. But Rāmānuja detected that there was a difference as well. He agreed with the oneness aspect, but he added a special clause—"the living being is obviously different as well." So this is an early Vaiṣṇava doctrine.

Then came Madhvācārya, who preached pure *dvaita*, or "dualism." This school teaches that there is absolute difference between God and his energies. But this teaching did not account for the similarities. God and His energies both *exist*, for example, so *in their quality of existence* they are indeed similar. It cannot, therefore, be said that they are absolutely different. Anyway, to make a long story much shorter, Mahāprabhu appeared with the perfect balance. Śaṅkara preached one extreme. Madhva preached the other. The truth—from the Gauḍīya perspective—was given by Mahāprabhu, and, thanks to Jīva Gosvāmī and others, his doctrine was couched in the most sophisticated philosophical jargon. For this, we are grateful.

But the most distinctive feature of Gauḍīya Vaiṣṇava philosophy, especially as opposed to other Vaiṣṇava schools, is the very developed conception of *madhura-rati*, or relationship with God in the conjugal mood. This includes laying stress on *bhakti*, or "devotion," more so than one can detect it in other Vaiṣṇava schools. And *bhakti* is most developed when understood in terms of *bhakti-rasa,* or relationship with God in a personal and loving way. There are five basic relationships like this, and Rūpa Gosvāmī explains them in great detail. They may be summarized: *śānta-rasa,* or "quiet devotion"; *prīta-rasa,* or "devotion of the faithful"; *preya-rasa,* or "devotion as a friend"; *vātsalya-rasa,* or "devotion as parents"; and finally *madhura-rasa,* also known as *ujjvala-rasa*—"devotion with the conjugal sentiment."

SR: These are the same as *śānta, dāsya, sakhya, vātsalya,* and *mādhurya.*

Dr. Chatterjee: Same thing. Just slightly different terminology. Yes. So the Vaiṣṇava *sampradāyas* have explained these things as a minute science—these are the five primary relationships, and then there are seven secondary relationships. So, in all of the world's religious literature, you will not find such an elaborate explanation of God and his relationship with the living beings. Then, to go further, the special contribution of the Gauḍīyas is this very developed conception of *mādhurya-rasa*—how one can emulate the highest devotee in the spiritual world, the maidservant, the *gopī,* and attain the most intimate position in the kingdom of God. It is a developed theological science.

First, *vidhi bhakti*—following rules and regulations. Then, while continuing to follow the rules and regulations, one learns from the *guru* how to model one's life after an inhabitant of Vraja. The inner meditation. This is called *rāgānugā bhakti,* or "spontaneous devotion," or, rather, it is "following an eternal associate who has spontaneous devotion." In any case, it is quite an advanced theological system. One can read all of the Gauḍīya literature on the subject: *Govinda-līlāmṛta, Caitanya-caritāmṛta, Ujjvala-nīlamaṇi, Bhakti-rasāmṛta-sindhu.* There are so many. But they are mostly in Sanskrit and Bengali.

After a thorough study of these books, I will tell you this: In order to best understand *mādhurya-rasa,* the ideal of Rādhā and her love for Kṛṣṇa must be introduced. The culmination of the Gauḍīya Vaiṣṇava experience is the service of Śrī Rādhā. Exactly how this is done is revealed in the esoterica of the tradition. Śrī Caitanya has stated that as a young man yearns for his sweetheart, in the same manner, the human soul must yearn for Kṛṣṇa. This is symbolically represented by Śrīmatī Rādhārāṇī.

SR: But according to the tradition she is not an ordinary human soul, and she is certainly not a symbol. She is the female counterpart of the male absolute truth. She is "the Female Moiety," as Śrīla Bhaktisiddhānta used to say.

Dr. Chatterjee: Oh, I am not denying her existence as a separate divinity. No. The Gauḍīya texts are quite clear on that count—she is Kṛṣṇa's better half, so to speak. But this symbolic imagery is there in Govindadāsa's diary. It is so the soul can see what the ideal situation is. It is not making a statement about Śrī Rādhā's ontological position. It is simply saying that this is something that the ordinary human soul can learn from her—how to develop one's relationship with Kṛṣṇa. And this is certainly true. Although her relationship is no doubt unique, it gives us a very substantial paradigm—something to follow. In essence, what we are referring to is her single-minded devotion to Kṛṣṇa! As the soul now, in the material world, may cherish some intense affection for her sweetheart, she must transfer that affection to Kṛṣṇa, just as Rādhā has done. This is there in *Govinda Dāser Kaḍacā.*

Yes, Rādhārāṇī's position is the highest. Gauḍīyas have the highest regard for her. This is traditional and historical fact. The devotee seeks to follow in her *mādhurya-bhāva,* and that's how I would relate it to the outline I have just given. But this is on the advanced level. First, one must approach an accomplished master, rendering service and learning the science of spirituality. Then, very gradually, one can advance to these other levels. On the highest level one must love God in intimate union, which is called *sambhoga,* and, on an even higher level, one must learn to love God in separation, which is called *vipralambha*—this allows one to truly appreciate union. Rādhārāṇī experiences both. She is the example—the very emblem—of these two ultimate experiences in God realization. Caitanya Mahāprabhu, too, in the mood of Rādhārāṇī, was experiencing these exalted states of spiritual attainment. The scientific procedure with which to accomplish this ultimate goal of life is the great secret of Gauḍīya Vaiṣṇavism.

The Vedic Literature

Michael Witzel

Michael Witzel is currently Chairman in the Department of Sanskrit and Indian Studies at Harvard University. He is the author of the text-critical edition of Das Kaṭha Āraṇyaka *(Kathmandu, 1974), translating it from Sanskrit into German and adding his own commentary. He is also the author of "Tracing the Vedic Dialects" in C. Caillat, editor,* Dialectes Dans les Littératures Indiennes *(Paris, 1989), and he has written numerous articles for well-known Indological journals.*

SR: Perhaps we can begin by defining the Vedic literature.

Dr. Witzel: Well, the Vedas are ancient texts that were given to particular *ṛṣis.* The Vedas are therefore called *śruti,* meaning, "that which is heard." In other words, it was directly heard by the sages as a sort of revelation. As far as the actual history of the texts are concerned, it is difficult to come up with a consensus of opinion. In the view of those who study the Vedas from various angles, according to various disciplines—religion, sociology, linguistics—the story looks a little different. Very often, the world of scholarship judges the dating of Vedic texts based on linguistic evidence. Sanskrit changes slightly from era to era, and so we know if a text is old—or not so old—based upon how it is composed, on its phraseology, and so on.

So, from the linguistic point of view, the Vedic texts are arranged in a certain order, and it is not exactly the same as that which is presented in the traditional Indian scheme: the four Vedas, with each Veda subdivided into Saṁhitā, Brāhmaṇa, Āraṇyaka, and Upaniṣad. In a sense, that system is also historical, but it is not quite correct in terms of philological and inner textual evidence.

SR: Okay. I guess from the linguistic point of view we would begin with the Ṛg Veda.

Dr. Witzel:: Correct. After that, we would have the Atharva Veda, which we might call a "*mantra* text," because it belongs to the group of texts composed in *mantra* language, which differs in dialect from that of the Ṛg Veda [and is later than the Ṛg Veda]. Also composed in *mantra* language are the Yajus—which are the *mantras* of the Yajur Veda—and the Sāma Veda, which is basically the same as the Ṛg Veda. So, in terms of dating, these three would come after the Ṛg Veda.

After this, you have the prose contained in the Yajur Veda Saṁhitās. These are Brāhmaṇa-type texts, although they significantly differ from what later came to be called the Brāhmaṇas. Then, after that, come the actual Brāhmaṇas, which are somewhat different in language. The Āraṇyakas basically belong to this same period, and the older Upaniṣads do as well. We can say that they belong to the later Brāhmaṇa period. These texts, as a whole, are known as the *śruti* literature.

SR: Can you tell me more about the contents of the Veda?

Dr. Witzel: Well, you will find more than one thousand hymns to the various gods, personifications of certain (social) concepts and of forces of nature; you get instruction for the recitation of *mantras*; there is profuse discussion of solemn rituals; there are complicated melodies that are to be used in the rituals; there are elaborate details of how to conduct a plethora of Vedic ceremonies and sacrifices; and then, in the Atharva Veda, especially, you get these interesting hymns and spells, a type of sorcery, if you will. This is really very elaborate—there is a spell for every conceivable situation. Perhaps you want to heal a broken leg, or you want to plan a clandestine visit to your girlfriend's room and you want to make sure that her dog will not bark. [laughter] You don't want her father to wake up! Or perhaps a king has been expelled from the country—there is a magical *mantra* that will get him reinstated. In fact, I remember one that was very interesting: there is a spell that a woman who was soon to be married could put on her future rival—a person who does not yet exist! There are magical spells for every imaginable situation. This is an extremely interesting portion of the Veda, although it has not been studied extensively.

So the early parts of this Veda deal with this sort of sorcery business, and the latter portion deals with the so-called "mystical" hymns. Actually, I am quite sure that "mystical" is not the appropriate word. But certainly there is esoteric knowledge that comes to the fore. It reveals the inner meaning of many of the sacrifices, and it expresses it in terms that reflect the magical mode of thinking that was representative of that particular time period. This Veda also deals with what might be called philosophical issues as well—the beginning of the world, and things of that nature. This part of the Atharva Veda is more complicated, but at least I want to say that there are basically two strands of thought in the Atharva Veda, and they are sorcery and esoteric knowledge. To this is added a third portion dealing with certain domestic and royal rituals.

But the next stage in the Brāhmaṇas and also in the prose of the Yajur Veda Saṁhitās is what we might call a "theological" discussion of the meaning of the rituals, and of each verse, melody, action, etc., used in the rituals. These texts discuss the secret utilization and meaning of all of these things, and just why certain items are employed at certain points in certain rituals. It is really quite elaborate.

SR: Where does secular learning or the Upavedas fit in?

Dr. Witzel: Well, traditionally, all of that is viewed as supplementary to the earlier Vedic texts. You have what is known as Arthaveda—statecraft and politics; Dhanurveda, which is the art of warfare; Āyurveda, which deals with medicine; Gandharvaveda—music and the fine arts; these are associated with the four Vedas as well, but are of much later date.

And while we are discussing it, you might be interested in the Vedāṅgas, which are not part of the actual *śruti* but are considered indispensable for the performance of Vedic rituals. *Kalpa* discusses detail of ritual; *Vyākaraṇa* is the study of grammar; *Śikṣā* deals with proper pronunciation; *Nirukta* elucidates etymology and the use of obscure words; *Chaṇḍa* focuses on meters; and *Jyotiṣa* explains astrology and astronomy. These auxiliary sciences are a very elaborate feature of the Vedāṅgas, showing that the ancillary texts are quite scientific and more profound than they might at first appear.

SR: Perhaps the next stage we should discuss is the *smṛti* literature, since this is where Vaiṣṇavism really ties in to all of this.

Dr. Witzel: That's right. Some say that these texts are not revealed to seers but are the compilation of human authors. In our Western view, and even among many Indian scholars and practitioners, certain of these texts can also be included among the many texts of the Vedic literature. They are closely enough related to the earlier *śruti* to be taken seriously by scholars and to be revered by adherents. By the way, some of these *smṛti* texts, such as the *Baudhāyana-Śrauta-sūtra*, are actually quite old. So it gets a little confusing.

But linguistically speaking and also in terms of inner textual evidence—that is to say that an early text might mention another text, and in this way we know that the texts were pre-existent—*smṛti* comes later in the sequence and history of the Veda as such. Now, I have just given you a rough outline. Actually, there are volumes and volumes of research material—but this is the basic idea.

Now, the next period, which scholars define as post-Vedic—this, again, is clear from the language, which is no longer Vedic Sanskrit or even classical Sanskrit—is where we get Itihāsa and Purāṇa literature. This is written in what we call "epic" Sanskrit, which is strongly influenced by Prākṛt. In any case, these works are very hard to date because, for example, we only have late manuscripts of the Mahābhārata. And they are obviously copied from and based on a much older work, but we do not have access to these things.

SR: So there may even be a much earlier basis, perhaps co-existent with the Vedas themselves?

Dr. Witzel: I would not necessarily go that far, but, you know, the basic story of the Mahābhārata can even be found in the Ṛg Veda.

SR: Oh?

Dr. Witzel: Yes. It is quite interesting. In the Ṛg Veda, we have a battle of ten kings. Now, the names and even the story change quite a bit, but I think the similarities are there. Bards who tell the stories over the centuries have a tendency to add things or take things out or adjust things—but we can see that there is a basic storyline that keeps coming to the surface.

SR: What do you think about statements in the Mahābhārata and the Purāṇas referring to themselves as "the fifth Veda"?

Dr. Witzel: That is a very interesting topic. In some of the later Vedic texts, like the Upaniṣads, you get a whole list of sciences. It mentions the various kinds of texts, and it mentions the Itihāsa and Purāṇa.

SR: Yes. The *Chāndogya Upaniṣad* (7.1.4), for example, mentions the Itihāsa and Purāṇa as the fifth Veda. So if we base our understanding on this idea, as Vaiṣṇava teachers such as Madhva and Rāmānuja do, then the later oeuvres can carry the same weight as the *śruti*. .

Dr. Witzel: But the problem is that we do not have any of it. We have no early examples of this later literature, and so, for scholars, in general, we find it difficult to accept the Vedic roots of these later texts. None of it currently exists. There are a few obscure examples, but nothing to build a conclusive theory upon. So it has to be concluded that these are later things, simply because of the lack of documentary evidence and, of course, because of the post-Vedic language of these texts. This does not mean that we are always correct in our assumptions, but scholarship deals with these things in a particular way, and so we abide by those rules. Still, there is some evidence that there may be ample reason for calling these things "the fifth Veda." Then, again, there may be no justification whatsoever. We simply do not know.

Now, in the original Vedic texts, there are individual verses that talk about great deeds of kings, even of Dhṛtarāṣṭra! But these are only stray verses, not a full storyline. In this way it is quite different than the Purāṇa or Itihāsa tradition. But the seed is there. We have bits and pieces in the Vedic texts which show that there is a tradition afloat, one that carries over into *smṛti* literature, albeit with certain elaborations and modifications. In other words, one can see that there is an often neglected connection between early Vedic writings and their later "non-Vedic" counterparts, but there are differences as well.

SR: Now, where does Vaiṣṇavism fit in? Scholars often say that it is not Vedic in the most literal sense because it is only based on the later texts.

Dr. Witzel: Well, there is ample justification for this point of view. Nonetheless, if you study the texts closely enough, you can see that there are very definite connections as well. Viṣṇu, you know, is even mentioned in the Ṛg Veda. So it goes back to the earliest texts. Now, the problem is this: in those texts he is considered a minor Vedic god whose basic feat is that he took three steps. Vaiṣṇavism took the Viṣṇu conception to much greater heights than one would naturally extrapolate from the original Veda. I think it is clear that as far as the Ṛg Veda goes, Indra is a much more prominent god. This, of course, has to do with the prevailing mythology and also with the needs of the people at the time. Different divinities are emphasized according to the insights of various seers and the requirements of the local people.

To simplify this very complex issue, let us just say that Viṣṇu undergoes a long development or unfolding, if you will, and by the time you get to latter-day Vaiṣṇavism, of course, he is identified with the supreme god. Now a practitioner might say that this truth was there all along, but you cannot really get that from Vedic texts proper. You would need a *guru* who reads the tradition in a very particular way, perhaps.

From a strictly scholarly point of view, however, Viṣṇu goes through a transformation, from what is perceived as a minor god to the all-important divinity one sees today in the practice of Vaiṣṇavism. One can debate this subject from various angles of vision. But if you are going by modern scholarship, particularly in terms of inner textual and philological evidence, you would have to concede this point. In any case, Viṣṇu is there in the earliest part of the Veda, and that cannot be ignored.

A further note of interest is this: some of the various Vaiṣṇava schools have direct links to the ancient Vedic texts and ideas, and others have rather indirect links, and, in some cases, no links. There is a South Indian school of Vaiṣṇavism that is very closely aligned to the original Vedic idea.

SR: What are they called?

Dr. Witzel: The Vaikhānasa. They are connected with the usual southern Indian Rāmānuja group: the Śrī Vaiṣṇavas. Now, every Veda is handed down through a particular school, called *śākhā*, or "a branch," and in this case the branch comes from the Yajur Veda. Of this Yajur Veda, you see, there are "white" (*śukla*) and "black" (*kṛṣṇa*) groupings. From the black side, there is a branch called "Taittirīya," and the Vaikhānasa is a sub-division of that particular group. The Taittirīya people are known all over the Dravidian countries and in Maharashtra.

What I want to say is this: the Vaikhānasa have all the Vedic texts, much like the other traditional schools, and they also have the *mantra-pāṭha*, a collection of *mantras* for the house rituals. All such groups in South

India have these collections. And the Vaikhānasa, too, have this neat little handbook that has all of these things. But the second part of their handbook is totally Vaiṣṇava—it contains the *mantras* for temple construction and various forms of Vaiṣṇava worship. Now I find that very interesting. It ties the Vedic school with Vaiṣṇava doctrine. Consequently there may be more of a general connection than we normally assume.

SR: Right. So the early Vedic connection to authentic modern-day Vaiṣṇavism should be more thoroughly researched. I believe that in South Indian Vaiṣṇavism one might find the answer—this Vaikhānasa idea reinforces my beliefs. And, you know, you have Prabodhānanda Sarasvatī and Gopāla Bhaṭṭa Gosvāmī, who were, of course, associated with South Indian Vaiṣṇavism. They could have brought these ideas up north when they were later influenced by Caitanya Mahāprabhu.

Dr. Witzel: It is not unlikely. I cannot say if it happened in this particular case. But these medieval *sādhus* travelled quite a bit more than we generally suppose. You can trace a South Indian text or tradition and see how, within twenty or thirty years, it migrated to the north, or elsewhere in India. So these things were circulating quite a bit. My point is this: while a Sanskrit scholar or academician may not be able to see overt influences of what we have come to accept as ancient Vedic ritual or culture in modern Vaiṣṇava religion, there may be more of it there than we initially thought. This Vaikhānasa tradition certainly has direct Vedic influence. Others may also, although it may be less obvious. The formal structure of *pūjā* as "guest worship" is a good example.

SR: Can you discuss a little bit more about the Vaikhānasa handbook and how it relates to Vaiṣṇavism?

Dr. Witzel: Well, right after the house rituals, it contains the *mantras* for temple rituals. So that is how they make the link. But the details of this are largely unstudied. Nonetheless, if you look at the *mantras* that they use in this handbook, they are half Vedic—they are recited with the accents of the Veda. So this is the only Vaiṣṇava school, at least of which I am aware, that maintains such a direct link to earlier Vedic traditions. For this reason alone, it would be worthwhile to study this school more closely.

In my research I was astounded by some of the Vaikhānasa *mantras*. I remember one in particular wherein Viṣṇu is described—his limbs and his form—with distinct Vedic language, in terms of accent and meter.

That is a thing which you will not find anywhere else. Most forms of Vaiṣṇavism, at least as it is viewed by the academic community, can only be tied to the Veda through the Mahābhārata, or the Purāṇas, or, at best, the Upaniṣads. But here, with the Vaikhānasas, you have something quite a bit more substantial in terms of direct Vedic connection.

So this subject really needs to be researched. Generally, scholars see only a very indirect connection between Vaiṣṇavism and the earlier Vedic tradition. But here you see something quite different, and it may eventually force the academic world to reassess some of its conclusions. The insider, or the practitioner, of course, already feels a direct link to Vedic tradition. To them, certain forms of Vaiṣṇavism are deeply rooted in the Veda, and no one can tell them otherwise. However, our methods are different, and it may take us some time before we will concur with the believers. And, then again, that day may never come.

The Rāmāyaṇa

H. Daniel Smith

H. Daniel Smith is Professor of Religion at Syracuse University, where he has introduced undergraduate students to Valmīki's Rāmāyaṇa for over a decade. In addition to his teaching, Dr. Smith has completed two bibliographic reference works on Rāmāyaṇa-related subjects and, working with two Madras artists, produced a Picturebook Rāmāyaṇa, *his own contribution being an easy-to-read synopsis of the entire epic. He also has contributed two volumes detailing contents of the neglected Pañcarātra corpus of Vaiṣṇava tantric texts to the prestigious Gaekwad's Oriental Series.*

SR: The Rāmāyaṇa is not a Gauḍīya scripture per se. But it *is* the classic epic of Rāma, who is an incarnation of Viṣṇu, or Kṛṣṇa. So it is related. I would like to talk about the structure and history of the Rāmāyaṇa and, among the things we should discuss today, also, are the later versions of the Rāmāyaṇa, like Tulasīdāsa's *Rāma-carita-mānasa.* These works always seem to add their own slant. They change the story a little bit here and there. Do they not?

Dr. Smith: That's right. They often do. I don't know how you want to move with that.

SR: Well, let's start with Valmīki's Rāmāyaṇa—the original story. What does "Rāmāyaṇa" mean? What is the basic storyline? Maybe you want to go through each of the *kāṇḍas,* or books, of the Rāmāyaṇa. There's a nice outline in your *Picturebook Rāmāyaṇa.* I have it here.

Dr. Smith: Yes, that was well-received. Well, what can I say? The Vālmīki Rāmāyaṇa is, in a sense, the granddaddy of all the Rāmāyaṇas, the one against which the others seem to be measured, at least from the literary point of view. As for the meaning of the Rāmāyaṇa, it's probably okay to just say it means "The Story of Rāma." But it's in fact two words put together: "*Rāma*" and "*ayana.*" Now, *ayana* refers to a course, such as the celestial course of a planet.

SR: A course. . .like a path.

Dr. Smith: Right. And, indeed, when they speak of *uttarāyaṇa* and *dakṣiṇāyana*—you know the two halves of the year as the sun travels north and south—it's that kind of a course. And so "*Rāma*" plus "*ayana*" refers to Rāma's course. By convention, then, Rāmāyaṇa means Rāma's travels—his "trek," if you will.

SR: "Rāmatrek. To boldly go where no *avatāra* has gone before."

Dr. Smith: [laughter] Exactly. And the Rāmāyaṇa depicts his travels from Ayodhyā out into the unknown reaches beyond. And in the story his course to and from those farther reaches have to do with Kiṣkindhā and Laṅkā.

SR: Laṅkā.

Dr. Smith: Yes, and then back again. The going out and coming back—both together—that is his "*ayana,*" or course. The end of the story is when he comes *back* to Ayodhyā and institutes the glorious *Rāma-rāja*—the ideal kingdom.

SR: Is that in the *Uttara-kāṇḍa*?

Dr. Smith: No, that's at the end of the *Yuddha-kāṇḍa* in Valmīki. It's at that point that many of the other treatments of the Rāma-story end it. They prefer not to go into the matters covered in Valmīki's *Uttara-kāṇḍa.*

SR: Why is that?

Dr. Smith: Well, you better ask all those who leave it out. I have my theories, and they have to do with the fact that some of those matters, in a sense, did not reflect well on the character of Rāma. That is to say, what he does in the end is to—I forget the word they use—to send Sītā off.

SR: He banishes her.

Dr. Smith: Right, he banishes Sītā—thank you—and he does it when she's pregnant. Now, on the face of it, that is not a very nice thing to do.

SR: Is it the *Uttara-kāṇḍa* where she goes into the fire and she comes out of the fire, or is that at the end of the *Yuddha-kāṇḍa.*

Dr. Smith: That's at the end of the *Yuddha-kāṇḍa,* although there's also a movement up to something like that later in the *Uttara-kāṇḍa*—it becomes almost a doubling on it, but then, in a surprise ending, instead of doing that, she descends into the earth, calling upon her mother. But at the end of the earlier *Yuddha-kāṇḍa,* she—having lived in the house of another man, not in control of her own destiny—is suspect, her chastity is suspect.

So then, at this penultimate point in the *Yuddha-kāṇḍa,* before one and all, she has to prove that she was *not* unchaste. This is a very interesting element in the Valmīki version; it's a very dramatic moment because they've been reunited and Rāma has sent for Sītā, and, I forget, I guess it's Hanumān who brings her back. But anyway, Rāma stands there silently and doesn't say anything. A telling verse describes him as deep in thought. What's he thinking about? Well, clearly what happens next is that he rejects her. She's broken by this, but what he's thinking is that he *has to do this* as a king, so that they won't suspect him of sentimentality.

He then orders her to demonstrate that she is chaste, and asks her to perform a "truth vow," namely, to enter a huge blaze. She enters saying, "If I have been true to my Lord, may the fire not harm me." Of course, she does survive because she *is* chaste. Only after that point has been made clear—after everything else that transpired in the story—is it possible to suppose that they could live happily ever after.

SR: That's all in the *Uttara-kāṇḍa.*

Dr. Smith: No, that's all in Valmīki's *Yuddha-kāṇḍa.*

SR: Oh, I see.

Dr. Smith: Then, having done that, after having lived 10,000 righteous years of rule, only then does the *Uttara-kāṇḍa* start in Valmīki. This is the reason so many people think that the entire seventh, or last, section of Valmīki's version is a later interpolation. In the *Uttara-kāṇḍa* of Valmīki, the narrative continues as various sages and holy men gather to congratulate Rāma, the newly-crowned king. It is early evening on what I interpret to be the *same* day as the coronation day. The festivities are over. As evening progresses they were all sitting up telling stories and Agastya—a very mysterious figure throughout the whole epic—narrates. He weaves in and out of the story at several different points. And since this is a big event—the coronation—he is there and he tells this story. It has to do with some of the past histories of the individuals who are involved. He tells who Rāvaṇa is; who Hanumān is; who the wonderful Indrajit is; and so on.

SR: He tells who they are in relation to Rāma?

Dr. Smith: Well, he explains why they are incarnated. You see, the *Uttara-kāṇḍa* puts an interesting "spin" on the story. What it does is that it provides an overall perspective, to wit, that so much of what has transpired is the result of fate, of destiny.

SR: So it does seem like a later comment.

Dr. Smith: Oh yes. There have been very complex studies of the structural layering of Valmīki's Rāmāyaṇa. And the reasons why some scholars propose that there are layers has to do with the presumed chronology of certain teachings. Clearly, to many of them, this "spin" that points to fate and destiny is a later type of teaching, a kind of brahminical recasting of the *meaning* of the story. And besides, it just sounds like an afterthought!

So, anyway, once Agastya's story is finished, they all sit in amazement—I suppose, while the force of the ideas sinks in! Then the story picks up again and, some time later, Sītā and Rāma are out under an arbor and she says something like, "Oh, by the way, I think I'm pregnant." Rāma, of course, is overjoyed—until he goes into his court and begins hearing what people have to say, what his subjects have to say. At that time, one of them—it is one of a number of subjects who are joking around—turns serious for a moment and voices a complaint. His name is Bhadra in the Valmīki version. He grumbles that if Rāma takes back Sītā after she lived for so long in another man's house, then he and all his kind will likewise have to take back their wives whenever they roam from righteousness's path, so to speak. Consequently, Rāma decides that he has to do something to show that he is king and a worthy model for everyone else.

So he calls Lakṣmaṇa in and reminds him of an event that transpired when they were crossing the Ganges River together, way back at the very beginning of their exile. At that time, he recalls, Sītā, in the middle of the river-crossing, made a prayer to the Ganges, saying, "If we get out of this safely, I shall come back to visit the holy men in the *āśramas* along your banks." And so Rama says at this point in the *Uttara-kāṇḍa* something like, "Well, she's wanted for so long to visit those holy men, let's just see that she manages to do this. Why don't you go take her, and come back alone."

SR: He just wanted to leave her?

Dr. Smith: So it appears. And that's exactly what Lakṣmaṇa does. He takes her to the Ganges and then stoically even to the farther shore. But as he is about to leave, he breaks down and tells her what's really happening and leaves her there. And she's weeping and wailing, and, I think, even rolling on the ground in his last view of her.

SR: Why? Is there any explanation of why Rāma wants to leave her?

Dr. Smith: Well, that has to do with some of those dark thoughts that he had earlier. We have to assume, I think, that it's part of a larger plan. But the one thing that it seems clear he wanted to do was to prove that he is more of a proper, exemplary king than a husband.

After all, in traditional India this is a book on *dharma*. Characters in it make choices about duty and act out of consideration for their responsibilities to those around them. Events are introduced to illustrate the difficulties of living according to the demands of propriety, or *dharma*. And don't think that the demands are the same for everyone. If anything, the story brings to the fore the ambiguities of understanding appropriate behavior, or *dharma*, in the abstract—for there are many verses which suggest that each individual's *dharma* is different in different situations, and the challenge is to deport oneself in any given circumstance according to one's own peculiar *dharma* (called *sva-dharma*).

Getting back to Rāma, I think that in the version of Valmīki that comes down to us Rāma is there presented in such a way as to show the ascendency of the royal, *kṣatriya* side of the *avatāra*, and, in the ultimate analysis, it is this identity that commands on him over and against the demands of him being a doting husband. So it is part of the story, I think, that one is supposed to ponder at the same time that the characters within it ponder it also. Rāma embodies a particular aspect of divinity—God as a responsible, circumspect king.

In any case, Valmīki is one of the sages who lives on the banks of the Ganges, and, after Lakṣmaṇa abandons Sītā there, Valmīki takes her in. After some time, she gives birth to twin sons, Lava and Kusha. Meanwhile, Rāma has ruled well, and in demonstration of his worldly sway as a great monarch he prepares to perform an elaborate *aśvamedha* sacrifice—you know, the ancient horse sacrifice. Are you familiar with that?

SR: Yes. I've read about it in various texts.

Dr. Smith: So here it is again. And Valmīki sends to the celebrations the two young boys that Rāma doesn't know about—Rāma's own twin sons—to whom has been taught the entire story we have rehearsed here only in part. And they sing the story in front of Rāma. [laughter] It's really rather amusing. I don't think it's meant to be, but as he sits and listens to it, he begins to think that these kids look kind of familiar. [laughter]

And, lo and behold—not to forget that the Rāmāyaṇa is also the story of adventures in self-discovery—as Rāma hears this story he realizes it's being told about him. And when he finally puts two and two together, he calls for Valmīki and tells him to bring Sītā with him to the royal enclosure. So when she comes in front of Rāma again, he's quite apologetic and says he's ready to take her back. But, he tells her, she'll have to prove herself yet again in another fire ordeal. As if once wasn't enough! [laughter]

To make a long story short, she protests. She too is torn. But through her tears she comes to a resolve. She has had enough! She realizes, I guess, it's time to go home—back home, back to her mother. Recall: Sītā was a foundling discovered as an infant in a furrow of earth; her very name "Sītā" reminds us of her grounding in the earth's soil. So she calls upon her mother to witness to her. And of course the earth opens up—it's a wonderful scene—Mother Earth comes up on a throne through a cleft in the ground, and beckons Sītā to come sit on her lap. Then the throne descends back down—just like the mighty Wurlitzer at Radio City Music Hall! Then the Earth closes over, and Rāma is left without Sītā, bereft. He wanders around in a daze, for some time with the boys, Lava and Kuśa. In the end, he hands over his kingdom to others.

SR: How does Rāma leave the planet?

Dr. Smith: Very important concluding episode! There are several complications in the plot at that point, because Lakṣmaṇa has to die, Bharata has to die, Śatrughna has to die, and Rāma has to die. And they all do. And, in fact, it's by a kind of ritual suicide, in most cases. Lakṣmaṇa, as it were, gives up breathing. He had disobeyed Rāma's orders to guard a door. As a consequence he is asked to go and suspend his breath—which he does. As for Rāma, he enters into the Sarayū River, followed by Bharata, Śatrughna, and hosts of devotees. They just walk into the river. It all culminated in an utter transfiguration scene, where they ascend to heaven and Rāma resumes his celestial throne.

That's the end of the Valmīki story. . .well, almost. It remains only for the *phala śruti* to be recited: anyone who hears this story will be blessed and so on and so forth. Because the same had been done at the end of the *Yuddha-kāṇḍa*, when we hear of Rāma and Sītā's ten thousand years' reign, many text-critical scholars feel this repetition in the *Uttara-kāṇḍa* is but another indication that the latter book is a later addition onto the original.

SR: What does "later" mean? It's obviously been part of the Rāmāyaṇa for as long as people can remember. It's part of the tradition. I think we need to be careful when we assume that something is a later addition, even if a good deal of evidence seems to point to that conclusion.

Dr. Smith: I agree with you. The *Uttara-kāṇḍa*—which means, literally, the "later section"—has been a part of the Valmīki version for, well, it's difficult to say how long. It may indeed be a later addition, however much later "later" means. The Valmīki Rāmāyaṇa has been handed down with that concluding section as part of it for many centuries. And to me that testifies to the wisdom of the folk tradition, because it really provides a kind of dimension to the story that matches up with the opening of the *Bāla-kāṇḍa*, which, of course, text-critical scholars see also as an addition.

SR: Oh, they do?

Dr. Smith: Yes.

SR: I didn't know that.

Dr. Smith: Well, when you get into the text-critical analysis of Valmīki's poem, the seven *kāṇḍas* become quite a complicated set of considerations. Both the *Bāla-kāṇḍa* and the *Uttara-kāṇḍa* may be taken to be additions to the main storyline. The earlier tells about the incarnation of divine personalities into the major, royal figures—their earthly childhood and youth—and the latter, the *Uttara-kāṇḍa,* tells about the events after the "story" has reached its culmination, after the abducted princess has been rescued by the prince and the lovers have been reunited—when the incarnated divinities return to their supernatural origins.

And then those middle five *kāṇḍas* which remain are not whole in themselves, either. But within them, the Rāma *kathā,* the basic story that's known far and wide, is revealed. Within those five there is one—what is it, the *Ayodhyā-kāṇḍa*?—which is obviously different because it's about human individuals engaged in palace intrigue.

SR: *Ayodhyā-kāṇḍa,* that's the second one.

Dr. Smith: Yes. And then when you enter into the third one . . .

SR: *Araṇya-kāṇḍa*?

Dr. Smith: *Araṇya-kāṇḍa.* That's when you enter into what I call a kind of Walt Disney world—truly another world altogether . . .

SR: [laughter] I see.

Dr. Smith: What I mean is that in it there are talking birds, and talking animals, and demons, and witches, and all sorts of wondrous, wonderful things.

SR: Seems like Walt Disney would be envious of some of these things.

Dr. Smith: Well, I think he certainly missed the boat by not making it into an animated spectacle, which leads to a footnote here. There is supposed to be, under production in Japan, an animated version of the Rāmāyaṇa.

SR: That would be incredible.

Dr. Smith: I read that some time back in *Hinduism Today,* where it was just one of the notes on the back page one time. And, unfortunately, I've never seen anything since.

SR: Okay. So I didn't want to interrupt. You were going through the *kāṇḍas. Araṇya-kāṇḍa. . .*

Dr. Smith: All right. And so they go off to the forest and run into all kinds of goblins and witches. They show heroism, love, compassion, chivalry, and things of that nature. Next to it you have the very similar. . .

SR: *Kiṣkindhā.*

Dr. Smith: *Kiṣkindhā-kāṇḍa. . .*which is also much like the fantasy-world of the *Araṇya-kāṇḍa.* But when you come to the *Sundara-kāṇḍa,* once again there is a discernibly different tone and texture. The setting is the remote and beautiful kingdom of Laṅkā. Here we see two figures. One is an energetic interloper who bounded there secretly—he goes by the name of Hanumān. The other is the forlorn princess held helplessly captive—and this, of course, is Sītā. These two are glorified throughout this section. One repeatedly hears the manifold virtues of Sītā while Hanumān is presented as the prime example of the devotee. . .

SR: Right. Hanumān—bringing it to the Gauḍīya tradition—is a very important person. You know, in the *Caitanya-caritāmṛta,* one of Mahāprabhu's prime followers, Murāri Gupta, has a strong fascination for Rāma—so he goes to Mahāprabhu to find out why he is attracted to Rāma and not to Kṛṣṇa. He points out that all of Mahāprabhu's other followers have this attachment to Kṛṣṇa, but somehow, mysteriously, he, Murāri Gupta, is attached to Rāma. And then Mahāprabhu tells him: "This is because in your previous life you were Hanumān."

Dr. Smith: That's counter to one tradition, at least, and that is that Hanumān supposedly never died!

SR: Oh, that's right. I think Murāri was an expansion or a removed incarnation of some sort.

Dr. Smith: Hanumān was given a blessing in Valmīki's *Uttara-kāṇḍa* that he will live as long as the story of Rāma is told. He is supposed to be living somewhere even now up in the Himālayas.

SR: They say the same of Vyāsadeva.

Dr. Smith: Who said?

SR: In the Gauḍīya tradition— Vyāsadeva has a cave in the Himālayas.

Dr. Smith: What is he continually uttering?

SR: They don't say what he is doing.

Dr. Smith: Well, Hanumān is believed to be continually uttering the name of "Rāma" or "Sītā-Rāma." A favorite theme in popular illustration, in fact, shows Hanumān in a kind of ecstatic trance-like state, sometimes with cymbals on his fingers, and sometimes with his heart, open, bleeding, with Rāma and Sītā revealed residing there. Usually his eyes are glazed while he sings the holy *mantra*.

SR: There's another interesting Rāma story in the Gauḍīya tradition wherein Mahāprabhu comes upon a Rāma *bhakta* who is crying. He won't eat; he won't even sleep, because he can't believe that Sītā went off with Rāvaṇa. And Śrī Caitanya says to him, "Don't worry. When she went into the fire, she stayed there and an illusory Sītā came out and went with Rāvaṇa." Mahāprabhu said that he had heard this from the *Kūrma Purāṇa*—it was an authorized story. So then the Rāma *bhakta* felt a lot better.

Dr. Smith: Right. You'll find it in the various traditions and re-tellings of the story. That's known as the "Māyā-Sītā" tactic. It's picked up by Tulasīdāsa, too, who may have known it from the widely-popular *Adhyātma Rāmāyaṇa*.

SR: Oh, Tulasīdāsa says that?

Dr. Smith: No, not in those words, but he uses the tactic: before Rāvaṇa comes for Sītā, Rāma has made Sītā enter a fire for safe-keeping. A phantom Sītā emerges, and that phantom is what is taken off to Laṇkā by Rāvaṇa. The reason why Rāma, in versions that employ the "Māyā-Sītā" tactic, orders the recovered Sītā to undergo a fire-test, is so that the phantom Sītā will return to the fire and that the real Sītā may emerge again—untainted by Rāvaṇa's touch!

SR: Right. It's also there in the Purāṇas. I believe Mahāprabhu cites the *Kūrma Purāṇa* when he mentions that story. There are seven Purāṇas that mention the Rāmāyaṇa.

Dr. Smith: Probably more. The late Dr. V. Raghavan has a whole book, *The Greater Rāmāyaṇa* (Varanasi: All-India Kashiraj Trust, 1973), in which he examines the Purāṇic recastings of the Rāma story.

SR: I'd like to see that.

Dr. Smith: It's really a thorough book.

SR: And also there's a section of the Mahābhārata that deals with the Rāmāyaṇa.

Dr. Smith: Right. And you know in scholarly circles one of the things that no one seems to be able to settle conclusively is which is older—the Valmīki version, or the *Rāmopākhyāna* of the Mahābhārata. I guess "ya pays ya money, ya takes ya cherce." But this is something that, you know, people writing books on the Rāmāyaṇa have to discuss and deal with in terms of sources of the Rāma story.

Well, enough said about the contents of Valmīki. I think that one has to acknowledge that if you go at Valmīki in a text-critical way, it's just replete with questions. And they're very interesting. But again, the real point is, Valmīki, whoever he or the school is, has been handed down in this seven-*kāṇḍa* form for many, many centuries. I forget who are the various authors that are pointed to as having quoted from the *Uttara-kāṇḍa*, which proves, of course, that it was there in their time. But I think early dramatists did, but that's not what we're talking about here. Okay. Where do you want to move then? Perhaps different versions after Valmīki?

SR: First of all, how long is the Rāmāyaṇa including all seven *kāṇḍas*? I have a figure here of 24,000 couplets. Does that sound accurate?

Dr. Smith: I really don't know. But that sounds pretty good. To be sure, it may be more or less than that amount depending on whether you are referring to the so-called Vulgate version or to the considerably reduced Critical Edition produced at Baroda University.

SR: Okay. Now, I have some information here about Rāmāyaṇas in other lands, like in China. There's a story of the wind monkey, *Ramakien*, in Thailand. And even a Sikh *guru*, Govinda Singh, wrote no less than 860 short volumes about the Prince of Ayodhyā.

Dr. Smith: Well, again, I don't know about that figure, but it's true that there is, if not a version of the Rāmāyaṇa by the last Sikh *guru,* then he certainly retells it and alludes to it, so that his audience clearly knew the allusion. I would be careful about citing numbers like that, though, because you've got to find those. . .

SR: I know. But that figure is given by more than one reliable researcher. Anyway, what about that wind monkey story?

Dr. Smith: Right. On the issue of the Rāmāyaṇa in greater Asia, there are a number of books out on that, and there have been some conferences on it. So it's pretty well acknowledged in scholarly circles that the Rāma-story surfaces in other cultures beyond India.

SR: Oh.

Dr. Smith: I have in my hand here a rather thick volume called *The Rāmāyaṇa Tradition in Asia,* which are papers from a conference in New Delhi in 1975—it was an international seminar. There are essays on the Rāma-story in Malaysia, in the Philippines, in Nepal, in Śrī Laṅkā, in Mongolia, and so on. That was only an early example: there have been a number of subsequent international seminars on the Rāmāyaṇa—in Delhi in 1981, in Lucknow in 1986, in Bonn in 1987, in Mauritius in 1990, to name only a few—and each one has served to shed new light on the dissemination of the Rāma-story in Asia and beyond.

And again, V. Raghavan, who was one of the great Rāmāyaṇa scholars, produced a book early on, called, *The Rāmāyaṇa In Greater India* (Surat: South Gauhati University, 1975). It is quite a useful introduction to the subject: he has different chapters on Ceylon, Tibet, Mongolia, China, Japan, Laos, Thailand, etc., in which he reviews the Rāmāyaṇa in those areas.

SR: Why do you think the Rāmāyaṇa has spread so far? It seems to speak to the sensibilities of a variety of peoples.

Dr. Smith: I don't know why, but *that it did* is certainly clear. Just for example, in Burma (now called Mayanmar), the capital city is named after Ayodhyā; I'm not sure how they pronounce it. But it's definitely named after the capital associated with Rāma's rule. You see, the Rāmāyaṇa is a very compelling story; it's one of the world's great stories. The only wonder is that it hasn't spread to the United States.

SR: Well, it's starting.

Dr. Smith: You bet! We're trying. We're working on it. Courses like the one I've given over the years for freshmen on the Rāmāyaṇa represent only the tip of the iceberg. Increasing numbers of both young and established scholars in North America have been turning to the Rāmāyaṇa traditions with critical interest. That movement is growing and has yet to peak. The completion of the translation project will help solidify this interest and bring it to newer and larger audiences.

SR: I'm just curious: What is the connection between Diwali, the Indian New Year's Day, and the welcoming back of Rama to Ayodhyā? I've always heard that there is some kind of connection.

Dr. Smith: There is, but I'm not very well prepared to answer that kind of question. The best I can do is to speak generally. Let me start by saying that holidays are times when believers celebrate their faith, oftentimes by employing rituals that help them to recapitulate a story, or part of a story, which relates to their faith, and this helps them to recall the story and reaffirm their faith. Be aware, however, that not all believers celebrate the same holidays in the same way; and some holidays are observed by only very few believers.

Now then, the Hindu year is punctuated by days which serve to remind followers of Rāma of him and his career. Early in the new year, in March-April, there are nine days of commemoration that lead up to the remembrance of Rāma's birth—this cycle is called "Rāmnāvmi." A few months later on a full moon is commemorated Rāma'ş crossing into Laṅkā. A month or so after that, on the tenth and last day of what's called "Navarātri," devotees celebrate the *Dussehra*-victory, which is recollected by many Rāma *bhaktas* as Rāma's defeat of Rāvaṇa. And, twenty days after that, observed by many Hindus on the fourth day of the five-day Diwali cycle, is when many of the faithful mark Rāma's return to Ayodhyā after his fourteen year exile. Other days in the year mark the birthdays of Hanumān, of Valmīki, of Tulasīdāsa, and so on. I wish I knew ıny religious history better—maybe I would be able to give you more specifics.

SR: Here's one for the historian: the relationship, if any, between Roma

(Rome), in Italy, and Rāma, and of Ravenna and Rāvaṇa. Perhaps it's more than coincidence?

Dr. Smith: Who can say? I'd rather not touch that one. Actually, your question about geographical locations reminds me of a whole other realm of scholarship over which oceans of ink have been spilled, and that has to do with the location of Laṅkā. The popular notion is that Laṅkā is Śrī Laṅkā, or Ceylon.

SR: Ceylon?

Dr. Smith: Yes, Ceylon. That's, after all, an Anglicized approximation of Śrī Laṅkā. But when you move back several centuries to more ancient times, and delve into what other names Śrī Laṅkā was known by, Śrī Laṅkā wasn't always called anything like Laṅkā! So that led some scholars to look for another offshore island that would fit the Rāmāyaṇa's description of Laṅkā. I remember reading one book that made a case that Valmīki's Laṅkā was none other than Australia.

SR: Australia! Really?

Dr. Smith: [Laughter] Another tried to prove that ancient Laṅkā was Sumatra.

SR: Are these people eccentrics, or are they respected scholars?

Dr. Smith: They are respected scholars in some Indian traditional communities. Quite a few Western scholars think they are a little off the mark, however.

SR: Right. Australia, that's . . .

Dr. Smith: Then there's another large group of very respectable archaeological-trained Indian scholars, who place Laṅkā up north, maybe in the Orissa area, not an island at all. Recall, there are remote, swampy areas around there that could just as well be the Laṅkā of the story. But, of course, the whole thing turns on the issue of the historicity of the story, that is, whether or not it is reflecting historical, i.e., real, events and places. And to some of us, that is a moot question, including some of us who may be Hindus. On the other hand, those committed literally to the faith claim that Rāma once walked the Earth. They feel they've got to find those places—Ayodhyā and Laṅkā have to be real places, they say. They are the ones who insist that present-day Ayodhyā was built on the ruins of the original, "real" Ayodhyā. And maybe Laṅkā is just over yonder...

I, as an historian of religion, take that quest very seriously. That is to say, there are many people who are committed to the absolute historicity of the story—whether I share that belief or not, really, is immaterial. For sure, one of the real areas of scholarly inquiry for those who consider themselves scholars of the Rāmāyaṇa has to do not only with the location of Laṅkā but also with the identity of the Rākṣasas. You wouldn't believe some of the stories you get about that!

SR: That's another big question.

Dr. Smith: Right, but I think it's brutally obscured by pseudo-anthropology, and fantasies having to do with coccyx bones.

SR: What do they say?

Dr. Smith: Well, that the Rākṣasas had tails. There are articles, "Did the Rākṣasas have tails?" The assumption is, of course, that the Rākṣasas actually existed, and since they did the question must be addressed whether those beings were the precursors of the human race, or subhuman? They try to justify those kinds of speculations with what we know about physiology and developmental anatomy.

SR: And they talk a bit about the coccyx?

Dr. Smith: Quite a bit. You know, right down at the base of your spine, when you fall down on the ice or something, what gets hurt is sometimes the coccyx. What they say is that the vestigial coccyx was, possibly, originally, the tails of the Rākṣasas, those precursors of the human race.

SR: Right.

Dr. Smith: Yeah. But I think we should give some time in this discussion to attitudes concerning the historicity of this story, of the *kathā*.

SR: We can discuss that now.

Dr. Smith: Well, to get right down to basics, it has to do with how one understands the word *avatāra*, more specifically, in what sense, if any, the *avatāra* of Rāma was historical. If so, when? If so, where?

SR: They say Tretā yuga.

Dr. Smith: That's the answer given. And the literalists can even give a date, in July or something of such-and-such a year. And that's fine for the believer—but it's only one of several possible perspectives. You see, it's that literalist commitment to the historicity of it, just like Christians are absolutely committed to the historicity of Jesus, that is at the crux of the matter.

SR: Right.

Dr. Smith: Just as many Christians affirm that Jesus really did exist in Jerusalem in the year One, also many Hindus say with the Rāmāyaṇa: Rāma really did exist and he lived in Ayodhyā, and when he went, he went out to Laṅkā, and there he fought and defeated Rāvaṇa and laid low all the Rākṣasa hosts. Now that's a real tight bind that people put themselves in. Whereas on the other hand, another way of dealing with it, is to say that it is all a myth. Now please don't misunderstand me: this view doesn't necessarily hold that the story is fictional; what it says is that the Rāmāyaṇa is telling a story that doesn't have to be taken literally on all counts, and that it is basically a story, if nothing else, that tells us quite a bit about human nature.

SR: And some believers take it like that?

Dr. Smith: Oh, indeed. Quite a few Hindus share that perspective—not many but there are definitely those who do. For example, how do college-educated Hindus deal with it? Well, some, to be sure, just go back to their childhoods, saying, "Oh Rāma. Bless Rāma." Others, however, *do* try to think in terms of mythic meaning, and try to probe for deep, psychological references in their own experiences.

In fact, I gave a lecture in India one time on Rāma Pāda-Yātrā—following in the footsteps of Rāma—and dealt with all the wonderful temples that have been built to commemorate places between Ayodhyā and Rāmeśvaram, where Rāma "rested" during his sojourn to Laṅkā. And I really got called—challenged—by a very sophisticated, urban Hindu, who asked, "Why are you committed to this Rāmāyaṇa story being historical?" I was astonished! Because, actually, I thought I was playing to the audience. And it taught me a lesson. From that point on, I became more self-conscious about my presentation: I have since tried to identify what is for me myth, and what aspects of the story might in fact possibly reflect what one might call historical reality. It's not so easy for me; but it's a better presentation.

SR: You have to be careful about using a word like "myth"...

Dr. Smith: I know. Unfortunately the word "myth" has generally negative connotations. Some people think that if something is a "myth," it is necessarily untrue. And that's not what I mean at all. What I'm saying is that the commitment to an historical literalism in dealing with the story has its implications. You have to find out where it was, when it was, who were the Rākṣasas, and it just opens up a whole gamut of questions, many of which seem themselves to run counter to the general tenor of the tradition.

SR: Right. So you're not questioning the story's veracity—on some level you see it as true. But you would say that we should look more deeply at its implications. The how, where, and when are secondary considerations. But it's the deeper aspect that is to be considered important.

Well, there's certainly truth to that. But I wonder how much of that is just resignation: "We can't possibly, at this time, find the answers to the how, where, and when questions. So we're going to say that this story can't be understood in that context. Rather, it is to be understood in terms of its deeper implications. So it is not a subject for historians."

Of course, there are some questions that would only be of concern to believers. For instance, did you ever come across a text saying that Rāma has a greenish complexion? Traditionally, he seems to be painted like that.

Dr. Smith: So far as I know, that's in Valmīki—and it's stated more than once. Now one of the things I have to level with you on, in terms of why you're talking to me about the Rāmāyaṇa, rather, than, say, Robert Goldman: Dr. Goldman could probably quote to you in Sanskrit from Valmīki the passages where it says that Rāma is green. I know from a translation, or I think I know from a translation (if the translation is correct), that he's described as green in Valmīki. That's a big, big difference.

So, of course, I'm waiting with bated breath, as are most scholars interested in the Rāmāyaṇa, for the completion of Goldman's translation of the Baroda critical edition. Several volumes are released already by

Princeton University Press, and altogether there will finally be seven volumes—one for each of the *kāṇḍas* of Valmīki. I may not agree with every word, but I have to hold it in high regard because those volumes will represent the most informed opinion of the scholarly community to date.

SR: One *kāṇḍa* we didn't really discuss is the core of the *Yuddha-kāṇḍa*. I think we should speak about the war. That's a very important section.

Dr. Smith: That's where we are in my class right now. We're smack in the middle of the *Yuddha-kāṇḍa*, just finished Kumbhakarṇa getting killed off.

SR: Maybe you could give some highlights of the war.

Dr. Smith: Well, I'll tell you, I'm interested in reaction to the war in the *Yuddha-kāṇḍa*. For village folk across the length and breadth of South Asia, the battle scenes are absolutely entrancing. They can't seem to get enough of the blood and gore. They even want to hear it over and over again. Now, as a teacher of Rāmāyaṇa, especially to undergraduates who know little about India, Rāmāyaṇa, Indian cultural history, or just about anything, I find it interesting that one of the young girls, a student in my class, said yesterday, "You know, it's all so tedious." Of course, as a teacher, I then tried to think, "Well, how can I make it not tedious?" But she said, "It's just one battle after another, and they all sound alike." Which is absolutely true. That student's boredom and frustration, however, is not unusual for those distanced from things Hindu and Indian.

The North American undergraduates new to the Rāma-story, who approach the battles of the *Yuddha-kāṇḍa* so differently from the South Asian villager, have required some special teaching strategies. For them, it's necessary to stress the drama of the continuing battle. It's in that context, then, when we're reading about the battles in class, that I try to raise some simple questions: is it indeed all of Rāvaṇa's kith and kin who are sent into the battle? Is everyone destroyed before Rāvaṇa enters the fray? I suggest that one dramatic way of looking at all these ensuing battles is that Rāvaṇa is sending out his emissaries and lieutenants, and they get killed off one by one as an onion gets peeled, layer after layer. Finally he's standing alone and has to fight Rāma—because there's no one left. In that sense it's very dramatic. And I try to get my students, even the bored ones, to appreciate that.

Another point I try to make is when you start reading these portrayals of the battles, they do become rather formulaic. You can almost recite how they're going to transpire. Someone has to get down out of his chariot. Then he's killed by a weapon that flashes through the sky. You know, all that sort of stuff.

SR: Predictable.

Dr. Smith: You said it. They certainly are. So there's a formulaic element that harkens back to the orality of the tale, when it was told around the campfires and so forth. And then there is also the possibility that I suggest to my students—in part I do it to make them read more carefully—that there may be some pattern behind this seeming repetition. I haven't figured it out yet myself, but why should the carnage just be meaningless or random? Eveything else in the story seems to relate organically or symbolically or in some way to other things, so why don't the battles relate either to one another or to some other elements in the story in some way? And I tell them to look for it. I don't know whether they do or not. . .In fact, that's one of the reasons I'm looking forward to the appearance of the *Yuddha-kāṇḍa* in that Princeton translation series of the critical edition.

SR: To see what they come up with?

Dr. Smith: What they come up with, yes, if anything. Alas, they don't always come up with everything I'm looking for. [laughter]

SR: It will be interesting, yes. Now, let's just talk a little bit about things like the *Rāma-carita-mānasa,* which Gauḍīyas, in general, don't accept. I've heard Śrīla Prabhupāda say that when Tulasīdāsa translated the Rāmāyaṇa into Hindī—which is the *Rāma-carita-mānasa*—he inserted some things that could be considered impersonalism, a philosophical school which, of course, runs counter to the Vaiṣṇava doctrine.

Now I don't know exactly what he means by that, or just what text he's referring to. But there are, in fact, many Gauḍīyas who sort of frown upon the Tulasīdāsa Rāmāyaṇa.

Dr. Smith: Well, I find that very interesting. That's about the only comment I can make. Does it mean, perhaps, that Tulasīdāsa uses philosophy in a Vedānta sense?

SR: Perhaps. Advaita Vedānta. Or as you were saying before—I think he gives room for the rare Hindu who would say that the historicity is not that important. Maybe he endorses the idea that Rāma can be seen as an abstract principle. Apparently there are verses to that effect in the *Rāma-carita-mānasa.* That's why Gauḍīyas sort of frown upon it. Gauḍīyas tend to be very fundamentalist in this sense.

Dr. Smith: Well, standing back a little, I would say that it is significant that the Gauḍīyas feel they must deal with the *Rāma-carita-mānasa* at all. Perhaps because it is such an important text throughout all of North India—Hindī-speaking India—they simply cannot ignore it. There is, it appears, some kind of grudging acknowledgement of it.

SR: Right.

Dr. Smith: Incidentally, there is a book in Hindī that you might want to look for. . .it's by Father Camille Bulcke. Ever heard that name?

SR: It sounds vaguely familiar.

Dr. Smith: He recently, well, within the last decade, he died.

SR: He wrote in Hindī?

Dr. Smith: And in English. He has this book called *Rāma Kathā,* published out of Allahabhad in 1950, in which in Hindī he surveys early Rāma literature and modern indigenous Rāma-type literature. And he identifies some 300 versions of the Rāma *kathā.* Now that has been a rather, well, I won't say seminal, but a very important synthesis in Hindī. It is referred to a lot. In fact, there's an English translation of it under way in Australia. But why am I telling you about a Hindī book from the fifties when there's a recent book in English that would also prove helpful here? It's called *Many Rāmāyaṇas,* edited by Paula Richmond (University of California, 1991); it contains some excellent essays.

SR: I'm aware of that book. I think Phil Lutgendorf's contribution there is a first-rate piece of scholarship and an important aspect of the Rāma tradition as well.

Dr. Smith: That's right. It *is* quite good. And in the context of what we've been talking about, so are the very informative essays by A.K. Ramanujan and by Frank Reynolds—one dealing with Indian variants, the other with retellings beyond India. But to return to where we were: you mentioned Śrīla Prabhupāda's misgivings about Tulasīdāsa's Hindī Rāmāyaṇa. I wonder if there have ever been any pronouncements by him on some of the Bengali Rāmāyaṇas?

Perhaps they just haven't had the popularity, you know, in Bengal that the *Rāma-carita-mānasa* has had in the Hindī-speaking areas. Although I am told that most Bengalis know their Rāmāyaṇa through the Bengali versions. Yet some of those versions vary considerably, if we can take the Valmīki as standard.

SR: Do you know anything about those Bengali versions?

Dr. Smith: Only that not too many of them circulate in the form of books. It's oral tradition, or it's fragments that one can find quoted in other texts. But if someone were into folklore, that would be the way to get at it, I suppose. There is a book called *Bengali Rāmāyaṇas* and it's by R.S. Dineshchandra Sen, an illustrious Bengali scholar. Although it was published way back in the 1920s or so, you might still be able to locate it in a library.

SR: Did you list it in one of your books? Maybe I can look it up.

Dr. Smith: I listed it in one of my Rāmāyaṇa-related bibliographies, yes. Are you familiar with those works?

SR: Yes. I've often referred to them. I think that's where I got a lot of information for an article I once wrote for *Back to Godhead* magazine.

Dr. Smith: Well, it was probably from the one called *Reading the Rāmāyaṇa.* That was originally planned as a two-volume effort. Then two different publishers published them, so that plan didn't work. Thus we have two quite differently formatted books. But the first one is on various translations in English, just trying to sort them all out and identify them, and give some order to students who might be interested. That came out in 1983 in Syracuse. And then a much more recent one, I think it appeared in '89 in Bombay. It's called, *A Select Bibliography of Rāmāyaṇa Related Studies.* And that has to do with simply trying to list studies *about* the Rāmāyaṇa. I don't discuss Gauḍīya-related Rāmāyaṇas per se, but I suppose you could get some useful material out of it. To my knowledge, there haven't been many studies on the Rāmāyaṇa's relation to the Gauḍīya tradition. But I guess there are some important connections.

SR: One way to tie it into the Gauḍīya tradition, of course, is through the Hare Kṛṣṇa *mahā-mantra*—Hare Kṛṣṇa, Hare Rāma.

Dr. Smith: Yes. That's a self-evident connection.

SR: And the tradition often teaches that the "Rāma" in the *mahā-mantra* refers either to Balarāma, Kṛṣṇa's older brother, or to Lord Rāmacandra, the hero of the Rāmāyaṇa. So Gauḍīyas see it as applying to both.

Dr. Smith: Balarāma being Kṛṣṇa's older brother. Right. And they say it doesn't matter. Rāmacandra is also called upon in the *mahā-mantra.* Yes.

SR: If you're a Rāma *bhakta,* you can chant it and think of Rāmacandra. If you're a Kṛṣṇa *bhakta,* you can think of Balarāma. But there is an interesting statement in the *Caitanya-caritāmṛta.* It says, "As far as the holy names of Rāma and Kṛṣṇa are concerned, they are on an equal level. But for further advancement, we require some specific information from the revealed scriptures. The holy name of Rāmacandra is equal to 1,000 holy names of Lord Viṣṇu. The pious results achieved from chanting 1,000 holy names of Viṣṇu three times can be attained by only one repetition of the holy name of Kṛṣṇa. The great Vedic teachers have thus concluded that for every three times one chants the name of Rāma, one can attain the same results by chanting the name of Kṛṣṇa once."

Dr. Smith: So that would be three times the *Viṣṇu-sahasra-nāma.*

SR: Right. That equals one Kṛṣṇa. Or three names of Rāma.

Dr. Smith: Well, that makes sense within the tradition, because they are extolling the virtues and the power of the name of Kṛṣṇa. The Gauḍīyas see Kṛṣṇa as supreme, the source of all the *avatāras.* So, although they do not understate the position of Rāma, or the power of Rāma, they see him as subservient to Kṛṣṇa. In one sense, on the absolute platform, they see Rāma and Kṛṣṇa as equal. But when you get down to it, they bring out the supremacy of Kṛṣṇa.

Mahābhārata

Alf Hiltebeitel

Alf Hiltebeitel is a frequent contributor to academic journals around the world and has written several important books, such as* The Ritual of Battle: Krishna in the Mahābhārata *(Ithaca: Cornell University Press, 1976) and* The Cult of Draupadi *(Chicago: Chicago University Press, 1988). One of the world's preeminent authorities on the Mahābhārata, Dr. Hiltebeitel has written entries on this subject in the* Abingdon Dictionary of World Religions *(Nashville: Abingdon, 1982) and Mircea Eliade's* The Encyclopedia of Religion *(New York: Macmillan Free Press, 1987). He is currently Professor of Religion at George Washington University.

SR: Let's first discuss the Mahābhārata as literature and then we can see how it relates to the Gauḍīya Vaiṣṇava tradition.

Dr. Hiltebeitel: Well, the common statistics are that it is three times the size of the Judaeo-Christian Bible and about seven times as long as the Iliad and the Odyssey combined. So you're dealing with quite a formidable work.

SR: It is usually described as being roughly 110,000 Sanskrit couplets. . .

Dr. Hiltebeitel: Yes. Now, there are problems that scholars face when dealing with such a massive text. If you go back to the late nineteenth century, you find the beginnings of a debate over whether the Mahābhārata had developed from a core, accommodating various accretions, interpolations, and additions. They say it developed from some original kernel to something much more massive.

Then there was the other side, which argued that all of the stories and sections of the Mahābhārata had a sense of unity and could possibly be the work of a single author.

SR: You're talking about the "Inversion View" and the. . .

Dr. Hiltebeitel: That's right. The first idea was later called the Inversion View. This view was basically worked out by two German scholars named Adolf Holtzmann and Adolf Holtzmann the Younger. They claimed that the Mahābhārata has many authors—little or no unity. You might find it interesting, too, that according to these two scholars the original story was one in which the Kauravas were the "good guys" and the Pāṇḍavas were the "bad guys."

SR: How did they come up with that?

Dr. Hiltebeitel: Well, the way they came up with it was by recognizing that the portrayal of the Kauravas and the Pāṇḍavas is ultimately ambiguous. And so at many points Duryodhana, the chief Kaurava, is portrayed as a noble kind of hero, with even the gods acknowledging his greatness. There is even one episode, just before Duryodhana dies, where he boasts that he was a great king, and Kṛṣṇa doesn't deny it. He could have, but he doesn't. So it is accepted on some level.

SR: But ultimately this view was countered.

Dr. Hiltebeitel: Yes. Dahlmann argued that the unity of the Mahābhārata lay in the complementarity of its two aspects. First it tells a story, which according to him is the epic aspect, or *Epos*. Then, too, it delivers teachings on *dharma*, or religious duty, and this he called *Rechtsbuch*—literally, "lawbook." So these were the two aspects. And Dahlmann, among other scholars, felt it was quite natural that one author could have easily written all of the stories, pausing occasionally to elucidate the religious meaning of the stories. And this is indeed what you have in the Mahābhārata.

SR: So these are the two prototypes that scholars tend to debate.

Dr. Hiltebeitel: Exactly. It still rages on. In fact, it has become even more complicated. For example, in Edward W. Hopkins's *The Great Epic of India,* he totally dismisses the synthetic view. He denies that the Mahābhārata has any unity whatsoever and he says that it could never have possibly been written by one author.

Hopkins said that the work developed in stages, which is more or less the Inversion View all over again. Although he didn't accept the Inversion View as it was, he developed a new version, if you will, and, in many ways, it focused directly on the personality of Kṛṣṇa. As far as Hopkins was concerned, in the original story there was no Kṛṣṇa—Kṛṣṇa came into the story at a later date.

Originally, says Hopkins, the story merely focused upon the fight between cousins. Then, later, there are stories introduced in which Kṛṣṇa is a kind of human teacher of righteousness and statecraft and things like that. And then Kṛṣṇa is *Vaiṣṇavized,* or at least turned into a kind of demigod. Finally, Hopkins says, Kṛṣṇa is turned into the "All God." A fully developed divinity. This gradual and time-conscious view, particularly as it applies to Kṛṣṇa, still seems to have many adherents.

If you assume that Kṛṣṇa has been gradually theologized, perhaps by the influence of late sectarian traditions like the *pañcarātra,* then you're going into it with a particular view. This is argued by Ruth Katz, from Harvard, who wrote a book called *Arjuna in the Mahābhārata.* She accepts the view of Kṛṣṇa's gradual Godhood. So there is quite a scholarly tradition for this and it has abided for some time.

But I see no reason for it. Even in the several Mahābhārata passages where Kṛṣṇa is considered to have been somewhat human, he still has four arms—and you've got to contend with that! [laughter] No. I would say that he is exactly who he is supposed to be—God. It all really comes down to your perspective. But I don't think you can really find texts in the Mahābhārata that imply he is anything other than a divinity. God. That's it. If you look at the texts objectively, it is clear, sometimes tacitly and other times more obviously, that he is who he is—and that's definitely God.

SR: I would be surprised if there were many scholars who held that view.

Dr. Hiltebeitel: It's certainly *my* view. And M. Biardeau could also be counted amongst those who tend toward this position. And even one of India's greatest Mahābhārata scholars, V. S. Sukthankar, who was the general editor of the Poona critical edition of the Mahābhārata and the author of a book, *The Meaning of the Mahābhārata*—he also upheld this view. There are many. Let's face it—to try and read beyond the text, to prior stages, is risky, speculative.

SR: It's purely hypothetical. It takes a certain *chutzpa* to come up with these theories, and even more *chutzpa* to vehemently defend them.

Dr. Hiltebeitel: [Laughter] Right. Sukthankar has this wonderful passage in which he says that Kṛṣṇa is the *Paramātmā*—the Supreme Lord—who is "winking" at all of these scholars who struggle to figure him out. Or it's something to that effect. [Laughter]

Basically he's saying that Kṛṣṇa is there on a number of levels, but that these levels are not historically emergent. They are levels in which the text is reflecting its theology, which is quite comprehensive. So on some levels Kṛṣṇa is operating in a human-like way, and he says this himself. At other times, he functions in a divine way, showing who he really is. This is revealed in a number of theophanies throughout the Mahābhārata.

SR: Does the Vedic tradition accept this? I mean, the Mahābhārata is not *śruti*—it is not Veda. Yet it is accepted as scripture, especially by the Vaiṣṇavas. Sometimes it is described as the "Fifth Veda."

Dr. Hiltebeitel: Oh, yes. It is widely accepted. And, yes, it's true that it is known as the "Fifth Veda." *It calls itself* the "Fifth Veda." Of course, this is not unique to the Mahābhārata. A good deal of later Indian literature is known by this same handy title. But I think the Mahābhārata was the first to be given this distinction.

Now, by placing emphasis on the Mahābhārata are we saying that the four Vedas were not enough? No, it's never taken in this way. The idea is that the Vedas were to be brought into a new formulation for a new age. This is the Mahābhārata. This is the Veda for a new population, for the masses and for people of all castes and persuasions.

SR: For Kali-yuga, the Iron age. It makes Vedic teachings accessible and relevant for the current epic in world history.

Dr. Hiltebeitel: Exactly. It is for a new time and for an extended population. And of course it teaches *bhakti*—devotional love—to that population. This is the special contribution of latter-day scriptures, and it is meant especially for this age. According to most Indian texts, the methods of self-realization in previous ages were sacrifice, meditation, knowledge, *tapas,* and austerities of that nature. But in this age it is *bhakti,* giving, sharing—all with a sense of love of God.

SR: In the Gauḍīya tradition this is emphasized. *Kīrtana,* especially *saṅkīrtana*—the congregational chanting of the holy name of God—is the recommended process for this age. *Bhakti* and giving, or sharing, in its highest form, centers on sharing the holy name, to chant with love and devotion, alone and with others.

Dr. Hiltebeitel: That's the Gauḍīya perspective. Yes. But this sense of *bhakti,* in general, is essential, and this is a central teaching in the Mahābhārata. So as the "Fifth Veda," it introduces the process for the age. This is important.

Another feature that ties the Mahābhārata into the Vedic tradition is that the personalities of the Vedic literature manifest as the characters of the Mahābhārata. First of all, Kṛṣṇa is clearly identified with Viṣṇu in a number of passages. Droṇa is the incarnation of Bṛhaspati; Bhīṣma is the incarnation of the celestial sky-god; Aśvatthāman is a portion of Śiva; the Pāṇḍavas are the sons of major Vedic gods; and so on, ad infinitum. So, in a certain sense, you can say that the whole Vedic pantheon is reactivated in the story, or the stories, of the Mahābhārata. This of course is all centered on the figure of Viṣṇu, or Kṛṣṇa.

The basic story is as follows: the goddess Earth comes to Brahmā first and complains that she is being overrun by demons and is sinking in the ocean. And then Brahmā says, well, go to Viṣṇu. So she does go to Viṣṇu and pleads with him to rescue her from her plight. Viṣṇu then takes two hairs—a white hair which becomes Balarāma, and a black hair which becomes Kṛṣṇa. This, of course is another way of identifying Kṛṣṇa (the black hair) with Viṣṇu. So there are different ways to conceptualize around the notion of *avatāras.* But, in any case, Viṣṇu is the central figure around whom the Mahābhārata is envisioned as a text which introduces *bhakti* as the teaching for everyone, and as the teaching more specifically for the Kali-yuga.

SR: Now the *Gītā* occurs about five or six chapters into the Mahābhārata?

Dr. Hiltebeitel: It's in the sixth so-called book or *parvan.*

SR: I saw the nine-hour play of the Mahābhārata by Peter Brook and I was very disappointed that when they came to the part of the *Gītā* they just showed Kṛṣṇa whispering to Arjuna, covering his mouth, and that was all there was to it. But it seems as though the *Gītā* should be a very significant segment.

Dr. Hiltebeitel: Well, you'll very soon get the chance to see the TV version of that. Barbara Stoler Miller was one of the advisors and she sent Peter Brook all the best lines from the *Gītā* and strung them together. So there's more *Gītā* in the new Peter Brook variant.

SR: Her version of the *Gītā* is quite good. I think her translation pretty much captures the spirit.

Dr. Hiltebeitel: Yes.

SR: What did you think of the Peter Brook play?

Dr. Hiltebeitel: Well. I thought it had a lot to recommend it—especially the nine-hour version. He managed to come to it with a very rich, imaginative, explorative tone. And I liked the fact that he had actors from around the world, different voices. Some of the scenes I thought were quite wonderful. But there were a number of things I had reservations about. One of them was that throughout the play Kṛṣṇa was made to appear kind of dour, wan and almost whiney. [Laughter] It's as if he felt, "Well, you know, I've got to do all this stuff." Also, Kṛṣṇa, you know, schemes with a smile. But this was missing in the Brook version. Kṛṣṇa is supposed to set the stage for some kind of catastrophe with the most subtle grin. That's one of the things that you can't miss if you know what the iconography looks like. That's a statement about seeing what Kṛṣṇa's up to in a *bhakti* kind of mode. But Peter Brook doesn't develop this subtlety, his player doesn't have this Kṛṣṇa smile. Rather, he looks like he's a figure who's going through one long weary scene of dire disaster, and the Mahābhārata is not really like that. I thought that this was a failure. And there are a couple of things that he has Kṛṣṇa do that are not in the classical Mahābhārata at all—like he has Kṛṣṇa tell Bhīṣma to be quiet at the dice match, or he has Kṛṣṇa carry the arrow across the stage that hits Bhīṣma. These are extra charges that we don't need.

SR: What about the later portions of the Mahābhārata, maybe we can discuss that—the war, the Battle of Kurukṣetra and how it finishes. I don't know much about how the battle ends. I had heard that the five Pāṇḍavas survive and that's it, but that there were some six hundred million people in that battle.

Dr. Hiltebeitel: Well, that's a number that I don't have, but maybe there is a number somewhere in the text. I forget.

SR: But are there some stories about that battle that come to mind, something to give the spirit of the Mahābhārata.

Dr. Hiltebeitel: Well, you see, the way the war works is that it is set up over eighteen days and the main Kaurava heroes lead the army through its various stages. At each point where one of them dies, Duryodhana has to name a new general. All these are major heroes—they are either incarnate gods or sons of gods or whatever, and they are on the bad side. So that is one thing, the Mahābhārata always plays with ambiguity and uncertainty. There are good divine forces who are in the Kaurava camp as well as in the Pāṇḍava camp.

Like Bhīṣma—he dies on the tenth day. Well, he's the grand old man, and he doesn't really die on the tenth day. He's filled with arrows and he lies on this bed of arrows for fifty-six more days waiting for the point at which the sun begins to ascend toward the north. It's basically the winter solstice, when the sun begins to get higher and higher in the sky. So that is the auspicious time to die, and the Mahābhārata war is taking place a couple of months before that. So Bhīṣma postpones his death, and the whole time that he is lying on the bed of arrows after the war is when he discourses to the Pāṇḍavas at Kṛṣṇa's insistence. He speaks about *dharma* and various aspects of salvation and so on.

So, in any case, it's hard to pick one hero, but the basic pattern is that there are a series of major Kaurava heroes who die, and in almost all cases, Kṛṣṇa, Arjuna, Yudhiṣṭhira and others sort of team together with various other heroes, particularly Draupadī's brothers. There are different ways in which the Pāṇḍavas, Kṛṣṇa, and then the brothers of Draupadī, team together to dispatch most of the major Kaurava heroes. And then certain major Pāṇḍava figures also die. The leading figure there is Arjuna's son, Abhimanyu. He is very, very crucial. And you saw that Peter Brook's dramatization of that scene was quite effective, with the chariot wheels, the staves, going here and there, closing in a circle. In other words, Abhimanyu ran into a circle that the Kauravas had made. And they made it, in effect, to entrap him. He can enter and fight within it but he has not learned the secret from Arjuna of how to get out of the circle. So they entrap him in the circle and finally he is clubbed to death.

And that then enrages Arjuna into making a vow: he will avenge his son's death. It sort of goes back and forth like this and you have all of these dramatic shifts in the course of the battle. But basically one of the strange things that happens in the course of the Mahābhārata is that while the Kauravas are decimated—there are only three Kaurava survivors, one of whom is Aśvatthāman, the most important, who is the incarnation of a portion of Śiva, or Rudra—on the Pāṇḍava side you have seven survivors, meaning the five Pāṇḍavas, Kṛṣṇa, and the relative of Kṛṣṇa, Sātyaki. The key thing that has to be noted here is that somehow all of the Pāṇḍava children die. All of Draupadī's children, all of the Pāṇḍava children from other wives as well, Bhīma's co-wife, etc.

Anyway, the sad fact of the matter is that Kṛṣṇa plays a scheming role in bringing about the deaths of all of these children. So not only is he helping the Pāṇḍavas decimate the Kauravas, but he is leaving them in a dynastic crisis wherein they will have no heirs at the end of the war. But the interesting thing is that the killing of Draupadī's children involves Aśvatthāman trying to kill the Pāṇḍavas. Kṛṣṇa plays a prominent role in this, taking the Pāṇḍavas off to a special camp where they will not be found by Aśvatthāman, but their children will be found instead.

So Aśvatthāman kills the Pāṇḍavas' sons. Then, Draupadi, realizing this the next morning, goes into a fury and says that she wants the head of Aśvatthāman. So Bhīma sets out to try to kill him, but he can't. Arjuna and Kṛṣṇa set out behind Bhīma, and Aśvatthāman releases this great weapon, the *brahmaśiras* weapon, on them. He has learned how to do this from his father Droṇa. Meanwhile, Arjuna also knows how to use this same weapon, which he had received from Śiva. So Arjuna releases the weapon as well and the two weapons meet in the sky, ready to cause the destruction of the universe.

By the way, Peter Brook does not give us this scene; he gives us an alternate one, kind of like *Apocalypse Now*. It's not the Mahābhārata's version. Anyway, while these two weapons are in mid-air there are various *ṛṣis* who appear in the air between them—Nārada and Vyāsa, for example—and they plead with the two heroes to withdraw their weapons. Now, Arjuna, because he is a perfect *yogin* and very disciplined, can withdraw his weapon, but Aśvatthāman cannot.

The uncontrolled Aśvatthāman, still enraged, wants revenge against the Pāṇḍavas, and so he utters a *mantra* that gives his weapon a new destination. The *mantra* is *apāṇḍavāya*, which means "for the nullification, or the destruction, of the Pāṇḍavas." He directs this into the wombs of all the Pāṇḍava women—to make them barren. They are all affected by this in terms of becoming barren, but one of them is pregnant, Abhimanyu's young wife, Uttarā. Abhimanyu had been killed in the battle, but now Uttarā is afflicted by this weapon and her fetus is destroyed. So Kṛṣṇa hears that this baby has been destroyed and he promises that he will revive it. He says that it will be born stillborn but he will breath life into it.

This is, in effect, how Kṛṣṇa sees to the renovation of the world. The renovation of the Kaurava-Pāṇḍava line—the Pāṇḍavas are actually Kauravas in the sense that Kuru was the ancestor of both branches of the family. So, after the line has been divided, after all this destruction has taken place, the miraculous revival of the child, which, in a certain sense, represents the renovation of the world and the inauguration of the Kali yuga, at least in an auspicious direction, is overseen then by Kṛṣṇa.

SR: Now the child in the womb was Mahārāja Parīkṣit, and I know the story is told in several different ways. *Śrīmad Bhāgavatam* (1.8.15) says that the weapon was neutralized, or *samaśāmyat*, by Viṣṇu, or Kṛṣṇa, *before* the child was killed. But whether Parīkṣit was revived, as you say, or initially saved, is really only a detail. The fact is this: Parīkṣit was born and his existence is vital for the retelling of the story in the context of the *Bhāgavatam* revelation. This is important from the Gauḍīya perspective. And Parīkṣit came out of the womb as an "examiner," or someone who was looking for that personality—Kṛṣṇa—who saved him. Therefore he was called *Parīkṣit*, or "examiner." This reflects a central tenet of Gauḍīya theology: that everyone in this world is really looking for Kṛṣṇa.

Dr. Hiltebeitel: And there is one other note which would be important for the Gauḍīya school as well. Another thing that has become a standard comment in a discussion of the Mahābhārata by scholars is the notion that you have really two Kṛṣṇas. You have the Mahābhārata adult Kṛṣṇa, and then you have Kṛṣṇa Gopāla, the younger Kṛṣṇa. There are arguments against that. In other words, the argument can be made that even though these two parts of Kṛṣṇa's career are dealt with in different texts, for the most part, these texts are very much aware of each other. The whole story was always known; there's never been a purely pastoral tradition about Kṛṣṇa, or a purely martial tradition.

SR: You would opt that it is the same Kṛṣṇa.

Dr. Hiltebeitel: Yes, for me it is the same Kṛṣṇa. Kṛṣṇa is Kṛṣṇa.

SR: It's interesting because in the *Gītā* he's called "Govinda," which refers to him as a young cowherd boy. So there you have an overlapping of the so-called "two" Kṛṣṇas.

Dr. Hiltebeitel: Exactly. There are all kinds of little details. When Kṛṣṇa makes a deal with Arjuna and Duryodhana that he will not fight as a warrior in the battle, he becomes a non-combatant chariot driver. He says that Arjuna can have him, Kṛṣṇa himself, on his side, and he tells Duryodhana that he can have all his warriors, Kṛṣṇa's warriors. Well, Duryodhana thinks that this is great. Anyway, this is a separate issue. But who are Kṛṣṇa's warriors? They are called the Nārāyaṇa *gopas*. So what is this? Why *gopas*—cowherd boys? This is clearly an allusion to the "earlier" Kṛṣṇa.

SR: That's interesting!

Dr. Hiltebeitel: Clearly the passage is aware of this connection. And when Kṛṣṇa's sister Subhadrā marries Arjuna, and Arjuna brings her home and she meets Draupadī—she dresses up as a cowherd girl, a *gopī*.

SR: This hearkens to Kṛṣṇa's younger life or, as they would say: the "other" Kṛṣṇa. . .

Dr. Hiltebeitel: I would say so. There are a number of other allusions I can make, but those are some of the clearer ones.

SR: I guess scholars would say that those are later interpolations.

Dr. Hiltebeitel: Exactly. So there you have it. That's the quick answer. [laughter] But there's no way to prove it. All of those passages are right there in the so-called critical edition. So there's no way to get a text prior to that. Meanwhile, the *Harivaṁśa* story, which is the first version that tells you the youth of Kṛṣṇa, has countless references to episodes that will occur in the Mahābhārata, that foreshadow the Mahābhārata. Anyway, that's one thing and then the other thing, another cliché that I think *is* a cliché, perhaps no more than that. And these are certainly conventional wisdoms that can be challenged—there is this major distinction between emotional *bhakti* and intellectual *bhakti*. If you read the *Bhagavad-gītā*, you see that it's an intellectual text, to some degree. But if you look at what happens at the end of the eleventh chapter, or throughout the eleventh chapter, particularly after Arjuna sees who Kṛṣṇa is—Time Incarnate. So he says, "I bow to you, having treated you as my friend, I now realize that you are God." He basically mentions all the possible ways in which one can relate to Kṛṣṇa—as a lover, friend, all these kind of things.

SR: *Rasas.*

Dr. Hiltebeitel: Right. They're basically like the *rasas,* although they're not called that in the *Gītā.* In any case, Arjuna has clearly undergone a deep emotional experience. I think that that distinction is overdrawn. To be sure, it's one that you can make in terms of increased emphasis on emotional *bhakti* in the later tradition. But I don't think it's a very close reading of what's going on in the Mahābhārata.

SR: But it *is* there. And so the Mahābhārata reveals a good deal of the essential truths that were developed in the Gauḍīya tradition. Śrī Caitanya's followers use this text, as they do the Purāṇas and many other works, as a basis for their theological stance. And when you get down to it, they have created an abiding tradition, one that has a formidable basis in Indian culture and spiritual philosophy.

Dr. Hiltebeitel: That's clearly a fine conclusion.

Bhāgavata-purāṇa

Clifford Hospital

Since completing his Ph.D. thesis in 1973 (Harvard), entitled, The Marvelous Acts of God: A Study in the Bhāgavata Purāṇa, *Clifford G. Hospital has written two books,* The Righteous Demon: A Study of Bali, *and* Breakthrough: Insights of the Great Religious Discoverers, *as well as numerous essays on Kṛṣṇa, Purāṇic Hinduism and inter-religious relations for prominent academic journals in America, Europe, and India. Since 1971 he has taught at Queen's University at Kingston in Canada, where he has been Principal of the Theological College since 1983. He also served as Head of the Department of Religion from 1983 to 1991.*

SR: The *Śrīmad Bhāgavatam,* or the *Bhāgavata Purāṇa,* as it is also known, was the first Purāṇa to be translated into a European language. It was translated into French in 1840 by E. Burnouf.

Dr. Hospital: That's correct. And it has remained a standard accepted translation. Another celebrated translation from the nineteenth century was that of the *Viṣṇu Purāṇa* by H.H. Wilson. Obviously Vaiṣṇava Purāṇas early attracted the attention of Western scholars.

These are fine translations. If I have any reservations about them, it has to do with a general problem in the translation of the Epics and Purāṇas into modern Western languages. As you know, these are all written in Sanskrit verse forms. These verse forms, as in the case of the epics of ancient Greece and Rome, are integral to the tradition. The question is, how does one best communicate the meaning and flavour of these texts into English or French. The most convenient method is to translate them into prose. An entire translation of these long texts in verse would seem to us quite artificial.

On the other hand, there are sections, particularly in the *Bhāgavata*, which cry out for a verse translation if one is to do justice to the poetic rhythms. I don't mean just the sound rhythms, but also rhythms of symbols and juxtapositions. And as well, the uses of imagery and a certain quality of mystery, of the epiphanic, that pervades the text.

SR: A certain poetic beauty that is intertwined with the essential meaning.

Dr. Hospital: Exactly. In many passages of the *Bhāgavata*, if you try to pick up in a translation the musical quality of the Sanskrit verse, and the *rasa*, the flavour of the text, it is necessary that the translation be in verse. So I hope that some time soon, someone will present us with a translation that is at least partly in verse. The problem is that to sit down and translate the entire *Bhāgavata* is a daunting task.

SR: Well, Prabhupāda's translation doesn't approach it in verse form, but it is a valuable contribution in the sense that it provides an English rendering with authentic Gauḍīya insight or perspective. What do you think?

Dr. Hospital: Well, what can I say? It was quite an achievement. I have certainly found it useful to see the way in which certain words are rendered in that tradition. I am not always convinced that his translation best presents the meaning of the *Bhāgavata* text. For example, *līlā*, or "play," is generally translated "transcendental pastime." Recent scholarship related to this word would suggest that that is a bit too high flown. And that correlates with another feature of the translation as a whole: the English seems to me rather Victorian, old-fashioned. And from what I said before, you can guess that I would wish he had tried some English verse.

There is also the fact that the translation is so guided by what you called "the authentic Gauḍīya insight." I prefer to try to understand the *Bhāgavata* on its own terms. Part of what is involved here is trying to understand the integrity of the *Bhāgavata* as a whole. Nevertheless, his translation is a significant contribution.

SR: Yes. I wanted to ask you about the original nature or structure of the

Bhāgavata. How many Cantos and verses, and things of this sort, and I also want to know why it is such an important text for the Gauḍīya Vaiṣṇava community.

Dr. Hospital: Right. I prefer to talk about the entire work. Then it becomes clear that what the Gauḍīyas pick up, very significantly, is the picture of Kali-yuga, which comes at the end, and what's required at that time, particularly focusing on the name of God as the way to liberation. That seems to me to be the distinctive emphasis that the Gauḍīyas pick up. As for the rest of the text, I think, they regard the *Bhāgavata* as primary because it gives the account of Kṛṣṇa's life. Beyond that, they, more than any other single group, seem to me to pick up the flavor of the *Bhāgavata*, in general, but that's subjective. . .

In fact, in this, I'm probably exaggerating, if one thinks of it more seriously. Certainly some of the Hindi poets, Sūradāsa, and so on, have profound insight and understanding as well. But what I find most interesting about the *Bhāgavata* is the flavour, what I would call the *rasa* of the text. The emphasis upon the playfulness of Kṛṣṇa and the tying of various devotional moods into that. The stories of Kṛṣṇa become—via the response of the *gopīs* and the cowherd people particularly—the way in which one understands devotion. But I should go back and talk about the text more broadly I think.

SR: Right. I'd like you to explain the background. Or maybe you can give a broad overview of the content.

Dr. Hospital: I think the initial thing to say about the *Bhāgavata,* from an academic point of view, is that it seems to be essentially based on the structure of the earlier *Viṣṇu Purāṇa,* which consists of six books, or Cantos. The *Bhāgavata,* of course, is divided into twelve. In both cases, however, you have a consensus about what a Purāṇa involves. Stories about creation, primal creation, the creation of our world, in our age, with particular emphasis then on the Varāha-yuga, which begins with the Boar *avatāra* of Viṣṇu.

SR: Is that Satya-yuga?

Dr. Hospital: Excuse me, did I say Varāha-yuga? Varāha *kalpa,* I should say. This begins with the Satya-yuga and the declining ages of four *yugas.* Beginning with that account of creation, one then has, as it were, a history of our great age, of our *kalpa.*

As we go on, we see that there's a combination of essentially three different things in both the *Bhāgavata* and *Viṣṇu Purāṇas.* Stories or histories of great kings, well-known kings of the past. Undoubtedly, from a scholarly point of view, these are not so much historical accounts as accounts which were intended to reflect the ideals of Indian society at the time.

Intertwined with those you have two other kinds of stories. The first of these is stories of great saints. (Some of these kings clearly act in that category as well.) I'm using the word *saint* in the broadest sense of ideal figures for the tradition. In this context you have figures like Prahlāda, or Dhruva, who pick up on the portrayal of virtue and devotion in these texts.

The third set of stories elucidate the various *avatāras,* incarnations of Viṣṇu, and these are greatly increased from the *Viṣṇu* to the *Bhāgavata Purāṇa,* as are the stories of saint figures, I think. There's considerably more detail and a lot more material in general.

Now, I guess there's a fourth thing that runs alongside as well, and that is a considerable amount of direct teaching about the nature of devotion, or *bhakti.* It's often actually incorporated within one of the others, but sometimes it appears on its own. In the *Bhāgavata* there is a large section on Kapila, too—a detailed account of Sāṁkhya philosophy. The *Bhāgavata* draws quite a bit on that particular *darśana* or that philosophical tradition.

What you have, then, is quite an extensive piece of work. We're talking about some 18,000 Sanskrit verses. Now, what intrigues me about the whole piece is the way in which it holds together. If you spend a lot of time with Purāṇic literature, you find they are extraordinarily diverse in the ways in which they are constructed. I am certain that in the case of many Purāṇas, a basic text was used, and then other materials were added to the basic text. You can see, in some cases, that they're added in slabs, and then the main text continues on. In other cases, the nature of the text changes completely—at a certain point you have what is clearly an addendum to the original piece.

What's significant about the *Viṣṇu,* and then the *Bhāgavata Purāṇa* following it, is a very clear construction from beginning to end which presents a kind of sacred history. Westerners often think about Indians as not being interested in history per se; and when they're being accurate about that, what they mean, I guess, is the kind of interest in detailing actual historical events in a datable kind of fashion, in the way in which we do it in the West. That interest doesn't seem to be in evidence. But if you look at the way history has functioned traditionally in the West, in terms of the way in which it provides an account of the past, and the way in which people learn their heritage, I think texts like the *Viṣṇu* and the *Bhāgavata* function in a similar way. They give you this account, a very extensive history, going back a long time, and via this story of the ancient past, they mediate the messages from which people could benefit.

SR: So, even among Purāṇas the *Bhāgavata* is special. But perhaps you can give an overview of the basic contents, delineating the fundamental structure of the work.

Dr. Hospital: In the Second Book, the structure in regard to subjects covered is laid out something like this: you have *sarga,* or primary creation; then *visarga,* secondary creation; *sthāna,* law and order; *poṣaṇa,* welfare and protection; *manvantara,* the lineage of earthly rulers; *ūti,* the explanation of enjoyment; *īśānukathā,* stories of the Lord in his various manifestations; *nirodha,* annihilation; *mukti,* liberation; and *āśraya,* or the ultimate refuge. This is how it's traditionally broken down.

SR: Good. Now maybe we can discuss why, according to the Gauḍīya tradition, the *Bhāgavata* is considered the natural commentary on the *Vedānta Sūtra.* And then they talk about the three sittings of the *Bhāgavata.* Are you familiar with the three sittings? How first it was divinely revealed to Brahmā, and then from him to Nārada to Vyāsa to Śukadeva, and Parīkṣit, and so on.

Dr. Hospital: Oh I see. Yes. It's an elaborate story of transmission—to the sages at Naimiṣa Forest. In a sense, I think that goes back to the kind of thing one finds in the Mahābhārata, where you get. . . .Well, take a sidetrack on this. Obviously the Purāṇas are on very much the same order as the Mahābhārata and the Rāmāyaṇa as epics.

SR: *Smṛti* and *itihāsa.*

Dr. Hospital: Well, yes, that's true. But what I meant is that they are the same general genre in their construction and what they try to present. In the case of all of these texts, you usually have something which is seen as coming from a great seer—but then that seer has received it from somebody else. There's a line of authority that's established. And the line of authority usually goes back to one of the gods. From a scholarly perspective, I would see the *Bhāgavata* as fitting into that kind of pattern. The other question? Oh, the *Vedānta Sūtras.*

SR: Right. They say that the *Bhāgavata* is a natural commentary on the *Vedānta Sūtras.*

Dr. Hospital: I'm trying to think what that means. Obviously there are different ways that one could talk about a commentary on the *Vedānta Sūtras.* The standard form of commentary, of course, is to explicate serially the various *Sūtras.* If you're talking about a "natural" commentary, though, I suppose what you mean is that the general world-view that the *Brahma Sūtras* present is dealt with in the *Bhāgavata* in the process of working through this sacred history, as I've been referring to it.

I mentioned that a lot of teaching is incorporated into the sacred history. One could certainly see that teaching, if you put it together, as a particular interpretation of the *Vedānta sūtras.* If one is talking about direct links, a very interesting question is raised by the idea of *līlā* and the way in which it is related to the creation of the world In the *Brahma Sūtra.* In a sense, creation is *līlā* in the Brahma Sūtras.

SR: In fact, there's a *śloka* like that in the *Vedānta Sūtra.*

Dr. Hospital: Yes, it is verse 2.1.33: "But as in ordinary life, creation is mere sport." Now "sport" is Radhakrishnan's translation of *līlā.* In the *Bhāgavata,* too, when there's reference to creation—or more broadly, the three-fold process of creation, preservation, and destruction—very frequently the word *līlā* is incorporated with the description of that or with reference to that. It's clear that in the *Bhāgavata* version the Lord creates as a part of his *līlā.*

Now what that means—whether it's intended to mean the same as in the *Brahma Sūtra*—is another question. One of the difficulties, of course, is that in the *Brahma Sūtra* itself you have only cryptic statements into which people can feed a great variety of different interpretations. The interpretation of that particular piece from the *Brahma Sūtra* by both Śaṅkara and Rāmānuja, for example, uses the analogy of a great king who is completely fulfilled and who therefore plays not to fulfill some hidden inner need, but rather as a spontaneous act.

This explanation is an attempt to deal with the theological problem of why God, who is complete and fulfilled, comes to create. And the emphasis is on the fact that God doesn't need to create, that this is not something that is done because there is a lack in God. Rather it is something which just comes spontaneously out of who that Supreme Person is. It comes from His inherent nature.

SR: There is also Baladeva Vidyābhūṣaṇa. . .

Dr. Hospital: I was going to explain that, too. There is another kind of interpretation that's given to *līlā*, which is worth mentioning because it comes from the Bengali Vaiṣṇava tradition. Baladeva of the eighteenth century, commenting on the word, as Radhakrishnan puts it, "makes out that *līlā*, or sport, is the overflow of joy within. As in ordinary life, a man full of cheerfulness on awakening from sound sleep dances about without any motive or need, simply from fullness of spirit, so is the case with the creation of the world by God."

Now what you can see there, in effect, is the typical Bengali version of *līlā* as in fact an outcome of the joy of God. There's a great deal of emphasis on that emotional component, as it were, in the whole tradition, and of course within God Himself. What interests me is that the term *līlā* is used, in these cases, in a slightly different way than the way it is used in relation to *avatāras* of the Lord. And I think while discussing *līlā*, we should get into the whole subject of *avatāras* as they are presented in the *Bhāgavata*.

SR: Yes. So let's take a sidestep for a moment. When the *Bhāgavata* gives the list of *avatāras*, it concludes that list with one verse, *kṛṣṇas tu bhagavān svayam*, which is made much of in the Gauḍīya tradition. Jīva Gosvāmī, in fact, declares this to be the *mahāvākya* of the Purāṇa. Correct me if I'm wrong, but this verse clearly states that Kṛṣṇa is Supreme among all the incarnations—the source of all these incarnations. Perhaps you can talk about that a little bit.

Dr. Hospital: Well, I think the *Bhāgavata* is very interesting on the whole idea of incarnation because, clearly, you have in the text itself major detailed treatments of what were to become the standard ten incarnations. (That standard ten, of course, varies from tradition to tradition in India.) Then there are lists which include a considerable number of other *avatāras*, and in some cases it looks as though Kṛṣṇa is just being treated as one along with all the others. However, in the *Bhāgavata* list, which includes Jīva Gosvāmī's *mahāvākya*, Kṛṣṇa is seen as in some sense being in a class of his own, superior to the rest.

Indeed what seems to be going on there is a picture of *avatāras* as generally a lower level manifestation of God. But when you come to Kṛṣṇa, he is not just "a manifestation." He is God Himself. Of course, this is picked up by the Gauḍīya tradition, who then say, "Yes, and in fact Kṛṣṇa is the Supreme Reality. All this reference to Bhagavān throughout the text is really a reference to none other than Kṛṣṇa. And when Viṣṇu is being talked about, it is the lower level. . ."

SR: They say expansion. . .

Dr. Hospital: Okay. My point is that the Gauḍīyas see Kṛṣṇa as the highest level of Viṣṇu and I think that the *Bhāgavata* is slightly more complex than that. What's really going on in the statement, "But Kṛṣṇa is Bhagavān Himself" is that there is an identification of Kṛṣṇa and Viṣṇu so that they are seen as really one and the same being. And, as I see it, the writer of the *Bhāgavata* wouldn't make a distinction between the two. Perhaps it could be said that in Kṛṣṇa you see the full nature of Bhagavān, who's most often called Viṣṇu. You see the full nature of that being in the person Kṛṣṇa, who comes down to earth at a particular time and place. What you see then at that particular time and place is the fullness of God.

SR: There are Gauḍīyas with this perspective as well. . .

Dr. Hospital: Yes, but I may be influenced too much by the Rāmānuja tradition there, because I think the Śrī Vaiṣṇavas tend to present it in that sort of way.

SR: Well, if the emphasis is on Kṛṣṇa somehow reflecting Viṣṇu, then it does have a South Indian flavor.

Dr. Hospital: That's a possibility, yes. But can we return to *līlā* for a moment? What intrigues me is the way in which the *avatāras,* including Kṛṣṇa, are incorporated into a series that's referred to generically as *līlāvatāras*—distinctions are made between these and other kinds of manifestations of God. This is in 2.6 and 2.7, where the list of twenty-four *avatāras* is introduced by that term. What intrigues me is that the idea of play is included within the list a number of times. There and elsewhere, it's clear that part of the way in which Kṛṣṇa is so important is that the whole movement of the Purāṇa is towards a focusing on Kṛṣṇa as the fulfillment of that playful *avatāra* activity. The *avatāra* for play. Again, of course, you have an interesting puzzle because you don't know what, precisely, is being meant by *līlāvatāra*. One might again assume that this is just a way of saying, "Well this doesn't need to be done. It's all just the Lord's outflow of joy." Yet the term *līlā* is used so often in connection with the major incarnations. The idea of the playfulness of the act—even when it's the destruction of the demons, or Kṛṣṇa's lifting up Mount Govardhana. There are frequent references to this kind of activity being done with play, or *līlā*; and there are other more specific images: "like a child with its playthings, its toys, Kṛṣṇa smashes the demon;" or he holds up Govardhana "like a child with a play umbrella."

SR: The *Bhāgavata* uses that analogy?

Dr. Hospital: Directly, yes. So you are given a range of images which suggests that every act is indeed playful activity. When you look at the details of the account of Kṛṣṇa, there is an extraordinary amount of emphasis on the childhood playfulness and the way in which that captivates all of the people in Vṛndāvana. The more I have looked at this, the more I've been convinced that the use of the idea of play in relation to these—whatever its origin—comes gradually to be built into a picture where these stories are told in such a way as to re-evoke, as it were, the response of the cowherd people in Vṛndāvana as they see what Kṛṣṇa does. When I was working on my thesis on the *Bhāgavata*, I was intrigued by a term that's used so often there, the "marvelous acts," or the "wonderful deeds," of God; and the picture that comes out in the Kṛṣṇa materials of the response of the cowherd people as being continually wonder, love, joy. And, of course, these emotional responses, which are central to the *Bhāgavata* view of *bhakti*, have been picked up and elaborated upon by the Gauḍīya lineage.

When you put this together with other things, like the idea of māyā, not illusion, of course, but "marvelous acts," again, or "divine power". . .

SR: Not Bhadrā but Subhadrā. Not Mahā-māyā but Yoga-māyā. Divine energy. *Śakti.*

Dr. Hospital: Divine energy. Yes. When you put it together with that idea, there certainly is a quality of illusion there. A divine illusion, a quality of the magical, I think, is still there in the notion of *māyā*. But what I think you get here is a picture of God coming into the midst of his people, the Vraja-loka, performing these acts—some of which are simple childish acts, some of which are naughty acts that little children perform.

But all of them have a magical quality to them that calls forth this response, that, well, parents have toward their children. The way one watches in amazement.

SR: An endearing quality. Befuddled by love.

Dr. Hospital: Yes. There is something about this child that you cannot but respond to. And, of course, this is expressed very poignantly in the story of Brahmā's stealing the calves and the children and enclosing them in a mountain cave because he wants to see Kṛṣṇa perform some charming marvel. There is this account of Kṛṣṇa, by means of his *māyā*, creating a series of replica children and calves; and there's a marvelous section in which it says that love of the parents for their children—their "illusory" children—increased beyond measure. They love them almost as much as they formerly loved Kṛṣṇa himself. [laughter]

There's a wonderful play there, because I think what's being suggested is the love that Kṛṣṇa draws forth is indeed of the same order as the natural love that parents have for their children. But it's carried to a much greater extent. It's an extension beyond that—to a kind of perfection of love for Kṛṣṇa.

SR: In the later literature, Rūpa Gosvāmī analyzes that. That's when he goes into his *rasa* theology: that one will have love for Kṛṣṇa as a parent in *vātsalya* mood, if that's his eternal relationship with God, and so on. Or *mādhurya rasa,* or *sakhya rasa,* etc.

Dr. Hospital: Oh yes. Clearly the Gauḍīya tradition draws that out, though it's equally clear that in the *Bhāgavata* itself there is no developed typology such as you have in the Gauḍīya tradition. Still, all the elements of the Gauḍīya tradition are there. And if you follow through that section of Book Ten, you see what the Gauḍīyas pick up: a sort of movement or flow from the *vātsalya* or parental mode to, eventually, the intimacy of the divine lover, the beloved relationship or the *mādhurya* phenomenon. This is more developed toward the end of that section.

SR: Let's take a slight detour and talk about the date of the *Bhāgavata.* Wilson, Colebrooke, and the Arya Samajists say that the *Bhāgavata* was written by Vopadeva in the thirteenth century, and that's been a big controversy. Now, there are scholars who refute Vopadeva's authorship. The opinion that the *Bhāgavata* is Vopadeva's creation is so untenable that historians like J.N. Farquhar, who wrote for Christian missionaries, had to admit that "it is quite impossible to believe that Vopadeva was the author, for, Madhva, who regarded it as fully inspired and used it in the creation of his sect, lived at least fifty years earlier than Vopadeva." What would you say about that?

Dr. Hospital: I think he's absolutely correct on it, but probably the most important work that's been done on that has been by J.A.B. van Buitenen and Friedhelm Hardy.

SR: And it predates Vopadeva?

Dr. Hospital: Oh yes. Absolutely. On a separate note, though, what's interesting about their work is that they do detailed analyses about the relation between certain parts of the *Bhāgavata* and the South Indian Āḷvār tradition. I think they make a very good case for what people have long suspected: that many of the ideas of the *Bhāgavata* are coming out of the South Indian tradition.

And I suppose the way the theory goes, then, is that the full blossoming of the Gauḍīya tradition really comes through the contact that Caitanya had had in the South when he had gone there and brought back a version of the *Kṛṣṇa-karnāmṛta,* which, as you know, is a South Indian text.

SR: And *Brahma Saṁhitā.*

Dr. Hospital: Right. And there are a few verses in the *Bhāgavata* (11.5.38-40), which van Buitenen describes as "a *post factum* prophecy," and in which there is reference to "devotees of Nārāyaṇa in great numbers everywhere in Tamil country. . . ." So this suggests that the author knows the flourishing development of devotion to Viṣṇu which is represented for us by the Āḷvārs. And the verses are detailed enough geographically to suggest that the author knows the area quite well. But as well, to expand on what I said before, Friedhelm Hardy in his book, *Viraha-bhakti,* has shown strong similarities of detail between passages in the *Bhāgavata* and certain poems of the Āḷvārs, which are not found in other texts of that period.

One of the other significant questions is that if the *Bhāgavata* came out of the south, why is it that Rāmānuja clearly doesn't place a great deal of emphasis on it. Instead, he places emphasis on the *Viṣṇu Purāṇa.* He appears to view the *Viṣṇu* as authoritative, but not the *Bhāgavata.* Now,

Rāmānuja was living in the early twelfth century?

SR: That's right.

Dr. Hospital: So that might suggest that the *Bhāgavata* was a bit too new.

SR: Or else it could suggest that it was not in line with Rāmānuja's emphasis, which was Viṣṇu.

Dr. Hospital: Very good. Yes. This is the other possibility. That is—and this in a way is related to your question about the *Brahma Sūtras*—the particular view of God in the *Bhāgavata* is not quite Rāmānuja's view. There is the Kṛṣṇa vs. Viṣṇu factor, but also the *Bhāgavata*, at times, promotes a conception of God as being beyond the acts he displays. In some places, there are pieces that lend themselves to an Advaitin interpretation, and Rāmānuja would never stand for that. So these are also acceptable reasons why he preferred the *Viṣṇu Purāṇa*.

There's one other thing worth mentioning, I think. The Gauḍīya tradition is basically *bhedābheda*, correct? Distinction in non-distinction. I think maybe that is an accurate picking up of what I was just talking about—the inscrutable relation between God and the world. You know, that there is an incomprehensible. . .

SR: *acintya*, or inconceivable. Yes. . .

Dr. Hospital: The incomprehensible holding together of difference and non-difference. In the *Bhāgavata*, God is both beyond action and he is acting, beyond qualities and at the same time he is the one who bears all magnificent, auspicious qualities.

SR: Well, that's interesting. What you're saying, in effect, is that the *acintya bhedābheda* concept of the Gauḍīyas is indirectly found in the *Bhāgavata*.

Dr. Hospital: Oh, yes, I would say so. Not using terms, but it heavily implies it. When the *Bhāgavata* moves into philosophical, or theological, thinking—it doesn't often because, really, it is so much more focused on what is actually taking place, that's where the center of attention actually is—but when it moves into more abstract thinking, you do occasionally get something that can well be seen to be the foundation of the Gauḍīya version.

SR: One thing about the Gauḍīya tradition: as much as Kṛṣṇa *līlā* is important, jumping to the Tenth Book of the *Bhāgavata* is considered taboo. They often warn that one needs to read the first Nine Cantos to properly understand Kṛṣṇa *līlā*. Only then would one pursue it with the proper reverence. Did you run up against that in your studies?

Dr. Hospital: No I haven't, but that *is* interesting, isn't it? Because I think the outside view is that the Gauḍīya tradition focuses almost totally on Kṛṣṇa.

SR: It is humorous, in one sense, yes. But they would insist on the proper development. One should know *Bhagavad-gītā* and the first Nine Cantos, and one should study them under a bona-fide *guru*. Then, and only then, does Kṛṣṇa *līlā* become accessible.

Dr. Hospital: That you really only see the significance of what's going on when you go through the process of these earlier traditions. Well, I'm not exactly sure what they mean by it, but I can see that the important themes of the *Bhāgavata* develop methodically, according to a scheme. As an aside—but perhaps along the same lines—it's quite magnificently constructed as a text. It's very well thought out, although you get little introduction to the great vision that you will get when you reach Kṛṣṇa, or the Tenth Book.

You do get foretastes of it as you go through earlier stages. And this is perhaps what they mean. You need to understand the philosophy and the themes and the personalities that lead up to it. In order to interpret adequately what's going on, say, with the *gopīs* and the others in Vṛndāvana, you really need to know what the *Bhāgavata* has been saying on occasions beforehand.

SR: Exactly.

Dr. Hospital: And, of course, this all relates to the nature of devotion—so that you don't misinterpret what's actually taking place there.

SR: Right. Right.

Dr. Hospital: If you think that there's just some licentious sort of activity that's going on in Vṛndāvana, you've completely misunderstood it. And to avoid this misconception there are many earlier examples—in the materials focused on Prahlāda, for example—where you have a detailed exploration of the nature of *bhakti*.

Look at Book Seven, for example, Chapters five to nine. In Chapter Seven, verses thirty to thirty-six, you have this extraordinarily important statement: "By service to a *guru* with devotion, offering him all one has acquired, by joining with pious devotees and by worshipping the Lord, by narrating with faith the accounts of his glories and deeds, by meditation on his Lotus Feet, by beholding and adoring his image, with the thought in one's mind, 'Hari, the blessed One, the Lord is present in all beings.' One should regard all creatures as good. In this way conquering the six passions, devotion to the Lord is attained. One finds joy in blessed Vāsudeva."

SR: This is the *śravaṇaṁ kīrtananaṁ viṣṇoḥ*. . .

Dr. Hospital: Well, it's based on the same idea.

SR: Very famous verse.

Dr. Hospital: Further, "When a man has heard the incomparable glories and heroic deeds performed by Hari, in bodies assumed in play, and when from too much joy the hairs of his body stand on end, with tears in his eyes, and uncontrolled speech and neck stretched out, he sings out loud, lets out a yell and dances. When like one possessed, he laughs and cries, he meditates and pays homage to men, often sighing, engaged in introspection, all bashfulness gone, and 'Hari, Lord of the World, Nārāyaṇa,' he cries, then is a person released from bondage." That's my translation.

SR: That's beautiful! That's very beautiful. And it brings to mind a lot of Gauḍīya concepts, like the *sāttvika bhāvas*, the transformations of the body that arise from intense love.

Dr. Hospital: So I guess what I'm saying is this: if you come to the Tenth Book and haven't read this, you know, you've completely missed what you were supposed to learn, what the Tenth Book is about. So I presume that's part of what the Gauḍīyas are saying when they demand a reading of the preliminary literature.

SR: I would say that's basically it. And, you know, things like the apparent sensuality of Kṛṣṇa and the *gopīs*—unless you've read the Nine Cantos and you've seen all the warnings against gross sensuality, you're likely to misinterpret the later texts. There's a similar phenomenon, I think, in *Gīta-govinda*. It begins with establishing the divinity of Kṛṣṇa, and then it goes into the erotic-seeming *līlā*.

Dr. Hospital: Yes. So you learn right in the beginning the frame of reference in which you are to understand this profound exploration of the relationship of the person to God.

SR: Right. The only other note I have here is to discuss the Eleventh and Twelfth Cantos of the work and why it comes after Kṛṣṇa's pastimes. It seems as though Kṛṣṇa's *līlā* would be the crown jewel, the concluding episode, but then there are two more cantos. What would you say about that?

Dr. Hospital: Well, if you go back to where we began, I guess the simple answer is that one has to see it as basically following the structure of the *Viṣṇu Purāṇa*, which I think it does. I could have given more detail on that, but in fact, with one or two minor displacements, the actual order of the stories is the same. So I can't imagine that it's not fairly closely dependent on the *Viṣṇu Purāṇa*. And the *Viṣṇu Purāṇa* certainly ends in that way.

I think the intention in both cases, then, is to bring one down to our time, Kali-yuga, and to point forward to the future coming of Kalki. That's there in both of them. What that then does, of course, is set the frame of reference for where we human beings are in our lives. How are we to relate to all this? And, in my view, that's where this idea is picked up by the Gauḍīyas in a most coherent way. At least I would see the Gauḍīya interpretation as a fully acceptable one.

They say that, according to the *Bhāgavata*, under the conditions of Kali-yuga the easiest process of God realization is made available. In fact, the Twelfth Book of the *Bhāgavata* directly states that what was attainable in Satya-yuga by meditating on Viṣṇu, in Tretā-yuga by performing sacrifices, and in Dvāpara-yuga by worshipping the holy feet in the temple—all these can be attained in the Kali age by chanting the names of Hari. In our evil age the simplest form of devotion will suffice. There are often paradoxical things that abound in the Kali age, and this is one of them: that it's easier to find the bridge in the Kali-yuga, even though it's the worst age. In the earlier ages, people were capable of more, somehow, and so more was expected.

SR: Right. Śukadeva Gosvāmī says: "Although Kali-yuga is an ocean of faults, there is still one good quality about this age; simply by chanting

Kṛṣṇa's name one can become free from material bondage and be promoted to the transcendental kingdom."

Dr. Hospital: Right. Well, one of the wonderful things about this literature is that it continues to re-make itself, as it were. You get all kinds of nuances developed within accepted structures. What starts out saying, "Oh we live in a terrible, terrible, wicked age, compared with the way things were in the past," includes a later reflection which says, "Yes. That's true. But in our time, chanting is all that is required of us." And so, in Kali-yuga, there is the potential for an even more wonderful focusing on God, because the method is so simple. Just contemplate the name, we are told, and perfection is assured. It's as simple as that.

Now, Books Eleven and Twelve, after the high point of Kṛṣṇa *līlā,* do, in a sense, seem a bit anti-climactic. True, there are sections that are essential for a complete understanding of what one has encountered in the other cantos. But in Book Eleven it's as though the writer is just continuing to tell the story of Kṛṣṇa without having the same kind of emotional, devotional interest in it. Do you know what I mean?

SR: Well, sort of. In the Eleventh Book I think there is some discussion of Kṛṣṇa's departure. So that might be one reason why the author seems to lose enthusiasm.

Dr. Hospital: Yes. But then it moves into the Twelfth and you certainly see that it's going somewhere. It's coming to us, to our time, and setting the frame of reference for that. What's more, it's not that the Eleventh doesn't have pertinent information. The Eleventh Canto also has a good deal of important instructions to Uddhava. Well, let's see. The Eleventh and Twelfth Books are said to deal with *mukti* and *āśraya,* predominantly. They contain the *Uddhava-gītā,* as I've mentioned, which is very deep, the legend of the destruction of the Yadu dynasty and, yes, Kṛṣṇa's ascent to his own kingdom. This is the Eleventh. Then the Twelfth deals with the Kali-yuga, as I've mentioned, and it ends with the long-awaited death of Parīkṣit. And then it gives a summary of its own contents.

Kṛṣṇa in the Performing Arts

John Stratton Hawley

John Stratton Hawley is the author of many books, including At Play with Krishna: Pilgrimage Dramas from Brindavan *(Princeton, New Jersey: Princeton University Press, 1981), which he wrote in association with Shrivatsa Goswami;* The Divine Consort: Rādhā and the Goddesses of India *(Berkeley, California: Berkeley Religious Studies Series, 1982), a collection of papers co-edited with Donna M. Wulff;* Krishna, the Butter Thief *(Princeton University Press, 1983); and* Songs of the Saints of India *(New York, Oxford University Press, 1988), a book of poems for which he contributed text and notes and shared translations with Mark Juergensmeyer. In addition he is published in many academic journals and is chairman and professor of religion at Barnard College, Columbia University.*

SR: I would like to begin with an understanding of how you became interested in *rāsa līlā* performance. And how you became interested in Kṛṣṇa as the butter thief. Your book, with Shrivatsa Goswami, *At Play with Krishna*, was a very important contribution in the area of Kṛṣṇa in dramatic performance, perhaps on a par with Norvin Hein's *Miracle Plays of Mathurā*. . .

Dr. Hawley: Oh, I don't think so. . .

SR: Well, perhaps you can talk about your introduction to the themes associated with *rāsa līlā* performances.

Dr. Hawley: Sure. You might be interested to learn that it wasn't at all what I went to India to find out about. I had gone intending to do a dissertation on Sūradāsa. Alas, I'm still doing that dissertation. And I was based in Benares, of all places, which clearly proved to be the wrong place. So I was very lucky to be introduced, by Donna Wulff, to Shrivatsa Goswami, who then welcomed me to Vṛndāvana. And once one goes to Vṛndāvana in the *rāsa līlā* season, as I did, you know, you are just surrounded by dramatic performances of the *līlā*. So there I was, staying in the heart of Vraja, and the *līlās* were being performed day and night.

SR: You were staying with Shrivatsa.

Dr. Hawley: Right. Well, I was staying in what has come to be called the Śrī Caitanya Prema Saṅsthāna. Near the Yamunā and the Rādhā-ramaṇa temple. But you know this—you've been there, haven't you?

SR: Yes, he has really developed it. I was there just recently. Shrivatsa's library is one of the best I've seen, and he's made it quite comfortable for guests—he has a ping pong table and everything.

Dr. Hawley: Really? [laughter] I wasn't aware of that. But, in any case, the whole thing is built around the stage, so even if you were interested in other things, as I was, the *līlās* were your constant companion. And they were just wonderful. They also actually involve a fair amount of the poetry of Sūradāsa, so it was good on those terms, as I saw it then.

But it was a wonderful medium for sensing what was really important to people. And what happened in the course of my stay there—and it became much clearer than it had been to me from the reading of books—is that I discovered that the motif of Kṛṣṇa stealing butter was terribly important to people and related to all sorts of areas you might not expect from a reading of books.

Līlās were performed on many diverse topics. And it would be possible for the sermonizer, who often was Shrivatsa's father, Purushottama Goswami, to take the Sudāmā *līlā*—to take one that would apparently be a great distance from the butter thief—and introduce that *līlā* to the audience by means of a sermon that would involve some reference to Kṛṣṇa in his mode as butter thief. Then, once you came into the confines, so to speak, of the *līlā* itself, once again, Kṛṣṇa himself assumes a position of the one who's giving an introductory speech, with music, as you know. That's the way these dramas are performed. And there, again, very often

the "Kṛṣṇa" personality would refer to his own activity as a thief of butter.
So the *līlās* themselves were the deciding factors, leading me to what I ultimately would work on. That's how I came to focus on the butter-thief theme and to bring in the Sūradāsa material in relation to it.

SR: This is prior to your dissertation?

Dr. Hawley: Well, the dissertation was what utimately became the *Butter Thief* book.

SR: Right.

Dr. Hawley: So this book was the outcome of the dissertation itself. I was trying to feel my way toward it. And then the book of plays—*At Play with Krishna*—came out as a kind of, I don't know what you would say, sort of a labor of love. The book of plays was a way for me to try to say something publicly about what it had felt like to be in Vṛndāvana and at the same time to try to say something about the fair disparity between what one read in books about Kṛṣṇa in Western countries, at that time, and what one experienced of Kṛṣṇa's personality in a more dramatic mode, specifically through plays, but also in the whole ritual panoply that surrounds Vṛndāvana. It seemed to me that there was a gross disparity between those two. So what I tried to do was to write an introduction to Kṛṣṇa as he seems when you go to Vṛndāvana, rather than the typical approach, as when one studies the *Bhagavad-gītā,* and then tries to deduce from that who Kṛṣṇa must be.

SR: I see. So you were concerned about conveying the "real" Kṛṣṇa as opposed to just some academic counterpart. There's a related thing, too, that I think you are getting at here. Correct me if I'm wrong, but it appears as if you were also trying to express the difference between the Mahābhārata Kṛṣṇa and the Purāṇic Kṛṣṇa, the Kṛṣṇa from the *Bhāgavatam,* for instance—his early *līlā* in Vṛndāvana—as opposed to the Kṛṣṇa who comes out in the *Gītā*—a very different side of Kṛṣṇa.

Dr. Hawley: That's right. What I was trying to express was that at least from the point of view of Vṛndāvana, and therefore from the point of view of pilgrims who come there as a religious observance—and that's a substantial number of people—and actually for a major contingent of other people who live in India, Kṛṣṇa's childhood is much more important than his manhood. I mean, Kṛṣṇa's "childhood," broadly conceived—his eternal childhood and adolescence—are much, much more important to people than other phases of his life, though the other side had appealed more to Western interests, especially academic interests. I don't want to put it too strongly. I may have done so. Clearly the televising of the Mahābhārata in India has made a difference in the way in which many people think about Kṛṣṇa. But I'm convinced that the Kṛṣṇa who was projected by Gandhi and the Hindu reformers, English-speakers who read the *Gītā,* is not the Kṛṣṇa who matters most to the majority of people who live in India.

SR: Right. And theologically that certainly holds true for people in the Gauḍīya tradition.

Dr. Hawley: Oh? why?

SR: Because their emphasis is on most of Kṛṣṇa's early *līlā* with Rādhā, before leaving Vṛndāvana to go to Mathurā and Dvārakā. This is considered the sweetest and most elevated. . .

Dr. Hawley: Of course. Sure. And, as you say, for theological reasons, all very clearly spelled out. One does now see such a thing as the *Gītā līlā* performed, but it is very much a recent creation and has a different tone and feel from the other *līlās.* And it requires, as a matter of fact, costuming that is different from the rest of the *līlās.* Now it is true that you will see the court of Kaṁsa in Mathurā in the course of the *rāsa līlā* as it is performed in Vṛndāvana. But it is always ancillary; it is only in the birth *līlā* or because you need that scene in order to understand why someone is coming from Mathurā to get Kṛṣṇa and take him away.

But you never see Kṛṣṇa himself, with but a few exceptions, actually leaving the Vraja country. That would be to break the mystery of it, to break the mystique. And to break the hearts of the devotees. The *gopīs,* as you know, do not like to see Kṛṣṇa leave Vṛndāvana; so why should *we* see it? Why should anyone see it? So, yes, the younger Kṛṣṇa in Vraja—this is the "real" Kṛṣṇa, if you will.

SR: In studying Kṛṣṇa drama, did you get at all involved in Rūpa Gosvāmī's writings, the *Lalita Mādhava,* for example?

Dr. Hawley: A little bit. My Sanskrit is not as good as Donna Wulff's by any stretch of the imagination. The butter-thief theme took me into Jīva Gosvāmī a bit. But my focus, increasingly, though I studied Sanskrit at Harvard, was Hindi, well, that's to say Brajbhāṣā.

SR: Studying poets like Sūradāsa, and Mīrābāī as well?

Dr. Hawley: Well, I'd read a bit of her. I've read more of her in years since. Why do you ask me about her? She's not a primary focus for the Gauḍīya tradition.

SR: Well, there's a Gauḍīya controversy about her. There are many unresolved questions about her meeting with Jīva Gosvāmī and/or Rūpa Gosvāmī.

Dr. Hawley: In fact, which one do you understand it was? Did she meet Rūpa or Jīva?

SR: Prabhupāda mentioned a meeting with Rūpa, and there is a more popularly known meeting with Jīva. The story with Jīva is the. . .

Dr. Hawley: That's the older tradition.

SR: Right. But it is certainly questionable. That story is related in Nābhājī's *Bhaktamāla*, I think.

Dr. Hawley: That's right.

SR: But there was sort of an insult to Jīva, wasn't there? Jīva Gosvāmī had said something to her about not coming to Vṛndāvana to meet with him because she was a woman. Her famous response was biting: "I thought the only male in Vṛndāvana is Kṛṣṇa."

Dr. Hawley: That's the story. Correct.

SR: Is there more to it?

Dr. Hawley: Well, that's basically it. He refused to talk with her, having taken a vow not to speak to women. I would have imagined that the Gauḍīyas would not accept it, for obvious reasons. And perhaps it never happened. One never knows. Indian religious writers like to connect popular personalities—say that they have met—but that doesn't mean they ever really did.

SR: There is another reason to doubt the story. First of all, it portrays Jīva Gosvāmī as a fanatic, in a sense, in regard to women. And he clearly was *not* a fanatic. According to both *Prema-vilāsa* and *Bhakti-ratnākara,* Jīva Gosvāmī met with Jāhnavā-devī, Nityānanda Prabhu's wife, and had extensive discussions with her. It was she who established *mūrtis* of Rādhā next to the Kṛṣṇa images in Vraja and it was she who influenced Jīva to send the *bhakti-śāstras* to Bengal with Śrīnivāsa, Narottama, and Śyāmānanda. So there is some evidence to suggest that Jīva was not extreme in this regard. If he did not turn away Jāhnavā because she was a woman, it is unlikely that he would have turned away Mīrā. After all, she was a respected Vaiṣṇavī of the time. To this day, she is remembered and there are even courses taught about her devotional poetry. . .

Dr. Hawley: Yes, well, as I say, I don't know how to adjudicate that one ultimately. The whole business about Mīrā is puzzling. I did a chapter on her in a recent book called *Songs of the Saints of India,* with Mark Juergensmeyer, where I try to bring general readers up to date on the Mīrābāī tradition. There are very interesting questions associated with it. Her hagiography is old. She must have been known in the sixteenth century. But by my count, at the time that I wrote that book, I only knew of two poems that could be verified in manuscript sources as coming before the mid-eighteenth century. And, in fact, there is a question about one of those. So there is no Mīrābāī manuscript corpus at all. The number of old poems "signed" by Mīrā is just tiny in contrast to everybody else.

So when you're reading Mīrābāī, on the whole, you shouldn't necessarily think you are reading a poem that would have been known in any century, reliably, before the nineteenth. I mean, she definitely was known, but the great mystery is why there is no corpus associated with her. There are many possible answers one could give, but there is a dissertation there and it is still to be written.

SR: One thing I've heard is that she is frowned upon because she is not linked to any *sampradāya* as such or any genuine spiritual master. So maybe this is why she was somewhat neglected. . .

Dr. Hawley: Well, that, of course, is disputed. The Ravidāsa people say that he was her teacher. But then many of Mīrā's followers would dispute that. But why would that affect a manuscript tradition?

SR: I don't know if it's directly related. I was just speculating as to why she might have been neglected. She was never emphasized in the Gauḍīya tradition because of this and other reasons—she never took formal initiation in one of the recognized *saṁpradāyas*. This is what I had heard, but I don't know if this relates to the mystery of the manuscript corpus.

Dr. Hawley: Well, there may be something to it, but then that would be problematic in several ways. Consider this: my opinion on Sūradāsa is that he didn't take such a formal initiation either, but he was claimed by the Vallabhites. Mīrā, on the other hand, was never claimed, in any way, by any *saṁpradāya*, except Ravidāsa's, if you would call that a *saṁpradāya*. I think it's something like that, but I wouldn't have put it quite the same way that you have, I guess. Additionally, probably because she was a woman, she didn't become a part of, or establish for herself, a lineage that would cause her poetry to be preserved by a group of people who would then come to be in a position of caring for it over the centuries. But you know, even with Sūra, who was a greater poet, pardon me for. . .

SR: [laughter] That's subjective, isn't it?

Dr. Hawley: [laughter] That really was. But I think, at the time, he must have been perceived in that way, and he was a different kind of poet. You have this great manuscript from 1582 in the city of Fatehpur in Eastern Rajasthan. It is an anthology, and many, many poets appear there, some thirty-five different poets. But it's primarily devoted to Sūra, apparently apart from any sectarian organization. And that just didn't happen for Mīrābāī.

SR: Why do you think the Vallabhites adopted Sūra? Is it because his poetry is theologically more along the lines of what they believe?

Dr. Hawley: No. I think this is a complicated question. It's one that in a way I'd rather not get into because I have written about it at length. But I think that Sūra's reputation in his own time, and in the decades immediately after—late sixteenth century and on into the seventeenth—was so massive that people of good taste, let's say, would have been singing him. Everyone would have been singing him, and would have known of him as the great Brajbhāṣā poet of Kṛṣṇa. So if you were building an anthology to be used in your ritual life, how could you exclude Sūra? I'm sure he was in some Gauḍīya settings as well. He certainly is today; it is impossible for me to imagine that he would not have been in the sixteenth century as well.

The Vallabhite tradition was in the process of defining a vernacular Brajbhāṣā corpus, a core of poets that would serve as the ritual basis for its tradition. In a way it didn't quite happen in the Gauḍīya sect. And it seems to me that Sūra and, perhaps, several others, were major poets who naturally would have been introduced. I wouldn't care to speculate about exactly how it happened, but the biographies or ḥagiographies of these poets did come to be associated with Vallabha. Clearly many of the poets and dramatists were Vallabhites themselves, and you can find this in certain internal elements of their work. But not in Sūra, and especially not in the poems that turn out to have been the older ones in the Sūra tradition. It may be a different story if you just pick up a copy of *Sūra-sāgara* as it's now published by the Nagari Pracarini Sabha, or some other major institution in Hindi-speaking India. But this is a complicated subject.

So I guess I'd just say this much. Normally it's thought that Sūra came to Vallabha and so forth and did take initiation from him. The popular story is that it is at this point that he shifted from his general poetry of despair and worship, written in the first person, so to speak, or, rather, spoken in the first person, to dramatic poetry that works from within Kṛṣṇa's world. But the oldest manuscript traditions don't observe that organization, and often don't observe that distinction.

Now I think—and I've written about this—that if one looks closely at the account that's preserved in the traditional texts, one can see that it probably was the other way around: Vallabha came to Sūra. But this perspective is quite unorthodox.

Still, even in the geography of it: in the hagiography you have Vallabha coming up the river from Allahabad, and he stops on the banks of the Yamunā River where, as it happens, Sūra was already dwelling. Well, if one takes that as a story rather than as an historical fact—and any look at North Indian hagiography forces you into that position because so many motifs transfer from the lives of one poet, or saint, to another—you have to begin to see it in less than purely historical terms.

In any case, to return to the story, if you don't get bogged down in the details that the hagiography loves so much, and look instead at the overall shape of the story, it was Vallabha who came to Sūra. And that's what I'm arguing would have made sense, actually, if you were trying to construct a ritual tradition that would form the nucleus for a new *saṁpradāya*. The Vallabhites came to Sūra.

SR: You know, whenever I speak to Gauḍīyas about Sūradāsa—and I've mentioned this to you before—it invariably comes to a discussion of Bilvamaṅgala Ṭhākura. That's a relation that I have trouble with because they seem so much alike—from the physical blindness to the depth and insight of the poetry—but it is said that they were different personalities.

Dr. Hawley: Yes. Okay. There's more. There are several poems which appear in Bilvamaṅgala which also appear in the *Sūra-sāgara.* Of course, Bilvamaṅgala is a Sanskrit poet, and a poem that is in the *Sūra-sāgara* is not going to be a Sanskrit poem; it's in Hindi, or, more specifically, Brajbhāṣā. But there are some very close relationships between the two. So what does one make of that?

SR: Are they roughly contemporaries also?

Dr. Hawley: Bilvamaṅgala is considerably earlier, and lived in a different part of the country, and as far as we know, he certainly wasn't writing in Brajbhāṣā. So that's a major difference. But I'd really like to know how far this connection goes back in time. The biographies of Sūra—the Vallabhite biography of Sūra and anything in the *Bhaktamāla*—the connection is just not there at that point. And whole aspects, particularly the sex life of Bilvamaṅgala, just don't arise in relation to Sūra. So I think they definitely were independent traditions up to a certain point.

Now, from the film point of view, if you see the movie on Sūradāsa—and there have been several—"Sūra" is half Bilvamaṅgala, because you need the sex to make the movie sell.

SR: You mean with the prostitute/*guru,* that whole . . .

Dr. Hawley: Of course. Sure. I mean blindness is okay for starters, but you need a little more spice—*masala*—to make the thing go. So anyway. . .

SR: So now in the dramatic performances of Vraja—the ones that you've seen in Vṛndāvana—do they make use of the poetry of Sūradāsa?

Dr. Hawley: Oh, sure. Shot through with it. All of the Kṛṣṇa stories, from childhood to *rāsa līlā*. . .

SR: Even *rāsa līlā*? Well, then again, I guess it all depends upon how you define *rāsa līlā.* I notice that in *At Play With Krishna* you seem to have a generic usage of it. I had always thought of it in terms of the *rāsa* dance between Kṛṣṇa and the *gopīs,* but it seems to be used in a broader sense in your book. Is it?

Dr. Hawley: Absolutely. You see, *līlā,* I mean, *rāsa līlā,* is the term that is used to describe this whole genre of performance. The reason it's all called *rāsa līlā,* of course, is that it cannot exist unless the *rāsa* is "imitated," to translate *anukaraṇa.* Unless the *rāsa* is represented, you cannot have an episode, an independent episode from Kṛṣṇa's life. You just cannot have it without the audience's having been prepared for it by seeing the *rāsa* itself. Because that's the core of the tradition.

SR: "*Rāsa*" meaning the circular love dance between Kṛṣṇa, Rādhā, and the *gopīs.*

Dr. Hawley: Right. So every *rāsa līlā* is composed of a *rāsa* performance and a *līlā,* and for that reason the whole tradition of dramatic performance, in this context, comes to be called *rāsa līlā.*

SR: Now I find that very interesting because the circular dance is considered to be one of the most esoteric parts of the tradition. What you usually hear is that one should study other parts of Kṛṣṇa *līlā* first—perhaps to more fully understand the theology behind Kṛṣṇa's activities—before you get into something like *mādhurya-rasa* or the circular dance. Kṛṣṇa's relationship with the *gopīs* is supposed to be very confidential and elevated subject matter.

Therefore, as in the *Padāvali kīrtanas,* they start with *Gaura Candrikā,* or praise of Lord Caitanya—often explaining who he is, theologically—and *then* they go on to Rādhā and Kṛṣṇa. Something to gradually lead up to the more esoteric aspect. But what I'm understanding from you, now, is that the circular dance is given first, at least in these dramatic performances.

Dr. Hawley: That's right. This region—it's at the center of the tradition obviously. Here the tradition is at its greatest depth. But that doesn't mean that from the point of view of most people who see these performances, or in general, or from the internal tradition of the worship of Kṛṣṇa in Vraja, you have to go through stages X, Y, and Z before your eyes are fit to see a performance of *rāsa līlā.*

But let's take it further. No one would question that those with a more refined sensibility can see more, can feel more, than people who are less well-prepared. But the tradition is acted out in a way that bars no one. So it is perhaps "better" to go into it with knowledge and a prepared sensibility, but it is not required.

SR: Does *rāsa līlā* always come first?

Dr. Hawley: The only *līlā* I know of in which the *rāsa* comes second, so to speak, or comes at the end, is the *Mahā-rāsa* itself, in which the subject matter of the *līlā*, the episode from Kṛṣṇa's life which is being presented, is the *rāsa* itself. There you follow the *gopīs* through what in the *Bhāgavata* is described as a rather elaborate process of testing and learning before you actually get to the *rāsa* itself.

Probably the *Mahā-rāsa* was always like that. The version that one sees these days is one of the more recent, and you will see it almost anywhere you go in Vraja. It's the creation of a man named Premānanda, who may be dead now, alas, but might still be alive. I'm not sure. It's something that he composed in, I can't remember exactly, but I would say somewhere in the 50s or even 60s. It hasn't been around that long. You would like it, though. It's a nice theological *līlā* and does the correct things. It's in fact a Gauḍīya *līlā*. That's his primary association.

SR: His name is Premānanda?

Dr. Hawley: Premānanda, yes. But with the exception of that one very wonderful *līlā*, I don't know any other that follows that program. The only analogue would be that before you ever get to the *rāsa* itself, at least in the dramatic *līlās* I have seen, Kṛṣṇa gives himself a kind of introduction, a musical introduction. He lets you know he's going to be seen. So there is a preparatory moment, but it's not at all so elaborate as you would expect on the basis of what you just described.

SR: Are there other *gopīs* who take a prominent role in these dramatic performances? Is Candrāvalī mentioned?

Dr. Hawley: Yes, there's a specific *līlā* for Candrāvalī. She does come up. Lalitā is probably more frequent, though, since she's the person who acts as Rādhā's main confidante. And the others are usually not mentioned by name, by contrast to what's done in the Gauḍīya tradition.

SR: So these dramas are usually in the Vallabha tradition?

Dr. Hawley: No, no, no. I'm not sure I would place them in any tradition.

SR: They are just general. . .

Dr. Hawley: They are Vraja, but one can still make distinctions. There are certainly some—we were mentioning Premānanda—which have a definite Gauḍīya feel to them, or sometimes a specific Gauḍīya debt, while other communities would claim, perhaps, a whole cycle of *līlās* for themselves. It does happen. But there's also this shared tradition, so that you can have *rāsa-dhārīs*, that is to say, people who lead or are leaders of troupes, who belong to one tradition or another. Many of them are Vallabhites. Quite in contrast to the actual representation of the Vallabha *saṁpradāya* in Vṛndāvana, which is negligible. It's definitely a minority community there, but the *rāsa līlā* tradition is usually thought of as having had its impetus farther west in the Vraja country—closer toward Govardhana, where the Vallabha *saṁpradāya* is stronger.

However—and I really don't want to stick out my neck on this because I don't know for certain—my feeling about it is that there is a still stronger force in both producing and sharing these *līlās*. It is more powerful than a *saṁpradāya* consideration. It is the knowledge that these troupes have of how other troupes are presenting their material. They have an interest in learning about the way in which other performers are presenting their *līlās*.

It is unmistakable that if someone has a good idea—Swami X's troupe has a good idea for embellishing *līlā* Y—it's not long before the new motif appears in the performances of just about everybody around town. It is a very fluid tradition—but it is fluid inside the general tradition of performers and not restricted, at least to my perception, not for the most part, by the sectarian ties that you would think would serve to create streams or bands of piety within a society like Vṛndāvana. While *saṁpradāya* considerations are important, a sense of sharing and learning is even more important, and the *līlās* themselves, of course, transcend all boundaries. So there is a sense of universality there. The truth of Kṛṣṇa's *līlā* is the bottom line, and exactly how one sees it may be dependent somewhat on one's sectarian affiliation, but it is even more dependent on that person's grasp of reality.

Bhakti Poetry

Richard Davis

Richard H. Davis is Assistant Professor in the Department of Religious Studies at Yale University. He alternately teaches courses in Sanskrit, Tamil, bhakti *poetry, and Hindu religious traditions. A specialist in Śaiva Siddhānta, he has written numerous academic papers and is the author of* Ritual in an Oscillating Universe: Worshiping Śiva in Medieval India *(Princeton University Press, 1991).*

Dr. Davis: Actually I could begin by talking about the class that I taught and the context of its material. For two years, at Yale, I've taught a course called "Devotion and Poetry in Medieval India," which focuses on *bhakti* movements from a social and historical point of view and from a religious point of view as well—but the course primarily uses the medium of poetry to get *bhakti* across to the students. And so in that context I've found that the focus on the Kṛṣṇa tradition in literature and in poetry is particularly effective, and it really gives students a good feeling for Indian religiosity as well as the kinds of techniques and strategies that devotional poets have used. It has also worked well, I think, because there are a number of good translations available, so they could really get a good feeling for what makes Indian devotional poetry so subtle and so special.

Now, in that class, so far, I haven't really dealt with the Gauḍīya tradition per se. A little bit. For instance, when your book on Caitanya was released, of course, you were invited to speak about the Gauḍīya tradition, and I really appreciated that. But beyond your presentation there wasn't much more that was specifically Gauḍīya oriented.

SR: However, you probably dealt with poets that were appreciated by Caitanya Mahāprabhu—earlier poets like Vidyāpati, like Caṇḍīdāsa, or even Jayadeva Gosvāmī. . .

Dr. Davis: Very much so, yes. So I would begin with the *Harivaṁśa* and look at the way in which the narrative tradition of Kṛṣṇa's younger life developed. From the *Harivaṁśa* we approached all kinds of related themes—the hidden nature of divinity in the world, the importance of being able to recognize divinity, and that kind of thing.

From there, we would follow the story to see the way it is changed in a later text, like the *Bhāgavata Purāṇa,* where you enter into a world that is really much closer to the world of *bhakti,* of the *bhakti* poets, where a kind of emotional devotionalism is being very forcefully set forth. We would show a number of contrasts between the two texts. For example, in the *Bhāgavata Purāṇa* the *gopīs* assume a much more important role than in *Harivaṁśa.* So we get the beginnings of an emphasis on the different characters in Vṛndāvana, who were to eventually act as devotional paradigms, as was explicated by later *bhakti* theologians. Then I like to go from there into the poetry that would have directly influenced Caitanya—*Gīta-govinda* and Caṇḍīdāsa and Vidyāpati—and the poetry that Dimock and Levertov translated. . .*In Praise of Kṛṣṇa.*

SR: Did your course discuss *Kṛṣṇa-karṇāmṛta,* the poetry of Bilvamaṅgala Ṭhākura, Sūradāsa, that kind of thing?

Dr. Davis: Oh, certainly, we would usually deal with Sūradāsa later on, though. Near the end of the semester, I would bring in the later North Indian devotional poets—Mīrābāī, Sūradāsa, along with others.

SR: Ravidāsa?

Dr. Davis: Right. I did that in the second year. Jack Hawley's and Mark Juergensmeyer's book, *Songs of the Saints of India* (New York: Oxford University Press, 1988), came out between the first and second time I taught the course, so suddenly we had a new text to work with. We tried to touch on as many of the devotional poets as was possible, though.

SR: In teaching Caṇḍīdāsa and Vidyāpati, or *Gīta-govinda*—how deep did you go?

Dr. Davis: Well, I would go into quite a bit of depth, focusing on two different angles. One angle would be poetic technique, and the other was theological content. Of course, the class has its limitations. But we tried to give the students a taste for the poetry—maybe even some entrance into the rich religious ideas discussed.

You know, it brings to mind something that Ken Bryant said in relation to Sūradāsa: in *bhakti* poetry, Bryant said, the central effort of the poet is to get the audience to participate directly in the reality that he's trying to convey. So in discussing *Gīta-govinda* and Bengali poets, we would focus a great deal on the kinds of rhetorical strategies that the poets used. *Gīta-govinda* turned out to be a very good example because of the kinds of shifts in style, the shifts in who was speaking, the shifts between the character speaking and Jayadeva himself speaking. So by studying these things we were able to bring out the kinds of ways in which Jayadeva would draw us as an audience into the poem and into this world of *bhakti*. Here, specifically, it was the world of Vṛndāvana.

SR: For me, the poetry of Prabodhānanda Sarasvatī, and perhaps Narottama Ṭhākura, is the best for absorption in Vṛndāvana. And the Ālvārs are just about the most intense, too, at least in relation to absorbing the reader in the realities of *bhakti*. Did you do the Ālvārs?

Dr. Davis: Definitely. I should say that we did poetry surrounding the Rāmānuja sect—there's some really outstanding work in that area. And we also did Śaiva *bhakti*.

SR: That's your specialty, isn't it?

Dr. Davis: Well, yeah. I'm mainly interested in Śaiva *siddhānta* and Indian Śaivism in general, so I was very keen on bringing Śaivism and its related poetry into the class.

SR: Did you discuss Jayadeva's *Daśāvatāra*, the Song of the Ten Incarnations?

Dr. Davis: This was essential, in a sense, and we discussed it in several different ways. Our approach to Jayadeva Gosvāmī was largely theological, in a kind of rough and ready sense. I mean, we had certain kinds of questions about the relationship between the soul and God, questions about the nature of God as he was portrayed, the kinds of methods that were advocated as ways of reaching God, the conflict or compatibility of social life with the religious quest. Actually, we asked every poet or every text those kinds of questions. But with Jayadeva, in *Gīta-govinda*, we asked in a more technical sense. So although we had already covered the *avatāras* early on with Nammālvār, we sort of went over that again and questioned how Jayadeva was using that to introduce his narrative.

SR: Which would seem important because the narrative itself might appear to be just some kind of mundane erotic literature. But to establish the divinity of Kṛṣṇa is very important, and I think that with the *Daśāvatāra* segment of *Gīta-govinda*, Jayadeva does this quite well.

Dr. Davis: Well, to my way of thinking, this is one of the things that's most interesting about the poem—the way that it shifts the audience's attention back and forth between those two conceptions. You can go through a whole song, thinking, "Oh, this is just an erotic poem, and a very beautiful erotic poem." And then suddenly Jayadeva will come in and say something to remind us all that, "Yes, it's a beautiful poem, but we should be thinking about this in another way as well." It's not that we should erase all of that eros that we've just experienced, but we should focus it and redirect it with a more religious leaning. To quote Barbara Miller's translation of *Gīta-govinda*:

> Make your heart sympathetic to Jayadeva's splendid speech!
> Recalling Hari's feet is elixir against fevers of this dark time.
> She [Rādhā] told the joyful Yadu hero [Kṛṣṇa], playing to delight her heart,
> 'Paint a leaf on my breasts!
> Put color on my cheeks!
> Lay a girdle on my hips!
> Twine my heavy braid with flowers!
> Fix rows of bangles on my hands
> And jeweled anklets on my feet!'
> Her yellow-robed lover
> Did what Rādhā said

His musical skill, his meditation on Vishnu,
His vision of reality in the erotic mood,
His graceful play in these poems,
All show that master-poet Jayadeva's soul
Is in perfect tune with Krishna—
Let blissful men of wisdom purify the world
By singing his *Gīta Govinda.**

You know, I thought it was very interesting to compare the Bengali poetry—Vidyāpati and Caṇḍīdāsa, for example—with *Gīta-govinda.* And I think that in terms of the sociology, the social setting of the two bodies of poetry, there are some interesting contrasts. *Gīta-govinda* really struck me and the students as well, because I got them to look at it this way—as a court poem, as a poem that was meant to be performed in a courtly setting before a very educated and refined audience, a royal court. And it required a great deal of knowledge of Sanskritic conventions. It was quite complex in a lot of the figures that it used, the kinds of rhythms and poetic devices throughout.

The Bengali verses were certainly more vernacular. They were composed for a different kind of audience. And a lot of the ways in which the content of the poems differ relate to that difference in the social settings. These poems were more for everyday folk, to relate complex theological ideas to the common people, perhaps, and I think they do it quite well.

SR: When you say Bengali poems are you speaking specifically about Caṇḍīdāsa?

Dr. Davis: Well I have in mind the collection of poems in the Dimock and Levertov book. That includes Vraja and Maithili poems, I suppose, or other related poems. I'm not sure. But let me elaborate on the differences a little more—this will give you an idea of what I'm talking about. Rādhā's situation, for example, is handled differently in *Gīta-govinda* than in the Bengali poems, where there's a lot more of a sense of her becoming estranged as a result of her passion for Kṛṣṇa. In those poems, there seems to be a greater disjuncture between living a social

* from *Love Song of the Dark Lord: Jayadeva's Gītāgovinda,* edited and translated by Barbara Stoler Miller (New York: Columbia University Press, 1977), p. 125.

life and living a passionate devotional life.

I think that Kṛṣṇa in the *Gīta-govinda* appears more like a human, and in the Bengali poems that kind of human aspect of him appears much less. That is, in the *Gīta-govinda* it's much more possible to hear the poem as a human love poem, with these periodic shifts. Whereas in the Bengali poems, we are always aware that Kṛṣṇa is something other, that he is not simply human and we should not understand him that way.

SR: That is interesting.

Dr. Davis: I think another interesting thing is the way in which the *bhanitās* are used.

SR: Those endings?

Dr. Davis: Yes, those tag endings where a poet will use his own name and say, "Vidyāpati says, 'By your own life you can gain the far shore of this sea of conflict.'" The author steps in to make a concluding, or summing up, comment. Now, in the Bengali poems there is a real tendency to do this. Some of them, as in the case I just read, the poet advises the actor, the character in the poem. But oftentimes the poet identifies himself with Rādhā, or a *gopī*, and I think that this growing tendency is there in the Bengali poems—it's a kind of precursor to the theological system wherein one identifies with an inhabitant of Vṛndāvana. This of course harkens to the Gauḍīya theologian—I'm forgetting his name—who explained the *rasa* theory.

SR: Oh, Rūpa Gosvāmī.

Dr. Davis: Rūpa Gosvāmī, in the Gauḍīya Vaiṣṇava tradition.

SR: I think the identification with Rādhā would be in the sense that Rādhā is the devotee par excellence, and the poet is also a devotee of Kṛṣṇa.

Dr. Davis: Right.

SR: A Gauḍīya can accept that kind of general identification—but anything else borders on mistaking the self as somehow being the Supreme Self. This is taboo to Vaisnavas—they see themselves as *servants* of the Supreme.

Dr. Davis: All I'm trying to say is that this kind of theological identification is worked out, or is exemplified poetically more often in these Bengali poems, and that to me was very interesting.

SR: Were the students able to follow these ideas? Did you have to give them some background? Did you introduce weighty Sanskrit themes? Complex Vedic concepts?

Dr. Davis: Well, in talking about *Gīta-govinda* and the Bengali poets, some basic background was necessary. But this is a course where I didn't try to introduce a whole lot of Sanskrit terminology. Still, I found throughout that there were certain kinds of Sanskritic distinctions, or sets of terms, that were really important to use and to introduce to the students. And in these poems the old distinction of the *śṛṅgāra* or *mādhurya rasa* having two aspects—the *sambhoga* and *viraha*—this had to be discussed, at least on a basic level.

SR: Love in union and in separation! You discussed this in your class?

Dr. Davis: To some degree. I did. So I had to introduce those kinds of terms, and I did so reluctantly, because they can become highly technical. But some of them seem crucial and these are a few of them. We had to discuss the way in which the old poetic texts, you know, secular poetry, the way in which they say that each of these—union and separation—is immanent in the other. A poem, to be a good poem, to be aesthetically pleasurable, has to show us that co-inherence of these two different aspects of love. I thought that the Bengali poems prove to be a very good way of showing that. They were very much involved with showing how even in those moments when Rādhā was in despair because Kṛṣṇa had left her—at the very core of her despair, the source of her despair, Kṛṣṇa was present.

SR: That brings to mind one particular poem. I don't know who the poet is; maybe you would know. But it's an old poem describing how Kṛṣṇa meets Rādhā at Prema Sarovara and, once they are together, he informs her that there's a bumble bee in their presence. So, in fear, she runs into his arms, and then he says, playing on words, "Madhusūdhana has gone," meaning that the bumble bee had flown away. But she takes it to mean that *he* has gone, since "Madhusūdana" can refer to Kṛṣṇa and also to a bumble bee. So she's feeling separation even though she's right there in his arms.

Dr. Davis: Right. Right. This is the kind of thing. . .

SR: Have you heard that?

Dr. Davis: It rings a bell; I don't know if I could find it. That may very well be in this collection. But there are. . .

SR: But that's the type of thing you are referring to. Correct?

Dr. Davis: That's exactly the type of thing. There's another poem where they have just finished making love, and she's laying in his arms, and suddenly she calls his name and weeps, burning in the fire of separation. And that's one of the most intense poems. And it's so intense that in the *bhanitā* the poet says, "Taking her beloved friend by the hand, Govinda dāsa led her softly away," as if the scene is so intense that we shouldn't even see it.

SR: The poet is Govinda dāsa?

Dr. Davis: Yes, Govinda dāsa. So that kind of distinction was important, and then I found also that Rūpa Gosvāmī's model of the five modes of relationship between the soul and divinity was very useful—more than useful—it was *central* to discussing these Kṛṣṇa narratives, particularly *Harivaṁśa* and *Bhāgavata Purāṇa*, and then also Sūradāsa.

SR: The *rasa* terminology. Well I think that it originated, or, shall we say, Rūpa Gosvāmī borrowed it, from the poets and aestheticians. Bharata, for example.

Dr. Davis: Yes. The language of *bhāvas* and *rasas* comes from Bharata, but the distinction of five relationships, in the peculiar way it is enunciated by Rūpa, is very much his own. And my students found it helpful to locate in the *Harivaṁśa*, for instance, or in the *Bhāgavata Purāṇa*, or to identify poems of Sūradāsa as reflecting or expressing one of those particular *rasas.* That gave them a way of getting a hold on what was going on.

SR: Did you do any of the poetry of the Six Gosvāmīs?

Dr. Davis: No I didn't, and the reason is simple: because I didn't know of any good translations.

SR: That is a big problem.

Dr. Davis: And for the most part, there was sufficient poetry available in good translation, and so I built a whole course around that. One exception where I used what I considered to be a really inferior translation was the *Bhāgavata Purāṇa*. What I had was an old translation, just of the five *rāsa* dance chapters. . .

SR: That's unfortunate. Of course, there's Prabhupāda's translation, with purports—pretty much the whole thing. But that's perhaps too lengthy for your class.

Dr. Davis: That's right. The one I had was by a fellow named Radhakamal Mukerjee, who, as I remember, had a kind of a commentary built into the text. So he would translate a verse and then give a commentary. And the commentary seemed to be an *advaita* commentary, which I thought was not really appropriate to the text. But that was what was available, and I thought that since the *Bhāgavata*, and especially the *rāsa līlā*, is of such central importance to the Kṛṣṇa tradition, the students should read it anyway. If somebody wants to do a good translation of that section someday, I would be very happy to use it in my class.

While we are on the subject of translational desiderata, I might mention that another thing I wanted to use, and couldn't really find enough of, was biographies. There are so many wonderful stories associated with the lives of Vaiṣṇava poets, but it's hard to find good translations, or even good summaries. . .

SR: Oh, right, you were thinking that you might even use my biography of Mahāprabhu.

Dr. Davis: I might very well do that the next time I teach this course. I believe hagiography is central to understanding the true spirit of *bhakti* poetry. One of the points that I wanted to get across in this course was that this was not poetry written in libraries; that it was poetry that came out of life. I wanted to show that many or most of the *bhakti* poets were intense practitioners, that the poetry was often an outcome of intense devotional experience. And one of the ways to show that is to look at biographies or hagiographies of *bhakti* saints. And there really aren't very many available.

SR: That's true. I'm actually working now on a book that discusses the lives of Narottama, Śrīnivāsa, and Śyāmānanda, who were seventeenth-century *bhakti* saints. Narottama is one of the most important Gauḍīya poets.

Dr. Davis: Oh, I should look at that. What I would be particularly interested in would be translations of . . .

SR: Early biographies?

Dr. Davis: Early biographies, yes, rather than our own versions of the biographies, because a lot of the miraculous events that we edit out in an attempt to make these seem more realistic to our way of thinking are often indicative of the kinds of themes that I want to bring out.

SR: That's difficult. There's not a whole lot of work in that area. You'd have more luck investigating the lives of modern *bhakti* poets. Did you do any discussion of contemporary poets in your class?

Dr. Davis: The first time I taught the class we basically ended with Sūradāsa and Kabīr. The second time, I taught Tagore. I thought that the situation of a "modern" *bhakta* would present interesting questions. For example, *should* we count Tagore as a *bhakti* poet?

I also found that it was very interesting to look at Tagore's relationship to the social world—British colonialism, for example—and his role in the Independence movement. So that for me was quite a bit of fun. I don't know how I would answer the question, though: whether or not Tagore should be considered a *bhakti* poet. Oh, and as a somewhat separate issue, I'm on the look out for contemporary *bhakti* poetry. I really don't know of any. I'd be glad to be told of some.

SR: I could send you some of Bhaktivinoda Ṭhākura's poetry, from the early twentieth century. Also Prabhupāda wrote some poetry. But, I'm just curious, of all the *bhakti* poets you have covered in your course—both modern and ancient—who would you say was your personal favorite?

Dr. Davis: I would say that of the poets that we read, I think Nammālvār was the most powerful poet for me.

SR: Interesting.

Dr. Davis: It surprised me. First of all, from the pedagogical point of view, I found that he's a difficult poet, and I thought he was going to be too difficult for the class. But in fact it turned out that the students really got into Nammālvār, really grappled with him. He challenged them in a way that some of the other poets really didn't, and that was very fruitful.

The other poet that I found really made a powerful impact on me was not a Vaiṣṇava poet at all, but was Rāmaprasāda Sen. I think there was something about the sense he conveyed of the world as a very difficult and chaotic place that was always in danger of falling apart. The sense of this divinity, Kālī, being a very fickle person, a divinity that you couldn't depend on. You weren't even sure if she was thinking of your own best interest; she didn't care. The devotee of the Holy Mother cries:

> I'm sweating like the slave of an evil spirit,
> Flat broke, a coolie working for nothing,
> A ditch digger, and my body eats the profits.
> Five Elements, Six Passions, Ten Senses—
> Count them—all scream for attention.
> They won't listen. I'm done for.
> A blind man clutches the cane he's lost
> Like a fanatic. So I clutch You, Mother,
> But with my bungled *karma*, can't hold on.
>
> Prasad cries out: Mother, cut this black snarl
> Of acts, cut through it. Let life, when death
> Closes down, shoot rejoicing up
> Out of my head like a rocket.*

All of that spoke to me very strongly of modern life.

SR: And it's related to Vaiṣṇavism, as well, it seems. The unpredictability of the material world—and the dangers of living here—this is a central tenet of Gauḍīya thought. The miseries of material existence, which are

---

* Leonard Nathan and Clinton Seely (trs.), *Grace and Mercy in her Wild Hair: Selected Poems to the Mother Goddess* (Boulder: Great Eastern, 1982), nc. 10, p. 25.

meant to show us that this is not our natural home—this is the subject of many a Vaiṣṇava text. This world is a place of suffering wherein repeated birth and death take place, but our real home, of course, is with Kṛṣṇa. And even there, Kṛṣṇa is sometimes a sort of scoundrel, a transcendental scoundrel.

Dr. Davis: Yes. Sūradāsa does a nice job with that, but somehow it does not have the same kind of edge with him. He's such a nice fellow, you know, and we find Kṛṣṇa playing with the world. But somehow it's much more benign when Kṛṣṇa does it. When Kālī does it, it can get nasty.

SR: What period is that poet?

Dr. Davis: Rāmaprasāda Sen? I think the eighteenth century. So it was a time in Bengali history that was quite chaotic. He had an odd life. Anyway, those I would say are the two poets that spoke to me most loudly and for very different reasons. Nammālvār writes in a much more stable world, in a way, but, more than any other poet, he was able to come out of the poem and reach me as a reader, and challenge me. Somehow it was harder for me to read him as a poet of the eighth century or the seventh century of India, of the Vaiṣṇava Ālvār tradition—there was something about his poetry that wouldn't let me historicize it. As a scholar, of course, that's generally my basic attitude toward the things I study. But Nammālvār didn't let me get away with that way of comprehending him quite so easily, and I think that made his work very powerful.

The Biographies of Śrī Caitanya and the Literature of the Gauḍīya Vaiṣṇavas

Tony K. Stewart

Tony K. Stewart is Associate Professor of Religion at North Carolina State University, Raleigh, North Carolina. His Ph.D. Dissertation was entitled "The Biographical Images of Kṛṣṇa-Caitanya: A Study in the Perception of Divinity," and Caitanyaite Vaiṣṇavism continues to be his field of expertise. As a respected authority in this area, he has published articles in academic journals worldwide, and he is the Director of the Triangle South Asia Consortium (an educational cooperative of Duke University, University of North Carolina, and North Carolina State University). He recently finished editing the Caitanya-caritāmṛta *of Kṛṣṇadāsa Kavirāja, which was translated by Edward C. Dimock, Jr. of the University of Chicago. This long-awaited translation is currently in press with the Harvard Oriental Series. Dr. Stewart is now conducting further research in Bangladesh.*

SR: I would like to discuss early Gauḍīya Vaiṣṇava literature. And I guess we can begin with the biographies of Śrī Caitanya. Now, as I count them, there are seven major biographies. You let me know if I'm wrong. There is the *Śrī Kṛṣṇa Caitanya-caritāmṛta,* in Sanskrit, by Murāri Gupta. The *Caitanya-caritāmṛta Mahākāvya,* in Sanskrit, by Kavi Karṇapūra. *Caitanya-bhāgavata,* the first Bengali biography, by Vṛndāvana dāsa Ṭhākura. And the two *Caitanya-maṅgalas,* Bengali works, by Jayānanda and Locana dāsa. Then there is also *Caitanya-candrodaya-nāṭaka,* a Sanskrit work, by Kavi Karṇapūra. And Kṛṣṇadāsa Kavirāja's *Caitanya-caritāmṛta,* in Bengali.

Now maybe you can talk about each of these in some chronological order. Which came first? Which came later? And perhaps you can talk about the particular theological view represented in each of these texts.

Dr. Stewart: Okay. These are the seven biographies extant today—that are complete. They all date back to the sixteenth century. And the last one, the *Caitanya-caritāmṛta* by Kṛṣṇadāsa Kavirāja—that was probably finished in the first decade of the seventeenth century, most people would say sometime by 1612. From about 1533 to about 1612 we know of about twelve or thirteen biographies of Caitanya that were written, but of those we only have seven. We have bits and pieces of some others. Every now and then another one will surface, sometimes questionable as to the date. But the seven that you have named are by far the ones that are considered to be the core of the tradition.

Murāri Gupta's Sanskrit work is the oldest. Most people seem to feel it was completed right about the time Caitanya died. There is a note in the second chapter of the book that tells of Caitanya's passing, just a single verse. That suggests of course that it was finished some time afterwards. There is also evidence in the book to suggest that he had started writing the book long before Caitanya died, and that he had actually gotten permission from Caitanya to do it. And this is, I think, pretty significant.

The book really forms the basis for the chronology that is adopted by almost every other author of a Caitanyaite biography. Several of the authors ended up translating or quoting extensively from Murāri and, almost without fail, he is the authority who is turned to when there is some question on the chronology of events in the life of Caitanya.

SR: Murāri, I think, was with Caitanya—as a personal associate—in the early *and* the later pastimes.

Dr. Stewart: Well, Murāri was actually his senior, and they were students together in the Sanskrit school of Gaṅgādāsa Paṇḍita. He is probably the only biographer who knew Caitanya really well. Everyone else was writing from second-hand knowledge, although "Kavi Karṇapūra," as the story goes, was given his name by Caitanya (he was originally called Paramānanda Sena). The young Paramānanda, son of the prominent devotee Śivānanda, was asked to compose an extemporaneous verse in praise of Kṛṣṇa. Well, the verse was so beautifully composed that Caitanya renamed him *Kavi Karṇapūra*, which means "the ear ornament of poets." That story is repeated in several places.

Another biographer, interestingly enough, also claims to have been renamed by Caitanya, and that's Jayānanda.

SR: Oh.

Dr. Stewart: That's right. Your response is not at all surprising. Most people have not taken this very seriously, but he claims that when he was very young, meaning, probably, three to six months old, Caitanya passed one night in his parents' house. Now his father was Subuddhi Miśra, who was in Nityānanda Vaṁśa, and his mother, Rodanī, was Nityānanda's personal servant.

SR: Rodanī?

Dr. Stewart: Rodanī. At least that's what the text says, and as it turns out, Subuddhi Miśra does show up in some of the other accounts of lineages. So that seems to be fairly accurate; at least it is corroborated. But it is possible, in fact, that Rodanī, while helping Nityānanda, may have somehow or other ended up hosting Caitanya, and then Jayānanda could have been renamed. According to the story, Jayānanda's original name was rather demeaning and unpleasant to the ear of Caitanya, hence the need for a new name. I have a sneaking suspicion that it is probably a device, though, in order to establish authority.

SR: I know that scholars tend to accept Jayānanda's biography of Mahāprabhu, largely because of its comparatively mundane explanation of the disappearance story.

Dr. Stewart: Some do, that is correct. I think that the text has been much maligned, and it's curious to me that the scholars who have looked at it, by and large, particularly *in* the tradition, have objected to it pretty seriously. Yet if you go back and look, there are huge numbers of manuscripts of this text, which means that it was a very popular text, at least on some level. Although it may not have been theologically acceptable to many of the people within the tradition, on the popular level, it undoubtedly met some kind of need, because it was copied and recopied. Today we have extant no fewer than seventy-five copies of the manuscript. I have waded through a number of these manuscripts, and it is often confused with Locaṇa dāsa's *Caitanya-maṅgala.* So together, those two books have about two hundred manuscripts between them—complete or partial. And a good number of them are Jayānanda's text.

SR: Why is it that three biographies, written within a short period, were given the same name: *Caitanya-maṅgala*? And maybe you could tell the story of how Vṛndāvana dāsa's *Caitanya-bhāgavata*, which was originally called *Caitanya-maṅgala*, came to be called *Caitanya-bhāgavata*.

Dr. Stewart: There are a couple stories in that regard, actually. I think that the underlying reason for Vṛndāvana dāsa's text being renamed *Caitanya-bhāgavata*, as opposed to *Caitanya-maṅgala*, was probably because of the epithet that Kṛṣṇadāsa Kavirāja continued to use for him. And Kṛṣṇadāsa, of course, writing last of those seven, says probably fifteen times in the course of his text that Vṛndāvana dāsa is the Vyāsa of Caitanya *līlā*. And by comparing him repeatedly to Vyāsa, I think that it is only natural that they would call his book the *Caitanya-bhāgavata*. Vyāsa, they say, wrote the *Bhāgavata-purāṇa*, and so the Vyāsa of Caitanya *līlā* wrote the *Caitanya-bhāgavata*.

Now there is a story connected to Locana dāsa's *Caitanya-maṅgala*, where a certain amount of animosity had developed between some of the lineages. This animosity seems to have been felt more by some of the disciples of the prominent *gurus* than by the *gurus* themselves, although that is difficult to judge. At one point upon the completion of his text, Locana dāsa took his book and gave it to his *guru*, Narahari Sarakāra. Narahari read through it and saw that Nityānanda had been essentially eliminated from the text. He sent it back, and said, "This is unacceptable because Nityānanda most definitely was there." Reading between the lines, he is saying, "even if you don't like him—that is unfortunate—you have to include him." And then, after revising it, Locana dāsa took the text back and it was approved by Narahari.

Then Locana dāsa's *Caitanya-maṅgala* was taken to Vṛndāvana dāsa to read. Now, Vṛndāvana dāsa accepted it, but did not particularly want to read it and, according to one of the stories, tried to put it down. But he was unable to do so. Another version of the story has it that each time he tried to pick it up, it was so heavy that it was difficult to lift. Just the opposite. But that seems to be an unsubstantiated story. I cannot find any textual reference for that except in secondary works. So, Vṛndāvana dāsa found that he had to read it. And when he read it he realized, so the story goes, that Locana dāsa had captured the *mādhurya*, the sweet side of Caitanya's incarnation, whereas he, Vṛndāvana dāsa, had primarily emphasized the *aiśvarya*, lordly, sovereign side, the majestic side. The outcome was that his book should be renamed because Locana dāsa's text was *maṅgala*; which means "auspicious": it was the more auspicious version of Caitanya's life because it had depicted the higher form of the deity: his sweet, loving side.

Now, the source for that story is the *Prema-vilāsa*, which is of course a disputed text. And this particular story comes out of those chapters in the end of the book, which are most disputed. So while it is a popular tradition, how accurate it is—this is another matter altogether.

SR: I had heard that one of the Six Gosvāmīs renamed Vṛndāvana dāsa's book *Caitanya-bhāgavata*. That is why it is such a respected work. It was considered a great honor. . .

Dr. Stewart: That seems to be another popular story. I have not yet found a textual reference for that. I do know that throughout the *Caitanya-caritāmṛta*, Kṛṣṇadāsa Kavirāja refers to Vṛndāvana dāsa's book as *Caitanya-maṅgala*. He never refers to it as *Caitanya-bhāgavata*. It's interesting that it has never been changed in any of the later printed editions. They have retained the older form. Comparing the manuscripts, the older manuscripts that I've looked at, they are all unanimous in that regard. The ones I saw all refer to it as *Caitanya-maṅgala*. So one would think that if one of the Gosvāmīs had done that, Kṛṣṇadāsa would have gotten the word. But it also may be that it is really not an important issue, that it is descriptively *Caitanya-maṅgala*, just as it is *Caitanya-bhāgavata*. I wonder if maybe we should reconsider the importance of names, because most of these seem to have several names, in fact.

SR: Okay. So let's move on to the *Caitanya-candrodaya-nāṭaka* of Kavi Karṇapūra, and then let's discuss Kṛṣṇadāsa Kavirāja's work.

Dr. Stewart: Well, actually, before we do that, you had asked something about the order of these biographies. I started with Murāri, and then we got side-tracked. Murāri's is the first text. Then probably Kavi Karṇapūra's *Mahākāvya*, the *Kṛṣṇa Caitanya-caritāmṛta Mahākāvya*, as it is called today—this was probably the second text. There seems to be pretty accurate dating on that. I think most of the scholarly tradition settles on 1542 as the date. But close on its heels was Vṛndāvana dāsa's *Caitanya-bhāgavata*, for which the most popular date is 1548, but it probably was written sometime between 1546 and 1550.

SR: And that was the first Bengali one—the first in the local vernacular. Correct?

Dr. Stewart: That was the first Bengali one, yes, and it is also the largest of all the biographies. *Caitanya-bhāgavata* is some 12,300 Bengali couplets, and that is, as you know, quite a huge work.

After that, the dating is less precise. There is a question, for example, regarding the dating of Jayānanda's *Caitanya-maṅgala,* which probably was written sometime between 1550 and 1560. Locana dāsa's *Caitanya-maṅgala,* in Bengali, is equally undatable. It is probably in the 1560s, but there is some evidence to suggest that it could be as late as the 1570s. Kavi Karṇapūra's *Nāṭaka,* in Sanskrit, is pretty clearly written some time in the decade of the 1570s. I would tend toward the middle or latter part, because of the more precise dating of his other work, the *Gaura-gaṇoddeśa-dīpikā,* which we can talk about in a little while. And then, finally, Kṛṣṇadāsa Kavirāja's text, which I mentioned before, is generally accepted as being completed in 1612, although some say as late as 1615. There does seem to be some evidence that it was started considerably sooner than that. Perhaps as much as ten, twelve, or even fifteen years before it was finished. And that is the second largest of the biographies—that is also the standard and most respected biography, only slightly smaller than Vṛndāvana dāsa's *Caitanya-bhāgavata.*

SR: There's a rather controversial story about the *Caitanya-caritāmṛta.* It is an apocryphal story: something to the effect that the Gosvāmīs had had some initial problem with Kṛṣṇadāsa Kavirāja's work because it was in Bengali, and they were trying to establish the tradition in Sanskrit.

Dr. Stewart: Well, there was clearly a tension, I think, between the two traditions. Of course, they say it is in Bengali. But when you read the text, you realize that Kṛṣṇadāsa cites more than seventy-five Sanskrit texts, and that accounts for something like thirteen percent—I would have to sit down with a calculator and figure it out. But well over ten percent of the book is in Sanskrit. So in that sense, it is really a mixed work, although it is not formally so. Nonetheless, the framework of the book is clearly in Sanskrit, and often the Sanskrit, usually in *sūtra* style, will give the basic text, and then it is explicated in Bengali. The narrative portions, of course, are in Bengali. But in that sense, it really is a mixed work. And secondly—and I think probably in response to the concern that it was written in Bengali—this is the only one of the biographies, and probably one of the few vernacular texts in all of India, that has a Sanskrit commentary appended to it. That gives it a sort of institutional authority that I think is pretty unmistakable. And it is the *only* biography that has a Sanskrit commentary.

SR: Commentary by whom?

Dr. Stewart: Viśvanātha Cakravartī.

SR: And this is in, for instance, the Gauḍīya Maṭha edition of *Caitanya-caritāmṛta*?

Dr. Stewart: No, it is rarely printed. But, you know, something further—most of the *Caitanya-caritāmṛta* has also been translated into Sanskrit, or at least part of it has. Again, it is the only biography to have been translated into Sanskrit.

SR: While we're talking about the biographies, let's just talk about a few others that we haven't mentioned—ones that are also quite important. The diaries of Svarūpa Dāmodara, Govinda and Raghunātha dāsa—I don't know if they are extant. . .

Dr. Stewart: Okay. Probably Svarūpa Dāmodara's diary, or *Kaḍacā*, as it is called, is the most controversial. If you go to Calcutta or Navadvīpa today, you will find publications that purport to be this book. Those tend to be considerably later publications or writings that very often have *sahajiyā* or other leanings that diverge from the Gauḍīya Vaiṣṇava mainstream.

Now it is pretty clear, based on the textual evidence from the biographies, that Svarūpa wrote something on the life of Caitanya. Kṛṣṇadāsa is constantly referring to Svarūpa's expertise in aesthetic theory, particularly in his interpretation of Caitanya's divinity. And if you carefully read the theological sections in the *Caitanya-caritāmṛta* that directly address Caitanya's divinity, you will discover that Kṛṣṇadāsa always prefaces these theories with some kind of homage to Svarūpa, and often says that Svarūpa is responsible for this idea. You will find it in the fourth chapter of the *Ādi-līlā* where he lays out the basic divinity of Caitanya. And you will find it in the very important revelation of the dual incarnation to Rāmānanda Rāya in *Madhya-līlā*, Chapter Eight.

From these texts, I have concluded the following: Svarūpa Dāmodara's

Kaḍacā was not very long. People call it a diary; I think that this is probably a misconception. Murāri Gupta's work is also called a *Kaḍacā,* a diary. But that is a very different kind of work than the kind I see coming from Svarūpa, what little bit we have. I think "jottings" or "notes" would probably be a better gloss on *Kaḍacā* in this context.

I do not think that Kṛṣṇadāsa had access to Svarūpa's complete text—he probably did not have the text proper but had a certain number of stray verses or basic ideas from his own *guru,* Raghunātha dāsa. Now Raghunātha was the special disciple of Svarūpa; he was handed over when he was in Purī, toward the end of Caitanya's life. Caitanya handed him over to Svarūpa's care, and said, "This young man is special; you watch out for him and train him. . . ," etc. What happened was that Raghunātha dāsa was apparently glued to Svarūpa, and one can reasonably speculate here that Kṛṣṇadāsa got directly from Raghunātha everything that he knew, or pretty much everything that he knew, about Svarūpa.

If you read modern editions of the *Caitanya-caritāmṛta,* you will find that there are attributions to Svarūpa Dāmodara's *Kaḍacā.* Probably eight or nine verses altogether. If you read the oldest manuscripts, those attributions are missing. Those citations have been supplied uniformly by modern editors. I would guess that it is probably, if not an actual quotation, very close to what Svarūpa was saying, based on the context. So it is not an unreasonable attribution, but I have my doubts as to whether it is an exact rendering of the text—with one exception. There is one verse which is—and again I can get the references if you would like—a verbatim quotation in the *Caitanya-caritāmṛta,* and also in Kavi Karṇapūra's *Gaura-gaṇoddeśa-dīpikā,* which is identical. There is no single aspect of the verse that is different. And Kavi Karṇapūra attributes it directly to Svarūpa, and that *is* in the manuscript tradition.

I would suggest that it really did come from him; that it was a verse that several people knew. Of course Kavi Karṇapūra was writing in Purī, where Svarūpa lived, not in Vṛndāvana, which would also suggest that it was legit.

SR: Now sometimes, although less often, we hear of Govinda dāsa's diary.

Dr. Stewart: Right. Govinda dāsa's diary has split the academic community. You are either for it or you are against it. The text, as you know, is not a complete biography, but rather a survey, or more of a diary of Caitanya's trip to the south, the pilgrimage that he took after his renunciation. Caitanya began in Purī and stayed there for a few months, and then he departed on his journey to southern and western India. And then, making a large circle going down the eastern coast, coming back up the western coast, and then cutting across, back to Purī.

This book—Govinda's *Kaḍacā*—has a very strange printing history, and that has created part of the controversy. The text has certain words that many scholars, who are philologically oriented, think could not possibly have been current when the text was ostensibly written. There were, for instance, Portuguese words in the body of the text. But then the Portuguese, as it turns out, were just coming into Bengal in the latter part of that sixteenth century. Some suggest even a little sooner than that. So it is feasible, especially if the text was composed later from memory, although it does raise some questions.

The late Professor B.B. Majumdar felt that the text could be legitimate in spite of the irregularities in some of the language. But there is one very curious anomaly, and that is that Kṛṣṇadāsa Kavirāja, in his text, names a different person, another Kṛṣṇadāsa, as the servant who accompanied Caitanya, and not Govinda dāsa. Now people generally assume that Kṛṣṇadāsa Kavirāja is always correct, and in this case there is no reason to assume that he is not, although there is no compelling reason to assume that he is correct and that everyone else is wrong. So, internal to the texts themselves, there is disagreement on who went with Caitanya to South India.

SR: Murāri says that the name of Mahāprabhu's companion was Viṣṇu dāsa. Others say the name was Govinda dāsa, and still others say Kṛṣṇadāsa, as you mentioned. But all three names basically mean the same thing: "servant of Kṛṣṇa." So these names can, feasibly, refer to the same person.

Dr. Stewart: It is possible, but I think that most Bengalis recognize those names as quite different, in spite of their common meaning. But something else interests me here, and I think it would be valuable if someone would do a little sustained research work on it. If you systematically go through Govinda dāsa's text and list the places that Caitanya visited, and then you go back and compare the places that Nityānanda visited on his pilgrimage in *Caitanya-bhāgavata* by Vṛndāvana dāsa—it could be quite interesting. You will find an amazing similarity in these two lists—a point first brought to my attention by my colleague, Robert Evans. This similarity suggests that the biographers must have been working with patterns that would not be considered historically accurate in a western, more positivist sense, but that are formulaic. Formulaic is not necessarily bad history, rather it means, in this particular case, that Caitanya went on pilgrimage and a proper pilgrimage would automatically include these important sites, and therefore Caitanya must have gone there—*did* go there. And that raises all kinds of questions about the way these texts are written, and specifically, whether Govinda dāsa's text is much more than a poetic version of "what must have happened."

Part of the problem is that these authors tended to write according to certain acceptable patterns. Things were always presented in a very predictable way. And to deviate from that in some respects would have at that time raised eyebrows. Now today, of course, we have a different standard for judging these things. So I would say in short that the text of Govinda dāsa's *Kaḍacā* is probably pretty old, but whether it is what it claims to be—I am not so convinced. I sort of bracket it in my own work. There is really not a lot to be done with it—there is no manuscript now, we have only the printed version.

Now you mentioned a third text, which was Raghunātha dāsa's diary. This was also probably a short work, and we have most of it, I'm sure, in the other, more well-known biographies. Raghunātha dāsa's works—if you look at his *Stavāvalī*, for example—are a number of *stotras* and *aṣṭakas*, and other kinds of short, very pithy eulogistic kinds of writings. They capture episodes out of the life of Caitanya, but certainly do not present any kind of narrative, so I would not call them diaries or biographies as such.

If you go back and look in the *Antya-līlā* of Kṛṣṇadāsa's text—of course, remember that Kṛṣṇadāsa was Raghunātha dāsa's student—each of the last ten or fifteen chapters of the book are structured around a single verse that is quoted from Raghunātha dāsa's writings. You will find that he generally uses a verse that is pretty dense, but has quite a lot of material in it about a particular episode. And then he will spend the next two hundred Bengali verses explaining what that Sanskrit verse meant.

It looks to me like the whole series of episodes that Kṛṣṇadāsa relates about Caitanya in his later years—of course that is what he was focusing on—seem to be structured primarily from the writings of Raghunātha. And I am sure it was filled in over the years by many tellings and retellings. So, in that sense, I would judge Raghunātha's texts to be pretty much as we have them. They are corroborated in manuscript form through several different versions, not only directly through *stavas* and *stotras* and *aṣṭakas*, but through texts like the *Caitanya-caritāmṛta* that quote them. They are very accurate and the manuscripts are very consistent. So that is probably all that we have by way of biographical information from Raghunātha.

SR: Now before we go on to the works of the Six Gosvāmīs, there are a couple of other biographical books that have come to my attention. *Caitanya-vilāsa* is one. And then there are the many *padas*, the songs about Caitanya, and then I think that this will wind up our talk about the biographies.

Dr. Stewart: There are a good many books that carry titles suggesting that they are hagiographical, or biographical. For example, there are several books bearing the title "*Caitanya-vilāsa.*" So I do not know the one to which you are referring. There are a lot of other books, too. Vaṁśi dāsa, for instance, has written a *Gaura-līlāmṛta,* which is only found in manuscript form; I have never seen a printed edition, or seen reference to a printed edition. We do have an incomplete *Gaurāṅga-vijaya* in Bengali by Cūḍāmaṇi dāsa, who was in Nityānanda's lineage. That actually looks like a very old text, but we only have about the first quarter of the book. It deals only with Caitanya's youth. And Sukumar Sen edited that lone manuscript, but it is 130 folios long. That is a massive work. But it is gone, so apparently it was not deemed to be very important.

We have some literature that I think really needs to be looked at closely. I am referring to the *pada,* or verse literature, the poems and songs in praise of Caitanya. There is quite a bit of it. For example, Narahari Cakravartī, in that early period, compiled a collection of *padas* dedicated to Caitanya called the *Gaura-carita-cintāmaṇī.* That is a very significant work that, quite frankly, has been pretty much ignored. Referring to such works, sometimes scholars say, "They are poems, so they cannot really have the kind of historical information that we are after."

Well, I would say that these scholars are quite mistaken. I would say that precisely *because* they are poetry, they might tell us a tremendous amount about the way people felt about this phenomenon—Caitanya—and his associates. These poems can tell us a great deal about how people in those days articulated their beliefs. And probably we will see a much greater theological variety in those texts than you would in the biographies. So that is an untapped resource that is really quite incredible.

You also have Prabodhānanda Sarasvatī's *Caitanya-candrāmṛta,* which is a Sanskrit work. There is a little bit of question as to exactly which Prabodhānanda Sarasvatī this was. But it seems to be fairly clear. He indicates in several of the verses certain popular theological notions about Caitanya. These differ slightly from the major traditions in terms of consistency. Rather, it diverges in a way, and it is really not linked together in any kind of methodical system; perhaps it was even reconstructed piecemeal over a number of years, reflecting the variety of beliefs within the community.

I think this is what often gets glossed over—people did not always know exactly how to interpret Caitanya's life. This is what makes this area of research so exciting. And there are very few biographical traditions where we have so much resource material. Moreover, we can see—and this is what I have spent the last fifteen years doing—how certain changes have taken place in the tradition until the community finally settles on what it finds to be an acceptable standard. And of course that is found, to a certain degree, in the last of the major biographies. I think that is why it *is* last. The *Caitanya-caritāmṛta.*

There is, by the way, another book that I am going to be looking at: Vraja Mohana dāsa's *Caitanya-tattva-pradīpa.*

SR: I've never heard of it.

Dr. Stewart: It exists in a single manuscript. It is complete—about forty folios long, which is a fairly short work. Half of it is in Sanskrit and half in Bengali. It was probably written in the 1620s, ten to fifteen years after the *Caitanya-caritāmṛta.* And the author quotes the *Caitanya-caritāmṛta.* It is pretty clear who Vraja Mohana dāsa was; he comes out of Nityānanda Vaṁśa.

Caitanya-tattva-pradīpa is a text, as I said, in a single manuscript, and I am going to be using that as a foil, in fact, to see what kinds of new issues were raised after the closing of the canon by the *Caitanya-caritāmṛta.* I think it does raise some new issues. But again, because there is but one manuscript, what he had to say did not seem to affect a whole lot of people.

SR: I'd be interested to see what you do with that.

Dr. Stewart: That is what my current work is on. I am looking at the biographies that have been used, how they develop the idea of Caitanya's divinity, or maybe not "developed." I think "explore" is probably a better word because they all felt pretty much the same way. But the ramifications were not always clear to some of the writers, and some, of course, were more sophisticated than others. And then finally, after the better part of a century, they land on what the community clearly seemed to feel was a good, systematic standard. From that point, with the circulation of the *Caitanya-caritāmṛta,* you no longer have major divergence within the ranks of Caitanyaite Vaiṣṇavas regarding the interpretation of Caitanya's divinity. Everyone more or less accepts the conclusions of that text. The canon closes, and what you have from that point on is primarily a restatement of those same basic ideas.

SR: Can you discuss some of those ideas and their development?

Dr. Stewart: Yes. Certainly. When you take the biographical tradition as a whole, there are several issues that keep coming up. There are things that suggest a certain amount of ambiguity and indecision at first, and then later that there was some tension involved. . .

SR: About what?

Dr. Stewart: Well, regarding Caitanya's divinity, for example. And, secondly, what devotees should expect from living a life dedicated to this divinity, or being a believer. The early biographies tend to present Caitanya in more of a Purāṇic mode. He is a majestic sovereign lord, and a part, an *aṁśa*, of Kṛṣṇa; or he is an *avatāra*. Of course those two theories tend to overlap pretty considerably.

SR: This conception is there in Murāri's work?

Dr. Stewart: Yes, it is in the very earliest forms. In fact the *aṁśa* theory is the very first one that Murāri articulates. And he says to his reader, "Look, this man is a part, an *aṁśa*, of God." And then he proceeds to explain what amounts to a rather basic Vaiṣṇava Purāṇic *avatāra*. Now this is very quickly understood to be the *Yugāvatāra*, the *avatāra* of the age, even in Murāri's own work. And, as you are probably aware, the first *avatāra* was in the Satya-yuga, and there are practices associated with that *avatāra* and so forth. So you go through the Satya, the Tretā, the Dvāpara—the Dvāpara age was Kṛṣṇa himself. Then finally here in the Kali age we get Caitanya. And the proper form of worship is *saṅkīrtana*, and the proper color that characterizes the age is yellow, and so forth. So it becomes part of that *Yugāvatāra* system.

Now what this theory or interpretation tends to do, though, is to emphasize Caitanya's celestial side, the *aiśvarya* or the majestic side of Kṛṣṇa. While on the one hand his message is one of *premā*, of loving Kṛṣṇa, on the other hand, the *mādhurya* or loving side is really not seen as embodied in the early conceptions of Caitanya as the sovereign lord.

At least it is not put in those terms. I think one of the reasons for this is that when Caitanya was first believed to be God, and was written about in those terms—shortly after his death—you had many people with the hope that he would lead them to an overthrow of the increasingly dominant Muslim community. This political dimension is most certainly present.

If you read the *Caitanya-bhāgavata* of Vṛndāvana dāsa, you will see over and over again where he envisions and actually describes confrontations with the Muslims. Now generally these confrontations were very tense, but tended not, by and large, to be violent confrontations, although there are a couple of exceptions. And several of these, and one of the most famous of course—and it is a wonderful story—is where Caitanya takes the *kīrtana* to the streets. He and his men are singing and dancing their way down the streets of Nadia. The Kāzī summons him, and they have a confrontation. Later the Kāzī has a dream, and Caitanya appears as the man-lion, Nṛsiṁha, and buries his claws deep into the chest of this poor old Kāzī, who is petrified. Then, of course, the next time they meet, the Kāzī says, "Look, you gentlemen go out and do exactly what you want because I've seen now the truth of who you are."

While on the surface these kinds of things would appear to indicate perhaps some local conflict, I think in fact they are more probably indicators of certain hopes and aspirations that did not come to pass. As you know, by the middle of the sixteenth century, I think it was 1556, the Gajapati dynasty finally fell in Orissa, and there were no more major Hindu rulers. There were minor rulers, but they too had lost control to the Moghuls. This shift, then, from emphasizing the majestic and potentially war-like and powerful sovereign side really gets downplayed as we progress through the biographies, for Hindu kings cannot guarantee the position of their own kingdoms, much less protect the Vaiṣṇava communities from Muslim domination and interference. Consequently, martial images proved completely untenable in the socio-political reality of post-Caitanya Bengal.

By the time you get to Kavi Karṇapūra's second biography, the *Caitanya-candrodaya-nāṭaka,* and Locana dāsa's *Caitanya-maṅgala,* you find that the *mādhurya* side comes increasingly to dominate. When you get to the *Caitanya-caritāmṛta* of Kṛṣṇadāsa—the *mādhurya* side is about all you see. So you have a shift from *aiśvarya,* the sovereign side, to an emphasis on *mādhurya,* the sweet side, from a form that was martial and threatening to a form that was innocuous and accommodating.

With this shift you have a concomitant shift in the perception of what Caitanya is teaching by way of ritual and so forth. So he always served as both a divinity and an object for emulation as the devotee. When he lived, he was believed to be the quintessential devotee, but he was always also believed to be God in whatever form. So that duality of being both the subject of devotion and the object of devotion, or the devotee and God, runs throughout. But the emphasis on what he was embodying as a devotee never really changes.

In the early biographies, there was a much greater emphasis on his early life, his life prior to renunciation. In the later biographies, the tendency is to emphasize his later life, the ascetic side. With that you get the shift in practices from an external *kīrtana*-based practice, to one that increasingly turned to internal modes of realization.

SR: Like *mañjarī sādhana.*

Dr. Stewart: Ultimately resulting in something like *mañjarī sādhana.* I think that is where it leads. There is evidence that they were heading in that direction by the time Caitanya died. There is no evidence per se to suggest that Caitanya practiced that exactly. *Mañjarī sādhana* seems to be an indirect response, again, to a different need, a need that would give you a style of worship that would enable you to locate your real and true personality in the realm of Kṛṣṇa. "Caitanya is not here anymore, so we want to go where Kṛṣṇa is." And that then is the interior landscape where the devotee works his way to heaven.

Conveniently—and I say this because there appeared to be some real pressure on these people—this kind of activity does not require a public performance. *Mañjarī sādhana* relies on an interior mode of realization. You do not have to go out onto the streets beating drums or anything like that—something that might upset the local rulers. It is done privately, behind closed doors. So you get a shift, then, from public practices to more and more private practices.

SR: Yet congregational chanting—out in the streets—was emphasized by Caitanya, and no less by his later followers, who became absorbed in *mañjarī sādhana* as well.

Dr. Stewart: Yes, it was. He proposed *nāgara saṅkīrtana,* too, but what I am saying is that the practices themselves, and the emphasis that is placed in the biographies, seem to shift. What Caitanya does increasingly in his later years really does not seem to be quite the same as what he was doing when he first had his experience at Gayā, and when he was living in Navadvīpa.

All I am suggesting is that the changing political climate probably helped devotees determine some of the forms that this new practice would take. On the other hand, the forms themselves seemed to change very logically and very much in accord with the theological position. So it is not as if they are forced into it at all, but rather we can see a very complex accommodation-process, where the form of ritual, the form of practice, adapts itself to a changing environment.

When Caitanya was physically present, it is clear that Vaiṣṇavas were allowed to do things publicly that fifty or seventy-five years later they probably were not allowed to do quite so freely. It is with this kind of change in political climate that you get the changes in the practices, and these are depicted somewhat in this shift from the early biogaphies, which emphasized his majesty, to the later biographies, which emphasized *mādhurya.*

SR: I think "emphasized" is a good word here. Otherwise, how would the tradition reconcile the conficting ideas that in the early biographies he is depicted as Viṣṇu, or as an *aiśvarya*-dominated *avatāra,* and the way they have come to know him now, as the perfection of the *mādhurya* side—the combined manifestation of Rādhā and Kṛṣṇa? I mean, Kṛṣṇadāsa Kavirāja and other later writers go so far as to describe Mahāprabhu as *avatārī,* or the source of incarnations.

Moreover, Gauḍīya Vaiṣṇavas, as believers, would quite naturally be disinclined to the idea that the conception of Caitanya Mahāprabhu's divinity "evolved." Rather, they would say that the earlier biographers "emphasized" a particular side—perhaps for the reasons you have mentioned—and that Kṛṣṇadāsa Kavirāja and the other later writers "emphasized" the more esoteric *mādhurya* side, for other reasons. But both things exist simultaneously. Truth, after all, is always true—it does not evolve. But if it is a question of emphasis, that is a different matter. . .

Dr. Stewart: Well, it *is* one of emphasis, you are correct, because every biography captures both sides of that tension—the *aiśvarya* and the *mādhurya.* But the earlier ones do tend to emphasize the *aiśvarya:* Murāri, Vṛndāvana dāsa, Kavi Karṇapūra's first biography, and Jayānanda. Those four really emphasize the *aiśvarya* side.

Then, starting with the *nāṭaka* of Kavi Karṇapūra and Locana dāsa's *Caitanya-maṅgala,* you begin to get an emphasis on the *mādhurya* side. Then with the *Caitanya-caritāmṛta,* that is the ultimate point that is made. Moreover, Kṛṣṇadāsa provides a way to reconcile these different positions;

he provides the entire biographical tradition with a structure. This structure hierarchizes the various forms of divinity—and here he utilizes so skillfully the theology of Rūpa and Jīva. *Aṁśas* and *avatāras*, those parts of God, are certainly legitimate, and Caitanya was those things, and the *Yugāvatāra* as well, but they were coincident with and subject to a much more important descent, which was *svayaṁ bhagavān*, God Himself.

SR: The original Godhead!

Dr. Stewart: Right. Kṛṣṇa comes down, not just as a part of himself, but in totality, the complete Godhead. You get then a hierarchical system of images. At the lowest end you get these smaller forms of *aṁśa*, of *avatāras*, generally, and specifically the *Yugāvatāra*. And Kṛṣṇadāsa Kavirāja includes or accounts, ultimately, for all of them—the *manvantarāvatāras*, the *guṇāvatāras*, the *līlāvatāras*, and so forth. The *catur-vyūha*, and all of it. But those are lesser forms. The highest form is *svayaṁ bhagavān*.

The preferred form here, of course, takes the conception a step further. And that is the androgynous form of Caitanya. We get good evidence in Locana dāsa's text that androgyny was very much perceived to be part of Caitanya's nature; except for Locana dāsa it tends to be serial, or alternating androgyny, and it is primarily understood through the manifestation of *bhāva*. So this emotional position that Caitanya would take as Rādhā, or as one of the *gopīs*, was seen to be his true nature as much as his other side. At one moment he would be deemed to be male, and the next moment, because of *bhāva*, he was understood to be truly female. Of course Kṛṣṇadāsa takes it a step further and says that this is going on all the time. . .

SR: Although at times Mahāprabhu is more gripped by Rādhā-*bhāva* than at other times.

Dr. Stewart: Well, especially toward the end of his life. Up to the time of his renunciation, Caitanya is primarily manifesting male *bhāvas*. After his renunciation, he tends more to reveal the Rādhā-*bhāva*, to the point where at the end of his life, that is just about all he is, at least according to most of the biographers, and especially Kṛṣṇadāsa Kavirāja. So what Kṛṣṇadāsa suggests is that both of these sides are present all the time, but the emphasis toward the end of his life is more toward the Rādhā side, which again emphasizes *mādhurya*. That emphasis, in turn, makes the point that it is the sweet loving nature that is really the dominant mode of divinity, more than the other side.

SR: The nature of *mādhurya-bhāva,* of course, was more systematically brought out in the writings of the Gosvāmīs of Vṛndāvana. So, if we can move away from the biographies for a moment, let us discuss the other Gauḍīya literature which, I think, even further develops the philosophical underpinnings of the Caitanyaite system.

Dr. Stewart: Right. Well, to continue along the same lines, though, it is really at this point, in reference to Caitanya's divinity, that Kṛṣṇadāsa brings to bear the full weight of the Gosvāmī theological system. He is the only one of all the writers who relies fully on this. Kavi Karṇapūra marshals a fair amount of very sophisticated theological and aesthetic works himself, but Kṛṣṇadāsa uses the *Ṣaṭ-sandarbha* of Jīva Gosvāmī. He uses the *Bhakti-rasāmṛta-sindhu* and *Ujjvala-nīlamaṇi* of Rūpa Gosvāmī. Those texts primarily provide the theological justification for interpreting Caitanya as he has.

I made the point earlier that when Kṛṣṇadāsa talks about Caitanya's divinity explicitly, he always refers to Svarūpa Dāmodara. But when he talks about *Kṛṣṇa's* divinity, he tends primarily to invoke the Gosvāmīs. I think this is an important distinction because what he is doing is relying on the designated theologians to structure his understanding of divinity, especially as it applies to Caitanya. Although at times he is willing to step outside that designated set.

The philosophical works of Jīva—the *Ṣaṭ-sandarbha,* or *Bhāgavata-sandarbha,* its alternate name—are very dense, very abstruse philosophical texts in a more traditional mode. They lay a foundation for establishing Gauḍīya Vaiṣṇavism as a *sampradāya,* an authorized lineage. This lends the group an institutional authority that is easily recognizable by any Vaiṣṇava or any other knowledgeable practitioner in India or around the world. Having that philosophical system at its base establishes an identity which is unmistakable, and I would go so far as to say that without it the Gauḍīya Vaiṣṇavas would have had to have turned somewhere and found it. Of course the place where most people look is Madhva, because there is such a close relationship in conception to the theological positions of the two groups. This is clear from the voluminous writings of the Gosvāmīs and from the strong associations we can see today in segments of the community.

SR: I have a couple of notes here regarding their writings. Let's see.

Raghunātha Bhaṭṭa did not write. He was the one of the Six Gosvāmīs who did not write at all, and I found that in his ontological form he is the *mañjarī* who takes notes and does various types of related service in the intimate *līlā*. Ironic—the one Gosvāmī who did not write, in his spiritual form, is the one who takes notes. I thought that this was interesting. Actually, both of the "Bhaṭṭas" interest me...

Dr. Stewart: Of course, the *Hari-bhakti-vilāsa* is a very controversial text.

SR: You mean the authorship...

Dr. Stewart: Right, it suggests that there was a collaboration where one of the Gosvāmīs, and even some of the others who were present, would work on something, and have notes, or have ideas about certain things, but then, for whatever reason, ended up not pulling it together into any kind of systematic statement. Gopāla Bhaṭṭa is often the one who gets credit for the *Hari-bhakti-vilāsa* and then others say, no, it was Sanātana. Again, we cannot really know. A lot of people want Gopāla Bhaṭṭa to be the author simply because he is the orthodox *brāhmaṇa*. And Sanātana was not; his status was brought into question by his work with the Muslim court.

SR: Of course, S.K. De has elaborately discussed this subject.

Dr. Stewart: Yes. Yes, in perhaps the most authoritative English-language scholarly book on the early tradition, *The Early History of the Vaishnava Faith and Movement in Bengal* (Second Edition, Calcutta: Firma K.L.M., 1961). So I think that the idea of collaboration and the notion that these devotees are working together is viable—probable. I have no doubt that there are parts of all of them in all of the books. I cannot imagine that Rūpa was the only person who thought about the material about which he wrote. The Gosvāmīs must have discussed these things constantly. And this is the beauty of community. It is unfortunate that scholars do not do this kind of thing more often. I think that when you do get together people, who have overlapping but different expertises, you get just this kind of creativity. In this case they are just like us—they worked on these ideas, they thought about them, and they explored them together. And, again, in terms of authorship—pride of authorship is a very Western concern.

SR: That is a very good point. After all, the important thing is the *content* of *Hari-bhakti-vilāsa.* This is why the book is still valuable: it sets out the ritualistic portion of Gauḍīya practice, or behavior. It's like a Gauḍīya *smṛti,* which is important. . .

Dr. Stewart: Oh, it is very important for the tradition. But as far as explaining the ritual process in relation to the transformations that take place in the individual, particularly in relationship to love of God, the *Bhakti-rasāmṛta-sindhu* and *Ujjvala-nīlamaṇi* of Rūpa become the key texts. Now, the *Bhakti-rasāmṛta-sindhu* lays out the step-by-step procedures for inculcating love for Kṛṣṇa. Love, then, is analyzed in great detail. You are given very explicit instructions as to how to create this kind of love, or how to invoke it.

Other people see the model somewhat differently—that the love is already there; it simply needs to be awakened. So whether it is created or given to you from the outside, or whether it is simply bubbling up from the inside—this is simply a matter of interpretation. But, in any case, you are led step-by-step. First through the outward mechanical rituals of devotion. These are the *vidhis*—sixty-four of them—five of which are most important. And of those *kīrtana* seems to be the one that most people have accepted as the real index to proper devotional activity because it will lead to all the rest. There is some argument about that, but there are five that are most important.

Interestingly, as you perform these outward rituals you may or may not even understand what you are doing, but you are hearing the name of God; you are chanting the name of God, of Kṛṣṇa; you are hearing the stories from the scriptures; you are associating with people who are good devotees; and, of course, if possible, you are living in Vṛndāvana, whether literally or figuratively. All of these things begin to transform you. They have an effect. From this continual practice they begin to take a life of their own, in a sense. I think it is fairly clear in the *Bhakti-rasāmṛta-sindhu* that they start off as purely mechanical rituals, perhaps, but fairly soon they become so second-nature that you cease to think about them as an act you must perform, but rather simply what you do naturally—it is what you are. And in that process you gradually assimilate these practices to the point where you could almost say they animate themselves.

Now, at this point you have a real subtle transition from a purely mechanical practice to a practice that is finally driven by what can only be described as a spontaneous, uncontrollable love.

SR: *Rāgā-nugā.*

Dr. Stewart: Yes. Exactly. So you move then from the *vaidhī bhakti* platform to *rāgānugā.* At this point, one is ready to follow in the footsteps of one of Kṛṣṇa's eternal associates—one is consumed by passion, which leads one irresistibly to discover one's true identity. Rūpa lays the foundation for this process in his *Bhakti-rasāmṛita-sindhu* and then follows up with very minute analyses of the highest love in his *Ujjvala-nīlamaṇi.* Here you develop your real personality, which is an eternal identity, your *siddha-deha,* or perfected body. This is a spiritual form that enables you to participate, hopefully directly, in the *līlās* of Kṛṣṇa.

David Haberman has written quite elaborately and insightfully about this process: how you transform a role that starts as alien and foreign to you, and through this acting procedure make it a part of your very existence. It becomes *you,* or you become it, or again, the alternate model is that you discover what is really in you.

SR: Yes. Now, there are three texts that I wanted to ask you about in relation to this, and these texts relate to the authors of the biographies. Kṛṣṇadāsa Kavirāja's *Govinda-līlāmṛta*; Kavi Karṇapūra's *Kṛṣṇāhnika-kaumudī*; and a much later work, Viśvanātha Cakravartī's *Kṛṣṇa Bhāvanāmṛta.* They deal with the *aṣṭa-kālīya-līlā,* and also the transition to *rāgānugā,* or let us say that *rāgānugā* is implicit in these texts. I thought maybe you could talk a little about those works and the esoteric way in which the Gauḍīya tradition understands them.

Dr. Stewart: Well, I have not read the *Kṛṣṇāhnika-kaumudī* and the *Bhāvanāmṛta* closely enough. Neal Delmonico would be a better scholar to question. But there are a lot of Gauḍīya works, especially from the seventeenth and eighteenth centuries, like Narahari's *Bhakti-ratnākara,* for example, that explicate the esoteric side of the tradition. There is a veritable storehouse of Gauḍīya literature. And I do think that Kṛṣṇadāsa's work, and especially his *Govinda-līlāmṛta,* which you have mentioned, is important for the *rāgānugā* tradition in the Gauḍīya line. Rūpa's dramas, too, are important for the tradition in the same way. *Vidagdha-mādhava, Lalita-mādhava*—these two dramas are not just dramas. And I think this is really important to understand. On the one hand, it is, yes, the application of *bhakti-rasa* theory—the adaptation of traditional dramatic aesthetics that Rūpa articulates to depict certain events in the life of Kṛṣṇa. And there is no question about that, because the texts can be well understood in those terms. But I think it goes a step further. I do not have sound textual confirmation for this, but there are so many indicators, so many red flags, that would suggest something else can be found in these texts. And I am confident in my conclusions. . .

SR: What exactly are those conclusions?

Dr. Stewart: Simply that these dramas are revelation, very directly. Let us say someone follows a *mañjarī*-style practice, goes into a meditative trance and shifts their point of consciousness to their *siddha-deha,* to their perfected body as the young helpers and *mañjarīs.* That practitioner witnesses things that other people do not see. Now, it is widely assumed that the *līlās* of Kṛṣṇa are infinite; it is also widely assumed that the *līlās* of Kṛṣṇa are constantly being played out throughout the cosmos. So in those instances, time, in effect, is collapsed, so that all of Kṛṣṇa's *līlās* are "going on" simultaneously.

SR: Prabhupāda said that in this spiritual context "time is conspicuous by its absence."

Dr. Stewart: Yes. Exactly. I think that is very well said. So you have someone entering into this *līlā* through the *siddha-deha* and then coming back to a mundane reality to report it serially. But my point is this: they are capable of reporting something that does not exist anywhere else in textual form. Now, the *Bhāgavata-purāṇa* reveals Kṛṣṇa's activities on this earth. But that does not describe every single thing that Kṛṣṇa ever did or does. So each time someone enters into this eternal realm through their *siddha-deha,* they are witnessing, potentially, at least, a "new" activity. Something that no one else has ever reported before.

SR: This is a wonderful explanation.

Dr. Stewart: And I think that the dramas of Rūpa, of Kṛṣṇadāsa, and of later Gauḍīya dramatists as well—every one of those are, really, revelations of a very high order. Now, again, I do not have any concrete evidence, but if you think about what the practice is supposed to produce, at some point you no longer simply relive the *līlās* that are described in the *Purāṇas* and so forth. Rather, you are really conducting yourself *as yourself* in those *līlās* directly. That gives you, then, the opportunity to see things never before reported.

SR: I think this is clearly seen in Narottama dāsa Ṭhākura.

Dr. Stewart: Definitely. I think that many of his poems regarding what he experienced as a *mañjarī* are probably direct reportings and, in that sense, are revelatory. This is someone who has been there! Someone who has seen it as an eyewitness, and who has now come back to reveal it to others. Again, I think that the *Bhakti-rasāmṛta-sindhu* and the *Ujjvala-nīlamaṇi* are really the keys for explaining how this is possible, the mechanisms of these transformations. And they leave it to you to figure out what has actually happened. I think that this holds true for all of the subsequent devotional literature, particularly the *padas,* the Bengali and Brajabuli writings, especially the very best—those to which people respond positively and on which they agree. You know that you are reading about the real event, not just a fanciful or imaginative piece of fiction.

When people read Narottama dāsa's *Prārthanā,* for example, they are genuinely moved. It is hard to avoid it. You know the Vaiṣṇavas read that and they say that these poems capture something that has the ring of truth—this is what makes them important. It becomes an index to the skill of the poet. But I think that in Vaiṣṇava terms the skill of the poet is in direct relation to the originality and sophistication of his *mañjarī* or related *siddha-deha,* shall we say, "experience." So the fact that Narottama dāsa moves people so much suggests not only that he is a good author or poet but probably that the source of his inspiration is a little more direct, or perhaps, maybe not so much more direct as simply from a larger pool of experience.

There is a wonderful little story that he tells in one of his *Prārthanā* writings where he says, and I paraphrase—"You know, there I was in my *mañjarī* form, finally getting to witness the *līlās.* And then all of a sudden Rūpa Mañjarī put her hand in the middle of my back and pushed me into the presence of Rādhā and Kṛṣṇa." Now, if that is not firsthand reporting, I have never heard it! What he describes in his poem is one of his *mañjarī* experiences, and he tells about the terror and the fear of possibly making a mistake. He tells how he was stammering and how it was so humbling to find himself in this ultimate sort of situation. It was also a joy, he says. A joy that was inexpressible.

So that is one of the things that hinted to me that we should rethink the point of the dramas. And I think that the way they are read and studied suggest that they carry at least close to the kind of weight that more widely recognized forms of revelation have carried.

SR: Oh definitely. The tradition itself fully accepts these as revelations, not just as dramas.

Dr. Stewart: Yes. So, in that sense, I think the role of drama is much greater than it would appear to be on the surface. Now, Kavi Karṇapūra, of course, could have potentially presented a lot of problems for this kind of theory. Well, let me rephrase that—it is not so much problems for this theory as problems fitting into the structure that the Gosvāmīs have created. Kavi Karṇapūra, significantly, is the only non-Gosvāmī to have generated, more or less, a complete set of Sanskrit compositions that would qualify one to be an esteemed *paṇḍita.* He wrote a *vyākaraṇa,* so he has a grammar to his credit. He has a *mahākāvya* to his credit. He has a drama to his credit. He has *Alaṁkāra śāstra,* a *rasa śāstra* text to his credit. He wrote the *Gaura-gaṇoddeśa-dīpikā,* which is another category of writing that I do not know quite how to classify. So Kavi Karṇapūra really serves, in my opinion, as the only serious rival—at least potentially—to Gosvāmī authority. But when you look at his work, you realize that though it differs remarkably from the Gosvāmīs', it frequently supplements or fails to conflict. What he does not do is advocate a particular *sādhana* or ritual practice, so he remains a theoretician without the practical application so noticeable in Rūpa's work.

When you think about when Kavi Karṇapūra was writing, and when the Gosvāmīs were writing, and then, when you realize what it meant in the sixteenth century to be separated by 800 to 1,000 miles—which is the distance between Vṛndāvana, where the Gosvāmīs were, and Purī, where Kavi Karṇapūra was—it is quite amazing that their positions do not conflict more. It is true that there was a fairly heavy traffic of devotees going back and forth. But it was not like it is today, where everybody can know exactly what everybody else is doing.

There seems to be some evidence that by the time Kṛṣṇadāsa Kavirāja wrote his biography of Caitanya, Kavi Karṇapūra's works were pretty well-known to the people in Vṛndāvana. But there really does not seem to be much evidence prior to that. So you have someone who, coming out of the same mindset, inspired in much the same way, and undoubtedly knowing many of the same people, attempts to systematize the life of Caitanya, and then to get that in accord with the life of Kṛṣṇa, and to apply that, then, to a devotional world. That work by Kavi Karṇapūra is noteworthy.

SR: So, if I understand you properly, you are saying that even though they were separated by geographical location, Kavi Karṇapūra came up with a theological and hagiographical theory similar to that of the Gosvāmīs and other Gauḍīya writers in Vṛndāvana.

Dr. Stewart: Complementary is perhaps better. Although, from what I have read, I would say that his theories are not nearly so sophisticated or detailed as those of the Gosvāmīs. His positions are in some ways analogs to the Gosvāmīs', for example, the elaborate explication of *siddha-dehas* in his *Gaura-gaṇoddeśa-dīpikā*. Now, what that suggests to me is that the foundation or source is the same for Gosvāmī theology, particularly that of Rūpa, and for Kavi Karṇapūra's systematic writings. And that source is probably Svarūpa Dāmodara. Again, this is speculation, but based on good history and comparative theology. There are enough similarities, and there is enough of an interest in applying aesthetic theory to the devotional experience, that it suggests that part of the community had this form of understanding firmly in mind. The Bengali biographies speak of *bhāva* when they try to explain Caitanya's religious experience, and this fact suggests that the aesthetic interpretation was understood by the community to hold the key to religious experience.

So, I think Kavi Karṇapūra probably was motivated by many of the same impulses as the Gosvāmīs, although his formulations assume a somewhat more formal shape, and a somewhat more traditional shape. The *gurus* of the Gauḍīya Vaiṣṇava community embrace Kavi Karṇapūra, but are mindful to rank him below Rūpa in matters of devotional exposition. Rūpa wrote what has become the standard interpretation of divine love, the life of the devotee. Kavi Karṇapūra is seen to augment that, in spite of certain disagreements of emphasis between the two authors' works. In this sense, there is a tremendous amount of theological consistency in the tradition as a whole, and that is one of Gauḍīya Vaiṣṇavism's most impressive points.

The Saṁpradāya of Śrī Caitanya

William Deadwyler III

William H. Deadwyler (also known as Ravīndra Svarūpa Dāsa) received his Ph.D. in Philosophy of Religion from Temple University (1980). He is the author of Encounter with the Lord of the Universe *(Washington, DC, The Gītā-nāgarī Press, 1984), and is published in numerous academic works. He is a lecturer and practitioner of Caitanyaite Vaiṣṇavism.*

SR: Most people who study East Indian philosophy don't know about the *paramparā* system. They've heard about *guru*/disciple relationships, of course, but they generally don't know about authentic preceptorial lineages—the various Vaiṣṇava *saṁpradāyas*—and the importance of being initiated into one of those traditions. So I thought that we could perhaps begin by explaining, philosophically and scripturally, the importance of the Vaiṣṇava *saṁpradāya.*

Dr. Deadwyler: The notion of *saṁpradāya*—it's also called *paramparā,* which means, literally, "one after another"—is found in the fourth chapter of *Bhagavad-gītā.* There Kṛṣṇa says that he originally taught the *Bhagavad-gītā* to the Sun god Vivasvān, who taught it in turn to Manu. And then Kṛṣṇa says, *evaṁ paramparā prāptam imaṁ rājarṣayo viduḥ:* this secret teaching was passed down in this way, one after another, in *paramparā,* and the saintly kings all understood it in that manner. Here we find the notion that sure and certain knowledge is *revealed.* And it is transmitted through spiritual sound—*śabda*—which is only truly given by Kṛṣṇa or his representatives in disciplic succession.

A tradition, or *paramparā,* is meant to preserve spiritual knowledge, or truth, through successive links in a chain that carries on over the years, one generation after another. And Kṛṣṇa implies in the *Bhagavad-gītā*—in the same verse from the fourth chapter—that if and when the disciplic succession is broken, and the knowledge is consequently lost, he himself descends to reestablish it.

Philosophically you can call this "a descending process," [*avaroha panthā*]—the knowledge comes down from Kṛṣṇa, who is God and therefore perfect. The purpose of a tradition, or a genuine *guru,* then, is to preserve the original and perfect revelation intact and complete. You can't improve on it. You can't add to it, but rather you preserve it and teach it.

SR: Now, there are a lot of *gurus* in India, and perhaps elsewhere in the world as well. But which *gurus* represent the genuine *paramparā* system? Or, more important than that—which lineages are authentic from the Vaiṣṇava point of view? I mean, if one were looking for a *guru,* which lines of disciplic descent should one be aware of?

Dr. Deadwyler: You're asking about the recognized *saṁpradāyas.* Well, the word *saṁpradāya* literally means "a community." A text from the *Padma Purāṇa* quoted widely in Vaiṣṇava writings speaks directly about these authorized communities. It says that "Those *mantras* which are not received within a *saṁpradāya* are fruitless; they have no potency." And then the text specifically names the *saṁpradāyas.* "In the Kali Yuga, there will be four *saṁpradāyas*"—we are talking about Vaiṣṇava *saṁpradāyas.* "They are the Brahmā Saṁpradāya, originating with Brahmā; Śrī Saṁpradāya, that is to say, it started with Lakṣmī; Rudra Saṁpradāya, starting with Śiva; and there's another one starting from Sanaka and the others, the Kumāras." Those are the four recognized Vaiṣṇava *saṁpradāyas.*

Each one has their main *ācārya,* or definitive teacher who enunciated the doctrine for that *saṁpradāya.* For the Śrī Saṁpradāya, there is Rāmānuja. For the Brahmā Saṁpradāya, there is Madhvācārya. The Rudra Saṁpradāya has Viṣṇusvāmī. And the *saṁpradāya* of the Kumāras has Nimbārka.

SR: In regard to the Viṣṇusvāmī Saṁpradāya—I've heard something to the effect that Vallabha and Viṣṇusvāmī were the same person. True or not?

Dr. Deadwyler: No. Viṣṇusvāmī was much earlier than Vallabha, and I believe that none of his works have survived. Now, Vallabha, who was a contemporary of Caitanya Mahāprabhu, said that he was associated with the *saṁpradāya* of Viṣṇusvāmī. But they are not the same person. In fact, Vallabha wrote his own commentary on Brahma-sūtra [the *Aṇu-bhāṣya*] and on Śrīmad Bhāgavatam [the *Subodhinī*] and founded his own group, called the Puṣṭi-mārga, although he is closely linked with the Rudra Saṁpradāya. Still, he doesn't seem to have really received much specific traditional teaching from the Rudra *saṁpradāya*. So Viṣṇusvāmī is the one that we often hear of as being the principle *ācārya* of the Rudra line, and he's from way back when. No one knows his dates. But Vallabha was a contemporary of Śrī Caitanya. The Vallabha line really has their own *saṁpradāya*; otherwise the Rudra line is not active, as far as anyone can see.

SR: So could you say Puṣṭi-mārga *is* the Rudra Saṁpradāya?

Dr. Deadwyler: In a sense, yes, although most people just call it the Vallabha Saṁpradāya. I've never heard anyone really refer to it as relating to the prior *saṁpradāya* or going back beyond Vallabhācārya. But formally they claim to be in the Rudra Saṁpradāya of Viṣṇusvāmī.

SR: Have you heard that this verse from the *Padma Purāṇa*—the one you quoted—has been brought into question by Stuart Elkman and even by O.B.L. Kapoor? They say that they can't find it, actually.

Dr. Deadwyler: Yes, present-day scholars have claimed that current editions of the *Padma Purāṇa* don't include that verse. That may be so. But it's quoted by Madhvācārya and other early writers.

SR: Kavi Karṇapūra quotes it.

Dr. Deadwyler: Right. So it may not be in modern editions, but it was found there somewhere along the way. That's the simplest explanation. Others will decide that the verse was fabricated or something of that sort. . . .Well, this is the virtue of accepting knowledge in disciplic succession. Believers will accept the verdict of their teachers, as it comes down through the tradition, the *paramparā* system. Others will be confused about this.

Unfortunately, there are different versions or manuscript traditions of various *purāṇas*—it's very difficult. There are many editions from various times and places. The *Padma Purāṇa* is huge, too. I don't know how many scholars have personally gone through it verse by verse. And the verse we're talking about may be there tucked away in some edition somewhere for all I know—for all anyone knows.

SR: Well, whatever the case may be, we do indeed find to this day that those four *sampradāyas* are in fact the major traditional lineages of Vaiṣṇavism in India. So let's move on from the four authorized chains of knowledge to how the Gauḍīya Sampradāya is aligned with them. It is said that the Gauḍīya school is connected to the Brahma-Mādhva Sampradāya.

Dr. Deadwyler: Yes. The claim for that is found in a number of places. The main reference is a list of the *guru paramparā* found in Baladeva Vidyābhūṣaṇa's *Govinda-bhāṣya* and *Prameya-ratnāvalī*. And also in Kavi Karṇapūra's *Gaura-gaṇoddeśa-dīpikā*, the earliest statement. And it's also in another one, a younger contemporary of Caitanya—Gopāla-guru. His work doesn't survive, but it's quoted somewhere else.

SR: B.B. Majumdar mentions eight.

Dr. Deadwyler: That's right. There are eight places in addition to Baladeva and Kavi Karṇapūra where the affiliation is brought out. But the really significant ones are the ones that I've mentioned. Gopāla-guru was a disciple of Vakreśvara Paṇḍita, but his . . .

SR: I think his work is called *Padya.*

Dr. Deadwyler: That's it. And it's also mentioned in the *Bhakti-ratnākara* of Narahari Cakravartī.

SR: Well, the other important place is Viśvanātha Cakravartī's *Gauragaṇ-a-svarūpa-tattva-candrikā*. That's a bit later, but it's an important reference because he was such an prominent *ācārya.*

Dr. Deadwyler: Now he was an associate of Baladeva Vidyābhūṣaṇa. Viśvanātha Cakravartī was the very one who sent Baladeva to debate the authenticity of the Gauḍīya Sampradāya. We can conclude that there was some agreement at that time that this list, with its Mādhva connection, was indeed the correct *paramparā.* At least these two important *ācāryas*—Baladeva and Viśvanātha—agreed. So, yes, Viśvanātha Cakaravartī also accepted it.

This comes from the Vṛndāvana side—they all accepted the Gauḍīya affiliation. So therc was some concensus of opinion. But the earliest writer to attest to the affiliation was Kavi Karṇapūra. In other words, the idea was there in Orissa as well. Of course, Baladeva was originally from Orissa himself. There's a work by a Mukherjee called *The History of the Caitanya Faith in Orissa.*

SR: Oh, Prabhat Mukherjee. He's a very important and well-known historian of Oriyan Vaiṣṇavism.

Dr. Deadwyler: Prabhat Mukherjee finds a number of Oriyan Vaiṣṇavas who affiliate themselves with Caitanya and give a *guru paramparā* that includes Madhva. So it seems to have been accepted in Orissa at a time soon after Caitanya's disappearance. Thus, there was a firm, early tradition that Caitanya's disciplic succession descended from Madhvācārya. And so it's called the Brahma-Mādhva-Gauḍīya Sampradāya.

Some scholars, however, have held that the affiliation was an invention of Baladeva Vidyābhūṣaṇa, who was originally a Tattvavādī, a Mādhvite. Then, through his spiritual master, Rādhā-Dāmodara, he became a Gauḍīya Vaiṣṇava. So some people think he had ideological motives for "affiliating" the Caitanya movement with Madhva. S.K. De, one of the big doubters of the authenticity of this list, even hints that Baladeva himself may have written the *Gaura-gaṇoddeśa-dīpikā* and attributed it to Kavi Karṇapūra, in order to back-date the affiliation.

SR: What is his evidence?

Dr. Deadwyler: There is no evidence whatsoever. S.K. De's "seminal" book, *Early History of the Vaishnava Faith and Movement in Bengal,* which is probably the most comprehensive early history of Gauḍīya Vaiṣṇavism in Bengal, at least in the English language, is full of forced conclusions. Yet it remains sort of the standard work on the subject, at least for scholars. De seems to bend over backwards to ape the manners of Western critical scholarship, and he tries to doubt everything conceivably doubtable. There's almost a presumption of falsification in the documents—guilty until proven innocent. He questions the historicity of *everything.*

So he cast doubt on this *guru paramparā*—the linking of the Gauḍīya school with the Brahma-Mādhva Sampradāya. Now he's not alone in this, nor did the idea originate with him. He was following some earlier

Bengali writers from the twenties and thirties. But you will find the first and one of the more prominent places where the affiliation is rejected is Surendranatha Dasgupta—*History of Indian Philosophy*. In the fourth volume of that work, in the section on Madhva, Dasgupta lists the succession of Mādhva *gurus*, and then he says that this list is largely at variance with the list given in the introduction of the commentary on the *Brahmasūtra* by Baladeva Vidyābhūṣaṇa.

After quoting Baladeva's list, Dasgupta tells us (on Page 56 of Volume 4): "We see that the list given by Baladeva is right as far as Jayatīrtha, but after Jayatīrtha, the list given by Baladeva is in total discrepancy with the two lists given from the Mādhva *maṭhas* in Belgaum and Poona." So Dasgupta rejects it.

But B.N.K. Sharma, in his *History of the Advaita School of Vedānta and Its Literature*, brings to light the miscalculation made by Dasgupta. You see, there are a number of Mādhva *maṭhas*. The one that Dasgupta quotes is the disciplic succession of the Uttarādi Maṭha. That Uttarādi Maṭha twice divided and so you end up with three *maṭhas*—the Uttarādi Maṭha and two others. But Dasgupta was ignorant of these two splits.

However, one of these offshoot *maṭhas*, called the Vyāsa-rāja Maṭha, records a line of disciplic succession that appears quite similar to the one Baladeva and Kavi Karṇapūra give. And *this* is an official Mādhva list. I can go over it with you. Here's what happened. After Mādhva, we find listed Padmanābha, Nṛhari, Mādhava, and Akṣobhya.

Now in the Mādhva tradition, these four are frequently regarded as direct disciples of Mādhvācārya, although some places say that Nṛhari, Mādhava, and Akṣobhya were all initiated by Padmanābha. At any rate, they're pretty much contemporaries. Then Akṣobhya's disciple was Jayatīrtha. He was the famous commentator and systematizer of Mādhva's teaching. All of these devotees, by the way, were the heads of *maṭhas*, *mahāntas*, or "pontiffs" as Sharma calls them. There may have been other advanced *ācāryas* during their time. But the list only contains the leaders of the *maṭha*.

After Jayatīrtha, the official Mādhva list mentions Vidyādhirāja. The list from Baladeva, however, has Jñānasindhu, Dayānidhi, and then Vidyānidhi. The list from Kavi Karṇapūra has Jñānasindhu and, instead of Dayānidhi, has Mahānidhi, and then it also has Vidyānidhi. So if you accept, as Sharma does, that Vidyānidhi and Vidhyādhirāja are the same person—just a variation of the same name—then what you have in Baladeva's and Kavi Karṇapūra's list are two names, Jñānasindhu and Dayānidhi or Mahānidhi, that are introduced between Jayatīrtha and Vidyānidhi.

After Vidyādhirāja or Vidyānidhi, assuming that it's the same person, the branching off from the *maṭha* takes place, and you get the distinctive Vyāsa-rāja Maṭha, named after Vyāsatīrtha, who was a later head of that *maṭha* and became very famous. Next in succession is Rājendra, who is in Baladeva's list; then the Mādhva list has Jayadhvaja whereas the Gauḍīya lists give a variation on that name—Jayadharma. And then it's the same: Puruṣottama, Brahmaṇyatīrtha, Vyāsatīrtha. So up to that point, everything's fairly consistent.

There's really not too much to fuss about—you've got two extra names and a few variations on names, which is common enough. Now, after Vyāsatīrtha, Baladeva lists Lakṣmīpati Tīrtha, Mādhavendra Purī, and Īśvara Purī, who was Caitanya's *guru*. And those first three names do not appear on any Mādhva list. So this is the problem. . .

SR: Right. This is where the real controversy begins.

Dr. Deadwyler: Exactly. Well, first of all, there's the controversy that concerns Surendranatha Dasgupta, which we've looked at—he didn't even recognize this list. But as we've shown, following B.N.K. Sharma, up until Lakṣmīpati Tīrtha there's not a whole lot of difference in the two lists.

SR: And minor differences shouldn't be all that shocking, because, for example, if two disciples of different *gurus* are writing books, let's say, five hundred years from now, and they each make a list of teachers, each list would be different, leading up to their particular *guru*. That's natural. It's like a tree with many branches.

Dr. Deadwyler: Sure. That's right. But at this point we should deal with the second problem, the one that arises after Vyāsatīrtha.

SR: You mean the one involving Lakṣmīpati Tīrtha?

Dr. Deadwyler: Right. Although Lakṣmīpati Tīrtha is indeed absent from the Mādhva list, there is a simple solution: this Lakṣmīpati Tīrtha wasn't a *mahānta*. He was an initiated disciple of Vyāsatīrtha, but he was not at any time the head of a Mādhva *maṭha*. I think that's a very simple and likely explanation.

SR: You're saying that his name isn't on the list because he was not a leader.

Dr. Deadwyler: Because the Mādhva lists don't contain every disciple. They list only devotees who served for some time as the heads of *maṭhas*.

SR: I'm interested in something related to this: how would you explain that Lakṣmīpati appears to be the last of the people with the "Tīrtha" titles? After him you have Mādhavendra *Purī*.

Dr. Deadwyler: That's the more interesting puzzle. All of those *ācāryas* up to that point have a "Tīrtha" in their names. Even Mādhva's name was Ānanda-tīrtha. The "Tīrtha" title originally came from a Śaṅkarite order, because Mādhva was initially initiated in the Śaṅkarite order, and it is characteristic of Mādhva *sannyāsīs*. So then you have Mādhavendra Purī, Īśvara Purī—you get a "Purī" title, which belongs to another Śaṅkarite order. Now how does that happen?

There are some plausible explanations for it. One of them is that Mādhavendra Purī, in fact, took *sannyāsa* initiation in an Advaita *sampradāya*—just as Caitanya Mahāprabhu did. Just as, as a matter of fact, Madhva did. And when people took *sannyāsa* sometimes, especially in those days, it didn't seem to matter so much. They took from whomever was handy. That seems to be a reasonable explanation. The change in title doesn't seem a sufficient reason to reject the lineage. And the testimony that there was a Mādhva connection is much older than Baladeva. And at least if you accept Kavi Karṇapūra and the similar traditions from Orissa, you can't say they had some "ideological motive."

Another plausible scenario is that Mādhavendra Purī could have already been a Māyāvādī *sannyāsī* and then met Lakṣmīpati Tīrtha. Vyāsatīrtha, by the way—this is interesting—is said to have died in 1539, so he was actually a contemporary of Caitanya also. Caitanya's lifetime was fairly short, but he was born before Vyāsatīrtha's demise. Still it was possible for Vyāsatīrtha to have initiated Lakṣmīpati, and that succession could have gone on during his lifetime.

According to the *Bhakti-ratnākara* of Narahari Cakravartī, by the way, Nityānanda was actually initiated directly by Lakṣmīpati. Baladeva, on the other hand, lists him along with Īśvara Purī and Advaita Ācārya as disciples of Mādhavendra Purī. This can be reconciled with Narahari's account, however, as Narahari says that although Nityānanda was Mādhavendra Purī's godbrother, Nityānanda always regarded him as his *guru*.

Incidentally, Kavi Karṇapūra states that one of Jayadharma's (or Jayadhvaja's) disciples was the famous Viṣṇu Purī, author of *Bhakti-ratnāvali.* In that case, we have the Purī title appearing earlier in the list, as belonging to an *ācārya* who was not a *mahānta.* B.N.K. Sharma speculates that this Viṣṇu Purī may have been the actual teacher of Lakṣmīpati, and so on, and thus the real link between Madhva and Caitanya. In some such way Sharma and others, like Stuart Elkman, accept an historical Mādhva connection, while having doubts about the exact list of Baladeva or Kavi Karṇapūra.

SR: There is another problem that needs to be addressed: if there is a connection between the Gauḍīya Saṁpradāya and the Brahma-Mādhva Saṁpradāya, why is there such a difference in the theology? O.B.L. Kapoor really brings out some divergent views. How would you explain that?

Dr. Deadwyler: Yes, this has been another reason for doubting the connection, and modern scholars have sometimes made much of it. But the differences are ones of emphasis, really. The essential teachings are in agreement. Mādhavendra Purī, it's true, is credited by the followers of Caitanya with introducing something new. Let me read you something from the *Caitanya-caritāmṛta.* This is *Ādi-līlā* 9.10: "All glories to Śrī Mādhavendra Purī, the storehouse of all devotional service unto Kṛṣṇa. He is a desire tree of devotional service and it is in him that the seed of devotional service first fructified." It says that he is "the storehouse of Kṛṣṇa *premā.*" In his commentary, Bhaktivedanta Swami Prabhupāda writes, "Śrī Mādhavendra Purī, also known as Śrī Mādhava Purī, belonged to the disciplic succession from Madhvācārya, and he was a greatly celebrated *sannyāsī.*" And then there's this critique: "The process of worship in the disciplic succession from Madhvācārya was full of ritualistic ceremonies, with hardly a sign of love of Godhead; Śrī Mādhavendra Purī was the first person in that disciplic succession to exhibit the symptoms of love of Godhead. . . ."

SR: Right. I have a few quotes about Mādhavendra Purī here: Vṛndāvana dāsa Ṭhākura, in the *Caitanya-bhāgavata,* refers to him as "the prime architect of the devotionalism in Bengal." Kṛṣṇadāsa Kavirāja calls him "the first sprout of the wishing tree of devotion." So It seems that Mādhavendra Purī moved the Brahma-Mādhva conception from awe and reverence, or worship of Nārāyaṇa (which was more common in the Mādhva Saṁpradāya), to worship in *mādhurya,* or the sweet loving aspect that's found in Rādhā-Kṛṣṇa. Apparently, there's some element here of moving from Vaidhī *bhakti* to Rāgānugā *bhakti*.

Dr. Deadwyler: Precisely. That's what the commentary is talking about here. Mādhavendra Purī, the commentator notes, was "the first to write a poem beginning with the words, *ayi dīna-dayārdra nātha he*." This verse is recorded in *Caitanya-caritāmṛta, Antya-līlā*, Chapter Eight, Verse Thirty-four. And I'll get back to that poem later. "In that poetry," the commentary continues, "is the seed of Caitanya Mahāprabhu's cultivation of love of Godhead." So that seed is contained in Mādhavendra Purī's verse, and that verse expresses Rādhārāṇī's anguished feelings of separation from Kṛṣṇa.

The *Caitanya-caritāmṛta* says that Mādhavendra Purī was reciting this very verse while passing away from the material world. I'll give you the translation: "O Lord, O most merciful Master, O Master of Mathurā! When shall I see You again? Because of my not seeing You, my agitated heart has become unsteady. O most beloved one, what shall I do now?" This is Rādhārāṇī speaking, expressing her most intense love in feelings of separation. The *Caitanya-caritāmṛta* (*Antya-līlā* 8.35-36) says, "In this verse Mādhavendra Purī instructs how to achieve ecstatic love for Kṛṣṇa [*kṛṣṇa-premā*]. By feeling separation from Kṛṣṇa, one becomes spiritually situated. Mādhavendra Purī sowed the seed of ecstatic love [*premā*] for Kṛṣṇa within this material world, and then departed. That seed later became a great tree in the form of Śrī Caitanya Mahāprabhu."

SR: But doesn't it go further? I remember. . .

Dr. Deadwyler: Yes! I'm getting to that. You're right, there's another discussion of this verse in *Madhya-līlā*, Chapter Four, in which Caitanya explained the story of Mādhavendra Purī and Nāthajī, or Śrī Gopāla. Here is *Caitanya-caritāmṛta*, beginning with Verse 192: "After saying this, Lord Caitanya Mahāprabhu read the famous verse of Mādhavendra Purī. That verse is just like a full moon. It has spread illumination all over the world.

"By continuous rubbing," the *Caitanya-caritāmṛta* goes on, "the aroma of Malaya sandalwood increases. Similarly, by considering this verse, its importance increases."

SR: This is a glorification of the verse spoken by Rādhārāṇī, the verse that reflects her mood.

Dr. Deadwyler: Yes. *Ayi dīna-dayārdra nātha he.* The *Caitanya-caritāmṛta* continues: "As the kaustubha-maṇi is considered the most precious of valuable stones, this verse is similarly considered the best of mellow poems. [*rasa-kāvya,* poetry about *rasa]*. Actually this verse was spoken by Śrīmatī Rādhārāṇī Herself, and by Her mercy only was it manifest in the words of Mādhavendra Purī."

So what is this saying? It's saying that Rādhārāṇī revealed this verse directly to Mādhavendra Purī, or that by her mercy it was manifest in the words that emanated from Mādhavendra Purī's mouth. And then Kṛṣṇadāsa Kavirāja says, "Only Caitanya Mahāprabhu has tasted the poetry of this verse. No fourth person is capable of understanding it." That is, only Śrīmatī Rādhārāṇī, Mādhavendra Purī, and Caitanya Mahāprabhu understood this verse. Then it says, "Mādhavendra Purī recited this verse again and again at the end of his material existence. Thus uttering this verse, he attained the ultimate goal of life." And then the verse is quoted in Text 197. Now I want to look at some of Bhaktivedanta Swami Prabhupāda's commentary on this text here. Prabhupāda writes, "Out of the four *sampradāyas,* the Śrī Madhvācārya Sampradāya was accepted by Mādhavendra Purī. Thus he took *sannyāsa* according to *paramparā,* the disciplic succession."

Here we see, by the way, Prabhupāda's statement that it was a *sannyasa* initiation. If so, the "Purī" title must have been used in the Mādhva order, at least outside of the formal *maṭha* structure. Kavi Karṇapūra's mention of Viṣṇu Purī as a disciple of Jayadharma [Jayadhvaja], gives some support for this idea.

At any rate, the commentary goes on: "Beginning from Madhvācārya down to the spiritual master of Mādhavendra Purī, Lakṣmīpati Tīrtha, there was no realization of devotional service in conjugal love." Then he says, "Śrī Mādhavendra Purī introduced the conception of conjugal love for the first time in the Madhvācārya Sampradāya." So here on the Gauḍīya Vaiṣṇava side is a frank recognition that there was something new with Mādhavendra Purī in this *sampradāya.*

SR: So is that to say that devotees before the time of Mādhavendra Purī could not attain Goloka Vṛndāvana? They only went to Vaikuṇṭha?

Dr. Deadwyler: Well, does it say that?

SR: That does seem to be the implication. . .

Dr. Deadwyler: In the Mādhva Saṁpradāya, the Deity that they were worshipping was Nārāyaṇa.

SR: So they go to Vaikuṇṭha.

Dr. Deadwyler: That's where they'll go; they'll go to Vaikuṇṭha. And if in the Śrī Saṁpradāya they were worshipping Sītā-Rāma, for example, then that's what they will attain—Ayodhyā—which is also Vaikuṇṭha.

SR: Well, was anyone worshipping Kṛṣṇa prior to that time?

Dr. Deadwyler: Of course. But even so, the worship was largely on the platform of *vaidhī bhakti,* that is, formal regulative service. Kṛṣṇa worshippers on that platform could attain the majestic feature of Kṛṣṇa in Dvārakā or Mathurā, but not Goloka Vṛndāvana. That is obtainable only by devotion on the spontaneous platform, *rāgānugā bhakti.*

But let me finish reading this commentary on Mādhavendra Purī's verse: "Śrī Mādhavendra Purī introduced the conception of conjugal love for the first time in the Mādhva Saṁpradāya." Now, the next comment is interesting: "This conclusion of the Madhvācārya Saṁpradāya was revealed by Śrī Caitanya Mahāprabhu when he toured Southern India and met the Tattvavādīs, who supposedly belonged to the Mādhva Saṁpradāya."

So the idea here, at least from the Mādhva-Gauḍīya point of view, is that there were potentialities, spiritual realizations, latent within Mādhvācārya, and these were fully brought out later by Caitanya Mahāprabhu and, before him, in a less manifest form, by Mādhavendra Purī. The implication here is that, for reasons of time and place, Madhvācārya may not have spoken these things aloud, or not have made certain things explicit, although they might still have been recognized by followers with realization.

What the Gauḍīya Vaiṣṇavas generally say is that Caitanya's philosophy of *acintya bhedābheda tattva,* and also his teaching on the *mādhurya rasa,* are a kind of synthesis and capstone of the philosophies of the four *saṁpradāyas.* Yet it's significant that Caitanya himself took initiation in the Mādhva Saṁpradāya. He singled it out, so to speak, because of his appreciation for its strong polemic against the Māyāvādīs. More than anyone else, Madhva and Jayatīrtha really were ferocious in their opposition to the Māyāvādīs.

Now, you can list a number of differences between what's commonly accepted as the philosophy of Madhvācārya and that of the Six Gosvāmīs. But you can make another list of similarities. If you ask me, the similarities are greater. So it's really a question of what you consider important, and what you consider secondary.

With a teacher as rich and profound as Madhvācārya, it's a question of what in his writings becomes emphasized, what becomes expounded upon by his followers, what becomes the prevalent mode of teaching. And there will be other things latent in those teachings which will not receive much emphasis, and yet may seem to be of greater importance at a later time. So it's a question of how you look at it. There are differences. And finally, that's why Baladeva Vidyābhūṣaṇa, who's one of the big proponents of the Mādhva affiliation, also had to write a separate commentary on Vedānta Sūtra specifically for the Gauḍīya Saṁpradāya. Because there are certain things in Madhva's works—relating to Gauḍīya practices—that you'll not find, such as the worship of Rādhā-Kṛṣṇa together. This won't be found in Madhva's works. The Mādhvites worship Nārāyaṇa, and they generally don't worship Lakṣmī-Nārāyaṇa either—just Nārāyaṇa alone. The fact that there are differences between the philosophy of the Mādhvites and the Gauḍīyas is no argument against historical affiliation.

SR: You know, in some ways, it always seemed to me that the Śrī Vaiṣṇavas—the Rāmānujites—were very close to the Gauḍīya idea. At least as much as the Mādhva teaching. You know, when Mahāprabhu met with Vyeṅkaṭa Bhaṭṭa—they seemed to really get on pretty well. And the *śakti* thing is there—Lakṣmī-Nārāyaṇa. So there is a closeness.

Dr. Deadwyler: Right. Well, it depends on what Mādhvite you talk to, you know. I've spoken to some who strongly remind me of a kind of Christian, actually, in their "this is the only way" mode of relating. Their emphasis on duality, a dualism that they have emphasized, also sometimes seems quite extreme—"there's no oneness between God and the living being, no similarity whatsoever." Well, I don't know if I can accept that.

On the other hand, a scholar like B.N.K. Sharma, who's a Mādhvite scholar, will say that Caitanya's *acintya bhedābheda tattva* is really just a variation of Madhva's category of *viśeṣa.* And he sees a clear development out of Madhva's teaching. Whereas some other scholar will say, "You know, they're two completely different things" and so on.

SR: I once read in an early *Harmonist* that the reason Mahāprabhu chose the Mādhva Saṁpradāya with which to align himself, as opposed to the other *saṁpradāyas,* was because Mādhvites emphasized duality—they taught that the living being is different than God. And when there's a difference, there's more of an aptitude for service.

Dr. Deadwyler: That's right. That's right.

SR: I thought that this was very nicely put.

Dr. Deadwyler: That's right. This reminds me of something I wanted to speak about. What gives some scholars problems—on the doctrinal level—with this Mādhva affiliation is the high respect Caitanya Mahāprabhu gives Śrīdhara Svāmī's *Bhāgavata* commentary. Most scholars regard Śrīdhara Svāmī as an Advaitin, and he was actually so regarded by Śaṅkarites, too; they accepted him as one of them, although he did get into trouble in that community. His commentary on the *Bhāgavata* was controversial, and it did seem as though it might not have actually been accepted because Śrīdhara Svāmī did recognize a difference, a quantitative difference, between the soul and the Supreme Lord. And, of course, there is a Mādhva idea here, as you mentioned.

So the Gauḍīya Vaiṣṇavas do not accept him as a real Advaitin. Even though he was apparently recognized by the Śaṅkara Saṁpradāya as one of them, they thought he was straying too close to Vaiṣṇava ideas. As far as the Vaiṣṇava *saṁpradāyas* are concerned, we have to recognize a great deal of overlapping. The *saṁpradāyas*—the four orthodox *saṁpradāyas*—teach basically the same thing. They all teach that one is an eternal servant of Viṣṇu or Kṛṣṇa, or one of his many incarnations. The emphasis and the details may differ, but the truth is ultimately one.

The Sahajiyā Tradition

Robert Sailley

Robert Sailley is the author (in French) of Le Bouddhisme tantrique indo-tibetain ou Véhicule de Diamant *(Paris: Editions Presence, 1980) and* Chaitanya et la devotion á Krishna *(Paris: Dervy-Livres, 1986), among other books, his latest being* Śiva et le Śivaisme *(1991), a detailed report on Kaśmīr Śaivism. Dr. Sailley received his Ph.D. from the Sorbonne, where he served as honorary librarian and researcher for many years. He was also affiliated with the l'Ecole pratique des Hautes Etudes, where he is called upon as an advisor and a pre-eminent scholar of Oriental Studies.*

SR: Your book on Caitanya Mahāprabhu is still quite popular in France, even though it was published over six years ago. Now, my French is not what it could be, but I can see that the book is quite thorough. Tell me, what inspired you to write that book? You are well-versed in a variety of Eastern traditions and, I believe, you practice Tibetan Buddhism. So Why Mahāprabhu?

Dr. Sailley: Well, there are two reasons. First, I had come across some very interesting books that elucidated the tradition. That started my interest. And secondly, in the early 1970s, I saw Bhaktivedanta Swami, the master of the Hare Kṛṣṇa movement, here in France performing a Vaiṣṇava initiation ceremony! Needless to say, I was more than intrigued. I could tell that this was a very deep tradition. So I set out for India—I had been there before, of course (I had gone to Puri in the 1960s)—to learn about the roots of Gauḍīya Vaiṣṇavism. Luckily, I had studied Sanskrit, Bengali, and other languages, so I was equipped to deal with some of the original source materials. I did a lot of field research, and the results were published in my Caitanya book, quite coincidentally in 1986, the year of his 500th anniversary.

Now, it is true that I am a Buddhist—I have been affiliated with a Buddhist fellowship here in Vincennes, near Paris, for over fifteen years—but this was no reason to avoid the Caitanya tradition. Besides, I had already written a book on Buddhism. And I saw many similarities between what I know of as Buddhism and Caitanya Vaiṣṇavism. The comparisons are clear. Of course, there are differences as well. Still, I thought that knowledge of Vaiṣṇavism could only enrich my own commitment to my Buddhist practices. And as a scholar, I have a thirst for understanding all religious traditions, particularly those of the Orient.

SR: Now, correct me if I am wrong, but is it not claimed that the Sahajiyā movement grew out of early Buddhist practices?

Dr. Sailley: There is a good case for it, but it can also be argued that it was actually just the opposite. The Buddhists were influenced by practices that were popular among the Hindus. You see, with the Muslim invasions, many Buddhists fled to the Himālayas. Eventually, though, teachers from Tibet sent their best masters back into India to learn Tantric secrets, which included many Sahajiyā doctrines. So it is very difficult to ascertain exactly what transpired. But it is certainly true that most scholars naturally assume that there was this Buddhist influence that gave rise to Sahajiyā values.

One thing is certain: there were popular songs in Bengal that are clearly associated with Sahajiyā origins. I had the good fortune of meeting a writer from Norway who translated a good deal of this material; he wrote a book about the *doha*, these popular songs that gave rise to Sahajiyāism. These songs are from seventh-to-ninth-century Bengal, when there was a large Buddhist population there. So that is where the ideas come from. I think that this is very clear.

Also, there were Tantric Buddhists at that time who followed the *Sahaja-yāna*, or the "path of the natural way." This was a system of Buddhism that grew out of the Vajrayāna ("Diamond Vehicle") school, and the adherents emphasized the use of the senses—including sex—veering away from all sorts of repression or abstinence. They considered the ascetic approach to be unnatual, and so they believed in sublimation, in a sense. Naturally, they employed left-handed Tantric practices and sexual rituals that deeply offended the orthodox among both Buddhist and Hindu communities.

SR: What exactly is meant by left-handed Tantrics?

Dr. Sailley: The technical term for right-handed is *dakṣiṇa,* and the term for left-handed is *vāma.* So we are talking about Vāma-Tantra. This is the spontaneous course, or the path of *rāgānugā.* The Sahajiyās say that this is better than Dakṣiṇa-Tantra, for that is the path of rules and regulations, or *vaidhi.* This is another reason that orthodox Vaiṣṇavism frowns on the Sahajiyās—they have totally ignored the *vaidhi* path, the important path of rules and regulations.

Another explanation of "left-handed" Tantrics involves male and female imagery. It is said that the left side of the body represents a person's "femaleness" and that the right side represents a person's "maleness." The two are to merge during ritual sex, and in this way the practitioner achieves a sort of universal unity, a oneness with the ultimate reality. This concept is severely scorned by the orthodox Vaiṣṇavas.

SR: Getting back to the Buddhist connection: I really do not see it. This does not seem like Buddhism as it is traditionally understood.

Dr. Sailley: You are certainly correct in that regard. You see, it arose as a reaction to Mahāyāna Buddhism, which accentuates discipline, austerity, and the serious practice of rules and regulations. This was the Buddhism that was known in those days. And whenever you have a tradition of severe discipline, you always have a counter tradition, one that reacts to the rigors associated with determined practice. It is an interesting sociological phenomenon.

Still, Sahajiyāism caught on, and today you can find it among Buddhist groups, Śaivites, Śāktas, Sufis and, yes, Vaiṣṇavas, although the Sahajiyā element is considered unconventional in all of these sects. A good deal has been written on this subject. You have Professor Dimock's book, *The Place of the Hidden Moon* (Chicago: University of Chicago Press, 1966); Dasgupta's *Obscure Religious Cults* (Calcutta: KLM Firma, 1976); and M.M. Bose's *The Post-Caitanya Sahajia Cult of Bengal* (Delhi: Gian Publishing House, 1986). These are about the best studies in the English language.

SR: How would you define Sahajiyāism in a modern Gauḍīya Vaiṣṇava context? What do they believe?

Dr. Sailley: Sahajiyāism is an interesting development that had existed on the fringes of the Vaiṣṇava movement from even before the time of Caitanya. But, you see, it was inadvertantly given additional impetus by Caitanya due to his emphasis on *mādhurya-rasa* and the various aspects of erotic love. Now, Caitanya meant something very internal and esoteric by this. But the Sahajiyās take it in a different way. The Vaiṣṇava-Sahajiyā believes that Rādhā and Kṛṣṇa exist, in a sense, in every woman and man. So when there is union between the sexes, as in intercourse, they are replicating, if you will, a divine occurrence. So the Sahajiyās see it as a spiritual phenomenon.

There are elaborate ceremonies, of course, and a whole series of detailed procedures wherein a Sahajiyā will have sex with a chosen partner and bring his *kuṇḍalinī*, or "serpent power," up to a certain point just before climax—and then he will stop. In this way he develops his self-control and sense of mastery over the body. It is a very involved process that culminates, supposedly, in *siddhi*, or perfection. In this, at least, they are very much like traditional Gauḍīya Vaiṣṇavas, who also seek perfection. However, the Sahajiyās' sense of perfection is more like the Śaṅkarites—they sort of *become* the supreme reality. By contrast, the Gauḍīya Vaiṣṇavas' sense of perfection revolves around *serving* the supreme reality: Kṛṣṇa.

Moreover, Sahajiyās tend to accentuate the *parakīyā* doctrine, which states that Rādhā and Kṛṣṇa enjoy the highest love because they are not married to each other. They take all risks to come together. This, too, is similar to the Gauḍīya Vaiṣṇava perspective. But, again, the Sahajiyās take it in a different direction. The practical ramifications of this, for the Sahajiyā, are ludicrous. They seek out unmarried partners for union. Well, naturally, the orthodox Vaiṣṇava community frowns upon this. The orthodox tradition promotes celibacy, or, at the utmost, sex within marriage. The *parakīyā* mode is *only* for Rādhā and Kṛṣṇa. *Not* for their devotees.

SR: What are some other differences between Sahajiyā-Vaiṣṇavas and the orthodox Vaiṣṇavas?

Dr. Sailley: There are many. Edward Dimock summarizes this nicely. He says that the Sahajiyā is primarily humanistic, whereas the Vaiṣṇava is theistic. He also says that Sahajiyās tend to be monistic, whereas the Vaiṣṇavas are dualistic. These words are understood in a variety of ways, but if you have an overview of Indian philosophy you can understand how they apply to Sahajiyāism in relation to regular Vaiṣṇavism. But the main difference, I would say, is in relation to sexuality and self-image. They approve of left-handed Tantric rituals involving sex with female *yoginīs*, and they often think of themselves as a sort of microcosmic Rādhā and Kṛṣṇa.

SR: I still cannot really see the Buddhist connection, though. How did the Buddhist ideal, which is not theistic, come to be accepted by a Hindu-based religion? How did Vaiṣṇavism incorporate Sahajiyā practices?

Dr. Sailley: Well, it is important to understand that orthodox Vaiṣṇavas never did, and probably never will, incorporate these practices. But I think you are asking something deeper: you are asking how a non-theistic tradition like Buddhism could engender conceptions that would be embraced or carried over to a fundamentally theistic tradition like Gauḍīya Vaiṣṇavism. This is a good question. And it deserves a detailed answer. Given the limitations of our discussion and our time constraints, I will do the best that I can.

You see, the Sahajayāna Buddhists did away with ritualistic conduct and practiced a "*yoga* of sex," if you will. Their goal was to experience heightened consciousness and to transcend duality. One way they hoped to achieve this is through the unity of male and female principles, which they called *upāya* and *prajñā*. Now, their songs, which I have mentioned, are collectively known as *Caryāpadas*, and they articulate these views in very esoteric language. This is how we know of their secret activities and practices.

This was going on during the Pāla dynasty—from about the eighth to twelfth centuries A.D.—and then the Sena kings came to power in Bengal. This was when Jayadeva won royal patronage from Lakṣmānasena, and Vaiṣṇava literature started to proliferate in Bengal. It was at this time that the Buddhist Sahajiyās and the existing Vaiṣṇavism of the day sort of blended into a rather twisted hybrid—they came to see their abstract *upāya* as "Kṛṣṇa," and their equally abstract *prajñā* as "Rādhā." This is one example.

But in a variety of ways the impersonal, non-theistic Buddhists came to merge with the more theological school of Vaiṣṇavism, and their conceptions became abhorrent to the orthodox people of both camps. In this way a sect of Vaiṣṇava-Sahajiyās developed that came to see the union of Rādhā and Kṛṣṇa as somehow paradigmatic of male-female union in this world. They saw the macrocosm reflected in the microcosm, which is fine, but they took it to levels that bordered on the absurd, at least from the traditional point of view.

SR: Traditionalist Vaiṣṇavas often refer to Sahajiyās as *Prākṛta*-Sahajiyās. That is to say that the Sahajiyās are not just on "the natural path," but on a "materialistic" natural path. They are considered materialistic in the sense that they are imitationists. They imitate Rādhā and Kṛṣṇa, and they also imitate the symptoms of *premā*, falsely exhibiting the ecstatic symptoms of true lovers of God.

Dr. Sailley: I am aware of this, yes, and there are certain sects, like the Sakhī Bekhī and the Cūḍa Dhārī, that are generally accused of these things. Also, the Kartā Bhajās, Ativādī, Āula, Bāula, and Sain sects—so there are a good number of them. And you are quite right: the orthodox community views them as cheap imitationists. So that happens to be the situation, and I am afraid that the orthodox and heterodox Vaiṣṇava groups will probably never see eye-to-eye.

However, sometimes Sahajiyāism is associated with Caitanya himself, with Nityānanda, Nityānanda's wife, his son, with Kṛṣṇadāsa Kavirāja, and so many others. Naturally, the Sahajiyās look for links in the orthodox Vaiṣṇava school. And sometimes it is difficult to disprove them. But the orthodox do not accept it, and it is unlikely that any of the Sahajiyā connections with members of the orthodox school are really valid. You know, Ed Dimock makes a pretty good case, though. . .

SR: Yes, but Joe O'Connell has reasonably refuted Dimock's arguments. His refutation appears in a paper called "Were Caitanya's Vaiṣṇavas Really Sahajiyās? The Case of Rāmānanda Rāya." A shortened version of this paper was published in Tony Stewart's volume, *Shaping Bengali Worlds, Public and Private* (East Lansing: Asian Studies Center, Michigan State University, 1989). I have the longer version, and there O'Connell gives convincing arguments that Rāmānanda Rāya, at least, was definitely *not* a Sahajiyā.

Dr. Sailley: I am not aware of this.

SR: Yes. Dimock had written in his *Place of the Hidden Moon* that there were Sahajiyā elements in the personality of Rāmānanda Rāya. Externally, this certainly appeared to be the case. And in Kavi Karṇapūra's *Caitanya-candrodaya-nāṭaka,* Śrī Rāmānanda is actually referred to as a *sa-*

haja-Vaiṣṇava. But O'Connell argues in his brilliant paper that in this case "*sahaja*" is not to be taken as the same as "Sahajiyā," even though the words come from the same root. He argues that here "*sahaja*" refers to a Vaiṣṇava who is situated in his "natural relationship" with Kṛṣṇa. It certainly does not refer to a Prākṛta-Sahajiyā. And he gives ample evidence to support his contention. In the reprint of *Hidden Moon* (1989), Dimock acknowledges the correction in this particular case but says that he stands his ground on other, related points.

Dr. Sailley: That is very interesting, and it is an important development in the scholarship of the tradition. But, you know, it can also be understood that Sahajiyā denotes a sect, a school of thought, advocating a particular access to spiritual reality. There are many traditional works associated with the Sahajiyā tradition. You may have heard of some of them: the *Vivarta-vilāsa,* the *Āmṛta-ratnāvalī,* and so on. These texts serve to define the concept of *bastu,* the sacralization of the body, which is so central to Sahajiyā practice. And there are many texts of this genre. To learn more about them, one can read the Bengali works of Paritoṣa Dāsa, for example.

But other works that are from time-to-time associated with Sahajiyāism—Kṛṣṇadāsa Kavirāja Gosvāmī's writings, the works of Raghunātha dāsa, and Narottama Ṭhākura's poetry, for example—should probably not be understood in this way. I would say that the Sahajiyā element in these works is really questionable. The names of these authors have been seized upon in order to give credibility to the Sahajiyā tradition, a credibility it otherwise would not have. And while there have been scholars who try to tie the two traditions together, I, for one, am quite pleased that O'Connell and others are finding that the orthodox Gauḍīya Vaiṣṇavas were not Sahajiyās in any pejorative sense of the term. I think that it is dangerous to mix the two traditions. I also think that it will shed a great amount of light on genuine Gauḍīya Vaiṣṇava practice if we come to fully understand the distinctions between the authentic Caitanya movement and its Sahajiyā counterpart.

Gauḍīya Vaiṣṇavism in the Modern World

Charles Brooks

Charles R. Brooks is author of **The Hare Krishnas in India** *(Princeton, New Jersey: Princeton University Press, 1989) and has published numerous articles on the sociological and anthropological aspects of Gauḍīya Vaiṣṇavism. He is currently teaching anthropology at City University of New York and New York University.*

Dr. Brooks: I think we can begin our discussion of Gauḍīya Vaiṣṇavism in the modern world with Bhaktivinoda Ṭhākura, or Kedāranātha Dutta, as he was known in his early life.

SR: Okay. That's the late nineteenth or early twentieth century.

Dr. Brooks: Caitanya's movement reached a highpoint with Bhaktivinoda; he rekindled the flame, so to speak, and he brought out, to newer heights, whatever excellence the tradition knew in earlier days. This is my synthesis of the movement, which, of course, was started by Caitanya and the Six Gosvāmīs, who revitalized *bhakti* at that earlier period—in the sixteenth century. And it was of course a very important social and religious movement in India at that time.

At the time of Caitanya, in fact, there were many similar movements responding to the same social and cultural needs. Thoughout the history of Bengal, and, throughout India, there have been many important figures, charismatic figures, or even prophets, who really revitalized *bhakti* in general, in particular the religion of Śrī Caitanya. There were very orthodox strains and then some that were less so.

But my impression is that, despite reform movements of all kinds, and significant religious reformers, things gradually decreased, if you don't want to say that they disintegrated. There was a gradual decline of fervor after the time of the Six Gosvāmīs, to such an extent that when Bhaktivinoda was going through what you might call his own personal religious crisis, when he tried to find a copy of *Śrīmad Bhāgavatam*, it was a difficult thing. He couldn't find it. So that let's you know the state of affairs—just how obscure the Gauḍīya tradition had become.

Bhaktivinoda was relentless, though, and he worked hard to reestablish the covered if not lost teachings of the Gauḍīya Vaiṣṇava *ācāryas*. He translated ancient texts and wrote new ones. He was really a visionary, in some sense, in the same way that Caitanya was. The parallels with Bhaktivinoda's rediscovery of Caitanya's birthplace and Caitanya's own visionary discovery of Vṛndāvana are uncanny. As Caitanya reclaimed Kṛṣṇa, so Bhaktivinoda reclaimed Caitanya.

Now I think that what I can talk about is the importance of Bhaktivinoda in this revitalization that ultimately culminated, or is still going on really, with the Gauḍīya tradition in India today and even with ISKCON around the world and the other factions of Vaiṣṇavism in the West.

SR: One thing we should insert here, although you did touch on it, is that there were some great teachers in between the Six Gosvāmīs and Bhaktivinoda Ṭhākura. It's often depicted that after the Gosvāmīs there was a big droop, and then at the time of Bhaktivinoda things started to get going again. And there is truth to that. But there were some very important personalities in the middle there. Some names should be mentioned: Kṛṣṇadāsa Kavirāja Gosvāmī, Śrīnivāsa Ācārya, Narottama dāsa Ṭhākura, Śyāmānanda Paṇḍita, Viśvanātha Cakravartī Ṭhākura, Baladeva Vidyābhūṣaṇa, which is a century or so before Bhaktivinoda, and, of course, Jagannātha dāsa Bābājī. So these were important personalities who kept the teachings alive.

Baladeva Vidyābhūṣaṇa, for example, was significant because the Gauḍīyas didn't have a commentary on the Vedānta Sūtra, and he wrote the commentary establishing the Gauḍīyas as a bonafide sect. So there were significant events like that, and these sort of need to be addressed.

Dr. Brooks: Well, that's definitely true. I'm actually not so familiar with that period. But there's no doubt that there were extremely important people that protected and legitimized the tradition, if you will. And the Baladeva Vidyābhūṣaṇa episode, the one that you mentioned, was a very important council, if you want to call it that. It addressed a conscious acknowledgement that they needed to keep this thing going, that it was a valuable religious tradition, with a rich heritage. So the *Govinda-bhāṣya*, Baladeva's commentary, was an important thing that came out of that. But, like I said, I really don't feel qualified to address the details around that. I certainly agree with you, though, that it remained, it continued, and it factioned as most religious movements do.

The various ways that the followers of Caitanya splintered off, and the different doctrines that developed around them—what we now call *sahajiyā*, for example—we can discuss whether or not those are legitimate forms of Gauḍīya Vaiṣṇavism. Certainly the adherents of the different factions felt that they were tapping into something that was essentially springing from Caitanya. And in some ways it clearly was. But, in many cases, it was just a sort of heterodoxical system that only loosely related to Caitanya's teachings or example.

I think that this is precisely what Bhaktivinoda was aware of and the problem he wanted to solve. With Bhaktivinoda we certainly see the negative attribution toward the *sahajiyās* that continues throughout the development of the Gauḍīya Maṭha and ISKCON itself. A lot has been written on that by people who specialize in analyzing that movement.

SR: So a lot of this comes from Bhaktivinoda. In your article in Weber and Chopra's book, *Shri Krishna Chaitanya and the Bhakti Religion* (Frankfurt am Main: Verlag Peter Lang, 1988), you mention Bhaktivinoda's education, how he worked in the government and how he was affiliated with the Jagannātha Temple. Maybe you can talk about that.

Dr. Brooks: That certainly spoke of his legitimacy. Someone who was in the world but not of it, Bhaktivinoda was a productive member of society and was in a sense integrated into the upper strata of British India. He knew how to give Gauḍīya conclusions to his contemporaries, to those who were given to, if we can use a vague term, *Westernization*. He himself was Westernized to a certain extent. He had received a Western, English education. He studied law and he was a civil servant. Along the way, part of his duties included overseeing the Jagannātha Temple in Purī. No doubt that had something to do with his rekindled interest in Vaiṣṇavism.

I think it's interesting to note that he studied Christianity and the other world religions. I imagine that there were these personal questions that he was trying to resolve himself. Ultimately, of course, he concluded that Gauḍīya Vaiṣṇavism revealed the same truth that is found in all religions but to a much deeper degree. But he did this after making a study of the other religions, which is significant, and he maintained a healthy respect for all genuinely spiritual revelations.

SR: I think it is also noteworthy that he was born in a family that was given to the Śākta form of worship—so he wasn't born into Vaiṣṇavism. This is significant on a number of levels. He wasn't biased in choosing the Gauḍīya tradition as the deepest revelation. That's one thing. Another point is that since he was converted, if you will, from Śāktism to Vaiṣṇavism, he makes a good role model for converts today, such as members of ISKCON, because like many of them, he was not born a Gauḍīya Vaiṣṇava but, instead, adopted the religion later in life. I believe he was forty-two when he took Vaiṣṇava initiation from Vipina-vihārī Gosvāmī.

Dr. Brooks: I see. That's interesting. But certainly, when he got copies of *Caitanya-caritāmṛta* and *Śrīmad Bhāgavatam*, a bit earlier, it was transformative for him. He studied the detail of the philosophy and theology there. It altered his way of thinking so much, in fact, that he was motivated to revitalize the religion of Caitanya. I think that, from what I understand, he felt that it had degenerated by this time. If you study the period, in the minds of the masses of people, the Caitanya religion was primarily associated with the *sahajiyā* sect and their particular *sādhana*—particularly the tantric aspects of their own *sādhana*.

SR: There's one *sannyāsī*, Suhotra Swami, who's currently writing a book about the *apasaṁpradāyas*, like the *sahajiyās*, that developed in between the time of Mahāprabhu and Bhaktivinoda, and he explains how Bhaktivinoda was preaching against them.

Dr. Brooks: That would be interesting. Basically, Bhaktivinoda's biographers and commentators paint the following picture: Bhaktivinoda felt that Vaiṣṇavism had been abandoned, at least by the educated people. The literature wasn't available to them. *Kīrtana*, particularly *saṅkīrtana*, was denigrated. The people in general felt that only those of loose morals followed these practices. So, he had a lot to contend with.

Again, we can see parallels with the life of Caitanya, who was contending with the same kind of negative feelings from the dominant society, and of course he was successful in converting so many people and winning the support of the leaders, the government leaders of the time. Certainly Bhaktivinoda was similarly a charismatic prophet, in a sense. . . .Now I'm using that term rather technically. When I look at the development or the resurgence of social movements and religious movements, I think a very apt model to look at is the anthropological concept of a revitalization movement. Rather than categorizing something as a cult, which has such a negative connotation these days, this kind of movement emerges when there is a breakdown in the culture, when the culture isn't working for a large number of people. In a sense we can look at every religion in its nativity and see it as responding to the dissatisfaction of the people involved. Now what is needed is a recognition by individuals that they are not satisfied, psychologically and materially.

SR: And spiritually.

Dr. Brooks: And spiritually, certainly. That's an important point. There are ultimate sorts of needs that people have to satisfy, and if the dominant religious system, or, more generally, the dominant culture, isn't providing the various mechanisms needed for providing this satisfaction, the people in general are going to be looking, they're going to be searching. That's the predisposition of what has to happen, what has to be there for something like that to arise, sociologically speaking. But it never happens unless there is some kind of catalyst, some kind of figure who has the answers.

Certainly, the ecstatic zeal that Caitanya displayed drew people to him like a magnet. And, likewise, although Bhaktivinoda wasn't the initial catalyst for the movement, he certainly was one of the few genuine instigators of it, and he had the vision. And I think that if we look at the spread of Vaiṣṇavism since his time, we have to say that he gave it real focus, and, certainly, he was the real generator of the idea that Vaiṣṇavism was a universal religion, that it had the potential to proselytize, to draw other people in. This not only echoes the mood of Caitanya but functions quite positively in Indian society, where some people are denied access to salvation because of their birth status. So it's appealing on that level. I think Bhaktivinoda was consciously prophetic in the sense that Vaiṣṇavism, Caitanya Vaiṣṇavism, wasn't limited to one section of India. It was truly universal in scope.

SR: Bhaktivinoda made some of those prophetic statements: "O for that day when the fortunate English, French, Russian, German, and American people will take up banners, *mṛdaṅgas* and *kartālas*, and raise *kīrtanas* through their streets and towns. When will that day come?"

Dr. Brooks: Right. That's certainly the famous one. But there were several others as well. There are obviously other prophecies here and there, in the scriptures, too. And people in India, even the poorest people, the most illiterate people, hook into the sacred texts, some rather obscure, and it's that ability that provides them the resources to deal with change, to deal with new ideas and revitalization of old ideas. The fact that Western devotees of Caitanya appeared in India was shocking to some people, but on the other hand, people also went to great lengths to find the scriptural precedent for this, and the mystical framing, the religious framing, to understand the meaning of the westward expansion. Certainly since the time Bhaktivedanta Swami Prabhupāda brought his Western *brāhmaṇas* to India, Indians themselves have had to delve deeper into their own culture and search for keys or clues to explain why this was happening.

So, Bhaktivinoda was really the instigator, one of the primary underlying architects of this scheme. And, you know, beneath all of this was what a lot of people would prefer to say is the social issue of caste. The way people deal with the concept of caste in India is very interesting, especially when you're talking about who can integrate into the system, who can be a *brāhmaṇa*, who cannot be a *brāhmaṇa*, and questions of this nature. That's the key issue here. Bhaktivinoda was anti-caste, in a sense.

SR: Like Caitanya.

Dr. Brooks: Like Caitanya. Yes. They didn't do away with caste conventions, with social conventions. They did seek to open it up, however, to whoever was able to exhibit the appropriate qualities and do the appropriate work. This was practical and, they said, supported by the sacred texts, such as *Bhagavad-gītā*. The scholars of the Bengal school went to great and effective lengths to prove their conclusions in reference even to the original Vedas.

Now, how did Bhaktivinoda visualize all of this symbolically? It's very interesting. Because you can look at someone and tell whether they are, well, at least whether they are twice-born; they wear the sacred thread. Some people say only *brāhmaṇas* should wear the sacred thread. In some areas, the three upper *varṇas* are accorded the sacred thread. But Bhaktivinoda basically said we need to get rid of all of these outward symbols of caste. He burned the sacred thread and said that, more or less, birth status, birth group or caste itself, doesn't matter; it's not important. What is important is the quality of your devotion.

SR: You know, this was a big issue in the time of Narottama Ṭhākura. He was a *kāyastha* and he was initiating *brāhmaṇas*. There were attacks on his life, and big debates, and a big festival, sort of an ecumenical council, at Kheturīgrām. Vīrabhadra, who was Nityānanda's son, gave an elaborate speech on the difference between a *brāhmaṇa* and a Vaiṣṇava. This was in the seventeenth century. Very significant issue.

Dr. Brooks: It *is* significant, because, in a very pragmatic sense, Vaiṣṇavism supercedes castehood. When you're trying to come to grips with categories that people actually use—and that's what the anthropologist tries to do—it causes problems. On the one hand, caste is an imposed concept. Although Indians use the concept of caste now, it's something that was more or less given to them. They have the word "*varṇa,*" and you have four *varṇas.* Some people say that's the same as caste. And you have the concept "*jāti,*" which are sort of sub-*varṇas.* But they are very flexible terms. Even outside of the *bhakti* religions, I think caste is more flexible than a lot of people presuppose. Still, most people, when they think about Indian culture, automatically think of caste. This is the repressive, rigid system.

SR: Right.

Dr. Brooks: But throughout Indian history, people have been dealing with just how important "caste" actually is. Certainly there are many contexts in India, and this is especially the case in sacred places like Vṛndāvana, where caste is completely superceded by other things. In Vṛndāvana, if you ask someone about their *jāti,* you get all sorts of different answers because the word primarily refers to the group to which they belong. And how people identify themselves will vary from situation to situation. So some people would say, "I'm Indian," some would say, "My *jāti* is *sanātana dharma.*" Some would say, "My *jāti* is Bengali;" "my *jāti* is human." Sometimes they say, "My *jāti* is *vaiśya.*" So I don't think that these are clearcut categories, at least empirically, in the Indian mind.

That creates a very flexible situation, especially when Indians themselves are trying to categorize other people, foreigners, for instance. And, because you have the debate already, within the context of the *bhakti* religion, it allows people to continue to debate about it. The question, for example, is not so much, "Can the ISKCON *pūjārīs* be genuine *brāhmaṇas*?" This is not so much the question for the people of Vṛndāvana. But the following question *is* on their minds: "Are these ISKCON people actually Vaiṣṇavas?" They generally consider that to be the more important question. And I think that the question is usually answered with "Yes, they are."

But, in any case, these underlying issues of inequality and stratification in Indian society were issues that Bhaktivinoda was dealing with. So Bhaktivinoda really laid the groundwork for manipulating, in a sense, what a person's identity was. His reading of Gauḍīya theology gave opportunities to people who were in the lower stratas of society to improve their status by proving, or showing through their behavior, that they should be accepted as *brāhmaṇa*. Or, further, as Vaiṣṇava. As I said, Bhaktivinoda wasn't so concerned with creating *brāhmaṇa* as he was in giving everyone access to the religion and de-emphasizing caste.

SR: Right, right.

Dr. Brooks: He refused to acknowledge caste distinctions and even burned the sacred thread. And when Bhaktisiddhānta Sarasvatī took over the reins of the movement in the early twentieth century, it was really a fortunate coincidence, you might say, that Bhaktisiddhānta was such an organizer and such a scholar. The organization that we call the Gauḍīya Maṭha was something new because it tried, really for the first time, to create a strata, or a category of Vaiṣṇava *sādhus*, Vaiṣṇava *sannyāsīs*. He took many of Bhaktivinoda's ideas a step further.

Now I'm sure that there were Vaiṣṇavas who lived as *sādhus* before this time, but as far as any kind of formal structure, that just didn't really exist. It was more or less relegated to the followers of Śaṅkara, who were outside the confines of Vaiṣṇavism. In fact, that may be one of the reasons why Caitanya himself took *sannyāsa* initiation from a Śaṅkarite, Keśava Bhāratī: it is possible that there were no or few Vaiṣṇava schools to take it from.

SR: Well, I think that the Śrī-saṁpradāya in South India had a structured system of *sannyāsa*. Prabodhānanda Sarasvatī was a *tridaṇḍa sannyāsī*. And in fact I think that's where Bhaktisiddhānta Sarasvatī got the rituals for the *sannyāsa* ceremony that he later instituted in the Gauḍīya Maṭha.

Dr. Brooks: Is that right?

SR: Yes. That's what I was given to understand from his biographers, like Bhaktikusuma Śramaṇa Mahārāja.

Dr. Brooks: Well, certainly, wherever Bhaktisiddhānta got the symbolism, or wherever he got the ritual, he didn't so much as his father de-emphasize caste, but he said, "If you qualify, you *are* a *brāhmaṇa.*" And anyone who exhibited the proper qualities, who was trained in devotional service, was, in fact, a *brāhmaṇa* and deserved to wear the sacred thread. So while his conclusions were the same as those of Bhaktivinoda, he manifested them, so to speak, or displayed them, with different symbolism. Bhaktivinoda did away with the thread, and Bhaktisiddhānta brought it back. Of course this certainly conflicted with other segments of the Gauḍīya Vaiṣṇava *saṁpradāya,* particularly with the caste *gosvāmīs* who were in charge of the temples. And that's a tension that still exists today. In a sense, this tension also prepared the Vaiṣṇavas of Vṛndāvana and of other places, particularly Bengal, for the advent of foreign Vaiṣṇavas.

SR: It seems the plan for Western converts could also be traced to Bhaktivinoda's writings—he *did* write in English as well as in Bengali. And he sent his books to the West. So we should say something about the phenomenon of Bhaktivinoda writing in English.

Dr. Brooks: It is important that he sent books to the West and began a sort of prosyletizing mission. It's an example of his vision that the Gauḍīya *saṁpradāya,* the religion of Caitanya, was capable of being the universal religion that the scriptures talked about, that it had the qualities, it had the attributes, of being one of the great religions, a panacea for all mankind.

For the average person in the West, whether he's well educated or not, he generally thinks of Hinduism as a sort of unified, great religion. And, of course, it's not. Hinduism is rather diversified. So certainly people in India are aware of that. There are a lot of different religious systems that come under the umbrella of Hinduism. But Bhaktivinoda saw in the religion of Caitanya something that was universal, something that would appeal, intrinsically, to the mind of anyone, regardless of whether they were born in India or not. That's a very complicated issue. How can something so rooted in one country, in a particular cultural tradition, be capable of translation into other places. And the amazing thing is that there hasn't been a lot of translation. There has been strict adherence to the basic principles, including language and cosmology—however you want to talk about it—and without major change it has attracted foreigners, Americans, Europeans, or whatever, who have become Vaiṣṇavas.

So Bhaktivinoda was quite correct. Certainly he had this insight that if some basic ideas about the Caitanya religion were available in English, it would attract at least the intellectuals. And, on some level, it did. Bhaktivinoda saw this, in a small way, even in his own lifetime. There was a slight resurgence, and he was successful in getting at least some of the books to Western shores.

SR: He sent books to some very important people, I think, like Emerson and Thoreau. And he received some favorable response. Also, one of his books was reviewed in the *Journal of the Royal Asiatick Society*. So there was, as you say, some modicum of success among the intellectual class.

Dr. Brooks: Right. Of course his *Jaiva Dharma* was sent, I think, to McGill University, in Canada, as was his *Shri Chaitanya: His Life and Precepts*. Now I don't have any idea how many people read those books at the time. Like you said, certainly some people read it, some people who were important in Western culture at the time. But the fact that he took on writing in English was a significant event. He was using his own English training to begin the process of disseminating cross-culturally what he felt was this universal religion. And I think a lot of people have pointed to his importance, not only as far as the resurgence of Gaudiya Vaisnavism in nineteenth-century India, but as far as setting in motion the things that would eventually culminate in the International Society for Krishna Consciousness.

You could also question why it didn't catch on before in other places, because, as Bhaktisiddhānta took over and organized the structure of the Gauḍīya Maṭha, he certainly challenged his own followers to proselytize in other places. He also had the idea, inherited from Bhaktivinoda, perhaps, to send his disciples to Western countries.

SR: He did, in fact, send some of them to the West. Do you know that history? Bon Mahārāja. B.P. Tīrtha Mahārāja. We should get into that a little.

Dr. Brooks: Well, I know a little bit about it. I do know that he sent some of his disciples to Germany, to England, and they had minimal success, really. You might just say the time wasn't right in these places. The success of ISKCON is, I think, largely a matter of timing. A believer, of course, could say that Kṛṣṇa was in charge, and the timing was precise because Kṛṣṇa wanted it to happen, and that he wanted to bestow this important service on his dedicated follower, Bhaktivedanta Swami. Whatever the case, ISKCON's founder succeeded in doing that which had remained only a dream for Bhaktisiddhānta's other disciples.

You know, I met Bon Mahārāja when I was in Vṛndāvana. He was near death at the time, and he died while I was there. But it was very interesting. I think that in the few conversations that I heard—I was present when he was speaking with other people—he was lamenting in a way, thinking about what he had done wrong as far as trying to spread the message in the West. Certainly the differences in the personalities between Bon Mahārāja and Bhaktivedanta Swami are significant. Bon Mahārāja was clearly impressed with England. That's where he went. And he managed to get audiences with the royal family and that was his idea. Start from the top. And, of course, they are going to be polite to this respected man from India, but they are not really going to be serious about delving into the philosophy.

Bhaktivedanta had a different idea. Start from the bottom and work upward. He wanted to attract intellectuals, of course, but he was anxious to give the message to *anybody*, and this is what worked. Also, he was unimpressed with Western culture. He saw it as spiritually backward, and so it had no sway on him. This, of course, separated him quite a distance from Bon Mahārāja, and this is what I think led to his success.

Now, Bon Mahārāja's production in England amounted to a few mature ladies, literally. He had a very small group of potential recruits. Certainly there were spiritualists in England, people who were interested in Hinduism. But these for the most part were people who were well-established in English society to begin with. They had no need to find something completely new. They had their own lives and it was more of a hobby for them. I think he initiated one disciple in England. Maybe, between him and Tīrtha Mahārāja, there were two or three. And I don't know any of the details about that.

SR: I think it's that woman, Mrs. Bowtell . . .she was given the name Vinodavāṇī Dāsī, and her friend, too, Stella Harris, who was called Viṣṇupriyā Dāsī. There were several men, too—Mr. Koeth Baron and

Mr. Schulze, who was given the name Sadānanda Dāsa. He was the one who shared Gauḍīya teachings with Walther Eidlitz, who wrote a couple of books. But that was about it. So there were maybe four or five disciples.

Dr. Brooks: It was Vinodavāṇī Dāsī. That's the one that I had heard about.

SR: Vinodavāṇī. I saw a picture of her recently, when I visited the English branch of the Gauḍīya Maṭha.

Dr. Brooks: Do you know if she continued her association with Bon Mahārāja?

SR: She did. She had a correspondence with a couple of his Godbrothers—Bhaktipradīpa Tīrtha Mahārāja. I have a copy of one of the letters she wrote to him in the 1930s. The late-30s—that's the time period here. She passed on in the seventies. But even if you go to that Gauḍīya Maṭha in England today, they have a big portrait of her on the wall and they garland it every day. It's very interesting. It's a small center and no one really knows about it.

Dr. Brooks: Meanwhile, Bhaktivedanta Swami's movement is worldwide—from America to the Soviet Union. And it's flourishing. You know, it was very interesting for me to talk to people in Vṛndāvana about Bhaktivedanta. He was there for ten years or so before he came to the United States. And even before then from time to time. But he pretty much lived there for ten years. And today, people who were living in Vṛndāvana at that time all have good things to say about him. In his day, most people just treated him like another *sādhu,* and didn't give him much credence. A lot of people will say, "I knew he was great."

There's one shopkeeper who always tells the story how Bhaktivedanta would come and sit in his store, years before he started ISKCON, and talk about the temples that were already there. He would say, "they just have to be revealed. They are already there; time just has to pass for us to see them." So he had this vision.

But for the most part, I don't think the people of Vṛndāvana really thought that he had the capacity to fulfill his vision. He certainly looked for support in every corner. The official word, especially among the other Gauḍīya Vaiṣṇavas, especially in the temples, was that he's a nice old man, a sincere devotee. But he has these pipedreams that will never be accomplished.

So looking back over what he did accomplish, there's certainly reinterpretation and reassessment of their views at the time. And all sorts of explanations arise, like, "Well, once he finally got on the boat, he was empowered by Kṛṣṇa." You know, that heart attack he experienced on the boat—some say that Kṛṣṇa entered his heart at that time. Kṛṣṇa entered him at that time. And of course, whatever the case may be, the results speak for themselves.

SR: Now, in retrospect, you can look at the *Bhāgavata Māhātmya* of the *Padma Purāṇa,* which predicted that personified *bhakti* would go south and then go to Vṛndāvana and then, finally, cross the ocean.

Dr. Brooks: Right. That's a very important quote that a lot of people in Vṛndāvana are familiar with. Intellectuals will take apart the exact words, deconstruct it and question whether or not the wording means "go to a foreign country" or "go to some other place in India." I think that, grammatically, the term is "*deśa,*" which means "land" or "country." So they ask whether it means that the religion will be spread throughout the land or countries of India, the different states of India, or to other countries.

SR: Shrivatsa Goswami gave me a good explanation of that: he said that in this particular section of the *Māhātmya,* all of the other places in India that *bhakti* visits are specifically mentioned by name. But when it gets to this controversial part, it doesn't give the specific country. . .

Dr. Brooks: Exactly. So that can be seen as another prophecy. The other followers of Bhaktisiddhānta didn't fulfill this demand, although, as a result of their missionary activities, I guess, some did make it to Vṛndāvana, as well as some other places in India and abroad.

SR: Klostermaier also went to Vṛndāvana for some time.

Dr. Brooks: That's true. And he did have a relationship with Bon Mahārāja. There's also another American disciple of Bon Mahārāja still living in Vṛndāvana.

SR: Oh, yes, I know who you're talking about.

Dr. Brooks: Right, and he was initiated by Bon Mahārāja, too, but, as far as I know, he is still working with Shrivatsa Goswami. You know, when you talk about Gauḍīya Vaiṣṇavism in India, you are not talking about something that's completely unified. I think that many of the Gauḍīya Vaiṣṇava spokesmen, whether they be in some other line of work, or whether they be a *gosvāmī*, or whatever, Gauḍīya Vaiṣṇavism is a tree with many branches. Besides that, you've got the *gosvāmī* families who run the temples. They have their own agendas. They have their own concerns about status, about who's in charge. These are rather pragmatic things, but inevitably they conflict with more spiritual issues about who's more advanced, who's more legitimate, etc. You've got the Gauḍīya Maṭha that is in many ways separate from ISKCON. It is still there, and you have factions of the Gauḍīya Maṭha that have emerged around various personalities. And you have other Gauḍīya movements as well.

But I think that on the level of the masses of people who basically integrate into a Kṛṣṇa *bhakti* religious system, you've got a lot of people who aren't organizationally included, but are spiritually included. In Vṛndāvana, for example, you have a lot of different temples that are run by various groups—you've got the Gauḍīya Vaiṣṇavas; you've got the Śrī-saṁpradāya; you've got Vallabhācāryas, who are huge; you've got the Haridāsīs; you've got so many. The average person who comes to Vṛndāvana on pilgrimage is simply seeking a relationship with Kṛṣṇa, an experience with God. They're going to look for that wherever they can find it. They will go to all the temples.

The model of religion, in all branches of Hinduism, especially, is a very individual experience. The model is the devoted individual seeking out a *guru*. And the relationship between the *guru* and the devotee is an individual relationship. People have different personalities and the *guru* has to be sensitive about how they can best be taken, throughout this life, and achieve *mokṣa* eventually, or, further, love for Kṛṣṇa. What is the best process for each individual disciple? That's up to the qualified *guru*. So, in a sense, the institutionalization of *bhakti* religion is something that a lot of people don't hook into. They may not even have a formal *guru*; they may not be integrated into any kind of organizational format; but yet the values, the ideas, the sentiments are still there and are still operating.

Back in the 1930s, there was a British man who came to Vṛndāvana looking for a *guru*. And, the story goes, he went to one of the *ghāṭs* and sat. The word got around that he was looking for a *guru*, and many people came and said, "consider me, consider me." Eventually he chose a *gosvāmī* from Rādhā-ramaṇa temple. His name was Bāl Mahārāja.

Even though the idea is there that anyone can become a devotee of

Kṛṣṇa, anyone can become a *brāhmaṇa,* if they study and learn the right things and behave in the right way, the Rādhā-ramaṇa temple fell into a crisis situation when the *gosvāmī* accepted this English man as a disciple. It caused the group of *gosvāmīs* there to seriously investigate whether or not there was any reason why this man from England should not be accepted.

There was a short period, even, of excommunication of this Bāl Mahārāja because he had allowed a foreigner access to the temple, and at the time, I am assuming, there were stricter codes of access even in the temple of Rādhā-ramaṇa. Anyway, this was resolved. The Englishman was accepted. It was concluded that there is no reason why an Englishman or any foreigner cannot have full access to the *gurus,* full access to the temple. The only stipulation, of course, is that one become a strict practitioner.

SR: What was this Englishman's name?

Dr. Brooks: His given name was Ronald Nixon; his initiated name was Śrī Kṛṣṇa Prema.

SR: Oh, the fellow who wrote books, a *Gītā* commentary, I think.

Dr. Brooks: Yes, he wrote several books.

SR: I have one of them.

Dr. Brooks: But what's amazing is that one rarely finds a mention about his stay in Vṛndāvana.

SR: I didn't know he was a Westerner. I always thought he was a native Indian.

Dr. Brooks: No. He was an English fighter pilot from World War I.

SR: [laughter] That's really interesting!

Dr. Brooks: Yes. He came to India as an English teacher at the University of Lucknow. And he refused to be British. He wanted to live like an Indian. And he lived with, I think, the vice-chancellor of Lucknow University, who was a very spiritual man. He was a Theosophist. And although he—I think his name was Mr. Chakravartī—didn't have the purity of a *guru*, his wife, evidently, was a very saintly person, and she did.

So Kṛṣṇa Prema took initiation from this woman, and then they left Lucknow and eventually wound up in Almora and established an *āśrama* there. It was called Uttar Vṛndāvana. She was a Vaiṣṇava, although this doesn't come out in Kṛṣṇa Prema's writings so much—still, he does write about Kṛṣṇa. You get the idea that he's more of a monist, at least that's what *I* felt after reading some of his work.

But, in any case, he was dissatisfied with the details that his *guru* gave him. Perhaps he, too, felt that her interpretation of truth was rather monistic, and he had a clear leaning to Vaiṣṇavism. So she took him to Vṛndāvana. This was in 1930. Evidently she had had a relationship all along with the temple of Rādhā-ramaṇa. But because he had already received initiation from her, and she had already given him a sacred thread, the process of his being re-initiated by Bāl Mahārāja was interesting.

They worked it as follows: Bāl Mahārāja re-initiated this woman into the Rādhā-ramaṇa *saṁpradāya*, which is essentially a Gauḍīya lineage, of course, and she in turn re-initiated him, Śrī Kṛṣṇa Prema. So it was an interesting course of events. He passed away in 1965 and by that time had quite a few Indian disciples.

SR: He was utlimately initiated by the woman, then, not Bāl Mahārāja.

Dr. Brooks: That's right. She was in fact his *dīkṣā guru*. Because of the specific situation—Kṛṣṇa Prema's *guru* was still living—she wanted him to study under this other man, this other *guru*, but to keep up the etiquette they did a series of initiations. According to Bāl Mahārāja's son, Jagdish Lal Goswami, that's the story. In simple terms: Kṛṣṇa Prema's *guru*—her name was Yashoda Mai—wanted him to take initiation directly from Bāl Mahārāja. He in effect said that this would not be proper, since Yashoda Mai was already his *dīkṣā guru*. Therefore, this indirect initiation ritual was done.

SR: That's very interesting.

Dr. Brooks: Yes. In any case, Bāl Mahārāja's son, who is an old man now (if he's still living), doesn't work as a priest in the temple but he runs a photography shop, at least when I met him. Now he took pictures of all of this, and he still has them. I even have some of the photos myself. Anyway, I asked him about the symbols that were given. Did Kṛṣṇa

Prema receive a sacred thread? What exactly transpired in that respect? He said, "The important thing—he already had a sacred thread, and that's not the important thing—the important thing was the *tulasī* beads." This certainly underlines our perception that Vaiṣṇava status is more important than *brāhmiṇical* status.

So, anyway, Bāl Mahārāja gave Kṛṣṇa Prema the three strands of *tulasī* beads. Now that in a sense predisposes, at least the temple of Rādhā-ramaṇa, which is one of the most important Gauḍīya Vaiṣṇava temples in Vṛndāvana, toward a relationship with foreigners. There have been other examples of people within ISKCON, for instance, coming to the temple of Rādhā-ramaṇa for advice of different sorts, especially in the refinement of ritual, because the Rādhā-ramaṇa *gosvāmīs* trace their lineage to Gopāla Bhaṭṭa.

SR: *Hari-bhakti-vilāsa.*

Dr. Brooks: And *Hari-bhakti-vilāsa.* Yes. The codification of ritual, so to speak. This is often associated with the Rādhā-ramaṇa temple. And that American disciple of Bon Mahārāja, whom we've mentioned, also sort of drifted from Bon Mahārāja's *aśrama* over to the Rādhā-ramaṇa temple. Today, he's closely linked with Shrivatsa Goswami. And he eventually started a relationship with another *sādhu* who a lot of Westerners meet when they come to Vṛndāvana—and this is Śrīpāda Bābā.

SR: Oh, from Vraja Academy?

Dr. Brooks: Correct. This American devotee pretty much considers Śrīpāda Bābā one of his *gurus* these days.

SR: I just missed meeting him the last time I was in India. Many people I know wanted to introduce me to him, but we just couldn't make the connection.

Dr. Brooks: Very interesting character. Very interesting, and very open to Westerners, especially if he perceives that they can help him along with his goals. He's a mysterious person. He just showed up one day in the classic manner. No one knows where he's from. He just emerged. A lot of people say he's quite old. But he certainly has some mystical powers that he's not afraid of using. . .

SR: Did you ever meet Nārāyaṇa Mahārāja of Mathurā?

Dr. Brooks: I did. I met him once.

SR: He's a great devotee-scholar, and I've sort of come to really admire him over the years. He is a great contemporary Gauḍīya Vaiṣṇava.

Dr. Brooks: I met several of Bhaktivedanta Swami's Godbrothers.

SR: You must have met O.B.L. Kapoor. Today, in Vṛndāvana, he is an important scholar of Gauḍīya tradition.

Dr. Brooks: Yes, I met him. But did we get off the track here?

SR: A little bit, but that's okay. I think in discussing contemporary personalities who are important in Vraja, like Śrīpāda Bābā and Dr. Kapoor, we're keeping right in line with our topic.

Dr. Brooks: Indeed. It's important to know the living scholars and practitioners in order to understand Gauḍīya Vaiṣṇavism in the modern world. They embody the tradition and all that it has become. You have ascetics, scholars, householders, traditionalists, innovators, mystics, and you have foreign devotees as well. If you look at the big picture, it seems that Gauḍīya Vaiṣṇavism is developing, growing, blossoming. It's here to stay, and it's spreading around the world at a rapid pace.

The Bengal of Śrī Caitanya Mahāprabhu

Richard Eaton

Richard M. Eaton has written numerous academic articles on Islam and Bengal, and is the author of several books, including Sufis of Bijapur, 1300-1700: Social Roles of Sufis in Medieval India *(Princeton, New Jersey: Princeton University Press, 1978) and* The Rise of Islam and the Bengal Frontier, 1200-1760 *(Berkeley: University of California Press, forthcoming). Dr. Eaton is currently Associate Professor of History at the University of Arizona.*

C. Life ✓

SR: Caitanya Mahāprabhu was born in 1486 in Māyāpura, or Navadvīpa (Nadīyā), in West Bengal, India. Let's discuss the religio-political climate at that time. Since you've done a bit of field work in the area, studying many of the Persian and Arabic sources, let's discuss the Muslim invasion of Bengal from the early thirteenth century to the time of Mahāprabhu.

Dr. Eaton: Well, it began in 1204. Now, there are many works claiming that when the Muslims first came to Bengal, they went to Navadvīpa. This is simply not true, at least not according to the latest scholarship on all this. You see, the word "Nadīyā" is first found in the *Ṭabaqāt-i Nāṣirī* by Minhaj al-Din. He was an historian who came to Bengal about forty years after the invasion. And he says that the Turks came to the royal city of Nadīyā, which was a name for Navadvīpa. This is where scholars get the idea that the Muslims first came to Navadvīpa.

But according to recent archaeological research, the Nadīyā mentioned here is not Navadvīpa but, rather, seems to be a city named "Naudah," which is in western Rajshahi. I've located that place, and apparently it was there in the twelfth century, whereas the present-day Nadīyā wasn't there back then. So this misconception is now being corrected.

SR: Okay. But let's talk a little about the Muslim invasion in general. What did they seek to accomplish by entering Bengal?

Dr. Eaton: Well, this was the continuation of a drive eastward by Turkish horsemen who were in the employ of Muhammad Ghuri, the sultan of Delhi. This was a slave dynasty—Turks—who came out of Central Asia. Now, the leaders didn't exert a good deal of restraint over their own men. So the people who were capable, feisty, and could mobilize horsemen, were able to accomplish a tremendous amount. Mind you, the big thing was that mounted cavalry enabled the Turks to sweep over northwestern Bengal with relative ease. From a military standpoint, mounted heavy cavalry were not known in that part of the delta.

SR: Did they peacefully co-exist with the Hindus at that time? Was there a lot of conversion going on?

Dr. Eaton: No conversion. No, not really. And there were certainly no conversion movements per se. In fact, there is no substantiated evidence of conversion in Bengal until the late sixteenth century. Of course, when the Turks first came they brought with them ideas of authority and government that were very different than those of the conquered Hindus. So, they did exist harmoniously to some degree, but what you had here in West Bengal was definitely a conquest dynasty of one culture ruling over a subject culture that was very different.

SR: Let's talk about that. I'd like to know about the dynasties that led up to Husain Shah—the time of Caitanya Mahāprabhu.

Dr. Eaton: Well, you have about three or four houses. Actually, until the end of the thirteenth century, you just have governors, sent down from Delhi, who were ruling over Bengal. Now, in 1342, you have your first independent dynasty. They're no longer merely governors—they're kings. And they're Bengali kings. The first dynasty—the Ilyas Shahi dynasty—was in power from 1342 to 1415, and that's a very important period in Bengali history. Why? Because the Bengali rulers were now isolated and cut off from patronage in North India—they were totally on their own, so to speak.

The implications of this were far-reaching: in Bengal's first centuries of Muslim rule, it was merely a province of Delhi, but after 1342, the Muslim kings become Bengali. So you have a whole new culture emerging—whether individuals were Hindu or Muslim, *they were Bengalis*, working together under the wider Muslim government.

SR: I see. So a sort of synthesis developed, a Muslim-Bengali culture.

Dr. Eaton: Definitely, and this becomes even more pronounced after 1410-1415, when there's a revolution, a civil war, basically, in Bengal. The last remnants of the old Hindu houses rebel and try to overthrow the Muslim government. They fail, of course. But they succeed in at least one sense: the chief Hindu power-broker, Rāja Gaṇeśa, manages to get his son on the throne.

There was a problem, though. In order to get the throne, Gaṇeśa's son had to convert to Islam. The son does this, under the name Jalal al-Din Muhammad, and becomes a devout Muslim. And he's an interesting character. Personally, I think he's one of the most fascinating rulers that Bengal ever knew. Although he clearly converted, he ruled as if he were a Hindu king.

SR: How so?

Dr. Eaton: For example, the architecture in his time started to change. The visual appearance of the Bengali mosque started to become heavily influenced by local vernacular Bengali conceptions of space and form. They completely depart from the old Delhi or Central Asian model. Moreover, Bengali became the official language—not Persian. This was noted by Chinese visitors at the time, which is, roughly, 1425. In other words, the Bengali language was patronized at the very highest level of government, and so, too, was Bengali literature. Later on, as you know, this patronage included the Vaiṣṇava literature. This, of course, prepared Bengal for Caitanya.

But the point I'm trying to make with Jalal al-Din is that the Muslim government was threatened with being shaken to the ground. This was a fascinating if also somewhat confusing period, for while it created a strange merger of Bengali, Hindu, and Muslim cultures, Jalal al-Din's conversion had diverse ramifications. In fact, he embraced Islam so tightly that he eventually pronounced himself the caliph of Islam!

SR: The political leader of the whole religion!

Dr. Eaton: Right. Now the Mongols had overthrown this institution in 1258—so there was no caliph in Islam. But here, in 1420 or so, Jalal al-Din starts proclaiming that he is the caliph. An absolutely incredible character. He also starts minting coins that have the Islamic confession of faith on them, which hadn't been done for hundreds of years. And he starts sending to Mecca and Medina lots of money for the construction of mosques. . .

SR: It sort of reminds one of Paul in the Christian tradition. He was a devout Jew, and then, when he converted to Christianity, he became a huge proselytizer on behalf of the Christian faith.

Dr. Eaton: Sure. You can make that comparison, but the difference is this: Jalal al-Din also minted coins that patronized the Hindu population, and he did the rest, as we mentioned earlier. So he patronized both. He was an affirmative action employer, so to speak.

SR: So this sense of egalitarianism is reflected in the numismatic evidence.

Dr. Eaton: It's all in the coinage, yes.

SR: Okay. So what happens after the 1420s, as we get closer to Mahāprabhu's appearance?

Dr. Eaton: Now, after the death of Jalal al-Din's son, there's a short restoration of the Ilyas Shahi dynasty, and in about 1433, you get about six or seven more kings. But in the exact year of Caitanya's birth, 1486, Abyssinian monarchs came to power in Bengal—Abyssinians are black slaves from Eastern Africa, and they had been imported as a kind of a slave caste by the last kings of the Ilyas Shahi dynasty.

SR: Ethiopians.

Dr. Eaton: That's what they were called later on. Anyway, one of the patterns of Islamic history is that slaves who are brought in to guard the royal house oftentimes wind up taking over the house themselves. It's an old pattern. And this is exactly what happens here, in the year of Caitanya's birth. So this opened it up quite a bit. Caitanya's birth coincided with this overthrow, which threw West Bengal into a period of social upheaval; class barriers became somewhat indistinct. Caitanya often preached to the lower classes, well, to all classes, but he really opened it up for all people. There's a parallel here. Something was brewing.

So, in any case, Bengal received a short series of Abyssinian or Ethiopian kings who ruled between 1486 and 1493—a brief period, actually. There's about three kings there, and they all assassinate each other—a bloody regime. Immediately after this, 'Ala al-Din Husain Shah emerges in 1493 and, of course, he's the fellow who was in power when Caitanya's movement really took off. Husain Shah, as you know, starts a new dynasty. Well, he was an Arab from Mecca who was brought in as a minister for the last of the Abyssinian monarchs, Shams al-Din Muzaffar Shah.

But, anyway, Husain Shah eventually took over, and he launched the last of these important dynasties. It was a brilliant dynasty. Remember: he was not an Abyssinian, but he was able to lead a *coup d'état*. History remembers him as the greatest sultan of Bengal. And he was in power until 1519. So this is in the height of Caitanya's missionary activity.

SR: Okay. So we should talk about this period. There was a brāhmaṇical revival at this time, which manifested in the writing of *Dharma-śāstra*, religious codes, and socio-religious codes. One of the important writers of this time was Raghunandana, who was Mahāprabhu's contemporary, I believe, and lived in Navadvīpa. Along with this, Bengal saw the development of Navya-nyāya, or the "new logic," which some people say originated in Mithilā. And the center for this, also, was Navadvīpa. So this was going on during the early days of the Gauḍīya Vaiṣṇava movement.

Dr. Eaton: Yes. These things were evolving alongside the political activity, as we were just discussing. You also had the more local religions as well. You had the composition of Maṅgala-kāvya literature, poems concerning the local goddesses, such as Mānasā and Caṇḍī. Remember, Bengal continues to be heavily *śākta*. This was the case in those days as well.

SR: Now what about Vaiṣṇava involvement in the court of Husain Shah?

Dr. Eaton: Right. We should mention that it was during this same Husain

Shahi dynasty that the Vaiṣṇavas came to be employed by the Muslim court. Actually, we should talk about the patronage of Vaiṣṇava literature which started much earlier. The work of Jayadeva Gosvāmī, Vidyāpati, and Caṇḍīdāsa influenced the Caitanya school quite a bit. And, you know, if you go back to Rukn al-Din Barbak Shah, who reigned from 1459 to 1474, before that brief Abyssinian rule, you get some royal patronage of Vaiṣṇava literature. Barbak Shah patronized the work of Mālādhara Vasu. So just a couple of decades before Caitanya's birth, you have this Muslim Sultan supporting an important Vaiṣṇava work. And there's no evidence that he supported any other literature, either. In other words, this might be seen as a significant event that paved the way for Caitanya.

SR: Yes. This is actually a very important development. Mālādhara Vasu, who was known among Mahāprabhu's followers as Guṇarāja Khān, wrote the *Śrī Kṛṣṇa-vijaya*, which was a Bengali summary of the *Bhāgavata Purāṇa*, in a sense. So this was critical. Actually, Guṇarāja Khān is mentioned in the *Caitanya-caritāmṛta*. He had fourteen sons, and the second one, Lakṣmīnātha, became a well-known follower of Śrī Caitanya Mahāprabhu. Gradually, he lost the name Lakṣmīnātha and they started calling him Śrī Satyarāja Khān. Who else was patronized by Barbak Shah?

Dr. Eaton: So far as I know, the rest of the literature was patronized by Husain Shah, or his son, Nasiruddin Nusrat Shah. They supported a work by Vipradāsa called *Manasā-vijaya*; Vījaya Gupta's *Manasā-maṅgala*; Yaśorāja Khān's *Kṛṣṇa-maṅgala*; and many other works as well, such as a Bengali adaptation of parts of the Mahābhārata, by Parameśvara. Actually, this work was financed by Parāgal Khān, a governor under Husain Shah. Also Caṇḍīdāsa's *Śrī Kṛṣṇa-kīrtana* was an important book that received patronage from the royal court in the fifteenth century. This was the immediate precursor for Caitanya, and it's a significant work because it develops the Rādhā-Kṛṣṇa theme.

SR: You know, it's interesting, because you get two conflicting views here. On the one hand, you get the idea that for the most part the Muslims and Hindus lived harmoniously—the Muslims even patronized the Vaiṣṇava literature. But on the other hand, there was obviously some friction, which continues to this day. And in the writings of Kedāranātha Dutta Bhaktivinoda Ṭhākura, I believe it's in his *Navadvīpa-dhāma Māhātmya*, you even have Husain Shah identified as an incarnation of Jarāsandha, Kṛṣṇa's mortal enemy.

Dr. Eaton: Is that right? You see, I'm more familiar with the other side of this issue. If you look at Joseph O'Connell's work, particularly the short piece called "Vaiṣṇava Perceptions of Muslims in Sixteenth-Century Bengal," which appeared in a volume called *Islamic Society and Culture* (Milton Israel and N.K. Wagle, eds., New Delhi: Manohar, 1983), you get an entirely different point of view. O'Connell cites *Caitanya-bhāgavata,* which was written early on, perhaps in the 1540s, and there you can find that the Bengali king was referred to as "*rāja,*" which is certainly a respectful title. And Jayānanda, in his *Caitanya-maṅgala,* refers to the Muslim ruler as "Īśvara" and "Indra," which would, of course, equate the king with a divinity. In any case, these fellows might have been patronized by the court, and that could account for their kind words toward the Muslim rulers. But I must admit that the side you are presenting does not appear to be historically accurate. There may have been some discomfort, naturally, but, for the most part, the Muslim kings allowed the Hindus to practice their religions.

I guess you can say that whatever the motives may have been, and whatever the exact relationship between Vaiṣṇavas and the Bengal court, the fact remains that it was Muslim kings who were most energetic in identifying themselves with Bengali cultural movements. This is confirmed not only in the patronage of vernacular Bengali, but also in the architecture of the time, where the mosques bear close resemblance to the Hindu temples in terms of their basic structure. We touched on this earlier. I think these things show a certain desire to assimilate and accommodate the existing traditions.

SR: And yet one hears of the destruction of the temples. Was there iconoclasm of any sort, the desecration of temple images perhaps?

Dr. Eaton: Not in Bengal. Well, the temple in Purī was attacked. That has to do with a very specific invasion that took place in Southwestern Bengal in the middle of the sixteenth century. You see, the popular myth is that the Turks just sort of went around on some kind of rampage and destroyed temples wherever they found them. The actual case, however, is that they were a bit more selective than that. Quite a bit more selective. They only desecrated those temples that were the principal temples of the ruling dynasty. In other words, there were strictly political motives behind their iconoclasm and it wasn't just wanton desecration. It was not a religious phenomenon, but a political one. This is important, although often misunderstood.

So this invasion of Purī was in 1568—led by Sultan Sulaiman Karrani. He took a force of Afghans and went down into Orissa, where the last independent Hindu house in all of North India was in power—the Gajapati. You can find a lot of this information in Hermann Kulke's book, *The Cult of Jagannātha and the Regional Tradition of Orissa* (Delhi: Manohar, 1978). Anyway, Sulaiman sacks the famous Jagannātha temple in Puri for political reasons. . .

SR: Is there definite evidence that it wasn't motivated by religious differences?

Dr. Eaton: Absolutely. You see, the Rāja of Orissa—Mukundadeva, at that time—had entered into a pact with Akbar. Now, Akbar was, theoretically, Sulaiman's overlord. But they were really rivals. Moreover, Mukundadeva also entered into a secret pact with Ibrahim Sur, one of Sulaiman's most likely opponents for the throne, telling him that he would help him along the way. In other words, Sulaiman went down to Orissa in response to what was clearly a threat to his own regime. So, to make a long story short, this was about keeping power, and not a Hindu/Muslim problem.

SR: But you also have the bloodshed in the Vraja region, with Aurangzeb and the Govindadeva temple—the deities had to be taken to Jaipur.

Dr. Eaton: That's North India, and much later. But not in Bengal. Aurangzeb is an abberation. He desecrated Vaiṣṇava temples, you are correct, and he even acted quite offensively to the Sikhs in the Punjab, who were hunted like animals. But this is a different story. . .

SR: Okay. Let's return to Bengal and the time of Mahāprabhu. You have his confrontation with Cand Kazi.

Dr. Eaton: Correct. But as I remember that story, the Kazi (Arabic: qāḍī) is simply trying to keep peace. He has nothing against Caitanya personally. But the local people start complaining to him, "Caitanya's men are making a nuisance of themselves with this loud *kīrtana*." Now it's interesting that Hindus are mentioned as the ones who complained to the Kazi, not the Muslims. You see, I think the true adversaries of the Caitanya movement at that time were the *brāhmaṇas* of the *śākta* cults—the devotees of Caṇḍī and Manasā. In their view, the whole *kīrtana* tradition not only caused public disturbances, but lacked scriptural authority. Secondly, they accused Caitanya of identifying himself with God. Thirdly, that he had usurped from brāhmaṇas their own monopoly over the use of *mantras.* And, finally, that his group was attracting followers from among the lower classes.

Now I find this last remark very significant because it hints at the social basis of the Caṇḍī and Manasā sects at the time. In other words, *śākta brāhmaṇas,* or *smārta brāhmaṇas,* seem to have viewed the low classes as their natural constituency, and they saw Caitanya as threatening to cut in on their potential clientele. So I think this, really, was at the basis of their complaints to the Kazi.

SR: I like that. Yes. That's an interesting point of view. The Kazi story is interesting. Apparently, at first, he took the complaints of his constituency very seriously, and he had his men disrupt the *kīrtana* party of Caitanya Mahāprabhu. He even had the *kholes* broken and he had the hand-cymbals thrown in the river. But then, at least as the story is recounted in *Caitanya-caritāmṛta,* the Kazi had a dream. Lord Nṛsiṁha, half man/half lion, appeared to him and said that if he again disturbed the *kīrtana,* he would be destroyed.

In addition, Śrī Caitanya himself came and confronted the Kazi, and they debated on the basis of Vedic texts, and also on the basis of the Qur'an, which I find very interesting. Anyway, to make a long story short, it appears that Cand Kazi came to accept Mahāprabhu's point of view, and he said that he forbade any of his descendants, in the future of his dynasty, to obstruct the *saṅkīrtana* movement in any way.

Dr. Eaton: Yes. That's the story. And, you know, by 1590, at least, the Gauḍīya Vaiṣṇavas were well established. City-dwellers. They were respectable workers in all fields of business, combining both ascetic and householder traditions around 1590, in the time of Mukundarāma, a *śākta* from Burdwan and author of the *Caṇḍī-maṅgala.* Anyway, Caitanya's movement wasn't really disturbed after that. It's true.

You know, when I did my research in Bangladesh, digging through old Persian records, I did discover references to Vaiṣṇava institutions being patronized by local *zamīndārs* in the mid-1700s and even earlier. I have evidence of grants given by Mughal governors in the extreme east, Sylhet district, to Hindus, or Vaiṣṇavas, specifically. And they refer to Vaiṣṇavas in the most respectful terms: they called them "masters of knowledge" and things of this nature. Muslim governors issued grants called "*Brah-*

mottar" and "*Bishottar*"—these are varieties of awards in terms of land and money. For example, in 1725, the Mughals in Sylhet gave away sixteen acres of jungle and a home to one Govindadāsa, who was a Vaiṣṇava. And they cite the reason: they're awarding him a grant because he's described as "a man who is worthy of honor." But the phrase they use, in pure Arabic, is *mustaḥaqq-i wājibu'r-ri'āyat*, which simply means, "worthy of honor." It's significant, though, because they gave them these Arabic praises that are associated with their own respected holy men, the Sufis.

The point I'm making is that the Muslims of Bengal were willing to patronize Vaiṣṇava holy men and there really didn't seem to be this overt prejudice that some historians try to reconstruct. Remember, a good deal of this Hindu vs. Muslim polemic is derived by twentieth-century scholars as they look back on the traditions of the sixteenth and seventeenth centuries. But you don't find this kind of hostility in the literature of the period. I think it's a later concoction, a fabrication by politically-motivated people.

Another point you might want to remember is that in the enforcement of law, or in the administration of justice, the Mughals in Bengal did not apply Islamic law to the Hindus. Rather, they rigorously upheld Hindu law with the full weight of their government. The famous case of two Muslims who killed a peacock in Midnapura comes to mind. This is a documented incident from 1640, about a century after Caitanya. The two men are hauled into court and they are tried for their crime. Now, this is a Muslim trying Muslims. And the judge orders that the hands of these prisoners be chopped off for violating Hindu law.

The rationale for this is that when Akbar had conquered Bengal he had agreed that he would rule it by Hindu law. Now, in the end, these two prisoners didn't have their hands cut off—there was some intervention by an Augustinian priest. But I think that the story is very telling. It shows us what the justice system looked like on the ground level. It was really good! And this might be another reason why you don't see this Hindu/Muslim polarity come out in early Vaiṣṇava literature: they were actually allowed to practice their religion.

SR: Well, I have one last reservation about this particular point of view: in the *Caitanya-caritāmṛta* and other, earlier biographies of Mahāprabhu, you do have Muslims referred to as *mleccha* and *yavana*, which are derogatory terms, implying that they are lowborn meat-eaters and such.

Dr. Eaton: Okay. But if you look at it carefully, it's not Muslims who are *mlecchas,* but Turks. The distinction is that Turks are identified as "foreigners." The Bengali word is "*turushka.*" So the Muslims of Bengal are not *turushkas.* They are Bengalis. And so to an informed person they're not *mlecchas* or *yavanas.*

SR: Unless, of course, these words come to be identified with certain practices, such as meat-eating. I mean, even if a Muslim is a Bengali—he's not a foreigner—if he eats a cow, I can see a believing Vaiṣṇava refer to him as a *mleccha.* Anyway, this is really a tangential issue. What I want to know is if the Caitanya movement is directly mentioned in Persian or Arabic sources.

Dr. Eaton: Not really. No. And it's interesting because Rūpa and Sanātana were highly posted in Husain Shah's court. They were known as Sākara Mālik and Dabīr Khāsa. And you'd imagine that there would be some reference to them. But, no, I've researched a good deal of the literature and I couldn't find anything. It's a hard one to figure out. Actually, it is a historiographical problem not just for Caitanya scholarship, but for Bengali history in general. For the entire period of 1204 to 1760 there is not a single regional history of Bengal. This means that in order to make any sort of historical sense out of religious movements such as that of Caitanya, or the far larger one of popular Islam, one must piece together scattered fragments taken from here and there. Bengal at this time is a jig-saw puzzle with ninety percent of the pieces missing. Nonetheless, both the Caitanya movement and Islam continue to exist, and remain powerful forces in the lives of their practitioners.

Śrī Caitanya's Pilgrimage to the South

David Kinsley

David R. Kinsley is author of The Divine Player: A Study of Kṛṣṇa Līlā *(Delhi: Motilal Banarsidass, 1979),* Hindu Goddesses *(Berkeley: University of California Press, 1986) and numerous other studies of the Hindu tradition. He is currently Assistant Professor in the Department of Religious Studies at McMaster University, Hamilton, Canada.*

Dr. Kinsley: After a brief visit to Purī, Caitanya started on a southern tour that was to last for about two years. We get our information from the *Caitanya-caritāmṛta*, but there are other traditional sources as well. Now, the southern tour is covered in chapters seven through nine of the *Madhya-līlā*, and parts of it are covered elsewhere. Do you have a date for this tour?

SR: Yes. It was not quite a year after he took *sannyāsa*. So, I guess, it was the following Spring, 1510 or 1511, after meeting Sārvabhauma Bhaṭṭācārya, in Puri, that he embarked on his 4,000-mile walking pilgrimage of the south.

Dr. Kinsely: Oh, so it was early in his renunciation. That's interesting. Only about a half-year after he took *sannyāsa*. That's very interesting. Anyway, you know, he goes south on the pretext of looking for his brother, Viśvarūpa. But he doesn't find his brother. Ever. It's interesting, though, that Caitanya seems to do things, in some cases, with his family in mind. When he first takes *sannyāsa,* for example, he wants to go to Vraja but instead he makes his headquarters in nearby Puri—because this is what his mother wants him to do. Then you have this huge trip to South India—all under the pretext of looking for his brother.

Now, to move on, when Caitanya leaves Purī to go south, one is reminded of Kṛṣṇa leaving Vraja. Just as the *gopīs* expressed distress at Kṛṣṇa's leaving, so you have Caitanya's associates feeling similar emotions. This all serves to tie Caitanya into the *avatāra* concept—to his followers, he is the embodiment of Kṛṣṇa. In fact, he is Rādhā and Kṛṣṇa combined.

But let's take this in a slightly different direction. Caitanya felt that the most appropriate way to take this tour of southern India is to do it alone. Here, it seems, he has in mind the ancient model of a lone, travelling ascetic, the *sannyāsī* who wanders from village to village. Of course, his disciples are concerned about this, too, because they know that he is prone to ecstatic fits of ecstasy. So they don't like the idea of him traveling alone—he might hurt himself. Apparently, they want him to take an attendant.

It's actually quite humorous how they convince him to take another devotee, for his own protection, on this tour of South India. "You'll need to take a change of clothes and to hold your waterpot," they say. "How will you do this if both your hands are used for chanting and counting *japa*?" In this way, they get him to take an assistant, a *brāhmaṇa* who, in the text of the *Caitanya-caritāmṛta,* is known as Kṛṣṇa dāsa. In fact, there's some trouble with Kṛṣṇa dāsa, and he leaves for some time. But this all gets resolved, I think, when they return to Purī. Now, I find it interesting that he takes a relatively unknown devotee, someone who does not figure prominently in the scheme of things, rather than a close associate. I'm not quite sure what to make of that. . .

SR: Well, remember, he really wanted to travel alone. It was a concession to take *anyone.* Besides, among his near and dear devotees, how would he decide? Whomever he chose—the others would feel slighted. Anyway, it's not uncommon that a *sannyāsī* will take a novice as a companion and in this way he can train the new fellow in the science of *bhakti.* It's interesting, though, that, at this point, Sārvabhauma tells Mahāprabhu to look for Rāmānanda Rāya. . .

Dr. Kinsley: Right. He warns him that there is this advanced devotee named Rāmānanda down south, and that Caitanya should search him out. But let's back up a bit. Caitanya starts his journey, and though he begins with several devotees who just can't leave his side, like Nityānanda, he does manage to drop them off in the first major town outside of Puri, a place called Ālālanātha. Then, of course, he carries on, and he meets a householder named Kūrma. He tells this man, who wants to leave hearth and home to travel with him, that it is totally unnecessary, that one can stay in the sanctity of one's home and still effectively practice the tenets of Vaiṣṇavism. So, this is instructive for those who are not inclined to early *sannyāsa.*

Then, as Caitanya goes a little further south, to Kūrma-sthāna, he meets a leper named Vāsudeva Vipra, and he cures him of leprosy. Now that's interesting, because you have Caitanya playing the role of a healer. And this episode reminded me very strongly of St. Francis of Assisi who, as you may know, developed a particular affection for lepers, especially after he renounced the world and became a holy man. He actually touched them and even lovingly hugged them in a way that is quite reminiscent of the way in which Caitanya is described as having hugged the leper Vāsudeva.

SR: After this episode, he meets Rāmānanda Rāya.

Dr. Kinsley: That's right. But these are a couple of the main stops before the Godāvarī River, where he in fact meets Rāmānanda. And I think we can jump to this meeting because this was clearly one of the most important attractions of his trip through the Deccan.

Now, I guess for our purposes we don't need to get into an elaborate discussion about the conversation that Caitanya had with Rāmānanda—which was actually quite profound and really does summarize the whole theology of Gauḍīya Vaiṣṇavism. I do want to mention, though, that this most articulate and revered devotee, Rāmānanda Rāya, was a *śūdra* and he was from the south. And yet he is so eloquent when it comes to Bengal Vaiṣṇavism. I think this is very significant, if also rather curious.

SR: Well, he was a minister for King Pratāparudra, so he had ties to Purī, or Orissa, which is close to Bengal. He was *stationed* in the south. Still, his close relation to Puri would have given him access to Gauḍīya doctrines. Also, you know, Friedhelm Hardy has proven that many northern ideas originated in the south. So there are several possible explanations. . .

Dr. Kinsley: Right. That's true. But I'm focusing in on something else. I think that Caitanya was looking for traditions that were preserved in the south. You see, the north had been dominated by Muslim rule for some time, even back then, so certain aspects of the earlier Vaiṣṇava tradition might have been lost. The Muslim presence was not as effective in the south, their penetration was not as strong.

There's some evidence that Caitanya went down there looking for something. This can be seen in the fact that he walks away with two important texts, texts that didn't survive in the north but were quite popular in the south. These two works, the *Brahma-saṁhitā* and the *Kṛṣṇa-karṇāmṛta*, later served to enhance the theological dogma of Caitanya's movement.

Also, he visits all of the ancient shrines in the south, impressive monuments that have few parallels in the north. So, I suspect that he had two feelings about the south—one was that the people there needed to hear the truth, Bengali-style, and his second feeling was that the southern devotees could give Bengal a link with older traditions. It's clear that he was looking for well-preserved traditions and texts that could elaborate the underpinnings of Kṛṣṇa *bhakti*. And he was quite successful. He was also successful in sharing the conclusions of Bengal Vaiṣṇavism, as can be seen in the documented portions of his trip, his proselytizing and conversion rate.

But before we stray too far from the Rāmānanda discussion, I want to mention this rather dramatic revelation that Rāmānanda gets: he sees Caitanya as Rādhā-Kṛṣṇa themselves, combined. This, of course, is an important Gauḍīya doctrine, one that was deeply ingrained by the time of Kṛṣṇadāsa Kavirāja. Now, you know, this revelation of the Rādhā-Kṛṣṇa form kind of reminded me of the *Bhagavad-gītā*, because you have a teacher-student sort of relationship, and then you have a revelation. They are very different revelations, to be sure, but I think the situation that precipitates the revelation to Arjuna and the revelation to Rāmānanda have certain things in common.

SR: This perception is interesting on a number of levels. First of all, according to Kavi Karṇapūra, Rāmānanda is a dual incarnation of Arjuna and Viśākhā, the *gopī*. And so it's interesting. When Mahāprabhu first asks Rāmānanda the question about the ultimate meaning of life, Rāmānanda replies with *Bhagavad-gītā* sort of wisdom—*varṇāśrama*, karma-yoga, jñāna-yoga, and so on. This was his Arjuna-nature coming out, and he was returning to Kṛṣṇa (albeit in the form of Mahāprabhu) what he had received on the battlefield of Kurukṣetra. But when Mahāprabhu asks him to go further, he begins to answer in the mood of a *gopī*—his

Viśākhā-nature—and that's when the highest truth comes out.

Dr. Kinsley: Oh. That's very interesting indeed. So there's kind of a reversal there, although not a complete one. Well, it's not that Arjuna is now teaching Kṛṣṇa. If you read the text of the *Caitanya-caritāmṛta,* you get the feeling that Caitanya in fact knows the answers to the questions that he asks. He's merely teasing them out of Rāmānanda, so to speak. So it's not a reversal, strictly speaking. It's more like the teacher testing the student.

But let's move on. I want to mention other things, generic things, that sort of make Caitanya's south Indian tour important or significant to me. As I reread this section of the *Caitanya-caritāmṛta,* I was struck, for example, by the way in which Caitanya sees Kṛṣṇa everywhere. He sees a pond or a river—it's the Yamunā. He sees a mountain—it's Govardhana. He sees a peacock—he faints or goes into elaborate fits of ecstasy. You see, what's happening here, from the Gauḍīya point of view, is that he's sacralizing the south. I think this is one of the things that Kṛṣṇadāsa Kavirāja is trying to get across.

And, to my mind, this relates to the concept of the *digvijaya,* or the person who conquers all quarters. Actually, *digvijaya* is a journey that a teacher undertakes to spread his or her distinct vision of truth. Now, there are many examples of this in the Hindu tradition, the most famous of which would be Śaṅkarācārya. In fact, there's a text called the *Śaṅkara Digvijaya,* and it details Śaṅkara's tour of India in which he sets up maṭhas, or monasteries, in the four regions of the subcontinent.

Now someone might ask, "How does one conquer the quarters?" Well, one conquers them by debating with opponents concerning traditional truths. And, of course, in the *Śaṅkara Digvijaya,* Śaṅkarācārya is depicted as defeating all comers with his *māyāvāda,* impersonal doctrine. Similarly, in the *Caitanya-caritāmṛta,* Caitanya, too, is depicted as defeating everyone who comes his way. There's actually a whole impressive range of opponents—the Buddhists, the Śaṅkara followers, Māyāvāda, Tattvavāda (a type of Madhva follower), Mīmāṁsā, Sāṁkhya, Patañjali, Manu, and also the Śrī Vaiṣṇavas, among others. Some he defeats outright. He explains to them that they are wrong—plain and simple. And he does this with logic, reason, and with the scriptures. Others, like the Śrī Vaiṣṇavas, he'll accept their doctrine, but he'll simply point out that the worship of Rādhā and Kṛṣṇa is higher than the worship of Viṣṇu. Maybe we can return to this later.

SR: I find it interesting that he takes many different positions when confronting these various. . .

Dr. Kinsley: Indeed. Yes, I was just going to point out that he defeats them by theological argument, in some cases, but, in others, he defeats them by his physical beauty, or. . .

SR: Well, some would argue that it is actually *spiritual* beauty.

Dr. Kinsley: Oh, I can see why the tradition would play that down, but in many cases it had to do with what people saw.

SR: Yes, I'm not arguing that point. But Gauḍīyas would question the term "physical beauty." Just because they could see it doesn't mean it was physical. Of course, it's clear from the texts that it was undoubtedly a *visual* beauty, but that doesn't necessarily mean *physical* beauty. Gauḍīyas would argue that what is being seen here is actually spiritual beauty.

Dr. Kinsley: That's very subtle, but, yes, I can understand that there might be that distinction here. In any case, Buddha is described like this in some texts, too. People are moved by his *visual* beauty. They saw him and they became convinced of his doctrine. So it was, in some cases, with Caitanya as well. Not that he wasn't a highly sophisticated *paṇḍita.* It's clear that as far as theological or philosophical argument and debate goes—he was a master! But sometimes he would get them with his beauty alone. He also converted people by the beauty of his devotion, and by miracles. So you basically have these four ways in which he defeats his opponents—debate, visual beauty, devotion, and miracles—at least that's how it's described by Kṛṣṇadāsa Kavirāja.

Now, these are not uncommon ways to be victorious in the *digvijaya* scheme of things. Often, the traveling *sādhus* would emerge victorious by displaying *siddhis,* or some form of yogic magic or mystical perfections. And, as I said, other times, they would engage in theological debate. Caitanya was clearly good at this, and he often defeated people in this way. Some of these debates are given a good deal of space in Kṛṣṇadāsa's work.

SR: Let's talk more about the shrines he visited while in the south.

Dr. Kinsley: Okay. Well, he clearly visited Vaiṣṇava shrines more than anything else. They represent the various incarnations—Kūrma, Narasiṁha, and several others are mentioned. But he doesn't visit *just* Vaiṣṇava shrines, and, of course, this is very interesting. He visits Śaivite and Devī shrines as well. And one wonders how he thought about these things, because the text doesn't tell us how he felt about these visits. I'm quite interested in the Goddess, as you know, and I would love to hear Caitanya's insights on the subject. But, alas, it was not given to us.

You know, in Bengal—at least when I was there in 1968, in Calcutta—I sensed a rather strong tension between the Gauḍīya Vaiṣṇavas and the Śāktas, and I found that the tension goes back a long way. Maybe you know something about this. Anyway, I found it interesting that Caitanya visited those shrines.

SR: Well, Gauḍīyas consider their tradition, in a sense, to be the ultimate in Śākta worship, because they are worshiping the *pūrṇa-śakti,* Śrī Rādhā. But Śākta worship as we know it, to the Goddess, was always frowned upon by Gauḍīyas. Yes. They see it like this: it's trying to take Sītā away from Rāma. So you become a sort of Rāvaṇa. [laughter] If you take the Goddess away from God, you are left with *māyā.* The separated Goddess is a manifestation of the illusory energy. You can't separate Rādhā and Kṛṣṇa. Otherwise you are left with Durgā. And this is Goddess worship. So that is one reason why the Gauḍīyas do not accept it.

Dr. Kinsley: Extremely interesting. Yes. But, it's interesting, too, you know, that Caitanya then goes to Śiva-kāñcī, or Kāñcīpuram, and the *Caitanya-caritāmṛta* says that he converted all of the Śaivites into Vaiṣṇavas. [laughter] Now that's quite a feat. And there's another episode wherein he apparently meets Śiva and Pārvatī themselves. But, okay, after that he goes to Śrī Raṅgam, the largest Viṣṇu temple, I believe, in all of India. Of course, that's not surprising, since he is quite fond of Viṣṇu, seeing him as a manifestation of Kṛṣṇa.

Now this Śrī Raṅgam temple complex is an impressive structure, even today, and I assume it was equally impressive, if not more so, back in the sixteenth century. So he stays there with a brāhmaṇa, Vyeṅkata Bhaṭṭa, for the four months of the *cāturmāsya.* In other words he spends quite a bit of time there. Unfortunately we are not told to what extent he takes part in the temple rituals, the worship of Raṅganātha, the image in the temple.

SR: Well, it says that he did go there and engage in worship. But, you know, there's also a tradition that he so missed the Jagannātha deities of Puri that he carved replicas with his own hands.

Dr. Kinsley: Is that right?

SR: Yes. And those deities are still there near the site of Vyeṅkata Bhaṭṭa's house—very odd-looking Jagannātha deities. The place is now called the "Shree Jagannath Mutt." These were Mahāprabhu's own deities of Jagannātha, Bāladeva, and Subhadrā.

His main purpose in Śrī Raṅgam, though, was his conversation with Vyeṅkata. This elucidated the difference between Viṣṇu and Kṛṣṇa, showing Kṛṣṇa's *mādhurya,* or sweet quality, as superior, in a sense, to Viṣṇu's *aiśvarya,* or majestic quality. This was important because Prabodhānanda Sarasvatī was there, and so he later became a follower, and so was the young Gopāla Bhaṭṭa, who later became one of Mahāprabhu's most important followers, one of the Six Goswāmīs of Vṛndāvana.

Dr. Kinsley: Right. That's true. And I think it's brilliant that Caitanya debates with Vyeṅkata on the point of the consort. After all, he was talking with *Śrī* Vaiṣṇavas—and Śrī refers to Lakṣmī—so it was correct to approach them with their central figure. He showed that even Lakṣmī wanted to enter the *rāsa-maṇḍala* but could not. So we see, in a sense, that Śrī is an inferior image to Rādhā, who, in many ways, is the central figure of the *rāsa-līlā.*

Anyway, to summarize, Caitanya tackled the subject from a very touchy position—from the heart. And, as Kṛṣṇadāsa Kavirāja tells it, he was quite successful. But what I find interesting is the phenomenon you alluded to earlier. I find the whole concept of developing an attraction for the local images, or the local manifestations of the deity, to be quite fascinating. I wanted to mention this earlier, going back to the beginning—the last place Caitanya visits before he leaves Purī for his pilgrimage to the south is the Jagannātha temple. He goes there as if to say "goodbye," and he asks Jagannātha permission to go on his lengthy trip. And when he returns after his two-year tour of the south—he goes right to the feet of this same Jagannātha deity and offers his prayers. So it really shows Caitanya's love and devotion for this particular form of Kṛṣṇa.

This whole episode reminded me of Anne Gold's book about Rājasthānī pilgrims, I believe it was called *Fruitful Journeys.* Oh, it's a beautiful book. Now she talks about village people, mostly women, who go to the shrine of the village goddess in order to get permission to go on pilgrimage, and they say "goodbye" in a disarmingly personal way—it's always the last place they stop before going on a long journey. And, then, when they return, the first place they go is to the shrine of the same goddess, and they offer prayers and enjoy knowing that the goddess is aware of their return. So, for me, this shows that the center of power and love is one's worshipable deity, and this is shown by Caitanya in the same way.

Of course, this goes on to the present day. Wandering *sannyāsīs* and, oh, all kinds of people go on pilgrimage to holy places—*tīrtha-yātrā*—and they carry their *iṣṭa-devatā*, the worshipable deity, in their heart. And it goes back a long way, too. In the Mahābhārata, in fact, we can see this whole tradition of making pilgrimage as an important religious phenomenon. You know, there's that huge section, when the Pāṇḍavas are exiled for thirteen years. Well, how do they spend those years? Largely on *tīrtha-yātrā*. They go right around the subcontinent visiting the sacred shrines.

And, to bring it into present context, this is particularly true for *sannyāsīs*, who renounce the world and wander about. But they don't wander aimlessly, at least not generally. They go to the sacred shrines. So, Caitanya clearly saw himself in this light. He had recently taken *sannyāsa*, and so along with the external pretext of searching for his brother, he decides to play the part of the wandering mendicant. And he visits all of the places we've mentioned and many, many more. While doing this, he accomplishes a great deal for his mission. All the time singing and dancing. That should be mentioned—he seems to sing and dance his way through South India. But he accomplishes a great deal. And I think this goes along with my initial point: he was looking for things that he couldn't find in the north.

So what does he find in the south? Well, he finds these important texts, *Brahma-saṁhitā* and *Kṛṣṇa-karṇāmṛta*; he finds serious followers, not least among them this wonderful Rāmānanda Rāya; he sees sacred shrines and rare deities, which give inspiration and encouragement; he finds this future theologian, Gopāla Bhaṭṭa; he converts Buddhists and many others to Vaiṣṇavism. It's a very successful trip, and one that was important for the future of his movement.

Śrī Caitanya's Tour of Vraja

Alan Entwistle

Alan W. Entwistle has worked with the International Association of the Vrindaban Research Institute and has contributed to numerous academic journals. He is the author of* Braj: Centre of Krishna Pilgrimage *(Groningen: Egbert Forsten, 1987) and is currently Associate Professor of Asian Languages and Literature, University of Washington, in Seattle.

SR: When Mahāprabhu was a very young householder, he sent Lokanātha and Bhūgarbha Gosvāmī to Vṛndāvana, to unearth the holy places that had become obscured due to the passage of time and Muslim influence. Some years later, he sent Rūpa-Sanātana there for the same purpose. So we see a persistent theme—from early on Mahāprabhu was interested in Vraja. My question is this: Why? What was so important about that region?

Dr. Entwistle: Well, obviously, the first thing that comes to mind is the connection with the adventures of Kṛṣṇa. Vraja would give devotees inspiration, especially for meditating on the infancy of Kṛṣṇa, his adventures as a cowherd boy, and his affairs or romantic adventures with the *gopīs* and Rādhā. All of these took place in the pastoral setting of Vraja, and Vṛndāvana, more specifically. It was outside the city of Mathurā—an idyllic, bucolic atmosphere.

You see, in Caitanya's time, it was felt to be more or less lost, as you mentioned, vaguely known, and so it needed to be reclaimed. Caitanya felt that this was very important for the tradition—to see the actual places of Kṛṣṇa's *līlā* in this world. And not just any part of his *līlā*, but his most intimate *līlā*, in the ideal setting of Vraja.

SR: Now, in 1515, or thereabouts, Mahāprabhu and an attendant named Balabhadra Bhaṭṭācārya reached Vṛndāvana through the Jhārakhaṅda Forest. . .

Dr. Entwistle: Right. He was coming from Puri, and he went through Jhārakhaṅda. That refers to the area south of Bihar and east of Orissa. It was largely a tribal area, with dense forests.

SR: And in those forests, the tradition tells us, he inspired the animals to chant and dance.

Dr. Entwistle: [laughter] That's right. That was on the way to Vraja. He went through wild country as he was making his way to Mathurā, which, of course, was his first stop before exploring Vraja proper. When he actually arrived in Mathurā, he bathed at Viśrāma-ghāṭa.

SR: It's now bordered by Dori Bazaar Road.

Dr. Entwistle: I do not know this name. But at the time of Caitanya, Viśrāma-ghāṭa—and this is documented in early *māhātmya* texts—was the central bathing place in the river, and it was very important for the Vaiṣṇavas of the area. It was important long before Caitanya's time. You see, people thought that Viśrāma-ghāṭa was so called because it was the place where Kṛṣṇa took rest ("*viśrāma*") after killing Kaṁsa.

SR: Oh. That's interesting. Then, from Viśrāma-ghāṭa, Mahāprabhu went to Janmabhūmi, Kṛṣṇa's birthplace.

Dr. Entwistle: That's right. Well, Kṛṣṇa's birthplace is in an area that is some distance from the center of modern Mathurā. There are lots of earthworks and mounds there, which are probably the remains of what we can call a "prehistoric Mathurā," going back well over two thousand years. There is also evidence to suggest that the course of the Yamunā has moved away from that area as well. So Kṛṣṇa's birthplace is in this area, just northwest of modern Mathurā, although as Mathurā expands it's beginning to incorporate this section as well. And there are a lot of important sites in the vicinity, too. The Śiva temple—Bhūteśvara—is there, as are remains of Buddhist shrines, monuments, *stūpa*, etc. It was once largely a Buddhist area.

In any case, at one point, a temple was constructed—perhaps in the early medieval period—that was recognized as the birthplace of Kṛṣṇa, and the deity there was given the name "Keśava." In those days images of Viṣṇu's incarnations were normally four-armed, just like Viṣṇu himself, and so an icon of "Keśava" could have been taken as a representation of Kṛṣṇa as well as Viṣṇu.

Then came the invasions in the time of the Delhi Sultanate. So there was some disruption in the worship of the deity. This leads us into the sixteenth century—so it's difficult to say exactly what Caitanya would have found there, exactly what shape it was in. He probably saw some kind of temple—exactly what state it was in, we cannot say. But it *is* true that the Mahārāja of Orchha rebuilt the temple early in the following century, and there are positively splendid descriptions of that particular structure. Nonetheless, it was demolished during the reign of Aurangzeb at the end of the seventeenth century. This was after the time of Caitanya, of course, and that's when a mosque was built—over the site that had been known as Kṛṣṇa's birthplace. That mosque still stands, although a new temple commemorating the birthplace of Kṛṣṇa has been built right next to it.

I was wondering: what are the other places that Caitanya visited in that particular area? I'm sure he must have gone to all of the popular pilgrimage sites. . .

SR: That's right. It's stated that he met a humble *brāhmaṇa* in Mathurā who showed him the various holy places. They went to Svayambhū, Dīrgha-Viṣṇu, Bhūteśvara, Mahāvidyādevī, and Gokarṇa.

Dr. Entwistle: Oh. Gokarṇa is a very interesting site. It's a Śiva temple, and is called *gokarṇa* because the deity there is a seated figure with what look like cows-ears on either side of its head. Scholars who have examined it think that it was a royal portrait statue carved almost two thousand years ago.

SR: As the champion of Kṛṣṇa worship, it's interesting that he went to so many Śiva temples.

Dr. Entwistle: It is. But there was a preponderance of them in those days, and I think, too, that Caitanya simply followed the existing pilgrimage circuit, without bias. When you go on pilgrimage, you see what there is to see. Perhaps you prefer to see certain things—Rādhā-kuṇḍa, etc.—but the other places have their relative value, too.

SR: Yes. Now, after Mathurā, Mahāprabhu travelled the forests of Vṛndāvana. Perhaps you could briefly talk about those forests.

Dr. Entwistle: It's difficult to say, again, in his time, exactly what was left, or what was there for him to see. Remember, the Gosvāmīs had hardly started their work, and much was done in the following generation. So it's difficult to tell. It's safe to say, however, that he was taken to the place that we now call Vṛndāvana. There is evidence that suggests that the area was accepted as Vṛndāvana several centuries prior to Caitanya. A Sanskrit poet from the early twelfth century named Bilhaṇa mentions this area—Mathurā and then the groves where Kṛṣṇa and Rādhā engaged in their love-play. So this might well have been the place to which Caitanya was brought.

Now, although there were not yet any widely recognized Kṛṣṇa temples, there was a sort of rural, forest expanse near the river, and this was recognized as the Vṛndāvana forest area. Vṛndāvana was one of the twelve forests of Vraja that are first mentioned together in texts of the twelfth or thirteenth century.

SR: Okay. So he went through Vṛndāvana, and the hagiographic material says that the animals recognized him, since he was actually Kṛṣṇa. Then, after that, he went to Āriṭagrāma, now called Aring.

Dr. Entwistle: Right. This was when he rediscovered Rādhā-kuṇḍa and Śyāma-kuṇḍa, which are not far from a small town, on the way to Govardhana, called Aring, Āriṭagrāma, or Ariṣṭagrāma, a puzzling name. Now, in the earlier texts, this is all sometimes referred to as the place of Ariṣṭa. But, in those days, who knows what names were applied to what places, whether Aring and Ariṣṭagrāma are separate or one and the same?

It is interesting that a Rādhā-kuṇḍa was known before the time of Caitanya. But he is credited with discovering it, or rediscovering it, if you will. There's a tradition, also, to the effect that there were two lakes lying neglected. And when Caitanya came to that place, his body went through the ecstatic symptoms, and he declared without any doubt that this was indeed the area of Rādhā-kuṇḍa, and that the lakes were those of Rādhā and Kṛṣṇa.

SR: I see. And then, from here, Mahāprabhu went to Sumana Lake, which is now called Kusuma Sarovara.

Dr. Entwistle: Right. Now that's a beautiful area. It's a pond, or a lake, which, I presume was, originally, a natural pond. But it's been provided with masonry *ghāṭas,* added much later, in the early nineteenth century, perhaps, by the royal family of Bharatpur. So Caitanya would have merely found a *kacca,* or a raw, barely paved pond.

Anyway, this pond was famous for a long time. There are stories involving this lake and the great devotee Uddhava. Anyway, it's a sacred spot for Caitanyaite Vaiṣṇavas, and for other local Vaiṣṇavas as well. Nearby is a small pond called Nārada-kuṇḍa, where Vṛnda, the Goddess of Vṛndāvana, told the sage Nārada to bathe, and when he did he was transformed into Nāradī, a female Nārada. This enabled him to join the *gopīs* in their dance with Kṛṣṇa. Now, where did Caitanya go after he left Kusuma Sarovara?

SR: After Kusuma Sarovara, Mahāprabhu went to Govardhana Hill.

Dr. Entwistle: Ah, there is an interesting story about how the hill came to be situated in the Vraja region. The story can be found in the *Garga-saṁhitā.* Initially, Govardhana manifested as a mountain range on the western island of Śālmalī. When the sage Pulastya saw it, he decided to convey it to Kāśī, or Benares, by his mystic potency. Govardhana was reluctant to go, however, and argued that he was too big to be transported. Anyway, Govardhana relented in due course, but only managed to be taken as far as Vraja. Once he was in the Vraja region, he remembered that Kṛṣṇa would soon be incarnate there, and that he—Govardhana, the hill—was destined to play a prominent role in his *līlā.*

Seeing that Govardhana would not budge an inch, the sage Pulastya became thoroughly vexed, and he cursed Govardhana to decrease in size by an amount equivalent to the size of a sesamum seed every day. Now, this is an ancient story. So, by the time of Caitanya, the hill would have decreased in size quite a bit. And, today, you can see that the hill is not very high at all. By the way, Nārāyaṇa Bhaṭṭa, who was an important *ācārya* and chronicler of Vraja tradition, offers an alternative story for how Govardhana came to Vraja. He says that Hanumān had brought the hill from the Himālayas. In any case, Govardhana came to be accepted as one of the holiest places in the Gauḍīya tradition, next to Rādhā-kuṇḍa. Naturally, this is because of Kṛṣṇa's *līlā* of lifting the hill to protect his devotees. Where to from Govardhana?

SR: After Govardhana, Mahāprabhu went to Brahma-kuṇḍa and Mānasī-gaṅgā. Anything about those places?

Dr. Entwistle: Brahma-kuṇḍa exists as a recognized tank, and it is named in older texts, in the older Sanskrit tradition. It's right near the Mānasī-gaṅgā, a name interpreted by some to mean "the lake created by Kṛṣṇa's mind." Mānasī-gaṅgā is the most important bathing place at Govardhana. After this, though, I believe Caitanya went to the village of Gāṅṭhuli to see the deity referred to as "Gopāla." Now this is presumably the Nāthjī deity associated with Mādhavendra Purī, who, according to Gauḍīya tradition, was the spiritual master of Caitanya's spiritual master. There was a temple atop Govardhana Hill, but Caitanya wouldn't set foot on such a sacred hill. Sources say that at the time, Muslim soldiers were causing trouble, and so the deity was in refuge, in the woods, perhaps. So, in any case, Caitanya didn't have to walk on the hill to see the image of Gopāla. He just went into the woods and was directed to the secret hiding place.

Now, there is quite a controversy—between the Gauḍīyas and the Vallabhas—about that deity. The first person who is associated with the deity is Mādhavendra Purī. Now, I don't think you can call him a Gauḍīya, but he was followed in his worship of the deity by people who were Gauḍīyas. Soon after, though, you get Vallabha and his son, Viṭṭhalnātha, and the temple, then, was really developed by the Vallabhas. So this is the story of the Śrī Nāthjī deity—it's actually very complicated—and the dispute continues to this day.

SR: Yes. There are a lot of problems associated with it. But, okay, we don't want to get into that too much. So let's move on. After seeing this Nāthjī deity, Mahāprabhu went to Nandagrāma and bathed in the rivers there, beginning with Pāvana-sarovara. . .

Dr. Entwistle: Now don't you find that interesting? Why does he seem to pass over Varṣānā, the place of Rādhā? Certainly it's one of the more important places for Gauḍīyas, but, perhaps, at the time Kavirāja Gosvāmī was writing, it wasn't developed enough to mention. In fact, in Caitanya's time, it was barely recognized, if at all. But, all right, you have Caitanya's visit to Nandagrāma, and there he found, in a cave, the deities of Yaśodā, Nanda Mahārāja, and the infant Kṛṣṇa. These are believed to be the deities that can still be seen in the main temple, called Nandabhavana, and they've added a Balarāma deity. So you have images of Kṛṣṇa along with his foster parents and his elder brother.

SR: Interesting. Then Mahāprabhu went to Khadiravana and Śeṣaśāyī.

Dr. Entwistle: It's a shrub, acacia, forest, one of the twelve traditional forests of Vraja. That's Khadiravana. Why that one is singled out, I do not know. Perhaps it's simply because it was on the way to his next stop: the Śeṣaśāyī temple. This is a Viṣṇu temple, where the deity depicts Viṣṇu lying on Śeṣa—that's how it gets that name. This is an important image.

SR: Next he went to Khelanavana.

Dr. Entwistle: That's the forest Kṛṣṇa and Balarāma used to play in together. *Khelana* means "playing." So he went to that forest. It's really a part of Sergarh, just outside of Sergarh, the town to the south of Śeṣaśāyī. The modern name Sergarh comes from Ser Shah, who came to power a few decades after Caitanya's visit.

SR: After this, Mahāprabhu went to Mahāvana, or. . .

Dr. Entwistle: Gokula. Yes. So he skips a few of the forests on the pilgrimage route, some of the places in between. . .or Kavirāja Gosvāmī fails to mention them.

SR: He may have gone. I'm just mentioning the places I can remember from the text. . . .But while in Gokula, he swooned upon seeing the Yamalārjuna trees. That I remember.

Dr. Entwistle: Right. Again, those trees are mentioned in very early texts, and devotees may exhibit these ecstatic symptoms at such holy places, just as you're saying about Caitanya. His swooning, though, was not some sedate or mild swooning—it was intense. At least that's how the texts describe it.

SR: Especially in Vṛndāvana. Kavirāja Gosvāmī says that Mahāprabhu was absorbed in ecstatic love in Purī. But it increased one hundred times when he set out on the road to Vṛndāvana. It increased one thousand times more when he entered Mathurā and one hundred thousand times again when he actually wandered the forests of Vraja.

One thing I want to point out is this: Vraja was so important to Mahāprabhu, and yet once he finally arrived there, after so many detours and problems getting there, he didn't stay very long. Now that interests me.

Dr. Entwistle: Yes. Who can say? Some suggest that he started to attract so much attention that, to maintain mental stability or public order, he went back to Purī. Besides, he had a fledgling movement there, one that, perhaps, required his personal presence. So maybe this was a reason. Who really knows?

You know, Kṛṣṇadāsa Kavirāja Gosvāmī was writing quite a long time after the events had actually taken place. So it is likely that he combined oral traditions with what he knew about the Vraja pilgrimage circuit, as it was developing in those days. So he was naturally giving a general or approximate account. I don't think you can hold him on every word. After all, he's trying to convey the "essence," or the "nectar," of the acts of Caitanya. That's literally what the title of his book, *Caitanya-caritāmṛta,* actually means.

SR: How did Vraja develop after the time of Mahāprabhu, say, in the time of the Gosvāmīs or even a little later, when Kavirāja Gosvāmī was an old man, or when Śrīnivāsa, Narottama, and Śyāmānanda made their way to Vṛndāvana?

Dr. Entwistle: It developed very rapidly, mainly on two fronts. The Vallabha *saṁpradāya* and the Gauḍīya *saṁpradāya* did much to develop the area. There were others as well, but these were, and are, the two main groups. As far as the Gauḍīya sect is concerned, we find them concentrated, at first, in the Govardhana area, and then at Rādhā-kuṇḍa. And of course, they developed Vṛndāvana, the main temples, like Govindadeva, Rādhā-Dāmodara, Rādhā-Gopīnātha, Madana-Mohana, and things of this nature.

Actually, Sanātana Gosvāmī's Madana-mohana temple holds the most interest for me. It's one of the earliest of the Gauḍīya temples there, if not *the* earliest. And it's actually proven to be at a very early and important site called Dvādaśāditya-tilā, where the sun was worshiped—there was probably a sun temple there. So Sanātana placed his temple on that hill. I can't say if there were any visible remains of the original sun temple when Sanātana Gosvāmī arrived.

The Vallabhites developed Gokula, Mathurā, and the controversial temple and adjoining places at Govardhana. So it was, and continues to be, to some extent, territorial. Now, other places in Vraja, like Kāman, Varṣānā, Nandagrāma. . .

SR: Who developed Varṣānā? That's a very important place.

Dr. Entwistle: That's largely the work of Nārāyaṇa Bhaṭṭa. He's a very important if often understated figure who came up from the south of India and did much to develop the Vraja pilgrimage circuit, especially from the Gauḍīya point of view. He settled at Rādhā-kuṇḍa, perhaps twenty or thirty years after Caitanya, say, in the time of Jīva Gosvāmī, and was tremendously inspired to discover Vraja. He proceeded to conduct extensive research, compiling a massive work called *Vraja-bhakti-vilāsa.* This is the most comprehensive book on Vraja to date. So Nārāyaṇa Bhaṭṭa should not be neglected when talking about the development of that area. He eventually moved to Uñchogaon, which is right next to Varṣānā, and so he should perhaps be given credit for its discovery and development. In fact, there are *gosvāmīs* who are considered to be descended from him, and they are the present-day custodians of the main temple at Varṣānā.

SR: What about Raval?

Dr. Entwistle: Right. Well, there's a dual tradition there. Some say that it was Rādhā's place of birth; others say that Varṣānā was her place of birth. It's pretty much agreed upon today, though, that she was born in her mother's home at Raval and was raised in Varṣānā, at King Vṛṣabhānu's palace.

SR: The palace. Now that brings to mind royal patronage. Maybe we can talk about that. Some names come to mind: Akbar, Man Singh. . .

Dr. Entwistle: Well, of course, Akbar was nobody's disciple, but he was willing to support all kinds of religious causes. Now, Man Singh seems to have favored the Gauḍīya sect, it's true, and, certainly, his later descendants were supportive of the Gauḍīya *saṁpradāya.* They were the ones who showed hospitality, shall we say, to the deity Govindadeva, when the image was transferred to Jaipura. So, yes, I would say that the royal house of Jaipur was particularly fond of the Gauḍīya sect and patronized it. Although the patronage wasn't exclusive.

You see, in sixteenth-century India, particularly in Vṛndāvana, I think, it wasn't so important which *saṁpradāya* one belonged to—it was more a question of the intensity of one's devotion. That's all. Well, there was, certainly, *some* sectarian consciousness. That's clear. But I think it was a little different than today. They weren't quite so provincial. But then, of course, the bickering started—*who* belongs to *which* sect. This kind of thing. But I think it really arose some time later, the rivalry between the sects. It's unfortunate.

They all, of course, had something to offer. The various sects of Vraja were merely emphasizing different aspects of the same cult, so to speak. Some focused on Kṛṣṇa's childhood sports; some on a parental relationship; some on the *mādhurya-rasa*. But they all shared the common bond of devotion to Kṛṣṇa. This is the real value of the religious traditions that arose in Vraja, and particularly in Vṛndāvana. So Caitanya was a forerunner, in a way, because it was his followers who developed the region, and much of what you see in Vṛndāvana today is a result of their efforts.

The Glories of Rādhā-kuṇḍa

Mohan K. Gautam

Mohan K. Gautam is the distinguished Director of the International Overseas South Asian Research Centre. He also serves as Chairman of the International Union of Anthropological and Ethnological Sciences. A prolific and respected scholar for many years, Dr. Gautam is a frequent contributor to religious and Indological journals throughout the world and is Director and Editor-in-Chief of the International Forum on Hindu Studies. *He is presently teaching at the University of Leiden in the Netherlands.*

SR: Dr. Gautam—your reputation precedes you. I have heard a good deal about your work in the area of Indological study. It is quite a contribution. In fact, I have just returned from a trip to Vṛndāvana—I heard that you were just there as well. Can you tell me a little about the research you are conducting in the Vraja region?

Dr. Gautam: Yes. In the 1960s, I discovered that although Western scholars were familiar with the stories of Rādhā and Kṛṣṇa, as revealed in the Vedic and later Vaiṣṇava literature, they actually knew very little about Vṛndāvana, or the Vraja area in general. This is significant, because unless one knows Vraja, the pastimes do not really come to life. If one really wants to understand Kṛṣṇa and the profound Vaiṣṇava philosophy that surrounds his activities, one will need to understand Vraja.

This begins by coming to terms with an important point: Kṛṣṇa's activities can be divided into two major categories. First, you have his youth, with the *gopīs,* and then you have his later activities, when he went to Mathurā and Dvārakā and so on. Now, that first period, which takes Kṛṣṇa up to the age of eight years, is very significant. And scholars have sorely misunderstood this period in Kṛṣṇa's manifest *līlā.*

SR: For example. . .

Dr. Gautam: For example, his love play with the *gopīs.* They try to attribute some mundane characteristic to these spiritual interactions. No. If you take the story as it is presented in the original texts, Kṛṣṇa is eight years old—where is the question of prurient interest? Aside from the theological perspective, which is quite clear, you cannot accept half the story. You cannot be consciously selective. If you accept that he had loving interactions with the *gopīs,* because it says so in the scriptures, then you also have to accept that he was only eight years old. Barring Freud's rather questionable suppositions, there are no grounds to look at this in a sexual way.

But we can move on from here. Afterwards, there is the historical development: Kṛṣṇa came back to his birthplace of Mathurā; he killed Kaṁsa; he handed over the entire empire to Ugrasena, his grandfather; he left for the kingdom of Dvārakā; and then you get the *Mahābhārata* story—a second part to Kṛṣṇa's activities—quite removed from Vraja. Okay. So what I found while doing my research in the '60s was that the *Mahābhārata* aspect of Śrī Kṛṣṇa was fairly well known in much of Europe and even in America, especially after the founding of the Asiatic Society of Bengal. But the early part of Kṛṣṇa's *līlā* was largely unknown. Rādhā was almost entirely unknown. An enigma. And since I originally come from the Vraja region, I initially wanted to set this straight. After all, the Vaiṣṇavas are especially fond of Kṛṣṇa's early *līlā,* especially the Gauḍīyas. And, then, the early *līlā* with Rādhā is particularly significant. So I set out to uncover these things for a Western scholarly audience.

Initially, I was interested in geographical information about the Vraja area, with special attention to Kṛṣṇa's early *līlā.* And then for the last sixteen years or so, I have focused in on Rādhā-kuṇḍa, the sacred lake of Śrīmatī Rādhārāṇī. This is in fact considered the most important holy place of Rādhā—the most important place in all of Gauḍīya Vaiṣṇavism—as it was rediscovered by Caitanya Mahāprabhu. It is true that the emphasis gradually shifted to other places, like Vṛndāvana, but Rādhā-kuṇḍa was the first place revived by Śrī Caitanya, and it remains the most important area for spiritual seekers of the Gauḍīya tradition.

SR: Do historians of Vraja support the idea that Mahāprabhu discovered Rādhā-kuṇḍa?

Dr. Gautam: Oh, yes, it is said that he discovered it in the year 1516. It was a small village—a pond—with not much to see. Later, it was developed by Raghunātha dāsa Gosvāmī. But, yes, during Kabīr, Nanak, Caitanya—they were contemporaries—and the history of that time is well known to researchers. The Muslim invasions. Aurangzeb's destruction of the temples. It is all in the history books. But my point is this: the Vraja region, especially Vṛndāvana, Mathurā, even Govardhāna, was not particularly well known to scholars, and the most important of these places—Rādhā-kuṇḍa—was least known of all.

SR: This is not without its virtues. Rādhā-kuṇḍa is quite an esoteric place. And if one tries to penetrate her mysteries without the guidance of a bona-fide spiritual master, it could be devastating. Even *with* the help of a *guru*, it can be devastating. In other words, one must be ready for that level of spiritual revelation. Bhaktisiddhānta Sarasvatī Ṭhākura said that if one prematurely tries to enter the understanding of Rādhā-kuṇḍa, one will instead be entering into the understanding of Naraka-kuṇḍa.

Dr. Gautam: "The lake of hell."

SR: Yes. It is considered very offensive. To go to the holy Rādhā-kuṇḍa and to act as though one were an advanced Vaiṣṇava. Most of them do not even follow the basic principles of spiritual life. Śrila Bhaktivedanta Swami Prabhupāda spoke out very strongly against this. Chant Kṛṣṇa's name according to a vow. And don't engage in illicit sex, intoxication, gambling and meat-eating. These are the preliminary qualifications. Then one requires some modicum of genuine advancement and the blessings of the *guru*. It is not a cheap thing. Otherwise it is not possible.

Dr. Gautam: Yes. I know—I am aware of the tradition's cautions. But a scholarly study can be useful. Not only useful, but it is invaluable. Most urgent. This is the point. The history, the geography, should be known. The world actually needs information about this very important holy place. Moreover, with proper education, one can learn what the qualifications actually are for genuine entrance there; one can learn to perceive Rādhā-kuṇḍa according to Vaiṣṇava doctrine.

SR: I agree. From that perspective, yes, it is of great use, both for scholars and for devotees. It is one of the most important parts of the Gauḍīya Vaiṣṇava heritage. And it should be explored in this way. But the cautions cannot be over-emphasized. . .

Dr. Gautam: Of course. So, as I see it, Rādhā-kuṇḍa can be studied in two ways. First and foremost, of course, is in terms of the books, the philosophy. What have the Vaiṣṇava saints written about it? What does it mean theologically? There is ample literature by Rūpa Gosvāmī and others. This will perhaps give us some insight into Rādhā-kuṇḍa. The basis can be found in texts taken from *Varāha Purāṇa, Brahma-vaivarta Purāṇa, Padma Purāṇa,* and so on. The basic story, as given in those *purāṇas,* is very interesting. It seems that Kṛṣṇa, after killing the bull-demon known as Ariṣṭāsura, had to make some kind of atonement. After all, Ariṣṭa was from the bovine species, and so Rādhā insisted that since Kṛṣṇa had indeed killed him, he must bathe in all of the holy rivers to purify himself from the offense.

SR: Yes. It might be argued that since Ariṣṭa was a demon, Kṛṣṇa should not have had to atone for killing him. But Śrīmatī Rādhārāṇī pointed out that even Indra, who is the king of the heavenly planets, had had to atone for the killing of the demon Vṛtrāsura, a *brāhmaṇa* by birth.

Dr. Gautam: Yes. [laughter] So Kṛṣṇa tried to please Rādhārāṇī by calling all holy rivers to that spot. He kicked his right heel into the ground, creating a large indent. Then he summoned all of the world's sacred rivers. In personified form it is said that they identified themselves: Godāvarī, Kāverī, Brahmaputra, Gaṇḍakī, Yamunā—all of them. With all of these waters, Śrī Kṛṣṇa filled what came to be known as Śyāma-kuṇḍa. He bathed, as Rādhā had suggested. But then he started to joke with her: "Now where is *your* lake?" Reacting to his statement, she found one of Ariṣṭāsura's big hoofprints on the western side of the Śyāma-kuṇḍa, and there she broke one of her bangles and started digging. With the help of her *gopī* friends, Rādhā-kuṇḍa was finally created. Still, there was no water—only a big concavity. Soon, all of the holy rivers again appeared and filled Rādhā-kuṇḍa. This is just a brief overview. But that's basically the scriptural story.

The other way to understand Rādhā-kuṇḍa—and this is the way in which I am pursuing it—is through historical or empirical study. In other words: not only through the scriptures, but through objective, observable research. This is also valuable. That means, as an anthropologist, I would like to see the situation *now*, by interviewing those who live there now and also by analyzing the physical territory now—the dimensions of the lake, etc.—and I would like to compare it to the same information that has been preserved by historians, documenting the same information from the past. In other words, how has it changed? In the minds of the residents, in the minds of scholars, in the minds of devotees, and in the objective historical records.

And this is the research that I started sixteen or seventeen years ago. So I have been continuing this work, on and off, since that time. I studied the maps of the area, from several historical periods, and I went from house-to-house making a survey of what local people had to say. Which of them were Caitanyaites? Which were general Kṛṣṇa devotees? What is their fascination with Rādhā-kuṇḍa? This sort of thing. The results are very interesting. And I will soon publish them as two scholarly studies, one directed toward scholars and the other for laymen who have an interest in such things.

SR: Is there a lot of work in this area? Did you get some assistance?

Dr. Gautam: It is growing, yes. You see, in the mid-1970s, there was a new wave in the anthropological and sociological world to locate the sacred places in the east, especially in northern India. It was a new interest. Of course, for me, it was an old interest. But I took advantage [laughter]. It really helped my research. There was a move to go through the records and to research. Like the Judaeo-Christian concept of "the Promised Land." A similar thing was there with Vraja. If not with the physical location always, at least conceptually. "I want Kṛṣṇa's name on my tongue when I die." Or sometimes they say, "I want Rādhā's name on my tongue as I leave this body." Why? Because it transports them to the Promised Land. Vraja. This goes on even today. So we are researching these places with renewed fervor. Like the Vrindavan Research Institute and Vraja Academy. All these things are going on. The British, in the last century, were concerned, too, and they started to put blue labels on temples, saying, "This is a monument—not to be disfigured." You can still see it on certain holy shrines. . .

SR: They did that? It was nice of them! [laughter] Of course, the Islamic leaders were often not as charitable. I'm talking about the prior invasion. They destroyed many temples. Even the Govindaji temple—five storeys were taken down. I know this smacks of Hindu chauvinism, but it did go on, at least in the Vraja region. To be fair, though, there were other Islamic leaders who were more tolerant, more liberal.

Dr. Gautam: You are referring to. . .the Mughals.

SR: Yes. And Sultan Barbak Shah. But Akbar, especially. Oh, definitely. There is that well known poem:

"Hail thee O Caitanya—the victor of my heart
Mark the rhythm of his mystic dance
In lofty ecstasy quite alone.
Merrily sounds the tabor
And the cymbals' notes keep time.
The joyous band following him
Sing and dance, merrily, merrily."

Dr. Gautam: [laughter] Beautiful. But there are a lot of things attributed to him. It is difficult to know what is authentic.

SR: Yes. That's true. Tell me, as far as your research into holy places, especially Rādhā-kuṇḍa, who initially inspired you in this work?

Dr. Gautam: The first person was a very good friend of mine, a professor at Ranchi University, Bihar, India. He did his doctorate on Gayā. At the time, he was studying under Dr. Milton Singer, a very famous anthropologist at the University of Chicago. The work on Gayā was one of the first works to inspire me. Of course, there were many others at the time. There were studies of Ayodhyā, Benares, and so many other places. . .

SR: These are important holy places. And it is interesting that various personalities will consider them important for different reasons. Gayā, for example, has become famous as the place where Prince Gautama Siddhārtha—the Buddha—had attained enlightenment. But for a Gauḍīya Vaiṣṇava, it is most important as the place where Mahāprabhu took initiation from Īśvara Purī. Or take Benares, for example. This is historically significant as a great center of Sanskrit learning and as a center for the worship of Śiva. Yet, to the follower of the Gauḍīya *saṁpradāya*, it is the place where Mahāprabhu instructed Sanātana Gosvāmī and where he defeated the impersonalist philosopher known as Prakāśānanda Sarasvatī.

Dr. Gautam: Yes. But the tradition teaches that of all holy places Rādhā-kuṇḍa is *most* important, does it not? Do you know those references?

SR: Yes. It is mentioned by Rūpa Gosvāmī in his *Śrī Upadeśāmṛta*. The ninth text tells us that Mathurā—even terrestrial Mathurā—is superior to Vaikuṇṭha, the spiritual world. This is because Kṛṣṇa took his birth in that holy land. Then it says that the forests of Vṛndāvana are even superior to Mathurā—because it is said that in *this* sacred area Kṛṣṇa's esoteric *rāsa-līlā* pastimes took place. But it goes further. It says that higher still is Govardhāna Hill, for it was raised by Kṛṣṇa's divine hand, and other loving pastimes occurred there as well. Rādhā-kuṇḍa is spiritually superior to even Govardhana, however, because this lake embodies Kṛṣṇa's love for Rādhārāṇī and her love for him.

Dr. Gautam: Yes. So the scriptures endorse that Rādhā-kuṇḍa is the holiest of places.

SR: But *Upadeśāmṛta* ends with a warning; Rūpa Gosvāmī says that the sacred place known as Rādhā-kuṇḍa is *asulabhaṁ*, or "difficult to attain." It is in the very last verse of the *Upadeśāmṛta*. What does this mean? Not that it is difficult to find by *rickshaw*. Nor will a mystical wand stop us from bathing in her waters. No. It means that we cannot really penetrate her mysteries—her inner meaning—unless we develop pure devotion. This is the thing.

Dr. Gautam: True enough. But as we pointed out earlier, the other information is invaluable and it is also inspirational, for devotees and scholars, and it will get them to stand up and to take note of this most important of all holy places. The history is enchanting. You can read in *Caitanya-caritāmṛta* of Caitanya's discovery, of Śyāma-kuṇḍa and Rādhā-kuṇḍa. Then, with his followers, how it developed. Specifically Raghunātha dāsa Gosvāmī. It is so interesting. How the original two paddy lands, Gaurī and Kālī, were purchased by Raghunātha dāsa for Jīva Gosvāmī. There are documents. The story of how twenty-some-odd steps were built on all sides of the lakes. How it was developed, in 1817, by Lala Babu, the rich landlord from Bengal. This information should not be withheld.

SR: I agree. This knowledge should be made available. . .

Dr. Gautam: Yes. So, as I said, I have been working on two books, possibly to be published by a major scholarly press, which will give all of the details, with much of the results of my last seventeen years of research. One book will focus on Rādhā-kuṇḍa from a scholarly point of view, and the other will be for laymen. So anyone can understand. In this, I am a supporter of ISKCON. The work that Swami Prabhupāda has done—making a rich, complex tradition accessible to people on all levels—is a major achievement. Whether we agree with every single translated word is another matter. But we must bow down to this major accomplishment. I see my work as a humble contribution to this same tradition. A humble offering, using my scholarly capabilities. Rādhā-kuṇḍa is a very confidential place, no doubt. But we feel that this information should be given to the world.

SR: It *must* be given.

Jagannātha Purī

Frédérique Marglin

Frédérique Apffel Marglin is Associate Professor of Anthropology and Women's Studies at Smith College. She is the author of Wives of the God-King: The Rituals of the Devadāsīs of Puri *(Delhi, New York, Oxford: Oxford University Press, 1985), which focuses on the temple dancers of Puri, and has written several articles on kingship, power, and the use of multiple media in rituals. Her more recent books focus on systems of knowledge and critiques of development, while her most recent field research in Orissa concerns the Festival of the Menses of the Earth: Rāja Parba.*

SR: Caitanya Mahāprabhu went to Purī and stayed there for the eighteen final years of his manifest *līlā*. While in Purī he exhibited the ecstasy known as *mahābhāva*, or the most intense form of love for Kṛṣṇa. Can you discuss the nature of Purī in the time of Śrī Caitanya?

Dr. Marglin: Well, first of all I want to say that Gauḍīya Vaiṣṇavism is only one tradition that is represented in Purī, where you actually find a vast array of religious beliefs—Śāktism, Śaivism, and various forms of Hinduism. This was so in Caitanya's time as well. Now, my particular introduction to Purī and Jagannātha was through the *devadāsīs*, the women dancers in the Jagannātha temple.

So perhaps we should start with them. As it turns out, they have two dancing rituals a day, one being a midday ritual and the other an evening ritual. The earlier one is a Śākta performance, and the later one is Vaiṣṇavite. I wouldn't specifically call it "Gauḍīya," because there are many strands of Vaiṣṇavism that one can perceive in the performance, but it certainly is performed through the Vaiṣṇava perspective. It's called *Baḍa-śṛṅgāra.*

SR: What are some of the themes conveyed in these performances?

Dr. Marglin: The evening Vaiṣṇava songs are sung by the *devadāsīs* while they stand on the threshold of the inner sanctum, the *garbha-gṛha,* literally, the "womb-house." This is where Jagannātha, Balabhadra and Subhadrā, as well as other deities, are installed. So it is from that place that a *devadāsī* will sing her song, either the *Gīta-govinda* itself or Oriya songs by local poets, in the vernacular, that are modeled on *Gīta-govinda.*

Now from these songs you'll see that the local people, in general, are hardly Gauḍīya Vaiṣṇavas—you'll notice the absence of Gaura-candrikā *kīrtana.* I think you'll find that the particular Vaiṣṇavism that is expressed by the people in Purī can more accurately be called "Oriya Vaiṣṇavism." It has its own emphasis and tradition. And if you read Prabhat Mukherjee's work, you can see the various distinctions, which, in some ways are quite subtle but in others are quite substantial.

SR: And yet some of Mahāprabhu's most important followers were found in Purī: Svarūpa Dāmodara, Rāmānanda Rāya, Śikhi Māhiti, and Mādhavī-devī, and there were many others, too.

Dr. Marglin: Yes. And I'm not saying that to this day they are not a very important presence. They are. They have their own *maṭhas.* And Gauḍīya Vaiṣṇavas come from all parts of India for Ratha-yātrā, or to visit the Gambhīrā, where Caitanya spent his last days, or to see the tomb of Haridāsa. These things are true. But I think you'll find that there are other important sects there as well, and, again, Oriya Vaiṣṇavas have their own traditions that are actually quite strong.

SR: But they all revere Mahāprabhu.

Dr. Marglin: Well, at least as a saint, yes, they all know of his adventures and his devotion to Jagannātha. That's clear. And, of course, Caitanya's presence is always felt due to the popular stories one inevitably hears while staying in Purī. For example, there is a Garuḍa pillar in the large audience hall that has a deep depression—it's worn—and they say that this is where Caitanya used to lean with his body while viewing Jagannātha. This was Caitanya's spot. He used to go there every day. From that particular area, when the doors are open, you can have a clear vision of the Jagannātha deity. Of course, I've never actually seen the Garuḍa pillar or the inside of the temple. You know, non-Indians are not allowed to go in. But we'll come back to that later.

Another local story you might hear: once, when Caitanya was standing near this pillar, a woman came and climbed up to see Jagannātha. In her enthusiasm, her feet touched Caitanya while she lifted herself up onto the pillar. Well, of course, Caitanya's servant would not have this, and he stopped her, "You cannot put your feet on Caitanya's holy body!" As the story goes, however, Caitanya calmed his servant, saying, "Since her enthusiasm is for seeing Lord Jagannātha, she can even stand on my head." You'll hear many such stories, and so, to this day, Caitanya is well-known throughout Purī as one of the foremost devotees of Lord Jagannātha.

SR: Okay. Maybe we could start with the story behind the Jagannātha deity, since this form of Kṛṣṇa was in fact so dear to Caitanya Mahāprabhu.

Dr. Marglin: Again, there are many different versions of the story, and I don't know that I would be able to recount any Gauḍīya versions. Well, the story is always variant on the same baseline. It begins by telling us that Jagannātha originally existed as Nīla Mādhava, a blue stone in the form of Kṛṣṇa. He was worshiped by the Śabaras, which is both a generic term for the tribals of Orissa and a specific name of one particular tribe. This is all to have taken place very long ago; it's difficult to say when.

Anyway, at that time, there was a great devotee of Viṣṇu, King Indradyumna, who wanted to worship his lord in a beautiful temple atmosphere. This was his prayer. So one evening, in a dream, Viṣṇu appeared to him and said: "You can find me on the eastern seaboard being worshiped by the Śabaras in the shape of Nīla Mādhava."

Immediately after this dream, Indradyumna delegated his *brāhmaṇa* deputy, Vidyāpati, to find the area where Nīla Mādhava was being worshiped. And so after many adventures, Vidyāpati made his way to the Śabaras and met their chief, Viśvāvasu, with whom he spent quite a bit of time. Now, in due course, two things happened: he fell in love with the chief's daughter, Lalitā, and he observed that the chief disappeared every morning and evening into the forest.

So Vidyāpati asked Lalitā, "Where does your father go everyday?" Well,

Lalitā proceeded to tell him about Nīla Mādhava, and that her father went off to worship him in secret. In any case, to summarize, they eventually get married, and he asks his father-in-law to take him to see this Nīla Mādhava. The chief Śabara agrees, but asks Vidyāpati to wear a blindfold, because Nīla Mādhava's whereabouts must remain secret.

However, Vidyāpati and Lalitā devise a plan wherein he is to drop mustard seeds out of his pocket as he journeys along with Lalitā's father. When they sprout, he would be able to find his way back to see the image again. The plan is carried out, but when he arrives for the second time, Nīla Mādhava speaks to him: "I will go with you to King Indradyumna by following behind you. My only request is that you do not look back. You'll know that I am behind you by the sound of my ankle bells."

So they leave. They travel a certain distance. At one point, however, Vidyāpati doesn't hear the ankle bells, and so he turns around. The deity vanishes. Now, there are many variations on this story, but when Vidyāpati returns to Indradyumna empty-handed, Indradyumna and his wife, Guṇḍicā, feel that they are the most unfortunate people in the universe and they decide to perform *tapasya*, austerities, for purification. The place where they practiced their austerities, supposedly, is right near where the present Guṇḍicā temple stands today. Anyway, they do the elaborate horse sacrifice, *aśvamedha-yajña*, and they collect thousands of cows to give in charity to the *brāhmaṇas*, and things of this nature. Actually, it is said that when he gathered all of the cows to give in charity, they were all kept in this one place and, together, they dug out what is today known as the Indradyumna tank. It's still there.

Anyway, to reward Indradyumna for his penance and austerity, Viṣṇu again appeared in his dream and explained that he had left the association of Vidyāpati because Vidyāpati approached him in the wrong way. But all was not lost. He would reappear for Indradyumna in the form of a log, *dāru-brahman*, that could be found in the sea. Now they have trouble bringing the *dāru* to shore, and so they have to evoke the goddess Maṅgala to bring in the *dāru*—this is a long story in itself.

When the *dāru* is finally brought to shore, the question arises as to who can fashion the log to look like Kṛṣṇa, or Nīla Mādhava. So, by Jagannātha's grace, an old man, Viśvakarmā, some say, appears and is clearly an expert in this field. He agrees to carve the deity, but insists that he must meditate on his service in perfect tranquility. If anyone disturbed his work, he said, he would leave the deities unfinished. Of course, this is exactly what happened. Some versions of the story say that Guṇḍicā was impatient and looked in on Viśvakarmā as he worked. Naturally, she found that he was gone and that the deities, Jagannātha, Balabhadra, and Subhadrā—Kṛṣṇa, his elder brother Balarāma, and his sister, at least from the Vaiṣṇava perspective—were left in an unfinished state. And this accounts for the peculiar look of the Jagannātha deities.

SR: So the deities were worshiped since that remote time in history?

Dr. Marglin: Again, there are various stories about that. One popular idea is that Indradyumna installed the deities and worshiped them, but, in the course of time, the temple was covered with sand. And everything gets forgotten. Now, the present temple, they say, is the second temple. Somebody sort of tripped on the tower, which was peeking out of the ground. So they refurbished the whole thing and reestablished the worship of Jagannātha.

SR: That was one of the Gajapati kings?

Dr. Marglin: Yes. That was a Gajapati ruler. That's their connection with the temple, at least as the story is often told.

SR: Right. You know, the Gajapati king from Mahāprabhu's time—his name was Pratāparudradeva—was said to be an incarnation of King Indradyumna.

Dr. Marglin: Some say that every Gajapati king is an incarnation of Indradyumna. Some say that because of their intimate association with the temple every Gajapati king is actually a partial incarnation of Viṣṇu or Jagannātha! There are many versions.

SR: I know. But from the Gauḍīya point of view, the identification of Indradyumna and Pratāparudra was substantiated by Kavi Karṇapūra in his *Gaura-gaṇoddeśa-dīpikā*. So that's part of their canonical literature, in a sense. Kavi Karṇapūra was also in Purī; his father was one of Mahāprabhu's intimate associates.

Dr. Marglin: Caitanya's followers in Purī, as you say, are remembered as great devotees, too. Rāmānanda Rāya, especially. He is given a special place, as is Yavana Haridāsa.

SR: What about the story of Rāmānanda Rāya and his activities with the *devadāsīs*? Since you've conducted quite a bit of field research on the *devadāsīs*, I'm sure you're familiar with the story. Is it known by the local people as well?

Dr. Marglin: Oh, his activity of bathing them and getting them ready for the dance. Some know it. Some do not. It's a controversial episode, but it's explained in *Caitanya-caritāmṛta*. You can look it up. It's interesting because the *devadāsīs* are also known as "courtesans" or even "prostitutes" (*veśyās, gaṇikās*), indicating that they are sexually free.

SR: Of course, the *Caitanya-caritāmṛta* says that Rāmānanda was above sexual attraction, and that although he bathed them and personally taught them the various dancing postures, he remained unagitated. We are told not to try to imitate Rāmānanda's risky behavior.

Dr. Marglin: [laughter] But as far as the *devadāsīs* go, their active sexuality was accepted, at least until the social reform movements of the late nineteenth century. In the past, the temple supported them, ideologically and financially, and their place in the society of Purī was very distinct. Now, the *devadāsīs* considered Jagannātha himself to be their husband, and Rāmānanda was a minister for the Gajapati king, who the *devadāsīs* considered a partial incarnation of Jagannātha and thus a genuine manifestation of their husband. So Rāmānanda, as the king's representative, may have taken some responsibility for training them while Caitanya was in Purī for Ratha-yātrā.

SR: Right. And while we are speaking about the car festival—I consider that to be an interesting aspect of Vaiṣṇavism in Orissa. It must seem really strange. Where else do you have devotees take their Lord out for a parade like that—with millions of people watching!

Dr. Marglin: You know, the Vaiṣṇava interpretation of the Ratha-yātrā *is* quite interesting. The deities Jagannātha, Balabhadra, and Subhadrā, go in a chariot, as you know, to the Guṇḍicā temple, which, by the way, is also the name of Indradyumna's queen, and they stay there for seven days and then they go back to Śrī Maṇḍira.

Now, before they had initially left to go to the Guṇḍicā temple, Lakṣmī, who is represented as a small metalic form on the *ratna-siṁhāsana* next to the image of Jagannātha, was left behind. And on the fifth day—that is, two days before the deities are to return—she is taken out on a palanquin by some of the local *paṇḍās* and they go walking down the road to the Guṇḍīcā temple where they will, of course, meet the other deities. At that time, though, Lakṣmī is also accompanied by the *devadāsīs*, who sing her glories.

When they finally arrive at the *rathas*, near Guṇḍīcā temple, the *devadāsīs* sing a song that is meant to reflect the mood of Lakṣmī as she sees the carts. The song says that Lakṣmī is angry because Jagannātha has neglected her. He has run off with his brother and sister and has left her behind. Actually, the song only mentions the sister, Subhadrā, because it is she who Lakṣmī is jealous of.

The *devadāsīs* act all of this out, and it's done symbolically—very beautifully. They break a piece of the chariot and tear a cloth from one of the priests—calling him the Gajapati ruler—to show Lakṣmī's anger. The song they sing then tells us that Lakṣmī has gone to the temple of the goddess Vimalā, which is found just behind Jagannātha's temple in the compound, to explain her predicament to the goddess. This Vimalā is the central goddess of Purī—a very important deity.

When Vimalā hears of Lakṣmī's plight, she gives her a packet of some sort of magic dust, and she tells her that if she throws this dust in Lord Jagannātha's face, he will turn his attention back to her and her problem will be resolved. In fact, the *devadāsīs* symbolically throw the dust in Jagannātha's face on behalf of Lakṣmī while he is in the Guṇḍīcā temple. Only after this occurs can Jagannātha begin his return journey to Śrī Maṇḍira. But during the seven-day stay in Guṇḍīcā temple, the *devadāsīs* perform their midday and evening rituals. So it's very interesting.

SR: I find it interesting that it is Lakṣmī who brings him back to Śrī Maṇḍira. Guṇḍīcā is often compared to Vraja and Śrī Maṇḍira to Dvārakā—so Lakṣmī is bringing him back to that *aiśvarya* mode, the mood of Dvārakā, or awe and reverence.

Dr. Marglin: Correct. The Gauḍīya Vaiṣṇava symbolism or interpretation of the Guṇḍīcā temple is that Guṇḍīcā represents Vṛndāvana and the *parakīyā* mode of worship—where the *rāsa līlā* takes place—and the Śrī Maṇḍira is contrasted with Dvārakā, where propriety or *svakīyā* reigns. So all of this is going on and, for the Gauḍīya devotee, has very deep theological implications. Now, these ideas hold true for the Gauḍīyas in regard to Ratha-yātrā. It's not that they are universally accepted or, even for the Gauḍīyas, that they are considered paramount all of the time. It's quite obscure.

SR: Yes. It's esoteric in nature. Like the ropes with which one pulls the Ratha-yātrā carts to Guṇḍicā—the symbolism suggests that one is pulling the Lord back to Vṛndāvana.

Dr. Marglin: Right. That would be a strictly Gauḍīya interpretation. But for the majority of pilgrims attending Ratha-yātrā, their primary belief is that if they touch the ropes they will attain *mokṣa,* liberation. That's the central idea for most people who attend. Conceptions of Jagannātha and his festivals vary quite a bit.

SR: I wonder what the British thought when they first saw it. There are ghastly descriptions. I understand that they brought back to the West reports about people crushing themselves under the wheels of the carts, and so they saw Jagannātha as some kind of blood-thirsty idol who wanted the death of his devotees! You mentioned earlier that foreigners are not allowed in the temple. Let's discuss that a little bit. Why do the temple priests keep foreigners out and what do foreigners generally think about Lord Jagannātha?

Dr. Marglin: Well, you know, that's where we get the English word "juggernaut." There was an extensive debate. When the British invaded Orissa in 1803 and took over the Jagannātha temple, the Christian missionaries in England argued that their government was supporting paganism. But the government didn't care for their complaints. They sort of latched onto Purī Jagannātha anyway, well, for two major reasons—they believed it was the Mecca of Hinduism, which is, of course, erroneous, and because of something very complex that occurred when they imprisoned the king.

SR: What's that?

Dr. Marglin: Well, they realized that they had to reinstate him (since they weren't allowed into the temple). The people believed in him—he was naturally in charge of the temple and the Ratha-yātrā festival, which brought in hundreds of thousands of pilgrims with a pilgrim's tax. So that was a sizeable piece of revenue that they didn't want to let go of. In order to get it, they had to reinstate the Hindu Gajapati ruler, and even give him funds, land and property. It was a political tactic, shall we say, to get exactly what they wanted out of the people.

Now, as far as the stories of devotees throwing themselves under the wheels of the Ratha-yātrā carts—that was just part of the polemic of the Christian missionaries. They took these isolated cases and tried to construct a nasty portrait of the Jagannātha religion. It was their way of showing what a terrible place Orissa actually was. It was supposed to be a den of iniquity, quite inferior to the holy places associated with Christianity and anything associated with Christian culture.

Anyway, Gajapati rule continued until 1963, when the state government of Orissa took over the management of the temple. This was the conclusion of an eight year court case—well, they started right after winning independence. In 1955 the Gajapati king entered a suit against the state government taking over. He lost. Since then, the administration has been headed by an appointed civil servant, and the king is only one member of a committee—he has lost his position as paramount authority in temple affairs. Before that, he had the last word in all decision-making. But they did, of course, take guidance from their teachers, the *rāja-gurus.*

Most *rāja-gurus* have been Śākta, at least for the last few centuries, although some may have been Vaiṣṇavite. It's difficult to reconstruct just who was Śākta and who was Vaiṣṇava. And, naturally, the further back you go, the more difficult it gets. But it's not impossible. There are records. You know, a lot of the records of this history are in the South Asian Institute at Heidelberg, and much of it hasn't really been looked at yet.

SR: Why is it in Heidelberg?

Dr. Marglin: Because the Germans conducted a six-year interdisciplinary project in Purī, and they gathered together quite a few capable scholars to research the Jagannātha traditions. In fact, Anncharlott Eschmann, Hermann Kulke, and Gaya Charan Tripathi edited a huge book about some of the findings. It is called *The Cult of Jagannātha and the Regional Tradition of Orissa* (Delhi: Manohar, 1978).

SR: Right. I have an ongoing correspondence with Professor Kulke. They've done a lot of work in this field.

Dr. Marglin: Oh, yes. They have a huge library of rare manuscripts and temple records. They brought it all back to Germany. It's tremendous.

SR: And, I suppose, they weren't allowed in the temple, either. It must have been difficult. . .

Dr. Marglin: That's true. But Professor Tripathi is a North-Indian *brāhmaṇa* and they hired local scholars as well. That's how you have to do it. I conducted my research with the aid of Purna Candra Misra, a local *brāhmaṇa.* Otherwise, it would have been quite impossible. They're very strict about keeping Westerners out of the temple.

SR: Well, let's discuss that. How did it all start? I mean, there are many temples in India that don't allow Westerners. But this temple is notorious for it. . .

Dr. Marglin: They've been particularly strict since the end of the Gajapati rule. I, in fact, once met a man—a Westerner—who was allowed entrance into the temple in 1959, when the Gajapati still had the ultimate say. Many voted against giving this man permission, but the Gajapati had absolute power in those days, and so this man was allowed in. But it could only be done in that way—by royal acceptance. And that was only granted occasionally.

There are two aspects to this peculiar rule against non-Hindus, Buddhists, or Jains entering the temple: first of all, the kitchen is very strict, according to Vaiṣṇava standards, and so no foreign elements are allowed in. They not only avoid meat, fish, eggs, onions, and garlic, as most Vaiṣṇavas do, but they also avoid vegetables whose origin is foreign. Consequently, they abjure the use of tomatoes, for example, which they call "foreign eggplant." That's what they call it. And in fact it doesn't grow indigenously. The same is true with potatoes, and possibly cauliflower. So, in the strict Purī Vaiṣṇavite kitchen, like the Jagannātha temple, they will not use these things. They feel that there is a reason why things do not have the virtue of growing in India, in what they consider to be the holy land.

Now, my understanding of this is that just as foreign food is banned because it is not grown indigenously, so, too, are foreigners—people—banned, because they did not have the good fortune of being nurtured on Indian soil, holy soil. They did not "grow" indigenously. Christians, Muslims, Jews, and others—all banned. So it has to do with this indigenous concept, not whether you are necessarily Hindu.

It also has to do with purity, which is a related concept. You know, if you travelled to foreign lands, for trading, or whatever, you lost a certain sense of purity, you were considered an outcaste. At least it used to be like that. So all of these things are related and they contribute to the Indian understanding or rationale for not letting Westerners in the temple.

SR: The whole thing just seems contradictory to me. *Jagannātha* means "*Lord of the Universe.*" So why should his *darśana* be denied to foreigners? Are they not part of the universe?

Dr. Marglin: What you say is absolutely true, and many have argued like that. But, you know, outcastes were also not allowed in the temple. So, as I said, it also has to do with purity. "Are you a part of *that* universe?" This is the question. Now, it's interesting because local songs and stories tell that Jagannātha *prefers* the lowborn, and he wants to show his mercy to them in particular. For example, there's the story of Baurī-bandhu, an untouchable, who was so devoted that Jagannātha came out of the temple just to see him. Then there is the story of an outcaste woman, Caṇḍālunī, who was also a great devotee of Jagannātha. When she used to sing while working in the fields, Jagannātha would come out of the temple just to listen to her.

So the conclusion is that Jagannātha is known as Patita-pāvana, or "Lord of the fallen ones." This is especially true at the yearly Ratha-yātrā, when he comes out of the temple and allows everyone—even foreigners—to see him and even to touch him. One year, I, myself, climbed his *ratha* and touched him. So I had firsthand experience of this phenomenon. In other words, at that time of the year, he comes down, and is immersed in the middle of the people; he is available to everybody, without distinction.

SR: So, then, if one is sincere, somehow, somewhere, they will get *darśana* of Jagannātha. This is the basic idea?

Dr. Marglin: Yes. Jagannātha will come to them.

Vaiṣṇavism and Christianity

Klaus Klostermaier

Klaus K. Klostermaier has published numerous academic articles and books, including his very personal story, Hindu and Christian in Vrindaban *(London: SCM Press Ltd., 1969). He is also the author of an important textbook, entitled,* A Survey of Hinduism *(Albany: State University of New York Press, 1989). Today he is Professor and Chairman of the Department of Religious Studies, University of Manitoba, Winnipeg, Manitoba, Canada.*

SR: People often prefer to understand a particular religious phenomenon from within the parameters of their own religious heritage. I think that Vaiṣṇavism, and particularly Gauḍīya Vaiṣṇavism, can in fact be understood by Westerners from within a Christian framework. The two traditions have quite a few things in common. Perhaps you would like to talk about that.

Dr. Klostermaier: Well, we should begin by pointing out that Vaiṣṇavism, like Christianity, is a living religion with millions of adherents. It is numerically the largest segment of modern Hinduism, with a history going back thousands of years. So we are not talking about some small sect but, rather, mainstream Hinduism.

Now, there are various Vaiṣṇava groups. You have the Śrīvaiṣṇava-sampradāya, whose main teacher, or founder, was Rāmānujācārya (1050-1137). This is found mainly in the south. You have the Brahma-sampradāya, which bases its teaching on the literature of Madhvācārya (1197-1276). And their important center is in Uḍipī, in Kannāḍa. There is the Kumāra-saṁpradāya, with Nimbārka (1125-1162) as the main teacher, and they are now primarily located in Vṛndāvana. Finally you have the Rudra-saṁpradāya, founded by Viṣṇu Svāmī (ca. 1200-1250), and this has turned into the Vallabha-saṁpradāya, or *puṣṭimārga,* under the charisma of Vallabhācārya (1479-1531).

It is important to note that Caitanya (1486-1534) is considered the founder of the Gauḍīya school, which claims affiliation with the Brahma-Mādhva-saṁpradāya. This affiliation was debated, and perhaps is still debated by scholars of the Mādhva tradition, but is nonetheless generally accepted by the mass of people.

The first point to understand, then, is that Vaiṣṇavism is as pervasive in India as Christianity is in the Western countries. It represents traditional Hinduism and claims to contain all that is genuinely Hindu. So Viṣṇu worship or, later, the worship of Kṛṣṇa, is something very much akin to the worship of God or, later, Jesus, in the Judaeo-Christian tradition.

SR: One can argue, though, that Śaivism has many followers, and they think of Śiva as the supreme.

Dr. Klostermaier: That is true. And there is some basis for this. But Vaiṣṇavism has a large following. If you look at certain texts, such as the story of Vikrāsura, the demon, you see that Viṣṇu has come to win a pre-eminent position in the scheme of popular Hinduism. You know the story: After practicing severe austerities, Vikra asked Śiva for a boon. He asked for the power to instantaneously kill a person by merely touching his or her head. Well, Śiva granted the boon, but realized his foolishness when Vikra chased both Śiva and his wife to try out his newfound power.

Śiva sought refuge in Viṣṇu, who, cunningly, induced doubt in Vikra. He told the demon that Śiva could not be trusted. "Śiva is fond," said Viṣṇu, "of joking and even lying. I am sure that he was not telling you the truth. Touch your own head and you will see. Nothing will happen." Vikra, of course, touched his own head and died. But the point of this story is the superiority of Viṣṇu over Śiva, who came to Viṣṇu for advice. Only Viṣṇu could solve this problem; Śiva could not. This story is known all over India.

SR: Okay. So Vaiṣṇavism is pervasive in India. And now it has come to the West as well. Christianity, for its part, has for a long time been the most prominent religion in the West. And it is practiced in India, too. Now I wonder about dialogue. Can these two great traditions find common ground? Well, before we get into that, I have a question: How do Vaiṣṇavas, in general, see Jesus Christ?

Dr. Klostermaier: That, of course, is a very difficult question. Vaiṣṇavas are not some monolithic entity. Rather than try to construct some global Vaiṣṇava doctrine on Jesus Christ, we can analyze how various groups of Vaiṣṇavas have viewed him over the centuries. Some Vaiṣṇavas consider him an *avatāra* or some kind of divine incarnation. Others see him as a great teacher of moral codes and ethical principles, a saint whose selfless spirit of sacrifice is a great inspiration to mankind. Then there are those who see him as a miracle worker, a sort of *yogī* like Ramakrishna or Sāī Bābā. There are quite diverse conceptions of Christ both in the minds of Vaiṣṇavas and in the minds of Christians.

The Hindi version of the famous passage in *Matthew* (16.16)—Peter's confession to Jesus, saying, "You are the Messiah, the Son of the Living God"—says: "*Āp Khrīst haiṅ jīvit īśvar ke putr.*" Now, this becomes a difficult passage to explain to Hindus as I have shown in my booklet *Krist-vidya: A Sketch of an Indian Christology* (1967). *Īśvar ke putr*—"the Son of God"—is a very common expression in Hindu India. In the epics and *purāṇas* there are countless stories of "sons of gods"—Brahmā, Viṣṇu, and Śiva beget sons from princesses and queens. Hindus will say: "What is so special about Jesus? We are all sons of God." So the idea does not convey the notion of uniqueness as it does in the West.

SR: There are diverse ideas about Jesus and also there are diverse ideas about the ultimate nature of reality.

Dr. Klostermaier: Precisely. Śaṅkara, for example, takes Upaniṣadic texts and explains them in an impersonalistic sort of way; Rāmānuja takes those same texts and gives them a personalistic gloss. The same sort of diversity exists in the Christian tradition, and there have been major theological schools that have emphasized one way of viewing things over and against another. Basically, of course, this all comes down to the failing of our language or our fundamental inability to understand the infinite. Neither the personal nor the impersonal image is fully adequate—God transcends all human conceptions. He or she must include both and exist beyond both.

SR: Would you say that Mahāprabhu's *acintya-bhedābheda* encompasses this idea?

Dr. Klostermaier: Well, you could say that, but Caitanyaites have been known to be rather hard on the Advaitins and the impersonalistic school of thought. But, yes, it is acknowledged in the *acintya-bhedābheda* school that God has both features. Gauḍīya Vaiṣṇavas do recognize that God is both personal and impersonal and, yes, is a blend of both.

This idea is there in the impersonalistic schools as well. Śaṅkara wrote hymns to Viṣṇu and Śiva, and Śaṅkarites, to this day, preach *bhakti*, devotion to God. You see, it is really a question of *emphasis* that separates the impersonalists and the personalists. Ultimately, the accomplished practitioners of both paths will recognize that God is a blend of personal and impersonal features. So the gulf may not be as wide as some would have us believe.

In Christianity, too, you have highly personalistic ideas, like those of the medieval Beghines—female devotees of medieval Germany. They envisioned the playfulness of God in highly personalistic terms, according to private revelations, and there were other, similar schools of thought. But then you have a counter theological idea, like that of Meister Eckhart, where you find striking parallels with the Advaita Vedānta of Śaṅkara.

SR: I am interested in these kinds of parallels. For example, I find that there are certain generic ideas that are discussed in both Christian and Vaiṣṇava literature.

Dr. Klostermaier: Absolutely. The *purāṇas*—like the Bible—deal with creation, history of dynasties, biographies of saints, moral laws, human wisdom, the first created being, a Noah-type personality, the birth of the saviour, miracles of all sorts. These things are there and they can be elaborated upon with volumes of commentary.

Now, if we want to specifically speak about *bhakti* or Vaiṣṇava sensibilities, we can also find them in the Bible. The Canticle of Solomon and the Gītagovinda of Jayadeva agree both in form and in spirit—and in a great variety of ways. You are familiar with the development of *bhakti* literature in the Gauḍīya Vaiṣṇava tradition, which is voluminous. There is also a *Christ-bhakti* literature, if you will, that arose in the late middle ages.

SR: You are referring, no doubt, to *The Imitation of Christ*. . .

Dr. Klostermaier: Right. The *Imitatio Christi* is a classic of *Christ-bhakti* literature. There are many other such books, too, which are classified under "*devotio moderna.*" You have St. John's *Dark Night of the Soul* as well. This could be seen as a Christian version of *viraha-bhakti* or love of God in the mood of separation.

SR: Oh, yes. St. Teresa speaks of it as "the great dereliction," and Madame Guyon calls it "mystic death." It is a temporary loss of the vision of God. Like Mephistopheles' description of hell: "Having once seen the Lord, to be denied that vision." Of course, this makes one mad with anticipation and increases one's sense of devotion. I believe Christian mystics not only experienced this very advanced level of God consciousness, but they also exhibited the bodily symptoms that go along with it.

Dr. Klostermaier: The *sāttvika-bhāvas.* Right. St. Teresa experienced loneliness and desolation, accompanied by a kind of catalepsy, with muscular rigidity and temporary cessation of the pulse. These symptoms are there in the Vaiṣṇava mystics as well. The last eighteen years of Caitanya's life include a particularly poignant display of these ecstatic symptoms—*viraha-bhakti* of the highest order. I explain these feelings at some length in my paper called "A Universe of Feelings" [in Weber/Chopra, eds., *Shri Krishna Caitanya and the Bhakti Religion* (Frankfurt am Main: Verlag Peter Lang, 1988)].

SR: Right. I read that paper. I thought it was an excellent summary of the basic Gauḍīya ideology. It was that paper, in fact, that really started me thinking about the similarities between Vaiṣṇava and Christian philosophers. After reflecting on the scholarship of these two traditions, I started to think of Jīva Gosvāmī as the Thomas Aquinas of the Gauḍīya tradition, since it was he who systematized the whole thing in a very coherent and methodical way.

Dr. Klostermaier: There are actually other Christian philosophers who come a good deal closer, like Bonaventure, for example. His perspective accentuates feeling and emotion more than the intellect. And I think if you look at the Gauḍīya philosophers, even a particularly rigorous thinker like Jīva Gosvāmī, you will see that feeling and emotion are considered much more important than the intellect. After all, it is *bhakti, bhāva,* and *premā,* emotional states, that are the desired goals of those who follow the Gauḍīya tradition, not *karma, jñāna,* or even *mukti.*

But I think you are looking for parallels in Christian and Vaiṣṇava traditions, and this can be found quite readily. In fact, if you look long and hard enough, you can find points of similarity all the way through; and you can even reconcile many of the obvious differences that the two religions have come to engender. You can see it in the basic practices of these religions. Certain key practices of Gauḍīya Vaiṣṇavism are found in Christian mysticism as well, and through this you can find many parallels. But, again, it is quite difficult to generalize. You see, Jīva Gosvāmī does not represent all Gauḍīya Vaiṣṇavas; and Bonaventure and Thomas Aquinas do not represent the mass of Christian believers.

Still, if you speak in general terms, there are certain generic spiritual practices and ideals that the two traditions share, especially if you look into the monastic communities. There is the sense of worshiping God in a regulated way; liturgical ceremonies; temple worship; subduing the senses; self-control; loving one's neighbor; communal worship; meditation; prayer. You can see these things, for example, in certain early Franciscan orders—a religion of song and dance. It is currently seeing some revival.

Here is a good parallel for what one might see in a Gauḍīya Vaiṣṇava community. It, too, is an exuberant sort of piety. Bonaventure was a Franciscan. So I do see a similarity there. You know, the Franciscans were even vegetarians—for a large part they still are. I think there are certain things you can look for in all genuinely spiritual traditions. The sense of love, compassion, commitment.

SR: What about chanting the holy name? You mentioned meditation and prayer. You know, for the Gauḍīya Vaiṣṇavas, this would be considered a central practice.

Dr. Klostermaier: Yes, certainly. And it is also important in the Christian tradition, at least for certain sects and monastic orders. Again, it is difficult to generalize. In the *Philokalia* and in the path recommended by *The Pilgrim*, you find thc tradition of the "Jesus Prayer," which may be unknown to most Christians today but was very powerful in its time. In fact, this, too, is seeing something of a revival. So people are aware of the potency of "the name" and the importance of focusing on it as a *mantra* or a repeated syllable or set of syllables. But it must be done with devotion.

In the Gauḍīya Vaiṣṇava tradition, this is the main consideration—to chant *japa* or *kīrtana* with devotion. Otherwise, it will not have the right effect. This same principle is there, of course, in the Christian traditions.

The idea of *logos*, or "the Word," has elaborate theological meaning that is intimately tied to the nature of Jesus and, indeed, to the nature of God.

SR: Let's talk about that: the nature of God. The Christian conception of the Father, the Son, and the Holy Ghost seems as though it has its natural parallel in Viṣṇu, his pure devotee, and Paramātmā, or the indwelling manifestation of the supreme. What do you think?

Dr. Klostermaier: Well, again, it really varies according to which conception of Vaiṣṇavism and Christianity you are referring to. For myself, I see more of a parallel between the Christian trinitarian concept of deity and the doctrine of Rādhā-Kṛṣṇa as such.

SR: Really? How so?

Dr. Klostermaier: The inner, divine relationship between the Father, the Son, and the Holy Ghost is fundamentally a relationship of love—profound, unending spiritual communication. Even though it is described in terms of a father/son interaction, it develops into the highest kind of *mādhurya* relationship. You see, there is a virtually unknown trinitarian theological system of emotional feelings. It was explored to some degree in the Middle Ages, but I think it needs further exploration. I hint at this in my *Kristvidya*, but it has yet to be taken up. The Western theological context in which the love of Rādhā and Kṛṣṇa could perhaps be best understood is precisely that of trinitarian theology. For the Christian, the Trinity represents the deepest mystery of faith. If one took literally the symbolism of the Son being eternally generated by the Father, for example, one could come up with all kinds of mundane crudities and perversions. Similarly, the Rādhā-Kṛṣṇa relationship cannot be fathomed by paralleling it with romantic love poetry or late medieval Marian devotion, as some writers have tried to do. The mystery of these things goes very deep, and there is no earthly symbolism that can accurately convey its truth.

SR: I think this is also true of *rasa* theology, which, again, has parallels in Christian tradition.

Dr. Klostermaier: It certainly does. There are so many different kinds of loving relationships among the characters of the Bible. There is the love of Abel and Abraham; the love of the prophets; the love of Moses and David; the love of those who were exiled in Babylon and the love of those who remained in Jerusalem; the love of the shepherds and the disciples; the love of Mary Magdalene and of Zachaeus; the love of Peter and of John; the love of Mary toward the child and towards the crucified; and then there is the love of Christ. Jesus says, "He who does the will of my Father, is to me brother, sister, mother." I think these various kinds of love adequately approximate the kinds of *rasas* that are developed by Rūpa Gosvāmī.

SR: Yes. This has been brought to light by several important writers. I think the first was Melville Kennedy, in his classic work, *The Chaitanya Movement* (Calcutta: Association Press, 1925). He was later paraphrased by Sudhindra Chandra Chakravarti, whose book, *Philosophical Foundation of Bengal Vaisnavism* (Calcutta: Academic Publishers, 1969), has some interesting statements about *rasa* theology in relation to the Christian tradition. Let me read this one section to you:

> Like the advocates of Bengal Vaiṣṇavism, Christianity has availed itself of the rich imagery of human relationship to represent the five stages of religious feeling. The quietistic type of Christian devotion familiar in all periods of Christian history corresponds to the śānta-bhakti of Bengal Vaiṣṇavism. The figure of Mary, sister of Martha, at the feet of Jesus is an apt illustration of this type of religious experience. The second stage called dāsya, which is characterized by the feeling of being a slave or a servant, has its counterpart in the devotion of Paul, the bondslave of Christ. An unbroken line of devout spirits following Paul is known to have expressed the utter devotion of heart in terms of slavery and servitude. Once, while washing his disciple's feet, Jesus said, 'I am among you as he that serveth.' This fact reveals Jesus's attitude toward the dāsya aspect of devotion. The sakhya stage has its counterpart in the relationship between Jesus and his disciples, indicated by his own words, 'No longer do I call you servants. . .but now I call you friends.' The devotion in terms of the parent and child relation is quite fundamental to Christianity. According to the Christian faith, God is the eternal Father, and all are His children. The vātsalya stage of Bengal Vaiṣṇavism, however, is concerned only with the parental feeling toward the Lord. It has its parallels in the New Testament picture of the wise men and the Christ child, and the worship of the Bambino as it obtains in the Roman Catholic Church. The mādhurya stage of bhakti finds its parallel in the mystical practices of mediaeval monasticism. The Roman Catholic nun is taught to regard her soul as the bride of Christ. In Protestant teaching, the church is regarded as the bride of Christ.

Dr. Klostermaier: Yes, I accept this idea completely. You have mentioned some of the paradigmatic figures, but there are many examples of this secret love affair with God in the Christian tradition. And another, related subject to explore is this: the more a devotee became absorbed in his or her distinct relationship with God, or *rasa*, the more the outside world had trouble dealing with it. Not only were many of the Christian saints so overwhelmed by their love for God that they never married—as you noted, nuns throughout the ages considered themselves the spouses of Christ!—but there are quite well-known instances where this development of inner taste, or *rasa*, led men and women to leave behind their mortal spouses, with whom they had been leading a perfectly normal and happy life. Such love of God led to the incarceration of St. John of the Cross by his fellow monks; it led to persistent abuse in the case of Teresa of Avila; it led to estrangement and suspicion in the case of many others. In the Vaiṣṇava context, Mīrābāī could serve as an example for such estrangement and misunderstanding. Caitanya himself was eventually seen as a raving madman by all but his most intimate followers.

This is the point: divine love cannot be understood by Everyman. It is a cherished goal, and one that is rarely attained. In Vaiṣṇavism and in Christianity you have examples of saints who have achieved this goal—but it is not so easily attained. What's more, when it *is* attained, it can make one an outcaste in the conventional world—in the reality to which we have become accustomed. One's consolation is that, when one achieves that goal, *one is no longer an outcaste in the spiritual realm.* And this, according to devotees of both traditions, is a reward that is more than worth the struggle.

Sādhana Bhakti

Joseph T. O'Connell

Joseph T. O'Connell is Associate Professor in the Department of Religious Studies, St. Michael's College, University of Toronto. He teaches Indian theology and religious history, his special area being Bengali religion. His Harvard Ph.D. Dissertation (1970), entitled, "Social Implications of the Gauḍīya Vaiṣṇava Movement," established the course of his career. A frequent contributor to academic journals, such as the **Journal of the American Oriental Society,** ***Dr. O'Connell has also contributed to such volumes as Bardwell L. Smith's*** **Hinduism: New Essays in the History of Religions** ***and Mircea Eliade's*** **Encyclopedia of Religion** ***(his entries focusing on Caitanya Mahāprabhu and Bengali religion). He is editor of*** **Bengal Vaiṣṇavism, Orientalism, Society, and the Arts** ***and other books.***

SR: Let's begin by defining Vaiṣṇava *sādhana.*

Dr. O'Connell: Well, let's discuss for a moment the meaning of *Vaiṣṇava.* It is a person who is devoted to the Divine in the personal form of Viṣṇu, or Kṛṣṇa, or Hari, or any of the directly related forms of the Lord—a Vaiṣṇava is a devotee of the Lord. Now, *sādhana* is basically a pattern or program of religious practices. The Sanskrit root, *sadh,* means "to accomplish" or "to attain" something. *Sādhana* is the means or the program that one goes through to attain the *sādhya* ("that which is to be attained") or the *siddhi* (the "perfection" or the "goal"). In this case, the goal is a yet more perfect experience of *bhakti*, or devotion to the Lord. The *sādhaka* is the person who is striving to attain such perfection.

Sādhana is a program, if you will, in which the Vaiṣṇava uses not only his or her mind but the physical senses also—eyes, ears, voice—to develop the underlying capacity for devotion into a more perfect culmination of it.

SR: It seems that there is some sense of *sādhana* in all forms of religion, in the various religious traditions.

Dr. O'Connell: I should think so. Certainly the major religious traditions that have expanded beyond any small tribal or ethnic base—and even those—have ways in which adherents are informed about the ideals of their respective religions. To pursue these ideals, they are provided with programs of training and practice and reinforcement.

You find a lot of this, of course, in the Christian tradition, where you have a great variety of denominations and religious orders which have their own specific ways of honing and reinforcing the devotional sensibility of the Christian. And even the average layperson is encouraged—especially in more traditional forms of Christianity—to have a program of daily or weekly prayer, or periodic participation in church services. They may be asked to do a certain amount of scriptural reading. For some laypersons this is done in a very systematic way, for others, it is more casual. All this can be seen as Christian *sādhana*.

SR: Perhaps you can elaborate on the early Vedic forms of *sādhana* and how it was eventually developed by the Caitanya movement.

Dr. O'Connell: In the Vedic setting, you really have two distinct dimensions of religion: the ritualistic dimension and the more reflective or philosophical one. *Sādhana* can be seen in both.

In the ritual aspect of Veda, there is *sādhana* in a limited and temporary form. When there is a ritual to be performed, especially a major Vedic sacrifice, there are certain preparatory practices one is supposed to follow. You may be expected to fast; to remain chaste for a certain period; to observe restrictions in sleep; and you would certainly be expected to concentrate or meditate on various aspects of the ritual.

But all this is focused on a specific ritual, and when it is over the *sādhana* ends. This is in contrast to Vaiṣṇava *sādhana*, which is meant to go on day after day, and lifetime after lifetime, if necessary, until the culmination of devotion is attained.

In the more reflective, philosophic form of Vedic *sādhana*, recorded in the Upaniṣad texts, there is this sense that one is probing into Brahman, the ultimate source and destination of human life. This is much closer to the kind of *sādhana* that you can find in the life of the Vaiṣṇava devotee. The practitioner is expected to sit down—*upaniṣad* means "to sit down next to," and it suggests an intimate or esoteric instruction from the *guru*—and study and reflect upon Vedic texts. This is done as a strict and continuing *sādhana*. Now, from the Caitanyaite point of view, the ultimate reality, Brahman, is understood to be the Supreme Deity—Kṛṣṇa—or Bhagavān, a more general term for the Supreme Person. This Caitanyaite tradition is quite explicitly theistic in its understanding of Brahman, more so than is the Upaniṣadic tradition as a whole. But the correlation is still there.

On the other hand, there is also a ritualistic dimension to Caitanyaite *sādhana*, one which has some of the parallels to the old Vedic rituals, for instance initiation (*dīkṣā*), fasting, *mantra* recitation and chastity. The main focus is on developing love for Kṛṣṇa, the personal Deity, the "Para"-Brahman or "ultimate" Brahman, if you will. So, in the Caitanyaite tradition, there is a sort of merger of both forms of old Vedic *sādhana*: it has its ritualistic side and its more probing, reflective side.

SR: Well what sort of rituals are you referring to in Caitanyaite *sādhana*?

Dr. O'Connell: To start with, there is the worship of the Divine in the form of the statue image, the *arcā-vigraha*, which is present in the temple, or in the home, perhaps as a small picture. Such worship is set out rather elaborately in the ritual texts, but there are abbreviated versions for those who have other responsibilities. There are many temple-related elements that become part of the devotees's personal *sādhana*, leading to absorption and surrender to the Deity.

Also, a very important part of Vaiṣṇava *sādhana*, especially for Caitanyaite or Gauḍīya Vaiṣṇavas, involves hearing, talking, or singing about the Divine pastimes (*līlās*)—the activities, qualities, and beauties of the Supreme Lord in association with other eternal beings, especially his confidential devotees. There are the stories of Kṛṣṇa's *līlās* in the Purāṇas, for example. To hear or sing about these, to recite, to read, to gather with others to celebrate these—develops a sort of "wrap-around awareness," if I can use that kind of expression, of the Divine. This is very much what *sādhana* is supposed to do from a Vaiṣṇavite point of view.

Use your ears, use your eyes to see the image of the deity! Use your voice—all of these senses—to build up and sustain an all-encompassing awareness of the Divine. It is called *smaraṇa,* or "remembrance." It is not simply looking back at the past. You make the awareness present, right here and now. And so a great deal of Caitanyaite Vaiṣṇavite *sādhana* is designed to enhance remembrance of Kṛṣṇa's eternal *līlā,* which is understood to be all-attractive, just like Kṛṣṇa himself. The more one hears, or visualizes, the more one becomes attracted and begins to remember. .

SR: Prabhupāda often compared it to amnesia.

Dr. O'Connell: How so?

SR: Well, if someone has conventional amnesia, he is given a daily regimen of gradual exposure to his former life. Hopefully, through this sort of sustained activity, the amnesia patient gradually remembers—he becomes cured. Similarly, by a certain routine, *sādhana,* one develops *smaraṇa,* or a kind of remembrance of one's constitutional position—his basic or original nature—as a participant in Kṛṣṇa's eternal pastimes.

Dr. O'Connell: Precisely. It's an exercise in *anamnesis,* or the reversal of amnesia. Sometimes it is said that certain saints recall their previous lives. Others recall the timeless community of perfected souls gathered about the Lord—into which one hopes to enter. Now, one partially enters this transcendent reality through the very hearing and chanting of the Divine stories. But the aspiration, or the *sādhya* that one is really aiming for is a definitive spiritual birth into such a realm, where one can relate to the Divine in a timeless and yet face to face way.

This is attained by *sādhana,* including the hearing and chanting about Rādhā and Kṛṣṇa's pastimes, and also the remembering of the life and activities of Lord Caitanya and his associates. These too are understood to be manifestations of the Divine, displayed only some five hundred years ago in India. Caitanya's *līlās* are dramatized, sung, and performed with the same enthusiasm that one would use for Kṛṣṇa *līlā.*

Both Caitanya *līlā* and Kṛṣṇa *līlā* come together in the Padāvalī *kīrtana.* Both are performed in group settings. And this suggests one of the most important aspects of Gauḍīya *sādhana—Saṅkīrtana. Saṅ* means "together." Although there are areas of *sādhana* that are performed alone—*japa,* or rosary-chanting, for example—the congregational glorification of Kṛṣṇa is considered most important. Cooperation and mutual support are integral to it. You see this very much in Līlā *kīrtana*, or Padāvalī *kīrtana*, where you have not only the lead singer and his musicians but also the congregation, who will sometimes sing along and shout and, in some cases, become quite visibly moved. And, of course, the reaction of the congregation stimulates the performers, as each one reinforces the other. The mood is such that one tends to transcend the current setting and be transported to the spiritual world, at least temporarily. For those who are advanced, there is experienced, I suppose, a more enduring state of Divine consciousness.

SR: Yes. This is the *saṅkīrtana* principle. According to Vedic texts, this congregational chanting is the recommended process for the present age. And Caitanya Mahāprabhu came to reveal this method as the most appropriate means for attaining love of God in the current epoch of world history.

Dr. O'Connell: There is certainly a scriptural basis for Vaiṣṇava *sādhana*, including *saṅkīrtana*, and the Caitanyaite tradition has developed this quite a bit. You have the *Hari-bhakti-vilāsa* and the *Bhakti-rasāmṛta-sindhu*, for example, which are two Gauḍīya texts that elaborate on the basic principles of *sādhana*. These are highly systematic texts, and they are intended in part at least to reflect the experiences which practitioners and religious guides have had in understanding human emotions and spiritual experiences. They set forth how, through very specific bodily activities and mental states, advanced levels of consciousness may be attained. These texts give detailed descriptions of how bodily and mental behavior can hinder or facilitate the rising of desired modes of consciousness or spiritual experience.

One of the key figures among the Six Gosvāmīs of Vṛndāvana—one of the important pastors of Caitanya's time—was Rūpa Gosvāmī. He was responsible for many such systematic texts, the *Bhakti-rasāmṛta-sindhu* being one. In that particular work, he develops very thoroughly the notion of *sādhana*. He discusses a generic sort of *bhakti*, or devotion, and then *sādhana-bhakti*, then *bhāva* and *prema-bhakti*, which are progressively more perfected modes of loving devotion. He also has a companion volume, called *Ujjvala-nīlamaṇi*, in which he continues these themes while going into greater detail in regard to *mādhurya-rasa*, or the amorous mode of devotion.

SR: Rūpa Gosvāmī deals with both Vaidhī *bhakti* and Rāgānugā *bhakti*. . .

Dr. O'Connell: Yes. Both are forms of *sādhana,* wherein you use your mind, body, eyes, hearing—all the senses—to train yourself for more spontaneous devotional experience, much like an athlete trains himself or herself. The difference between vaidhī and rāgānugā, in the beginning stages, is that vaidhī is said to be motivated by injunction, i.e., by advice, or command. The idea here is that if one has heard that devotional life is a good thing, if he or she is persuaded in that way, then as an act of *śraddhā,* faith, or trust, one will adopt the vaidhī-type discipline. One then submits to a daily regimen under the guidance of *guru* and scripture. This vaidhī may, in turn, ultimately lead to an intensified and more spontaneous level of devotion to the Supreme. But the point is this: at the early stage, devotion or *bhakti* may not be something that one is spontaneously feeling within oneself—one simply has faith that it does some good, and so one follows the injunctions. This is Vaidhi-bhakti-sādhana.

It becomes Rāgānugā when the motivation shifts. Externally, you might still do the same things. You might get up in the early morning; recite the holy name a prescribed number of times; you may take certain baths; you may go and make offerings to the deity in the temple. But the motivation has shifted from merely following good advice, or injunctions, to an inner longing, an intense desire. You really feel it. You *want* to do these things. If, when seeing the deity or chanting the holy name, there is this innate yearning to know more or to participate more fully in the divine *līlā,* then the motivation has shifted from injunction (*vidhi*) to longing (*lobha*). This is the shift from vaidhī to rāgānugā, or passionate, spontaneous *sādhana.*

There is another way of understanding rāgānugā. Passionate devotion, which has replaced the following of good advice as a motivation, often takes—and perhaps always should take—a form in which one yearns to model one's devotion after that of the personalities of Kṛṣṇa's kingdom. A rāgānugā devotee is thus one who follows in the footsteps of a Rāgātmikā *bhakta,* i.e., one of the perfect lovers of Kṛṣṇa in the transcendent Vraja *līlā.*

SR: This more specific kind of rāgānugā is a highly specialized sort of practice, or *sādhana,* which is given by one's *guru.* The spiritual identity of a disciple is revealed and one meditates on himself or herself in this ontological form. To accomplish this end, the *ekādaśa-bhāva* of one's mystical body (*siddha deha*) is given. These are the eleven items needed to engage in such meditation: knowing one's name; one's relationship to Kṛṣṇa or Rādhā; one's age; body color; group; dress; order; residence; service; highest desire or expectation; and under whom one serves. This last item is especially important, for one must know all of the details of the particular individual from Vraja *līlā* in order to serve them properly. But this is very advanced, and few have the good fortune to genuinely achieve these heights of God consciousness. Today, there are many Gauḍīya authorities who dismiss these things because too many have exploited the higher position of true rāgānugā. It is difficult to attain. So, in response to this, many prefer to recommend the safer path, so to speak, encouraging practitioners to strictly follow Vaidhī *bhakti*. . .

Dr. O'Connell: Yes, but the development of this rāgānugā system is a significant part of the Caitanyaite tradition, especially in the centuries immediately following Caitanya. It is an important elaboration on the principle of *sādhana*. Mañjarī *sādhana*, for example, is a very complex Vaiṣṇavite conception, wherein one assists the primary *gopīs* in their service to Rādhā. And while we are on the subject, there are two broad types of rāgānugā devotion. One centers on the *kāmānugā* idea, that one can follow the spiritually erotic mood of the *gopīs*; the other on the *sambandhānugā* idea, that one can follow the eternal inhabitants of Vraja in any number of relations of kinship and friendship. This has all been elaborated upon by David Haberman in his excellent study, *Acting as a Way of Salvation: A Study of Rāgānugā-Bhakti-Sādhana* (New York: Oxford University Press, 1988) and by Donna Wulff in her earlier book, *Drama as a Mode of Religious Realization* (Chico, California: Scholars Press, 1984).

Viśvanātha Cakravartī, an eighteenth century Caitanyaite theologian, in his *Rāga-vartma-candrikā* ("The Moonbeam on the Path of Passion"), stresses the more generic form of rāgānugā, the kind to which I was referring earlier, giving *lobha*, or internal desire, as the distinguishing quality of rāgānugā *sādhana*. He emphasizes that when and if one goes from vaidhī to rāgānugā, one may engage in all of the same practices of *sādhana* or discipline as before, but only if one finds them helpful. If not, one may drop them.

SR: Yes. Rūpa Gosvāmī also says that, ultimately, one should accept that which is conducive for devotional service to Kṛṣṇa and one should reject that which is not conducive. But one has to be careful. As you know, in the Gauḍīya tradition, there is a certain class called *prākṛta-sahajiyā*, or those who take cheaply the teachings of the predecessor *ācāryas*. The *sahajiyās* tend to say that because they have graduated to the rāgānugā stage, there is really no reason for them to follow the rules and regulations of vaidhī. But the greatest rāgānugā devotees—the Six Gosvāmīs of

Vṛndāvana, for example—continued to strictly follow all of the practices of vaidhī *bhakti*. The inner meditation may be different, but externally it would be difficult to tell who is a rāgānugā devotee and who is a vaidhī devotee.

Dr. O'Connell: What you call the *prākṛta sahajiyā* disciplines are a topic of their own, a tangent we cannot pursue here. But as for the relation of vaidhī to rāgānugā *bhakti* in the mainstream Caitanya tradition, there is some flexibility. In the early stages of rāgānugā it would certainly make good sense to stick closely to one's discipline and the rules of the vaidhī path. But there is also the principle, frequently enunciated in the texts, that if certain practices are no longer enhancing your devotion, you can let them go. Along these same lines, if you fail for one reason or another to do certain things that you ordinarily would have done, like getting up early for your *pūjā* because you were genuinely so enthused by hearing a *kīrtana* the prior evening, or something to that effect, there is no problem on that score.

This is all assuming, of course, that there is a genuine emergence of rāgānugā *bhakti*. The same texts that tell you that you can relinquish prior vaidhī-like disciplnes, also warn you to beware of false devotion, or *bhakti-ābhāsa*—counterfeits. It should go without saying, or perhaps it needs to be said from time to time, that just because somebody decides that he or she is now on a loftier plane of devotion and no longer needs to hear scriptural advice or the advice of the *guru*—it doesn't mean that one is really on such a level. In fact, if someone's claiming such a thing it is probably more likely the case that he or she is *not* on that level. The role of the *guru* is very important in this kind of thing. The *guru* is the experienced judge of the disciple's advancement. He or she is more objective and more accomplished as well.

You always get into this kind of problem, however, when spontaneity begins to rub up against regimentation. I think that in any religious tradition, as in most any humane activity, this is the case. In writing poetry, for example, you can ruin a good poet by insisting that he follow certain grammatical rules or conventions of metre. On the other hand, you can also waste a good talent if you encourage him to be too careless of these things. So one has to find one's own level and gain a sense of when one is being impeded by or gaining from continued discipline. But it certainly helps to have a good editor to advise you occasionally. In the same way, it certainly helps in spiritual matters to have a competent spiritual advisor to assist you.

This brings us back to something we discussed earlier: that Vaiṣṇava *sādhana* is community-based. It is important that Vaiṣṇavas help and reinforce each other, that they do it together. What we may call the *Saṅkīrtana* principle, shared devotion, association with *guru* and other Vaiṣṇavas, is crucial in developing Vaiṣṇava piety. If this is maintained, it will naturally minimize the likelihood of someone prematurely attempting rāgānugā *sādhana*, or any other devotional practices for which he or she is not ready, or not suited.

SR: *Guru*, *śāstra*, and *sādhu*. If one has a bona-fide teacher, the guidance of the scriptures, and the association of sincere Vaiṣṇavas, it seems that the goal can be readily achieved.

Dr. O'Connell: I should think so!

Personalism vs. Impersonalism

O.B.L. Kapoor

Oudh Bihari Lal Kapoor has served as head of the Philosophy Department and dean of the faculty of arts at B.R. College in Agra, India; as principal and head of the Philosophy Department at K.N. Postgraduate College in Benares; as principal of the Government College in Rampur; and as member of the Executive Council of Agra University. He has been residing in Vṛndāvana since his retirement in 1967 and is engaged at present in writing books, articles, and, currently, a screenplay, concerning the life and teachings of Śrī Caitanya Mahāprabhu. Dr. Kapoor's book,* The Philosophy and Religion of Śrī Caitanya *(Delhi: Munshiram Manoharlal, 1977) is considered an invaluable reference for scholars of Gauḍīya Vaiṣṇavism.

SR: The Gauḍīya Vaiṣṇavas acknowledge both personal and impersonal aspects of the absolute. In fact, their philosophy could, in a sense, be viewed as *transpersonal,* that is to say that it is beyond both personalism and impersonalism. And yet there is a distinct emphasis on the personal nature of the absolute, which is seen as Śrī Kṛṣṇa. Maybe you can discuss these ideas to some degree.

Dr. Kapoor: The Personal Absolute, or *Para-brahman,* enfolds even the the *nirviśeṣa* or formless and attributeless *Brahman.* Everything is included in the complete, absolute personality of God. This is the Gauḍīya view. The rationale behind the Gauḍīya view is that God has the inconceivable power of reconciling the irreconcilable. This enables the absolute to rise above our imperfect and contradictory notions of qualified and unqualified *Brahman* and allows them to be reconciled in a higher synthesis.

Even the concepts of identity and difference are transcended and reconciled in the higher synthesis. Transcendence and immanence are made the associated aspects of an abiding unity in God, or, in other words, in the doctrine of *acintya-bhedābheda,* which is the distinguishing feature of the school of Śrī Caitanya.

SR: I'm still trying to understand just where the impersonal aspect fits in.

Dr. Kapoor: The Nirviśeṣa Brahman, according to Śrī Caitanya, is but an aspect of the absolute, which by its very nature is endlessly qualified and perfect. The concept of the absolute as *merely* impersonal, which is beyond thought and speech, is dismissed by Śrī Caitanya as meaningless. Such an absolute cannot be made the subject of an intelligible proposition. Any intelligible proposition about it would cancel the concept itself. For, even to say that Brahman is inexpressible or unthinkable is to say or think something about it. This is the argument that Jīva Gosvāmī poses in his *Sarva-saṁvādinī,* and it is certainly a powerful one. He points out that the whole proposition is full of inherent contradictions.

SR: I can see that. Yes. And since the absolute is perfectly complete, his essential nature must include all conceptions and aspects of existence: male and female, personal and impersonal—if he were lacking any one of these he would be incomplete.

Dr. Kapoor: Precisely. But let's return to Śrī Jīva's argument. Think about the implications: the Advaitins themselves refer to Brahman by such words as *svaprakāśa,* which means "self-luminous," and *paramārtha-sat,* which means "transcendent reality." The use of these expressions to describe the absolute proves that it is not altogether inexpressible. To press their point, however, they sometimes say that these words only *indirectly* point to the absolute. But it is clear that these words *directly* imply the absolute because they do not have any other meaning outside Brahman and cannot signify anything other than Brahman.

SR: Isn't it true, though, that certain texts seem to affirm that Brahman is unknowable and ineffable?

Dr. Kapoor: There are, no doubt, some Upaniṣadic texts which seem to teach that Brahman is unknowable and inexpressible. But there are also passages which support the opposite view. In the *śruti* texts, for example, we find such expressions as *atha kasmāducyate brahman,* and *tasmāducyate paraṁ-brahman,* which clearly indicate that Brahman is the subject of thought and speech. Even the *Gītā* affirms that Brahman is the highest subject of speech.

SR: The impersonalists argue that the absolute truth must be beyond differentiation. I guess they mean that it is not subject to duality in any form.

Dr. Kapoor: According to the Advaitins, Brahman is a pure identity. It is above the application of all kinds of difference, whether *svajātīya* (which appears between things of the same category), *vijātīya* (which appears between things of different categories), or *svagata* (which manifests itself in one and the same thing, either between its essence and form or between its component parts). It is the absolute denial of the last of these three kinds of difference that makes the Brahman of the Advaitins devoid of all forms and attributes. Śrī Caitanya and his followers also recognize the importance of identity as a fundamental characteristic of reality. But while their denial of the first two kinds of difference is absolute, their denial of the last is not. They are adverse to the concept of the absolute as a pure and undifferentiated being. Their criticism of Nirviśeṣa Brahman bears a close resemblance to that of Rāmānuja, to whom Jīva Gosvāmī frequently refers in his *Saṁdarbhas.*

Having accepted the undifferentiated Brahman as the sole category of existence, the Advaitins fail to give a satisfactory explanation of the world of appearance, which necessarily implies *viśeṣa* or qualities in Brahman. How can a variegated world, with such diverse qualities, come from an undifferentiated Absolute?

SR: [laughter] Well how *do* impersonalists view the world? How do they explain its existence?

Dr. Kapoor: They regard the world as a sort of superimposition (*adhyāsa*), like the superimposition of silver in a conch-shell. But Śrī Jīva argues that there is always some object, or *adhiṣṭhāna,* upon which a superimposition must rest. Since, according to them, nothing exists besides Brahman, the *adhiṣṭhāna* must be Brahman itself. This implies some kind of *viśeṣa,* or quality, in Brahman. For if Brahman did not have this quality, it would not be possible to explain its tendency (*pravṛtti*) toward superimposition.

Again, as Jīva argues, looking at it from a different angle, we may ask, "Does Brahman actually have anything to do with the superimposition?" If not, then *ajñāna*, ignorance, alone explains the superimposition, and the existence of Brahman is ruled out as a gratuitous hypothesis. But if Brahman does indeed have something to do with the superimposition, its *śakti* and attributes follow. The very etymological meaning of the term "Brahman," as explained by *śruti*, shows that *śruti* accepts the *śakti* of Brahman. According to *śruti*, the term "Brahman" implies "greatness" as well as "expansive activity," and Brahman, in respect of its expansive activity, is dynamic and *saviśeṣa*.

SR: I must admit that I've always been uncomfortable with talk of an impersonal absolute. I mean, *I'm* a person. If my source is impersonal, then where do *I* come from and what am *I* in an ultimate sense? Moreover, even if one can have some kind of impersonal experience, such an experience always occurs to a *person*—it's a person who has the "impersonal" experience! In other words, even if you call it impersonal, because it happens to a person it must be considered a variety of personal experience.

Dr. Kapoor: Well said. Therefore we say that Nirviśeṣa Brahman cannot be proved. Firstly it cannot be proved because the object of proof is always *saviśeṣa*. Secondly, because all objects of proof, according to the Advaitins, are perishable. In the absence of proof, the Nirviśeṣa is unreal like the horns of a hare. Nor can it be accepted on the authority of the scriptures, because the scriptures depend on the various forms of speech and Nirviśeṣa Brahman cannot be made an object of speech.

SR: Yes, this sort of *via negativa* philosophy was seen in the Buddhistic thought of Nāgārjuna, the Advaita Vedānta conceptions of Śaṅkarācārya, and the Christian mysticism of Pseudo-Dionysius and Meister Eckhart, among others. I think, in the West, it's being carried on today by Matthew Fox, and even Fritjof Capra and Gary Zukav, to name a few.

The ideas of these philosophers and theologians are alluring, in one sense. Sometimes they take on an external appearance of embracing a *via positiva* sensibility, and their followers accept it as such. But all of these conceptions seem to fall to the wayside when contrasted with the ultra-positive Vaiṣṇava thought—the thought of a personal absolute.

Dr. Kapoor: Yes. The absolute is positive, and since nothing positive is without attributes, the absolute must be *saviśeṣa.* Not only must it be determined by certain qualities or attributes, but just because it is infinite, it must be determined or qualified in endless ways. There should be nothing in which it is wanting. If there is anything that in some form does not belong to it, then in so far as it is lacking in that, it is imperfect and cannot, properly speaking, be called absolute. This means that the absolute must be personal, beginningless, and the origin or the ground of everything else. *Brahma-saṁhitā* (5.1) says: "*īśvaraḥ paramaḥ kṛṣṇaḥ, sac-cid-ānanda-vigrahaḥ, anādir ādir govindaḥ, sarva-kāraṇa-kāraṇam*—Kṛṣṇa, or Govinda, the Supreme Godhead, who has an eternal, blissful, spiritual body, is the prime cause of all causes."

SR: Let me read this statement by Dr. John C. Cotran, who, before he retired, was Professor of Chemistry and the Chairman of the Science and Mathematics Division at the University of Minnesota:

> Chemistry discloses that matter is ceasing to exist, some varieties exceedingly slowly, others exceedingly swiftly. Therefore the existence of matter is not eternal. Consequently, matter must have had a beginning. Evidence from Chemistry and other sciences indicates that this beginning was not slow and gradual; on the contrary it was sudden, and the evidence even indicates the approximate time when it occurred. Thus at some rather definite time the material world was created and ever since has been obeying law, not the dictates of chance. Now, the material realm not being able to create itself and its governing laws, the act of creation must have been performed by some nonmaterial agent. The stupendous marvels accomplished in that act show that this agent must possess superlative intelligence, an attribute of mind. But to bring mind into action in the material realm as, for example, in the practice of medicine and the field of parapsychology, the exercise of will is required, and this can be exerted only by a person. Hence our logical and inescapable conclusion is not only that creation occurred but that it was brought about according to the plan and will of a person endowed with supreme intelligence and knowledge (omniscience), and the power to bring it about and keep it running according to plan (omnipotence) always and everywhere throughout the universe (omnipresence). That is to say, we accept unhesitatingly the fact of the existence of 'the supreme spiritual being, God, the creator and director of the universe'. . .

Dr. Kapoor: We must agree with this conclusion. The impersonalists, however, argue that a qualified and personal absolute must be limited, because to attribute certain qualities to it is to deny certain others, which are opposed to them. But the impersonalists must understand that it is not personification or attribution of character or qualities to the infinite that puts limitation upon it, but determination not carried to the fullest extent. The notion of personality is not only consistent with the infinite but essential to it. "The infinite" in mathematics, as Pringle Pattison points out, means something different than in theology. In mathematics it "means having no limits at all." But if it meant exactly the same thing in theology, no character or qualities could be attributed to God, and we cannot accept that proposition for reasons we have already discussed.

Given the mathematical definition, God would merely be an undifferentiated substance or *tabula rasa*. The Advaitins in fact accept this. But God is certainly not an empty concept. He is not something vague or indefinite, which the mathematical notion of infinitude implies. Instead, he has character, which implies something *definite*, and in this sense he is limited. He is unlimited in the sense that he is immeasurable and there is nothing outside him, whereby he may be limited.

SR: Can you give some early scriptural examples of God as a person with qualities?

Dr. Kapoor: *Chāndogya Upaniṣad* (7.14.4) describes Brahman as *sarvakarmā sarvakāmaḥ sarvagandhaḥ sarvarasaḥ*, which indicates that Brahman is not only qualified, but qualified in endless ways. The *śrutis* frequently describe Brahman as *vijñāna-ghana* and *ānanda-ghana*, as in verse seventy-nine of the *Gopāla Tāpanī Upaniṣad*. In texts such as this, the word "*ghana*" implies that Brahman is knowledge (*vijñāna*) and bliss (*ānanda*) personified. There are innumerable other *ślokas* that support this view.

SR: Then why do the impersonalists support the doctrine of the impersonal Brahman?

Dr. Kapoor: You see, there are also many texts that describe Brahman as unqualified. *Kaṭha Upaniṣad* (1.3.15), for example, describes Brahman as *aśabdam, asparśam, arūpam*, which means that Brahman has neither sound, nor touch, nor form. . . .In the *Bṛhadāraṇyaka Upaniṣad* (1.4.10), Brahman is described as *acakṣuṣkam, aśrotram, avāk, amanaḥ*, etc., which means that Brahman has neither eyes nor ears, nor speech, nor mouth, nor mind.

SR: How do you resolve the contradiction?

Dr. Kapoor: The apparently contradictory statements of the *śāstras* regarding the nature of Brahman are sometimes reconciled by saying that they are not all of equal importance. Those who believe that Brahman is qualified minimize the importance of the texts describing it as unqualified, while those who believe it is unqualified minimize the importance of the texts describing it as qualified. But this undermines the authority of the scriptures. The words of the scriptues must all be considered as equally authoritative.

Sometimes the contradiction is sought to be removed by taking the direct meaning of some of the texts and the indirect meaning of others. According to Śrī Caitanya, the Advaitin view of unqualified Brahman is based mainly on indirect meaning. The indirect meaning of words *(lakṣaṇā vṛtti)* is justified only where the direct meaning (*mukhyā vṛtti*) does not make any sense. Śankara's exclusive emphasis on unqualified Brahman makes him conceal the direct and real meaning of the scriptures, which describe Brahman as qualified.

Jīva Gosvāmī partly resolves the contradiction by showing that the word *nirviśeṣa* is often used by the scriptures to deny all *prākṛta* or worldly qualities of Brahman and not to deny qualities as such. If it were used to deny qualities as such it would not be possible to attribute to Brahman the qualities of *nityatva* (eternity) and *vibhutva* (all-pervasiveness), which are accepted by the Advaitins themselves as the qualities of the absolute. Jīva Gosvāmī also quotes from the *Viṣṇu Purāṇa* to prove that although Brahman does not have any ordinary or worldly qualities, it has infinite transcendental qualities.

SR: Do you mean to say that Śrī Jīva categorically denies the unqualified Brahman?

Dr. Kapoor: No, Jīva denies Brahman as *merely* unqualified. He describes such a Brahman as the subject of predication apart from its predicates, or the substance apart from its attributes. Since the complete (*samyak*) form of an object includes both its substance and attributes, the unqualified Brahman is only an incomplete (*asamyak*) manifestation of the absolute. Jīva insists that the personal Brahman *includes* the impersonal Brahman as the formless lustre of his divine form (*aṅga-kānti*). As the *Gītā* says, "the personal absolute is the basis of the impersonal Brahman—*brahmaṇo hi pratiṣṭhāhaṁ.*"

SR: But is it not natural to revolt against the idea of an absolute that is at once personal and impersonal?

Dr. Kapoor: Our thought revolts because we are inclined to think of the absolute in human terms. But the form of the absolute is different from our own. We have to bear in mind that there is an essential difference between the finite and the infinite and we cannot fetter the infinite with our human thought and terms. When dealing with any problem relating to the infinite, we have to use the laws of our understanding with reservation and with the necessary precaution that they do not impair the perfection of the infinite or impoverish our notion of divinity.

It is the application of the law of contradiction that is mainly responsible for our crippled notion of the infinite. But the infinite, by virtue of its inconceivable potency (*acintya-śakti*), in a sense, transcends even the law of contradiction. The very infinitude of the infinite consists in its transcendence of this law and harmonious blending within itself of contradictory notions or qualities, while the very finitude of the finite consists in its subjection to it. The finite is finite because it is what it is and not its contrary. But the infinite is infinite because there is nothing that does not fall within it. The infinite logically excludes the possibility of the existence of anything other than itself.

SR: But does not such a view give credence to the Advaitin claim that there is nothing except Brahman?

Dr. Kapoor: It does. But the Gauḍīya Vaiṣṇavas interpret this to mean that whatever exists is a manifestation of Brahman and is internally or externally related to it as a manifestation of one of its infinite potencies (*śaktis*). Nothing exists apart from it and independent of it. Any other explanation would lead to absurdities! We are thus constrained to believe that the concepts of infinity and personality are both essential to the real nature of the absolute.

Henry L. Mansel, a nineteenth-century English philosopher who was Professor of Moral and Metaphysical Philosophy at Oxford, expressed the same idea in this way:

> It is our duty, then, to think of God as personal; and it is our duty to believe that He is infinite. It is true that we cannot reconcile these two representations with each other, as our conception of personality involves attributes apparently contradictory to the notion of infinity. But it does not follow that this contradiction

> exists anywhere but in our own minds; it does not follow that it implies any impossibility in the absolute nature of God. The apparent contradiction, in this case, as in those previously noticed, is the necessary consequence of an attempt on the part of the human thinker to transcend the boundaries of his own consciousness. It proves that there are limits to man's power of thought, and it proves no more.

To describe the absolute as merely *nirviśeṣa* or without quality and attributes is to make Him imperfect by amputating, as it were, the auspicious limbs of His divine personality. Once the absolute, complete, and perfect nature of the Divine Being is recognized, the Advaitin philosophy of impersonalism cannot consistently be maintained.

The real purpose of the scriptures is to describe the absolute as both *saviśeṣa* and *nirviśeṣa,* or rather as possessing infinite attributes and forms. When this is properly understood, the conflicting statements of the Vedas and the Purāṇas can easily be reconciled. But according to the primary and general sense of the scriptures, the absolute is essentially *saviśeṣa,* because only in a *saviśeṣa* absolute, possessing infinite and inconceivable potencies, can the infinite forms of Godhead, including the *nirviśeṣa* Brahman, inhere.

Acintya Bhedābheda

Shrivatsa Goswami

Shrivatsa Goswami hails from an ancient priestly family that to this day serves at Gopāla Bhaṭṭa Gosvāmī's famous Rādhā-ramaṇa temple in Vṛndāvana, India. An academician as well as a practitioner, Shrivatsa became renowned in the mid-1970s as a Visiting Scholar at Harvard Divinity School's Center for the Study of World Religions. His mangum opus centers around an elaborate study of Jīva Gosvāmī's Ṣaṭ-sandarbha, *the complex philosophy of which remains his life's work. Among other literary projects, Shrivatsa co-authored, with John Stratton Hawley,* At Play with Krishna: Pilgrimage Dramas from Vrindaban *(Princeton, New Jersey: Princeton University Press, 1981) and authored "Rādhā: The Play and Perfection of Rasa" in* The Divine Consort: Rādhā and the Goddesses of India *(Berkeley: University of California Press, 1982). He is also a member of the Board of Editors for* The Encyclopedia of Indian Philosophies *(General Editor: Karl H. Potter). Shrivatsa is Founder and Director of the Śrī Chaitanya Prema Sansthāna, an academic and cultural institute dedicated to the propagation of Vaiṣṇava philosophy and tradition.*

Shrivatsa Goswami: Are you familiar with the works of S.K. De?

SR: Oh, yes, of course. His research is admirable. He is quite thorough, especially as a historian of the Vaiṣṇava tradition. But his *siddhānta,* his perspective, leaves a great deal to be desired. . .

Shrivatsa Goswami: This is the point. Although he has, to date, given the best survey, or overall information, about the Caitanyaite or Gauḍīya Vaiṣṇava tradition, at least in the English language, he has no Caitanyaite perspective at all. He lacks the eye to see Caitanya.

SR: What would you attribute that to? I mean—he *did* do the research. . .

Shrivatsa Goswami: He was suffering from his own idea of objectivity.

SR: Pseudo objectivity.

Shrivatsa Goswami: [laughter] Well, it was certainly objectivity, of sorts, but it didn't allow him entrance into the spirit of the tradition. One has to know the limitations of such objectivity. Otherwise it is impossible to penetrate the tradition. Consider his approach to *Bhakti-ratnākara*, for example. S.K. De can say little more than "it is a pseudo historical work." Well, it is much more than that. It is an elaborate account of the Caitanyaite tradition in Vraja from sixteenth to seventeenth century. . .

SR: Well, I have to admit that, in my own research of books such as *Bhakti-ratnākara*, *Prema-vilāsa*, *Karṇānanda*, *Narottama-vilāsa*—there *are* historical difficulties. Dates, events—they don't tally. Śrīla Bhaktisiddhānta Sarasvatī Ṭhākura, in the Bengali introduction to the *Bhakti-ratnākara*, also says that the book may not, in all cases, be historically accurate. To some extent, then, De may have a point. How would you explain the historical inconsistencies of such works?

Shrivatsa Goswami: It all depends on how you define history, on your approach to history. You see, Śrī Caitanya gives the key: *acintya bhedābheda*. Yes, this is it—"the inconceivable difference-in-nondifference of reality." Generally, people think that this *acintya bhedābheda* is only applicable to the realms of metaphysics and ontology and so on. But I believe that the true beauty of Indian philosophical systems—especially Śrī Caitanya's *acintya bhedābheda* system—is that it can apply to all dimensions of human experience. If a philosophical system doesn't do that, it is only a partial treatment of reality. And no partial, relative, reality can be accepted as truth in Indian philosophy.

This is the case because, ultimately, philosophy is not just an academic exercise. Nor was it so in the West, at least in early times. It was accepted as the search for reality, or a guideline for living one's life. So Śrī Caitanya's system of philosophy, too, was meant to be implemented, and only by such implementation could one understand, with perspective, all facets of reality, including history. Otherwise, it is quite difficult to accommodate the perceptions of the historians of the Caitanyaite faith.

SR: This is my conclusion, too. It is obvious that for Vaiṣṇava historians—their point of emphasis was different. History, in the West, generally means facts and figures. But, in India, especially in the time of Caitanya Mahāprabhu and his first, second, and third generation followers—the sequence of events were not as important as the *rasa* or feeling conveyed. For Śrī Caitanya's followers, "history" meant pursuing the *bhāva,* the emotion, because if one can follow *that,* he can then truly understand the period—he can *enter into* the period in its truest sense. So these devotional "historians," if they can be called as such, were more concerned with conveying the truth of the period, not with time sequence and external events. This they documented, too, but it was given second place to the more important principle of divine *līlā.* So this is another consideration when we are judging historical accuracy.

Shrivatsa Goswami: Yes. Both are important. But, as you've stated, most important is the totality, the essence. That is *acintya bhedābheda.* You have made the connection. Good. When we are talking about history—how do we decide what is history and what is not history? Obviously when Kṛṣṇadāsa Kavirāja was writing his *Caitanya-caritāmṛta,* for instance, or when any of the other Vaiṣṇava scholars would produce religio-historical treatises, they were certainly aware that they were not writing history or biographies as such. No. They were giving the "nectar" of the history or biography. *Caritāmṛta.* You see?

And this means that what is important in historical processes, from the Vaiṣṇava point of view, from their experience, and their tradition—what they have imbibed, received, from their *gurus* and colleagues—is the essential truth. And they were trying to pass *that* on to us. Actually, it is only from that point of view that the whole Purāṇic tradition—or any tradition—becomes historically meaningful. But especially in the Indian historical tradition there is a tendency to give us the history of ideals. They are not interested in giving minor details. But they are giving the actual substance of a particular historical period and process. So, from that point of view, *Bhakti-ratnākara* is an important text. If *Caitanya-caritāmṛta* is an important text (and De admits that this is the case), then *Bhakti-ratnākara* should be accepted as important, too. And these works give the *siddhānta,* the conclusion.

If you don't have this holistic perspective, you cannot write an accurate historical account, at least from the Vaiṣṇavite point of view. For example, a very good friend and colleague, the late A.L. Basham, gave the world a monumental work—*The Wonder That Was India.* But why does he say "*was*"? He is writing in the twentieth century. And India *was*?! Is there no current reality called India?! He stops his study in the tenth century. India *was.* Not *is.* So, for him, the subject is finished.

SR: Why did he stop at the tenth century? Some of the greatest episodes in Indian history occurred after that time.

Shrivatsa Goswami: That's the whole point. You cannot dispute an historian's choice. And that's where subjectivity comes in. This is where *acintya bhedābheda* talks to us. Subjectivity/objectivity. Whatever the likes of Basham are doing is subjective as well as objective. Objective in the sense that he's trying to be quite accurate, quite faithful, scholarly, comprehensive, in regard to conveying the facts which he has gathered about India in the chosen time period of his study. But why does he stop in tenth-century India? He could have written up to the fifteenth century and described the appearance of Śrī Caitanya, or further. That is his subjectivity. And, materially, you will never see a totally objective piece of writing.

SR: Ideally, it seems that if someone reached a level of pure devotion, they would then have a spiritual, all-inclusive vantage point. They could then find that realm of perception where subjectivity and objectivity coalesce. The absolute platform. This would be the perfect retelling of history. No?

Shrivatsa Goswami: Of course. But in all fairness—what you are talking about does not pertain to the discursive realm. It transcends. We are now talking about the scholastic tradition of *śāstra,* scripture. *Śruti,* divine revelation, is another issue. It is a completely different subject. There we don't need histories. We don't need points-of-view. Of course, this is impractical. We are concerned as people living in *vyavahāra.*

SR: What was that word?

Shrivatsa Goswami: *Vyavahāra.* The mundane realm. The phenomenal world. And then there is the noumenal—the *paraloka, paramārtha.* So you are talking about the perceptions of those on the absolute platform. But we are, no doubt, in the realm of duality. In this realm, we have certain norms to deal with, certain intellectual processes with which to handle our everyday experiences. Here, again, *acintya bhedābheda* applies. We are spiritual beings functioning in a material world. Simultaneously different and nondifferent.

So, coming back to *Caitanya-caritāmṛta*, *Bhakti-ratnākara*, and works of that nature, works from the seventeenth and eighteenth centuries, they are giving both subjective and objective histories together. . .

SR: I see it slightly differently. I see those works as supra-mundane—very much like *śruti.* Supra-subjective and supra-objective. Nondifferent than *śāstra.* They are subjective in the sense that they convey, among other things, the particular *rasa* or mood of the writer and they are objective in that they convey the spiritual truth, in an absolute sense. As far as the historical inconsistensies—this is due to a different set of values, a different point of emphasis. Dates were not considered important. Philosophical conclusions and essential theological truths were considered the important thing.

Shrivatsa Goswami: This is clearly the orthodox view. But, critically, we have to deal with these works in a removed way. Scientifically. In China, for example, history begins with the Long March and ends with Mao. You may say that Confucius and the various ancient traditions should be regarded—but it doesn't apply to normative Chinese history. So who decides? That's the question: who decides? Who decides that you are a pagan? Who decides that you are a heathen? Who decides that you are an infidel? Who decides that you are a rascal? Can I sit in judgment and call other people rascals? Me, never. It is a subjective idea. From the point of view of those I call "rascals," I am absolutely wrong. [laughter]

SR: Well, sometimes a *guru* may call his disciple a "rascal," and they will naturally agree. [laughter] They would normally resolve to correct themselves.

Shrivatsa Goswami: Yes. That is your freedom. You have chosen to be that particular *guru*'s disciple. That is also subjective. And, yet, ideally, he is giving you objective knowledge of the absolute truth. So, you can see that *acintya bhedābheda* applies in every case. You give me any situation: political, historical, religious, devotional, cognitive, and I will immediately demonstrate to you how *acintya bhedābheda* applies and how it gives meaning.

Pure subjectivity will not do, nor will pure objectivity. Because, in the material sphere, these things do not exist in a pure isolated form. They just do not exist. A person on this plane cannot be purely objective, especially. Because this is begging the question. Logically speaking: what is objectivity without subjectivity? Objectivity begs subjectivity to be understood! And vice versa. There are many contradictory concepts that can only be explained by *acintya bhedābheda tattva.*

SR: This seems as though this is an apologetic or a rationale for *acintya bhedābheda.* Although *acintya bhedābheda* can be applied in varied ways and has the widest possible scope, as you have said, it is mainly used to define or characterize Kṛṣṇa and his various energies. It is ultimately quite particular in application: it defines the absolute and the energies of the absolute—their interrelation. But it is true that the principle of *acintya bhedābheda* finds universal application as well, because God, the supreme person, is present everywhere and permeates (in a known or unknown way) all of our experiences. Anyway, if it is *acintya,* inconceivable, how can it be explained in this way? How can it be explained at all?

Shrivatsa Goswami: It was considered inconceivable largely because, for those people, when it was formulated, it was a revolutionary thought. It could not be understood by the traditional methods.

SR: I see this a little differently. According to the original Sanskrit, *acintya* literally means "inconceivable," "incomprehensible, "inscrutable," and perhaps even "unexpected." For example, God and his creation are identical, since the creation emanates from him and not from anyone else. Yet he is also different from all matter, all spirit—he is different from everything that exists—since all the parts that make up the whole are never equal to him. So this is how simultaneous oneness and difference is *acintya,* or inconceivable. It is quite literal.

Shrivatsa Goswami: But for practical understanding, we have to talk rationally. *Acintya bhedābheda* may be inconceivable, but it is not irrational. It is supra-rational. And even then, it is only suprarational on a certain level, to the limited mindset of a particular people—to their standard of rationality.

In this connection, I would like to cite an example from the Western tradition. Aristotle gave us the logic of contradictions. "A" is not "B" and "A" is not "not A." Very simple. Logic of contradictions. And that has governed the whole of Western civilization. Of everything. But to progress they had to wait for Bertrand Russell and Alfred North Whitehead. They taught that true logic is not single-valued logic. It is a fallacy to think that logic is only the logic of contradictions. There can be multi-valued logic. And with Charles Hartshorne it was complete. Hartshorne showed that reality is multi-valued. *Acintya bhedābheda*—he detailed a very similar truth to what was expressed by Śrī Caitanya and Jīva Gosvāmī, but in Western jargon, of course.

The common mind, in this world, is governed by simple-valued, single-valued, logical systems. Even in India. It is not just a Western phenomenon. When Śaṅkarācārya said that reality is epitomized in the truth of "nondifference," *advaita*, then the other extreme automatically followed. If you say "A" is a reality, then someone else will automatically say "not A" is also a reality. And they will have good, well-thought-out reasons, too. [laughter] So immediately Madhva came and he said that duality is the only reality. [laughter]

But both Śaṅkara and Madhva gave simplistic conclusions—single-valued logic. So Śrī Caitanya came and said that both of you are partially correct and partially wrong. Neither of you are absolutely wrong, nor are you absolutely correct. He showed that *acintya bhedābheda* is the ultimate reality. And that had been shown, too, by Vyāsa, in the Purāṇic tradition. Nimbārkācārya had shown that as well. To a limited extent, also, Rāmānuja preached a similar doctrine. Many devotees and scholars were able to perceive this truth, at least to some degree. But Caitanya brought this idea to full fruition. It is beyond all mundane logical systems and it harmonizes them as well. It is supra-rational.

SR: What you're saying is, of course, true. But whenever you say that something is "beyond ordinary logic," you leave yourself open to criticism. People will accuse you of promoting blind faith. This has, in some cases, given *bhakti* a bad name. Antagonists sometimes say that devotees do not use their critical intelligence. Sometimes people accuse devotees of being anti-rational. It becomes especially dangerous if you reject the law of the excluded middle.

We require the law of contradiction to think. If there is some suspension of the standard laws of logic when we talk of *acintya bhedābheda*—some "higher logic"—then there must be very specific circumstances or rules for that suspension. It cannot be suspended in toto, nor can it be suspended arbitrarily, for this would lead to absurdities and the rationalization of sinful life: "sin is simultaneously sinful and not sinful!!!" I can hear it now. . . .You know, because of this some people define *bhakti* as "blind emotionalism."

Shrivatsa Goswami: [laughter] Therefore, one must be thoroughly trained in Vedic theology. If you look at the work of the Six Gosvāmīs, you will see living proof of six lives dedicated to intellectual work of the highest order. So the claim of blind emotionalism is unfounded. The Gosvāmīs, just those initial six, produced some sixty-seven volumes on every possible branch of Sanskrit scholarship, containing the most profound philosophy. Many other Vaiṣṇava teachers, after them, wrote many hundreds of other treatises as well. No. It is not the work of fanatic sentimentalists. Hardly. [laughter] It is the work of genuinely open, critical intellect, the likes of which are rare in this world.

But the real intellectuals are generally suppressed. They are accused of being religious fanatics or so many things. Who decides? Who is the fanatic and who is making a substantial contribution to humanity? Power and politics decide. And in the wrong hands, power and politics are dangerous. In the right hands, they are an asset. This is another dimension of *acintya bhedābheda-vāda.* The same phenomenon is either negative or positive, depending on how it is used. Caitanya Mahāprabhu was aware of this. He also used power and politics to spread the truths of his faith.

SR: How so?

Shrivatsa Goswami: Whatever organizational work he did—he took into account the politics of the time. It was brilliant. He utilized "power" for his own spiritual ends. For example, consider his selection of the Six Gosvāmīs. What was the deciding factor? Why were they considered his most prominent successors? Even Nityānanda Prabhu, ultimately, did not have the power and the authority that was given to these six, because they were the codifiers and formulators of Śrī Caitanya's doctrine. Why? They are considered more instrumental in spreading the message, more than Advaitācārya or Svarūpa Dāmodara. More than Rāmānanda Rāya. Why? They were given a prominent place even above Prabodhānanda Sarasvatī, a well-known *tridaṇḍī sannyāsī* and the author of many theological works. So, why were the Six Gosvāmīs given this special place? Can you follow?

Among other theological reasons, the answer can be found when we analyze the importance of power and politics. Śrī Caitanya knew of Prabodhānanda Sarasvatī's greatness. But Prabodhānanda was a simple *sannyāsī*. How would he ever manage a movement? It was not possible. So Śrī Caitanya chose those who were materially powerful—who were qualified for the project of resurrecting Vṛndāvana. They had the spiritual qualifications, too, no doubt, but Mahāprabhu did not underestimate the importance of power and politics.

If you look at Rūpa and Sanātana—they were from prestigious Karṇāṭaka *brāhmaṇa* stock. Their ancestry was royal. They were also known as powerful ministers in the Islamic government of the time. So, from two sides, they would be respected and followed by the masses. They were men of power. Ministers under the king Hussain Shah of sixteenth century Bengal. Their knowledge of power machinery was utilized by Śrī Caitanya. Jīva Gosvāmī, too, was from the same family. Now. Who was Gopāla Bhaṭṭa?

SR: He was from an important South Indian family.

Shrivatsa Goswami: Precisely. He was the *only* son of the *chief* priest of the *most powerful* Śrī Vaiṣṇava center. Power. Pure power. Money. Prestige. Scholarship. All forms of power. Prabodhānanda may have been a greater scholar, and he was from the same family as Gopāla Bhaṭṭa. But he was a mendicant. So Mahāprabhu did not choose him to be a leader.

Next was Raghunātha Bhaṭṭa Gosvāmī. He was nearer to the power center than any of the four Gosvāmīs I have already mentioned. He was *guru* of the Amber kings. . .

SR: Like Man Singh. . .

Shrivatsa Goswami: Yes, of course. Because he was living in Benares—a big spiritual center of the time. These kings built temples because of him, because of Raghunātha Bhaṭṭa, in Benares and, yes, Rūpa Gosvāmī's Govindajī temple was built under the guidance of Raghunātha Bhaṭṭa—he was so powerful. He had men, money—power. Benares was the power center. And Raghunātha Bhaṭṭa's father, Tāpana Miśra, was the big *guru* there. This was Śrī Caitanya's plan in sending Tāpana Miśra to Benares early on.

And then there was Raghunātha dāsa. He was filthy rich, if I may use slightly blasphemous language. A multi-millionaire. And he was a *kāyastha*—not even a *brāhmaṇa*! Śrī Caitanya didn't care about such things.

But Raghunātha was rich and enthusiastic. This was the thing. Rich—like some New York Jewish banker! [laughter] Mahāprabhu utilized the previous material assets of his most enthusiastic followers. This, of course, was also attempted by Bhaktivedanta Swami Prabhupāda. [laughter] So the method has seen a modicum of success.

SR: Nonetheless, the achievements of the Six Gosvāmīs, as scholars and as genuine *sādhus*, were considerable—glorious!

Shrivatsa Goswami: This is my point. You can't say that power and politics are necessarily a bad thing. It depends on their utilization in the service of Kṛṣṇa-*premā*. This is Śrī Caitanya's teaching. You see, we are suffering from an ill-conceived Western notion. Aristotle gave us the wrong idea: that reality can be compartmentalized. "This is chemistry. This is physics. This is mathematics. This is philosophy. This is logic. This is religion." But reality doesn't work in that way. Concepts overlap. Reality doesn't fit into neat categories. It is expansive, vibrant, alive. So, the human experience is holistic—everything is interdependent and included. As soon as you say one thing is all bad, or another thing is all good, you are talking in contradictions. Drawing artificial parameters. So this is resolved with *acintya bhedābheda*, how everything is different and nondifferent. In seedlike form, this is Śrī Caitanya's philosophy about the nature of reality.

SR: How do you see Śrī Caitanya's teachings coming down to contemporary society? What is the application of *acintya bhedābheda* today? This is a question, of course, with which modern devotees need to contend. ISKCON, for one, is trying to apply this philosophy on Western shores, which is no easy task. Do you think it is going on properly? What advice would you give?

Shrivatsa Goswami: I think that there is tremendous potential. Not that I am part of Prabhupāda's movement, although I am also a Caitanyaite. But, as a somewhat removed student of religious history, I can only admire the achievements and progress that this movement has made. In fact, this might surprise the casual observer, but I think that Prabhupāda's movement has greater strength and hope than ever before.

SR: That's interesting. I agree with you, but given the problems ISKCON has gone through, I wonder how it is that you have come to these conclusions. Why do *you* say that?

Shrivatsa Goswami: I know that ISKCON has had its problems—politically, spiritually. But I am quite impressed at the maturity the devotees have shown in dealing with these problems. Actually, problems are inevitable. Such is life in this material world. But Prabhupāda has taught his followers well, and the proof is *how they deal with their problems.* ISKCON has come of age. Matured. It shows tremendous signs of maturity. Because, as I mentioned to Śubhānanda dāsa, and as it was recorded in his book, *Hare Krishna, Hare Krishna* (New York: Grove Press, 1983), the real strength and glory of the movement lies in anonymous, obscure yet sincere devotees. It does not lie in temples, in distributing eighty million *Gītās,* in a huge bank balance, or in any of those things. Again, those things are laudable, when used properly. But the real strength and glory lies in just five or ten sincere—if also obscure—devotees. And ISKCON has many of them. The big people will come and go. But a sincere, simple heart will always be there, will always be ready to worship Kṛṣṇa with love and devotion. And that's what keeps the movement alive.

SR: Thank you.

Shrivatsa Goswami: Hare Kṛṣṇa! Jai Śrī Rādhe!

Sonic Theology

Guy Beck

Guy L. Beck's Ph.D. thesis, **Sonic Theology: Hinduism and the Soteriological Function of Sacred Sound,** ***explored the subject of sound in the various Indian philosophical schools, including the Gauḍīya tradition. This groundbreaking work will soon be published by University of South Carolina Press. Dr. Beck writes for numerous academic journals and currently teaches Introduction to Religion, Eastern Religions, Mysticism, and Hinduism at Louisiana State University.***

SR: I like the title of your Ph.D. dissertation, which is "Sonic Theology: Hinduism and the Soteriological Function of Sacred Sound." This sort of sums up the central point of Gauḍīya Vaiṣṇava philosophy—to develop love for Kṛṣṇa, or God, by chanting his holy name. *Japa* (quiet chanting) or *kīrtana* (loud chanting) or *saṅkīrtana* (group chanting)—this is really the heart of the Gauḍīya tradition. And to engage in this activity is the natural, healthy state of the living entity. Hence: "soteriological." I like it!

Dr. Beck: Thank you. What I've done so far is to study Vedic and Hindu theology in terms of sacred sound, and I'm grateful that you appreciate my work. But please don't misunderstand my use of the term "soteriological." It refers to healing and the healthy state of the living being, yes, but I'm using it in a more theological sense—it's more saving, salvific.

SR: Perhaps that's how we should begin this discussion—let's talk about how sound can have a salvific effect.

Dr. Beck: Good. Yes, because that's the intention here. We say that sacred sound not only heals material woes, but in fact it elevates the consciousness, elevates the soul, or elevates the being of someone and places him back in context with Brahman. However you define it—this is the purpose of the *Śabda Brahman*, or the spiritual sound vibration.

Now, the word *śabda* normally has two divisions: unlettered sound or *dhvani*, and lettered sound or *varṇa*. I think we need not get that technical here, but we should at least understand that the Vedic concept of sound is very developed.

SR: So, in the Gauḍīya tradition, the *Śabda Brahman*, the spiritual sound, brings one back in contact with the ultimate spiritual reality, which is seen as Kṛṣṇa.

Dr. Beck: Precisely. Brahman is Kṛṣṇa or Nārāyaṇa for the Vaiṣṇava Vedāntists. So the sound is transmuted through *dīkṣā* by the *guru* and then it is practiced by the disciple either through *mantra* repetition or recitation. And this way the whole soteriological theory takes effect.

Now in the Sanskrit grammatical tradition, there is something you might find interesting—the view that grammar is soteriological. The tradition teaches that if you polish your speech into perfect grammar, then you will elevate yourself to Brahman.

SR: That's interesting.

Dr. Beck: Yes. Grammar is not simply a pedagogical discipline, but it has a salvific dimension for the grammarian or for the one who learns the art of doing it properly.

SR: Interesting. You know, I think that the power of sound is highly underestimated. If you look carefully you can see the slightly disguised potency of sound in most areas of everyday existence. It can be seen in very mundane things, like advertising or politics—the world is controlled by sound, radio waves, TV, and we are totally manipulated by it. In most areas of life, it seems, you can more effectively get what you want if you choose your words properly.

Dr. Beck: Yes. That's all in the same utterance, performative utterance—when you speak, the thing occurs. In this work I tried to articulate, or flesh out, some of the issues which in fact occur when one looks at sacred sound—beginning from the Vedas through the Upaniṣads—and how it branches off in different schools of thought regarding the efficacy of sound, particularly as *mantra.*

Whether the *mantra* is simply a device to get you to a reality that is beyond sound (which for Advaita Vedānta is exactly what it means), or is something to connect you with the reality which is supersonic, God, through the amplified sound. It seems that the Gauḍīya Vaiṣṇava tradition would fall into the latter category, strictly into that category.

SR: Let's backtrack a little. Maybe you could talk about the Vedic roots of all this.

Dr. Beck: Recently, I've been looking at some of the texts which focus on the theory of sound and its manifestation or its personification as the goddess of speech, who is known as Vāk. And there are a number of hymns either mentioning Vāk, or directly centered on this goddess.

She takes on the form of someone who is related to Indra, but she's also the mother of the Vedas—the female potency behind the creation and manifestation of language. There's a hymn in the first book of the *Ṛg Veda,* hymn 164, and there's one in the tenth book of the same Veda, hymn 125, which is a hymn by Vāk herself. She proclaims herself as the female potency and the mother of the Vedas, etc. In this way, it sort of takes shape in the early part of the Vedic period. Gradually, Vāk becomes Brahman, by the time of the Upaniṣads.

SR: Now you're saying v-ā-k; is it v-ā-k or v-ā-c?

Dr. Beck: Well, "vāc" is the word as it stands itself, but very often the "c" is replaced by a "k" when it's in conjunction with other words. So, depending on which translation or edition you're looking at, it can either be "vāc" or "vāk," but it's the same word.

SR: Okay. So, you were saying. . .

Dr. Beck: One of the texts, the first one I mentioned, talks about sacred sounds having four parts, and three of those parts are hidden. The fourth part is the part that we hear in the world, and the other parts are hidden—they're the spiritual aspect, or, let's say, they're the unmanifest aspect of the sacred sound.

SR: I find that to be a fascinating subject. Many people will not even acknowledge the possibility of unexplored categories of sound. But for those with an open mind, even modern scientists have uncovered areas of sonic vibration to which few people gain access. I've done a little research in this area. Humans are sensitive only to sound waves of about 1,000 to 4,000 cycles per second (cps). Dogs and cats can hear up to 60,000 cps, and other creatures, like dolphins, can emit and receive sounds well over 100,000 cps. So there are known portions of the vibratory spectrum that humans cannot commonly penetrate. A natural series of questions arise: what about other dimensions of sound that we can't even imagine? And are we hearing all aspects of the sounds we do hear?

Dr. Beck: Exactly. Now, it is this unmanifest dimension that the *ṛṣis*, or the sages, have been able to tap into—the hidden areas of sound. The goddess of speech has priority or propriety over these aspects, but there are other aspects, too, like the phonetics and the meter, the metrical element in Vedic sound, which has a tremendously religious dimension in the sense that the pronunciation is of the utmost importance in manifesting the unmanifest.

Secondly, the metrical structure of the *mantras* has to be according to a variety of meters, the shortest one being the *gāyatrī* meter. Not the Gāyatrī *mantra* itself, but there's a meter of the *gāyatrī*—twenty-four syllables (three lines of eight syllables each)—and then it increases throughout the Vedic period. It increases up to over one hundred different types of meters. The most common one which we know in the later Purāṇas and the *Bhagavad-gītā* is the *anuṣṭup* meter.

SR: The familiar one. . .

Dr. Beck: Yes. That consists of four lines with eight syllables per line—thirty-two syllables. That's only one of nearly a hundred different meters you'll find throughout the Vedas. For some reason, that meter became standardized for recitation of the Mahābhārata, the Purāṇas, the Rāmāyaṇa, *Bhagavad-gītā.*

Now, going back to the Vedic period, we have in the metrical tradition a phenomenon that is called *chanda,* or meter in the Veda. It's often connected with the power of the *mantra,* and so a *mantra* of a particular meter would have a certain degree or certain manner of power associated with it. Other meters would be the *triṣṭup*, the *jagatī*, and they are also connected with different gods of the Vedic period, in terms of the Prajāpati. . . .You know, Indra, Agni. Agni's associated with a certain meter. It becomes fairly complex once you look at the texture of the *mantras* and how they're all structured and analyzed according to the different gods and different potencies.

And one interesting thing that you see at the time of the *Brāhmaṇas*, for instance, that portion of the Vedic literature known as the *Brāhmaṇas*, is that somehow the masculine aspects get polarized in Prajāpati, and the female aspects of the different *mantra* potencies are polarized into this mother/goddess figure, which then becomes more pronounced. And she ultimately becomes the wife of Prajāpati, and you have a genderization of male and female.

SR: That's interesting.

Dr. Beck: It sort of climaxes in the *Brāhmaṇa* literature. By the time of the Upaniṣads, at least, the personifying elements sort of recede to the background, and you just have this notion of Brahman—the all pervasive spiritual absolute—which is articulated more in the Upaniṣads. Although it's hinted at in the Vedas, it's not philosophized or developed into any kind of systematic theology. With the Upaniṣads you've got Brahman (especially in the *Chāndogya Upaniṣad*)—you've got Brahman equals Om, or the sacred syllable, and the *Udgītha*, which is the sound, song, melodious utterance of the Veda.

SR: Now, there are some related subjects we can discuss, and these, in turn, may lead us into the area of sacred sound in the Vaiṣṇava tradition. For example, what is *nāda*? In my studies I've come across that word quite a bit. "*Nāda*" and "*sphoṭa*."

Dr. Beck: Right. I might mention that there's no reference to *nāda* in the classical Upaniṣads. These are terms which have a different source than the Vedas directly. *Nāda* originates in phonetic texts, where it appears only as a word that signifies audible sounds, sounds of a vocal nature. But *nāda* has a metaphysical dimension in the Āgamas. Are you familiar with the Āgama literature?

SR: The various *Tantra* literature. Yes. I think there are about 108

Vaiṣṇava āgamas, or *saṁhitās,* although āgamas, per se, are often associated with Śaivite texts. Āgamas usually prescribe particular disciplines and guidelines for lifestyle—they are a sort of *sādhana* literature. . .

Dr. Beck: Precisely. *Āgamas* are a large collection of texts dealing with the earliest layer of theistic worship and temple rituals—how to conduct them. Now, there's an argument going on whether they originated in South India or North India, and, in one sense, that's a moot point. Today, there's even a large collection of them in Pondicherry at a French institute. Whatever the case may be, āgama literature seems to reflect a very ancient civilization—either devoted to Śiva or Viṣṇu. Some have argued that they are as old or older than the Vedas. Researchers say that they're a different substratum, a different source, than the Vedas, and they merged with the Vedas to become Hinduism.

So these texts, quite a lot of them, mention *nāda* and even *bindu,* meaning the "seed." I'll develop that further, because in the early *Yoga* texts you also have mention of *nāda.* And with the grammarians, from which the *sphoṭa* doctrine developed, they come together.

SR: What exactly does "*sphoṭa*" mean?

Dr. Beck: *Sphoṭa* is the aspect of the inner consciousness that is awakened when one reads a sentence or hears a *mantra* being chanted. It's something greater than the sum total of all the parts, or the syllables, of the *mantra,* and which is latent within human consciousness. They're flashes, of sorts, which open up inside the mind, kind of like the "light bulb" effect when someone understands something.

SR: *Mantra* means "mind release." Is it connected?

Dr. Beck: Oh, yes. Right. *Sphoṭa* is more of a philosophical idea, though. Let's say I read a verse from a text—from the *Gītā* or something—and suddenly something flashes inside of me: "Oh! I know the meaning!" or "I apprehend what they're saying." It has nothing to do with any of the particular words, as such, but it's something over and above the words which awakens a burst of insight or inspiration. Incidentally, *sphoṭa* literally means "a bursting."

Extending it further, the theorists, at least the grammarians, including, especially, Bhartṛhari, developed the idea that the *sphoṭa* is latent in human consciousness and it just needs to be awakened—the dust needs to be wiped away by constant recitation. So the theory of *mantra* is, at least theoretically, in many respects, related to *sphoṭa* doctrine. The way that repetition of *mantras* is supposed to reawaken one's sense of *bhakti*, or, for the Vedāntins, to give a flash of the *ātman* or Brahman, so also does the *sphoṭa* reawaken in one's consciousness.

Now I came across some problems. It's not all a neat and tidy system. Because you also have another school called the Mīmāṁsā school. That's a school of Vedic exegesis, Vedic interpretation. You might even call it a sort of fundamentalism, in the sense that it promotes strict adherence to the Vedas as being the eternal uncreated Word. And the reason they pose a problem, in a way, is that they argue as follows: they say that there is no such thing as the *sphoṭa* inside the human being—that everything is only in the Vedas. And when one hears a Vedic *mantra*, for example, one is understanding something that's directly caused by Vedic syllables. You're receiving impressions from the text—it's nothing that is already inherent in your consciousness.

So these two schools—the people who promote the *sphoṭa* doctrine and the Mīmāṁsās—have divergent points of view. And they've been at each other's throats for the last 1,500 years—but that's Indian philosophy.

SR: Of those two perspectives, which position would the Gauḍīyas take?

Dr. Beck: That's a very interesting question, because, as it turns out, Jīva Gosvāmī denounces the *sphoṭa* doctrine in one passage of his *Sandarbhas*. Now, that surprises me because it sounds like Jīva was just repeating what Śaṅkara had said. Śaṅkarācārya also denounced the *sphoṭa* doctrine in the same way.

SR: Where does Jīva Gosvāmī do that—where does he denounce it?

Dr. Beck: It's in the *Tattva Sandarbha*. He denounces it and he quotes Śaṅkara, who refutes it in his commentary on the *Brahma Sūtra*. Jīva uses that same passage and same reason, being that there's no independent entity over and above the words of a given text. The text itself is numinous.

It's interesting because although the *sphoṭa* offers a very convenient way of explaining *mantras*, it has been rejected by most of the traditions in India. Advaita Vedānta denounces it along with the Mīmāṁsās.

SR: And, apparently, including the Gauḍīyas.

Dr. Beck: Yes, including Vaiṣṇavism, Śaivism, the theistic traditions. Sāṅkhya philosophy. The only school that doesn't reject it is the *Yoga* school, particularly the minor commentaries on the *Yoga sūtra.*

SR: Is there any place in the Gauḍīya tradition where it is accepted?

Dr. Beck: There is some evidence that Bhaktisiddhānta Sarasvatī Ṭhākura published something, and in that work he attempted to close the gap or reconcile the *sphoṭa* idea with traditional *mantra* understanding. Apparently, he gave a lecture to this effect and it was transcribed and published in the *Gauḍīya Darśana.* He forcefully presented the point that the ultimate referent and nature of *sphoṭa* is God or Kṛṣṇa. This was later elaborated upon by one of Bhaktisiddhānta's disciples, Śrīmad Bhakti-vilāsa Bhāratī Mahārāja, in a Bengali work entitled, *Sphoṭa-vāda Vicara.* This information was brought to my attention by Gauḍīya historian Paul Sherbow.

As a side line, you know, there's also something called *nāda sphoṭa.* And this could easily be accepted by many of the schools we've just discussed. Very often you wonder, "Well, are a lot of these commentators familiar with all of the issues, or are they just repeating a line of argument that they've inherited from their teachers, etc."

SR: Right. Well, there's something to be said for absorbing the existing traditions. Abiding traditions continue to exist for a reason. . . .How would you summarize the different positions or points of view?

Dr. Beck: The fundamental premise of most of these doctrines is that sound or language equals consciousness. Consequently, it is understood, on the one hand, that human consciousness is latently sonic, whereas, on the other hand, the Mīmāṁsā school offers the more orthodox position that the syllable is potent in itself, and that this is the main center of attention—it's more traditionally Vedic. From the perspective of the *sphoṭa* doctrine, however, the sentence is the center. I think that's why it has been neglected—because in most *mantra* theory, in terms of Vaiṣṇavism, especially, they focus on the syllable as carrying impressions and by the repetition of the syllable, something is generated in the consciousness—whether it be *bhakti,* feelings of surrender, or piety, that's another question. Something is created in the mind; it's not awakening something that's there already. These are subtle distinctions. It touches on a very sensitive issue.

SR: This *is* a very subtle subject, and, I think, there's validity on all sides. In one sense, the *mantra* creates or triggers an inspirational realization; on the other hand, the realization is innate. It is something that already exists in the soul.

Dr. Beck: Well, some people do theorize like that. And it certainly has its strengths. As I said, there was an attempt to harmonize these concepts by Bhaktisiddhānta. Moreover, it can be taken further. The Mīmāṁsās, for example, say that the word is identical with the thing that it refers to, and this goes back to the early Vedic orthodoxy—when you pronounce a word, it is non-different from the thing that you are pronouncing. Like the name "fire." You say the name, "*agni*," and, in a sense, that *is* agni, especially if you know the proper *mantras* and have sufficient metaphysical know-how.

So, for the Mīmāṁsās, there is an eternal connection between the word and something out there in the universe which you manipulate through ritual and through proper pronunciation. This, by the way, is how they brought down the rain and did all those mystical things that occurred in Vedic times. By sharp contrast, in the *sphoṭa* doctrine, there is no such implicit connection between the word and the thing it represents, at least not in the same way. The word and the idea of the thing are connected.

SR: I see. But I'm curious about how all of this information was used by the early Gauḍīyas Vaiṣṇavas. How did they resolve these subtle conficts?

Dr. Beck: By the time of Caitanya—particularly his disciples, the *ācāryas*—you have two lines of argument reflecting this notion of *mantra*. And this is what they had to deal with in putting together a coherent philosophy—which was done quite successfully by Jīva Gosvāmī. Now in terms of the *Pāñcarātra* tradition, which is frequently quoted by Rūpa Gosvāmī, particularly in the *Bhakti-rasāmṛta-sindhu*, there's a great deal to say about all of this.

The *Pāñcarātra* are the ritual texts of the Rāmānuja *sampradāya* in South India, and there are at least 108 *Pāñcarātras*. Only a few of them have been translated. You may be familiar with some of the titles—*Parama Saṁhitā*, *Īśvara Saṁhitā*—and they all deal with Viṣṇu worship.

SR: Is the *Nārada Pāñcarātra* actually a *Pāñcarātra*?

Dr. Beck: There's one that is said to be; and that's one that Rūpa quotes. I did a little digging on that, and the verses that he quotes are not included in the published *Nārada Pāñcarātra*, the one that has been available for about one hundred years in Bengal. It's a different one. So I sort of came up against a dead end. Rūpa does quote from a *Nārada Pāñcarātra*, though, whatever that may be, and a number of other *Pāñcarātras*, too. There's no doubt that he was familiar with the tradition and felt it to be authentic. And it is a Vaiṣṇava ritual tradition of Nārāyaṇa worship, preferred over Kṛṣṇa. And Rāmānuja rejected the *sphoṭa* doctrine. Madhva made a comment against it as well.

SR: *Sphoṭa*, in its orthodox form, really seems to be rejected across the board.

Dr. Beck: Very few schools accept it in toto. Let me quote you something that's stated in the *Dvaita* school, or the Madhva school. "Madhva, in consonance with Rāmānuja and the *Pāñcarātra* texts, appears to have refuted the tradition of *sphoṭa-vāda*. The phonemes and the *varṇas* [meaning the syllables] are eternal and all-pervasive substances, according to Madhva. Though eternal they manifest themselves in primary sounds which are non-eternal. As soon as they reach the sense of hearing, they remind the hearer of the corresponding syllables or *varṇas*. The only type of order that the followers of Madhva recognized as the *varṇas* was the order imposed by the speaker, or the hearer. No other order is possible. According to Madhva there is no separate sentence meaning apart from the words as they are put together. [This is where the issue comes in.] Madhva criticized the *sphoṭa* doctrine on the grounds that there was no separate sentence apart from word sense and words denote their own sense as well as their syntactical relation. Language for Madhva is an eternal substance only because it is made up of separate syllables. And for the *sphoṭa* theorists, they would say that language exists within the mind in an ultimate sense, or that it is epitomized by the syllable *'om,'* which is latent within, and of course you find that in the *Yoga Sūtra*." So there are really some serious issues that must be dealt with, and I think they are unfortunately sort of glossed over too quickly. And Nimbārka—though he doesn't talk much about it—generally subscribes to that same line of thinking as the other Vaiṣṇava *sampradāyas*.

Now this all leads to the theologians around Caitanya, his followers, who developed the elaborate *mantra* theory of Gauḍīya Vaiṣṇavism. One professor had emphasized the "tantric" character of this aspect of Gauḍīya Vaiṣṇavism. By "tantric" he means the very broadly defined way of simply being ritualistic, or having a basis in the *Pāñcarātra* system. Not tantric in the pejorative sense. Because, as you know, there is a text called the *Gautamīya Tantra,* for example, which is used by the *ācāryas* and is in fact accepted as authentic revelation.

All right. Let me read this to you. It's from the prominent Bengali scholar Govinda Gopāla Mukhopādhyāya: "It must be remembered that the Vaiṣṇava cult, which stems from the *Pāñcarātra* system is, in its origin, tantric. The Bengal variety of Vaiṣṇavism is predominantly *śākta* in character, in view of its emphasis on elaboration of the worship of Rādhā. Even Śrī Caitanya, the founder of Gauḍīya Vaiṣṇavism, is looked upon as embodying in Himself the spirit of Rādhā. . ."

SR: I recognize that quote from your dissertation.

Dr. Beck: That's one that I pulled out. Right. Because the point I want to make is this: *tantra* often implies the genderization of the tradition, where you've got male and female, Śaktimān and Śakti—the potent and the potency—and that's really an important part of the tradition. Even Bhaktivinoda Ṭhākura writes of the *svarūpa śakti,* where you've got *hlādinī śakti*—the inner potencies, which would be the female dimension, and the energy—the energy and the energizer.

SR: This could bring us into a whole discussion about the *mahā-mantra.*

Dr. Beck: Right. It's all tied in. There's definitely something going on there between the, well, first, the gender, but then the *nāda* and the *bindu,* which are also genderized. *Nāda* correlates to the female dimension generally; *bindu,* then, is said to be the seed—masculine.

To connect it all, "Hari" is, of course, the energy of Kṛṣṇa and Rāma—Mother Harā. In this way, Gauḍīya Vaiṣṇavism has incorporated some of the seed syllables which we often associate with *tantra.* But it just broadens the definition. It doesn't mean that Vaiṣṇavism is indebted to Śaiva or Śākta types of worship; it just means that they all have family resemblances.

SR: So you have Pārvatī and Śiva, but you also have Lakṣmī-Nārāyaṇa, Sītā-Rāma, Rādhā-Kṛṣṇa. Yes. So the *mahā-mantra*—Hare Kṛṣṇa, Hare Kṛṣṇa, Kṛṣṇa Kṛṣṇa, Hare Hare/Hare Rāma, Hare Rāma, Rāma Rāma, Hare Hare—fits right in with earlier concepts of *tantra,* genderization and sound. Good. This, as you know, is the "great *mantra* for deliverance"—therefore it's called the *mahā,* or "great," *mantra.* Practitioners translate it like this: "Oh Lord! Oh Divine energy of the Lord (known as Harā, which is name for Śrī Rādhā, literally referring to 'the one who steals Krsna's heart')! Please engage me in your service." Pure. It asks for nothing in return.

Dr. Beck: This is extremely important for the tradition, and that's why you have millions of Gauḍīyas—not just Gauḍīyas but many branches of Vaiṣṇavas!—chanting it as their central *mantra.* But let's backtrack for a moment. We were talking about genderization and the seed sound. There is the syllable in the *kāma-bīja*—or the "*klīṁ*" syllable, which is the *kāma-bīja* of Kṛṣṇa. This is important when discussing the science of sound in the Hindu tradition.

SR: Gāyatrī.

Dr. Beck: Right, and then there's one for Rādhā—"*hrīṁ*"—which was used in some of the śākta traditions—the Śrī Vidyā śāktas. Then, in the *Hari-bhakti-vilāsa* there is more of a description of this *bīja*—the *klīṁ bīja.*

SR: k-r-i-m?

Dr. Beck: No! k-*l*-i-m. "kr" is Kālī. [laughter] You see, it's such an exacting science. And if you mispronounce the seed-*mantra,* you can be calling upon the wrong deity.

SR: I thought you used k-r-i-m for Rādhā.

Dr. Beck: Rādhā is "h-r-" or sometimes it's used for Lakṣmī. This is the tantric science of sound. Ed Dimock summarizes this nicely in his *Hidden Moon.* He basically says that *the bīja* has five letters KA, LA, I, M, and the sign of nasalization, which is the *bindu.* And they correspond to the five elements in the visible world: KA is the earth, LA the water, I the fire, M (or *nāda*) the wind, and the sky is represented by the *bindu.*

SR: I believe, too, that Dimock gives the corresponding spiritual levels: KA is Kṛṣṇa, LA is Rādhā, I is bliss, M is Rūpa and *bindu* is Vṛndāvana.

Dr. Beck: Right. Right. There are so many correlations—because sound pervades all of existence. And these seed-sounds are developed into very powerful *mantras*. Such Vaiṣṇava *mantras* can be found In the *Gopāla Tāpanī Upaniṣad*, which contains the Kṛṣṇa *mantra, klīṁ kṛṣṇāya govindāya gopījana-vallabhāya svāhā*, and this is a very important Gauḍīya *mantra*. It means "I offer oblations to Kṛṣṇa, who is Govinda, the beloved of the *gopīs*, the cowherd maidens." The *gopīs* are the most intimate associates of Kṛṣṇa, and so this *mantra* takes on profound implications.

Baladeva Vidyābhūṣaṇa, an eighteenth-century Gauḍīya saint and scholar, elucidated the importance of this *mantra* for the tradition: "Reciting this *mantra* of five words on the five parts of the body, namely, (1) the heart, (2) the head, (3) the *śikhā*, or tuft of hair, (4) the breast, and (5) the hands with the five elements heaven, earth, the sun, moon and fire, one assuming these forms attains Brahman, verily he attains Brahman!"

This same Kṛṣṇa *mantra* is also in the *Nārada Pāñcarātra*—the one which is available. And it's in some of the other *Pāñcarātra* texts. There's a Gopāla *mantra*, or I should say that this is what the Kṛṣṇa *mantra* is usually called. You know, it's also found in the *Hari-bhakti-vilāsa*.

SR: Oh, that brings something to mind. Let me interrupt for just a second. In going through Śrī Caitanya Mahāprabhu's biographies, it says that he's initiated into the ten-syllable *Gopāla mantra*. And I was wondering about that. You know, we hear so much about how Mahāprabhu emphasized the chanting of the Hare Kṛṣṇa *mahā-mantra*, and yet if you read about his initiation you find that he was initiated into the ten-syllable Gopāla *mantra*. So that would be very important to discuss.

Dr. Beck: Now the eighteen letter *mantra* is the "*klīṁ kṛṣṇāya govindāya gopījana-vallabhāya svāhā*." The ten syllable one is—a good question. [laughter]

SR: I always thought it was *gopījana-vallabhāya svāhā*. But it's not explicitly stated in the text.

Dr. Beck: That's it! The ten syllable. Cut in half. I remember that.

SR: Right.

Dr. Beck: That's what I would say. There's also something called the Siddha Gopāla *mantra*, which has an additional tantric syllable, like "*om śrīm*." That would be in *Pāñcarātra*. In the *Sāṇḍīlya Saṁhitā*, perhaps, which brings to mind another *mantra,* eighteen syllable. Baladeva Vidyābhūṣaṇa talks about it.

SR: If we can move away from these various *mantras* for a moment, I would like to discuss the *Kālī Santāraṇa Upaniṣad.* It's quite an interesting book. As you know, it's one of the main textual sources, perhaps an early source, for the Hare Kṛṣṇa *mahā-mantra.*

Now, in your dissertation, you mentioned that this particular Upaniṣad has the "Hare Rāma" part first—Hare Rāma, Hare Rāma, Rāma Rāma, Hare Hare/Hare Kṛṣṇa, Hare Kṛṣṇa, Kṛṣṇa Kṛṣṇa, Hare Hare. One might wonder, therefore, why modern Gauḍīyas, for the most part, chant it with the "Hare Kṛṣṇa" part first.

I once asked a Gauḍīya Maṭha *sannyāsī*—Maṅgala Mahārāja—about that, and he said that there are actually two early editions of that manuscript. One is a Bombay edition, and the other is a Navadvīpa edition. In the Bombay edition, he said, they have the "Hare Rāma" part first, and in the Navadvīpa edition they have the "Hare Kṛṣṇa" part first. And he said that because they are both early manuscripts, no one really knows which one is authentic, or which part should come first.

Sometimes it is said that Mahaprabhu switched the order of the words because common people were not allowed to chant Vedic *mantras.* So he switched the order, enabling people from all walks of life to benefit from the chanting. This is an apocryphal story, though.

One of Śrīla Prabhupāda's disciples, Acyutānanda Dasa, once asked Prabhupāda a related question, and Prabhupāda said, "It doesn't matter, if you chant enough—and sincerely—then it doesn't matter which words come first or which come second."

Dr. Beck: Right. That idea is related to the *sphoṭa* concept.

SR: Oh, is it?

Dr. Beck: Yes. Remember, according to *sphoṭa* doctrine, the order of the syllables isn't that important; it has the same effect in either case. On the other hand, the Mīmāṁsā view is that the order is absolutely crucial. They say the order of syllables or words in the Veda is critical. I have a question for you: is the *mahā-mantra* in other Vedic or Purāṇic literature?

SR: I had heard that the *mahā-mantra* is also in the *Brahmāṇḍa Purāṇa.*

Dr. Beck: I believe so, yes. I haven't seen that text, though. It interests me, because Vaiṣṇavas tend to chant this—as the central *mantra*—both quietly, to themselves, as in *japa* meditation, and aloud, in *kīrtana*. I think we should discuss this at some length, especially because sonic theology works its way into the Gauḍīya *sampradāya* primarily through these two methods.

The Vaiṣṇava method of *japa* generally employs the tantric implement of the *akṣa-mālā*, or rosary, of which the beads are normally counted at 108 and are made of Tulasī wood, sacred to Lord Kṛṣṇa. In addition, a work from the sixth century A.D., entitled the *Jayākhya-Saṁhitā*, contains in its Fourteenth Chapter—the chapter is called "Japa-Vidhāna"—many early references to the practice of *japa*. It says that there are three considerations in doing *japa* repetitions—employing the rosary (the *akṣa-mālā*), saying the words aloud (*vācika*) or repeating them in a low voice (*upāṁśu*). There are quite a few details in this text, garnered from early sources, and so a case can be made for a pre-Islamic, and even pre-Christian, use of beads or rosary in the Vaiṣṇava tradition.

SR: I believe the Roman Catholics started using rosary or *japa* beads in the time of St. Dominic. That's as late as the twelfth century.

Dr. Beck: That's correct. So the Vaiṣṇavas were chanting *japa* from very early on. But what I want to say is that in Gauḍīya Vaiṣṇavism, especially, there has always been emphasis on *Nāma-saṅkīrtana*—loud congregational chanting of the holy names of Kṛṣṇa. This was directly emphasized by Caitanya, who would be considered the father of the Gauḍīya tradition. Whereas other Vaiṣṇava groups had advised that the silent or low-volume muttering of *mantra* or *japa* was more efficacious than its loud chanting or singing, Caitanya and his followers proclaimed and argued that the loud singing or chanting of God's names was as much or even more effective in the requisition of salvation or, further, even love of God.

SR: Yes. Bhaktivinoda Ṭhākura and Bhaktisiddhānta Sarasvatī have both written extensively about the importance of loud chanting, and they base their proclamation on the authority of the Purāṇas and Rūpa Gosvāmī, who had even written in one text of eight verses, the *Prathama-Caitanyāṣṭaka* (5), that Mahāprabhu himself had chanted the *mahā-mantra* in a loud voice. So it's a long-standing tradition.

Further, the loud chanting is a prominent feature of Gauḍīya *sādhana*, practiced daily, and I think that it relates to much of the underlying sonic theology you spoke about earlier. For example, Gauḍīyas have a very developed philosophical system to explain that the named one and the name itself are identical. Jīva Gosvāmī calls this *abhinnatvān nāma-nāminoḥ.*

Dr. Beck: Oh, it's an incredibly detailed system, and, it's true, it centers around the loud chanting, or *kīrtana.* Let's explore that for a moment. This sense of volume in the chanting. The importance of loudness, literally blasting us into the numinous sonic realm. Consider this: the sonic realm is bursting with sound, and if one is in connection with it—one will of necessity chant loudly. That's the emphasis in some of the *ācāryas* that one should chant loudly rather than silently.

SR: But what about *japa?*

Dr. Beck: Even *japa,* because in some of the more Advaitin-influenced texts, they talk about *ajapa*—the silent *japa*—and that it's superior to audible *japa,* and ultimately that silence is the highest stage. This particular dimension, by the way, I try to expose in my thesis. For example, in the Upaniṣads there's nothing beyond AUM except the fourth element, *turīya,* meaning the fourth. And so in one Upaniṣad it says that the fourth element is called *aśabda,* or "without sound," and that has been interpreted by the Advaitins to mean that sound exists only in the manifest nature. They say that beyond that, on the higher level, you have silence.

Now, of course, there are those who say that Śaṅkara was influenced by Buddhists, and I sometimes agree with this, because Buddhism says that silence is the highest stage and that one should eliminate all types of language because of its connection with *saṁsāra, māyā* or illusion. On the other hand, in Mīmāṁsā Grammarian and Hindu theistic traditions, we never find that accent on silence. Not by any stretch of the imagination. There's always something, maybe it's inaudible to the material ear, but there's some higher power of sound behind that, and to use the word "silence" is very misleading. This is why I try to argue convincingly here, but there isn't much I can do. The Upaniṣads are very unclear and, in one sense, it's mainly a matter of interpretation. Nonetheless, the whole tantric dimension of Hinduism is built on *Nāda* and *Bindu*; it's overlaid upon the "om" as being the sort of primal sound or uncreated sound. And because the male deities (Viṣṇu, Śiva, Kṛṣṇa, etc.) are often said to be *nādānta* (or, literally, "at the end of *Nāda*") does not mean that *Nāda* or sacred sound is ever given up or discarded. *Nāda* is always regarded as the abiding female energy of God.

SR: So, just to see if I clearly understand what you are saying, in the Vaiṣṇava tradition, *japa* is always loud chanting, but not like *kīrtana*. Still, you have to make a sound. And this sound puts you in touch with the energy of God. It *is* the energy of God. In fact, it's God himself.

Dr. Beck: Right. There's a rather complicated theory behind it; anyway, the *guru*'s instruction is there and there's a philosophical argument based on Vedic and Mīmāṁsā and/or grammarian tradition. This is quite elaborate.

SR: And this is what you've been talking about, at least in summary form, in the first part of our discussion.

Dr. Beck: Right.

SR: Now, *kīrtana* is loud chanting, and its efficacy has been emphasized in numerous texts and by Bhaktivinoda and Bhaktisiddhānta. And also in the *Caitanya-caritāmṛta*, for instance, where Haridāsa Ṭhākura talks about the loud chanting and the incomparable importance of it. But why is it so important?

Dr. Beck: Right. The transcendental sound. What does that really mean? In short: something very powerful cannot be contained in ordinary human consciousness—not in full volume. So it has to be articulated at full throat. The intensity and sincerity with which one chants, under the direction of a spiritual master, will manifest in loud glorification of the Lord. Gradually, after strict practice and the unfolding of one's inherent spiritual nature, one will burst with enthusiasm, with passion, or *rāga*, for his subject, in this case, God, or Kṛṣṇa. *Kīrtana* will be inevitable. It's the natural cry of the soul. This is the Gauḍīya idea.

SR: Do the other Vaiṣṇava *saṁpradāyas* stress the loud chanting and dancing or. . .

Dr. Beck: This, of course, was popularized by Caitanya, and it continues to be associated with his name. But, yes, there are other examples. Sure. The Haridāsī and Rādhāvallabha sects of North India, founded by Swami

Haridāsa and Hit Harivaṁśa, respectively, while lesser known, do also emphasize singing and chanting.

SR: I notice that the Vallabhas, too, seem very close in doctrine and practice to the Gauḍīyas. They certainly chant Kṛṣṇa *mantras.*

Dr. Beck: The Vallabhas teach that Vallabhācārya received a very special *mantra* from Kṛṣṇa himself. It is called the Brahma-sambandha-*mantra.* And then Vallabha initiated Dāmodara dāsa with the same *mantra,* and the *saṁpradāya* was born, so to speak.

SR: *Śrī-kṛṣṇaḥ śaraṇaṁ mama.*

Dr. Beck: Exactly. That's the *mantra,* and it's still given to Vallabha followers. It means, basically, "Śrī Kṛṣṇa is my refuge." Nice. An eight-syllable *mantra.* All of the Vaiṣṇava *saṁpradāyas* emphasize the importance of chanting, and, in some of them, as we've noted, they emphasize the singing and dancing. The Gauḍīyas, though, are particularly known for ecstatic singing and dancing.

The world of all believing Vaiṣṇavas, however, is permeated by sound. Drums, bells, gongs, cymbals, conches, flutes, and a wide variety of vocalizations are often heard simultaneously, creating a sonic atmosphere in one's temple, home, or just, in general, in one's sacred space. The impression to the outsider, or to one who's ear is not trained, is that there is simply some useless cacophony and chaos, simply noise, without rhyme or reason.

On closer inspection, however, one will find that all of the sounds that surround Vaiṣṇava activity are clearly prescribed, backed by a long-standing oral and written tradition. Whole ranges of "unauthorized," or "non-prescribed," sound would be restricted from sacred enclosures. This is quite explicit. Some Sanskrit texts reveal a concern with the divine origin of sound, in fact, including speech, language, and music. Some of them describe the universe as an emanation of sound, while others prescribe methods of individual salvation via sound.

What I would add here is that Narahari Cakravartī, who had written *Bhakti-ratnākara* and who in fact is a major source for the lives of the *ācāryas,* devotes a whole lengthy chapter to music.

SR: Yes, I've been looking at that. It's quite detailed.

Dr. Beck: And he has some verses glorifying *nāda.*

SR: Oh. That's important.

Dr. Beck: *Nāda* as being the form or energy of Hari and Viṣṇu. Of course *nāda* as being the substratum for Indian music as well. So you have a real link between not only *tantras* in general, but with Vaiṣṇavism from the *Bhāgavata,* and then with Indian classical music, which without exception talks about *nāda* and *bindu* as being the ultimate musical experience—to come in contact with the *nāda.*

SR: Now, you mentioned the *Bhāgavata,* or the *Śrīmad Bhāgavatam.* I think we should talk about that for a moment. It's perhaps the most important Gauḍīya scripture. How does it fit into all of this?

Dr. Beck: Right. The connection actually runs very deep. The entire *Bhāgavata Purāṇa* (18,000 verses) has been traditionally believed to be an expansion of four "seed" verses, which themselves were considered to be an expansion of the Vedic *Gāyatrī mantra,* and we've touched on this *Gāyatrī* idea earlier. Now the *Gāyatrī* is an expansion from "*OM.*" So, properly chanted, the whole *Bhāgavata* is evoked with this seed syllable.

The role of sacred sound in the *Bhāgavata*'s creation scenario comes into view toward the end of the text, in the Sixth Chapter of the Twelfth Canto. In that section, the *Bhāgavata* describes its own sonic origin, including the theologies of *Śabda Brahman* and *Nāda Brahman.* When questioned regarding the origin of the *Bhāgavata Purāṇa* itself, Sūta Gosvāmī, the narrator, replies with an explanation of the origin of OM, the Vedas, and the Sanskrit alphabet. And Kṛṣṇa himself, talking to his disciple, King Citraketu, in the Sixth Canto, describes that he is the very embodiment of *Śabda Brahman.* According to the *Bhāgavata,* everything comes from Kṛṣṇa—everything comes from sound. And sound is eternal. . .

SR: This is interesting. Narottama dāsa Ṭhākura also writes about the eternality of sound and its identification with the Supreme Being. He states, in one of his songs, *golokera prema-dhana, hari-nāma saṅkīrtana:* which means that glorification of Kṛṣṇa, Hari *kīrtana,* is directly imported from the spiritual world. In other words, the sound is eternal, and it is coming to us from the higher stratum.

Dr. Beck: Yes. First of all, the Vedic notion of the eternity of sound rests on the following three philosophical axioms mentioned by linguistic scholar P. Chakravarti: "(1) Sound is eternal like space, since both are imperceptible to touch; (2) sound is eternal and not liable to perish immediately after its utterance, inasmuch as it is capable of being given to others, as in the case of a teacher communicating words to his pupil; (3) sound is eternal as there is no cognition of the cause that might destroy it." So, though there are standard arguments against these perceptions, they are strong enough to have abided and have been deeply discussed by the finest minds of Indian philosophy.

Now, you mentioned Narottama and the *ācāryas*—perhaps we should briefly explore Nāma-*kīrtana* and Padāvalī-*kīrtana.*

SR: That's essential.

Dr. Beck: In the present context, yes, it definitely is essential. You cannot truly speak of sonic theology in the Gauḍīya line without referring to these things. Let me give some background. Nāma-*kīrtana* is a stringing together of the names of Rādhā, Kṛṣṇa, Caitanya, the various incarnations, and that sort of thing, in very melodious ways, according to established standards. It centers on glorification of the name of God.

Now Padāvalī-*kīrtana* is a *kīrtana* that tells a story. Experienced performers will take the well-known stories of Caitanya and Rādhā-Kṛṣṇa and convey them with a band, instruments, and beautiful vocalization. Especially significant for Bengalis is the Gaura-candrikā part of the performance. Are you aware of this aspect?

SR: Oh, yes. I've seen these performances. When all is said and done, Gaura-candrikā, along with the Rādhā-Kṛṣṇa part of these *kīrtanas*—they can last three or four or five hours. Quite elaborate. Ed Dimock wrote an excellent article in the 1950s, I believe. It was called "The Place of Gaura-candrikā in Bengali Vaiṣṇava Lyrics;" it was published in *the Journal of the American Oriental Society.*

Why don't you briefly describe, though, exactly what goes on in these performances, and what is the purpose behind them.

Dr. Beck: Basically, Gaura-candrikā refers to the first part of these lengthy performances you are mentioning—the first part of the Padāvalī-*kīrtana.* It is always in praise of Caitanya and his associates. This prepares the audience for the next part, the Rādhā-Kṛṣṇa *līlā.* Now, the interesting thing is that there is always some thematic connection between the

Gaura *līlā* and the Kṛṣṇa *līlā*.

SR: I remember that. In the one that I observed, there was a story about Mahāprabhu's *sannyāsa*—when he renounced the world. So they sang about how the people of Navadvīpa developed a sort of attitude toward Keśava Bhāratī, the person who initiated Mahāprabhu into the *sannyāsa* path. They felt that Keśava Bhāratī had taken away their Mahāprabhu. In a sense, he had, for once Mahāprabhu entered the renounced order, most of the associates in Navadvīpa were bereft of his association.

Then, in the Rādhā-Kṛṣṇa part of the performance, there was the *līlā* of Akrūra taking Kṛṣṇa away from the *gopīs* of Vraja. When he took the Lord to Mathurā, the *gopīs* developed a sort of attitude toward him. Of course, they understood that he was doing his service for Kṛṣṇa by taking him, but they were all but pleased by this service, since Kṛṣṇa was being taken away and they might never see Kṛṣṇa again.

Now, it's interesting that in the Gauḍīya line, Keśava Bhāratī is considered a reincarnation of Akrūra. . .

Dr. Beck: Right. This is the kind of thing. [laughter] Right. So Caitanya and then Rādhā-Kṛṣṇa. And the correlation. Right. This is Padāvalī-*kīrtana*. And it corresponds to the function of sound in many other areas of Indian religious tradition. An interesting parallel emerges between the particular musical practices of certain Vaiṣṇava schools, Gauḍīya included, and the *Yoga* texts which describe musical sounds heard during meditation. The "divine sounds" of the drum, cymbal, *vīṇā*, and flute, which were enumerated in texts such as the *Nāda-bindu Upaniṣad* or the *Haṭha-yoga Pradīpikā* somehow appear to correspond with the instruments which are employed in devotional music, such as the Padāvalī-*kīrtana*.

All Gauḍīya *kīrtana*, in fact, emphasizes the loud playing of the *mṛdaṅga* drum and the *karatāla* hand-cymbals, as if to reflect externally what the advanced *yogī* should be perceiving internally. In the sitting *bhajans* of the Vallabha and Rādhāvallabha *saṁpradāyas*, maximum attention is given to the subtle sounds of the stringed instruments, almost as if each sound brought one closer to the activities of the divine. If nothing else, this is only to point out how sacred sound seems to function in ways which always suggest something beyond the normal visual realm.

Mysticism, Madness and Ecstasy in the Gauḍīya Tradition

June McDaniel

June McDaniel is assistant professor in the Department of Philosophy and Religious Studies at the College of Charleston in South Carolina. Her book **Madness of the Saints: Ecstatic Religion in Bengal** *(Chicago: The University of Chicago Press, 1989) is a breakthough discussion of* bhāva *and altered states in the various Bengali religious traditions.*

SR: Mysticism, of course, is found in all major religious traditions, but Gauḍīya mystics have a distinct quality. I think we could perhaps begin with a discussion of this sort of mysticism and how it relates to the ascetic and ecstatic nature of certain aspects of Gauḍīya Vaiṣṇavism.

Dr. McDaniel: One of the things that I think is unique about the Bengali or Gauḍīya Vaiṣṇavas is their emphasis on mysticism in relation to emotion, and just how deeply they enter into emotional states. There are lots of different kinds of mysticism in the world, and they deal quite a bit with altered states. Frequently, in the Indian tradition, it's very detailed: they explain how you get to these states; the *mantras* to chant; the physical gymnastics. They ask questions like: "Is it the result of *karma* that one can achieve such states?" But they really don't get at the personal experience of the mystic—they don't get to the heart of devotional mysticism. I think that the Bengali or Gauḍīya Vaiṣṇavas are quite distinct in their approach because they focus on the stages of emotion within mystical experience.

They have texts, like Rūpa's *Ujjvala-nīlamaṇi*, where they describe these emotional states in detail. And it's really very much a sort of love-oriented mysticism. To explain these things, the Gauḍīya Vaiṣṇavas have very systematic texts, delineating very complex and often conflicting emotional ideas in a way that I think is unique in the world of religious literature.

The Gauḍīya style is detailed and methodical. The texts explain a given saint's inner experience to such a degree that the reader can almost experience it for himself or herself, and, indeed, the goal of many of the descriptions is to enable the reader to attain these states. The Gauḍīya literature and tradition construct a sort of ladder to the divine, and one is encouraged to go step-by-step, until one reaches *siddhi*, or perfection in mystical experience.

Again, we might mention the *Bhakti-rasāmṛta-sindhu* and the *Ujjvala-nīlamaṇi*, which describe these emotional states in great detail. Of course, Rādhā and the *gopīs* are the ultimate paradigmatic individuals that those books deal with. But, ideally, devotees on the ritual path can follow their lead and attain similar devotional states. Perhaps one can never quite match the intensity of Rādhā and her inner circle of friends, but one can get the general idea and try to attain that state.

SR: Right. Because Śrī Rādhā and her inner circle are in the highest state of devotional ecstasy—*mahābhāva.*

Dr. McDaniel: Exactly. Now, this highest state is one that includes all of the emotions at once—simultaneously. This is something that's very unusual in world mysticism. If a person has some emotion toward the divine it's usually quite simple. The goal is to have a purity of that one emotion: humility, purity of heart, detached love. If it's love of God in a particular mode, say, as bride and bridegroom, one will seek to perfect that line of feeling, to embrace all of the aspects of that particular relationship.

But if you look at *mahābhāva*, it really includes all possible ways of looking at the divine. You've got the most intense of all relationships. The protective and loving feelings of a parent; the intimate comradery of a close friend; the desire to render service; and, of course, the most passionate erotic relationship. All possible emotions, even those which are mutually exclusive, are present. It is a state full of wonder and paradox.

And it gets more subtle as well. Those in the state of *mahābhāva* experience love that's like *ghee*; love that's like honey; love that's pure attraction; love that comes from indignation; love that's sulking—these refer to different types of love, or love at different levels of intensity. In *mahābhāva*, one experiences all of these different emotions as the *bhāva* shifts from time to time, or even from moment to moment. It embraces every conceivable emotion to express complete absorption in the divine. All of the variations of love-in-union (*sambhoga*) and love-in-separation (*vipralambha*) are brought into play.

This is a bit different than the yogic idea, where although you do seek to merge in the "ocean of consciousness (*citta*)," you want to let go of the *vṛttis*, which are basically "whirlpools" of emotion that are associated with past trauma—they are generally thought of as unwanted things, as something to be avoided. Now, in contrast with this, when you go toward the Gauḍīya tradition, the idea is to allow these whirlpools to emerge in as intense a way as possible. This, in fact, is what draws Kṛṣṇa down to you. The more intense your emotion, the more likely it is to attract Kṛṣṇa.

Now, while developing one's relationship with the divinity, there are many possible roles in the Gauḍīya tradition. You can be a devotee loving God; you can be a *gopī*, perhaps, or you can be a *bhakta*, in Caitanya *līlā*. There are complex emotional realities associated with all of these identities. This is especially true for those who reach the higher *bhāvas*, or the higher emotional states. It's really very rich, with many sides, and there are people practicing this today.

SR: Right, well, let's talk about some of those people, the mystics that you met or heard about in Bengal. While you were there, I understand, you met Gauḍīya saints who were on the path of perfection, people who were imbued with mystic powers, or whose meditation was very deep. That interests me because it shows that Gauḍīya Vaiṣṇavism is a living tradition; and one that works.

Dr. McDaniel: Oh, it is very much alive, and ecstatic phenomena are very much a part of the tradition. In Bengal, there were ascetics in the recent past who meditated upon Kṛṣṇa, and their meditation on a Kṛṣṇa *mantra* was so intense that the *mantra* was said to appear on their bodies, as if burned into their skin. *Mantras* would appear on their arms and legs, written in Devanāgarī script, and then disappear. There was one recent saint, Vijayakṛṣṇa Gosvāmī, who would visualize events from the Rāmāyaṇa or Mahābhārata, and then pictures or scenes from these epics would show up on his body, like tattoos, and then they would be gone. I also heard a description of a mystic who offered boiling milk to Kṛṣṇa in his meditations and, because he touched the imaginative pot of milk, he awakened from his trance with burn-marks on his hands. Other devotees claimed to have seen this. Modern Vaiṣṇava ascetics in the forests near Navadvīpa perform the same type of meditation today.

Of course, ascetics can be strange. One *sādhu* claimed he could eat rice and water—and then regurgitate them separately, in two separate piles! A woman near Calcutta claimed she could make bananas bleed—I won't even go into the Freudian implications of that!! [laughter] It is difficult to tell what to make of these claims. Religious traditions *do* have methods for testing whether someone is mad, lying, or telling the truth. However, the lines often blur—people believe they are telling the truth, but are often seeing with spiritual rather than physical sight.

Like the banana lady and the rice and water *sādhu*—Vaiṣṇava ascetics can be very unconventional saints. They are clearly more concerned with their spiritual world—*this* world is a secondary concern. Outsiders, in fact, would consider them quite mad. Actually, some are considered eccentrics even by their own tradition. You see, Vaiṣṇavism is practiced in various ways. There are ascetic traditions, householder traditions, scholar or *paṇḍita* traditions—there are many different orientations. Now, many of the ascetic mystics are considered outcastes, and they usually don't live with the more conventional devotees in the *maṭha.* They go out into the woods and forests. They're too different to get along even with members of their own religious orders.

That's always the case, though. People committed to the physical world naturally find it hard to relate to mystics, to people who are claiming another reality. And just because someone's a practitioner doesn't mean he is perceiving a higher reality. In fact, few attain such insights. Consequently, the mass of devotees do not understand the behavior of the mystics and often ridicule them, unless they are well-known or from a respected lineage. But the point is this: because many people can't find a point of comparison, something to relate to, they call it madness.

SR: In your book, you talk about this sort of divine madness quite a bit. You point out that madness is often caused by separation. In the conventional sense, the madman is separated from his ancestral home, or money, or a wife, or he lost his job—these are the kinds of things that cause madness. A person is separated from something that he or she finds it difficult to live without.

Dr. McDaniel: Well, sometimes it's said in Āyurvedic medicine that madness is the intoxication of the mind caused by an imbalance in the body's elements and qualities. The madness is relieved when the body is brought back to a homeostatic balance. Modern psychiatrists may say that madness comes from problems in the chemistry of the brain, or when neurotransmitters are deficient in certain necessary bio-chemical substances. . .

SR: Still, again, it's separation. Deficiency implies that you are "separated" from those needed substances.

Dr. McDaniel: [laughter] Well, if you want to use that metaphor.

SR: But this is the point that you make in your book. And that the ecstatic, too, experiences a kind of madness—*divyonmāda,* divine madness—due to separation. In their case, however, it is separation from God. This, of course, leads to the conception of *viraha-bhakti,* or devotional service in separation, which the Gauḍīyas conceive of as the highest kind of devotional love, for through that madness comes the sweetest level of divine union. So it could be said, in a sense, that this madness leads to the highest form of sanity: to be situated in reality.

Dr. McDaniel: Nicely put. And one test of genuine religious madness is the presence of the *sāttvika-bhāvas.* This is how the observer in India can tell if the alleged *sādhu* is a madman in a disoriented secular sense, or if he is mad out of divine love. And I might point out that secular madness leads the person who experiences it to pain, frustration, anger, and violence. Spiritual madness may exhibit these same qualities, but it is understood as ultimately uplifting, joyous, and full of knowledge. In Vaiṣṇavism, separation from Kṛṣṇa may cause a type of pain or longing, but it ultimately increases the sweetness of *sambhoga,* or union. So it always has a happy ending, so to speak.

Now, the *sāttvika bhāvas* are spontaneous manifestations of inner emotions that burst forth, often as a result of spiritual practices. The outward signs include immobility (the person is conscious but in such a state of ecstasy that he is unable to move); hair standing on end and gooseflesh; trembling, including quivering and throbbing; sweating; crying; changing skin color (usually paleness or ruddiness); and loss of consciousness. There are others, but these are the most common or well-known. For Vaiṣṇavas, they support the truth of the saint's claims of ecstasy.

SR: Now, these signs of spirituality, or ecstasy, were seen in Mahāprabhu's body. . .

Dr. McDaniel: Oh, these and many more. Caitanya was unusual in that he exhibited more than the typical number of *sāttvikas*. It's funny, you know, when the Gauḍīyas generally talk about *sāttvikas*, they talk about them in numbers: "Oh, he only exhibited two *sāttvikas*—but my *guru* exhibited four of them." That kind of thing. Competition. I found it interesting that saints in Bengal judged other *sādhus* by how many *sāttvikas* were displayed on their bodies.

Now, Caitanya exhibited many forms of ecstasy. And he did so, apparently, with both intense pleasure and severe pain. The interesting thing, though, is this: he displayed the commonly known *sāttvikas*, but in addition he exhibited ecstatic symptoms that no one had ever seen before. Caitanya's whole body would stretch out at times; joints coming out of joints, until he was elongated in a strange, unnatural way; and sometimes he appeared like a tortoise, and his arms and legs would shoot in and out of their sockets. No one could understand what was happening, including his closest companions. But they knew this: he loved Kṛṣṇa. In fact, they understood him to be Kṛṣṇa in the mood of Rādhā, and so it was quite believable that he would exhibit the highest ecstatic symptoms, even those which had never been seen before.

SR: Maybe you could talk more about Caitanya Mahāprabhu's specific ecstatic symptoms.

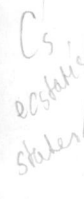

Dr. McDaniel: Well, Caitanya had an amazing collection of ecstatic states. He would laugh, cry, roll on the ground, shake and tremble, sweat, burn, roar, and act as if possessed. Taking on a variety of *bhāvas* or identities, his body would turn different colors, and various body parts would swell or turn rigid. The effect of these mental and emotional states upon his body was extreme. For the believer, they show the power of spirit over matter.

The states that were attained by Caitanya are considered by Vaiṣṇavas to be beyond the understanding of ordinary mortals, though it is believed that one can achieve a similar state by spontaneous love or the process of *līlā-smaraṇa*. *Smaraṇa* literally means "remembering," and the process involves a combined method of visualization and meditation. Through the rigors of this method, one becomes first familiar with the intricacies of Kṛṣṇa's ideal world, *and then enters into it.* This is Rūpa Gosvāmī's characterization of *rāgānugā bhakti*, the second part of the *sādhana* process (the first part being *vidhi,* where the practitioner scrupulously follows the rules and regulations). *Rāgānuga-bhaktas* may also be strict followers, but the inner meditation is more important for them.

Now, there are two forms of this *līlā-smaraṇa* practice, one that centers on the *līlā* of Rādhā and Kṛṣṇa, and the other focuses on that of Caitanya and his associates. Both forms of *līlā smaraṇa* involve visualized service to the deities, and the meditative techniques involved are given by one's *guru.* In most of these lineages, initiation by a genuine *guru* is quite important. The *guru* was compared by one informant to a bird who hatches the *siddha-rūpa,* or the disciple's perfected body. The *guru* has the spiritual heat, if you will, that is needed to crack the egg. So, through the grace of the *guru,* there's a new birth, in a sense, which bears many shamanic undertones—the death of the old self and the birth of the new.

SR: What are the meditations themselves like? What does *līlā-smaraṇa* center upon?

Dr. McDaniel: Primarily, the focus is the Vṛndāvana Rādhā-Kṛṣṇa *līlā,* where the devotee meditates on himself as inwardly female, a handmaiden to Rādhā, or, rather, to one of her immediate friends. This servant of the servant is called a *mañjarī,* one who is like a flower bud. So, under the direction of a *guru,* and according to the guidebooks on such meditation, like the *Govinda-līlāmṛta,* the practitioner will meditate upon himself as a *mañjarī*—who is twelve or thirteen years old, or, according to some, nine or ten, and who lives at a certain residence, with a certain family, and who tends to wear a certain color *sari.* The *mañjarī* becomes his (or her) true self, and identification with the physical body is left behind. The visualization is quite detailed. And according to these details, one goes deeper and deeper into the distant land of Kṛṣṇa's youth.

Now each day is divided into eight periods—this is how the practitioners have broken it up—and Rādhā and Kṛṣṇa are doing specific things at specific times. This is called the *aṣṭa-kālīya-līlā,* and there are elaborate blueprints for pursuing this kind of meditation. So, the practitioner of *līlā-smaraṇa* must place himself at the appropriate scene, doing his assigned service at the right time. And he must be in his feminine *mañjarī* body—his spiritual body. The successful practitioners know how to do this in such a way that they penetrate the boundaries of ordinary reality, and they understand themselves to actually enter into the divine *līlā,* the play of the gods.

A similar process is used for Gaura *līlā* or the meditation upon the activities of Caitanya and his associates. This is similar, in principle, to the visualizations of Rādhā-Kṛṣṇa in Vṛndāvana, but, here, one goes to Navadvīpa in his meditative body, and, instead of being a *mañjarī*, one is generally a *brāhmaṇa* boy. But the principle is the same—through the carefully divided eight parts of the day, they wake Caitanya in the morning, dress him, comb his hair, travel in a *kīrtana* group with him, and share his devotional ecstasies. This extends even to the point of seeing Kṛṣṇa everywhere and in everything. One sees a black tree and thinks of it as Kṛṣṇa; one sees a body of water and thinks it to be the Yamunā river. The ecstasy is so intense that the devotee's absorption in the *līlā* is total.

SR: But let's backtrack for a moment and deal with a fundamental question here. How is it that one can exist as a *mañjarī* in Kṛṣṇa *līlā* and as a young Bengali boy in Gaura *līlā*? I mean, someone would naturally ask, then, "Who am I really?" Presumably, the whole point is to find out who you really are. That's why it's called self-realization. But. . .

Dr. McDaniel: I know. But the tradition doesn't find anything wrong with it. After all, spiritual substance does not have the same limitations as matter. And remember, the Gauḍīya Vaiṣṇava school promotes the idea of *acintya-bhedābheda*—simultaneous and inconceivable oneness and difference. There's an answer there somewhere. [laughter] So, yes, at times, a person may do both forms of visualization and, indeed, take on two identities. In Vaiṣṇavism, there's no reason why he cannot be both.

There are others who question whether the visualization technique reveals a pre-existing identity, or gives a new identity to the devotee, or combines these. Bhaktivinoda Ṭhākura, a famous Gauḍīya saint, indicates that one can have two eternal identities, and that the highest realm, Goloka, has two divisions: Kṛṣṇa *pītha* and Gaura *pītha*. I'll read something from Bhaktivinoda's work, *Jaiva Dharma*. Listen to this:

> Those who are worshipers of Śrī Gaurāṅgadeva [Caitanya] alone during the period of practice, serve him only in Gaura pītha in their accomplished state; and those who as practitioners, worship only Kṛṣṇa do so, when accomplished, in the Kṛṣṇa pītha. Those, however, who are worshipers of Kṛṣṇa and Gaura during practice, are present, when accomplished, in both the pīthas simultaneously, adopting the two bodies at the same time; this is the great mystery of the inscrutable simultaneous distinction and non-distinction between Śrī Kṛṣṇa and Śrī Gaura.

So this is yet another application of the *acintya-bhedābheda* doctrine, which is usually used, in a more conventional setting, to define the person's relationship with the divine, how he is one with it and yet different as well. The visualization of two spiritual bodies at once is quite unusual for meditative practice—I cannot offhand think of another tradition that practices this.

SR: You know, the *līlā-smaraṇa* technique is accepted, of course, throughout the lineage or *saṁpradāya*, but more conservative devotees will de-emphasize it, quite naturally, because it is easy to cheat, and that, of course, can get us into a whole post-Caitanya *sahajiyā* discussion, which is not what this conversation is about. But the thing that interests me is the fact that those who emphasize *līlā-smaraṇa*—not all, but many—tend to move away from the chanting. Now I find that disturbing because chanting is at the very heart of Caitanya Mahāprabhu's process of God realization.

Dr. McDaniel: I see what you mean. There is often some tension between the proponents of different ritual practices. Those who focus their practice on chanting—and that is recommended in many of the texts—often place little emphasis on other ritual practices, like *līlā-smaraṇa*. For them, the name reveals everything, and nothing more is necessary. Visualization, in fact, can be seen as an attempt to force the issue, to bring the divine under one's control—to force entry into the *līlā*. Chanting, on the other hand, is seen as an act of submission. The devotee is glorifying the name of God and waiting for his mercy. And traditionally, the devotee is supposed to show humility and patient love. However, there is still debate in the Vaiṣṇava community over the roles of grace and free will.

In Sanātana Gosvāmī's *Bṛhad-bhāgavatāmṛtam*, he gives several arguments for the superiority of *kīrtana* over *līlā-smaraṇa*. He points out that in singing one uses all of one's senses, not just the mind. Also, it can be done with others, so it can benefit a multiplicity of people, not just oneself. That same work states that singing Kṛṣṇa's names is the safest, easiest, strongest, and most direct means to attain divine love and ecstasy—and the divine madness associated with it. The chanting is the dearest thing to Kṛṣṇa's heart and it immediately attracts him, at least when it is done with love. So there is a claim that chanting is superior to the visualization process. However, it's not that these two paths are always mutually exclusive. One can do both, be active and passive, as one may have both male and female spiritual bodies.

SR: Right. I just thought we should mention this. Also, I thought you should talk about some of the mystics you wrote about in your book. I started to ask you about that earlier, but we went off in another direction. . .

Dr. McDaniel: Well, there were quite a few. Pāgal Haranāth, of the late nineteenth and early twentieth centuries, was an interesting case. His life is full of shamanic experiences—dismemberment, death and resurrection, trances, miraculous powers. He was not part of an accepted lineage, and as such was not accepted by the mass of devotees. His authority, among those who respected it, came not from tradition or affiliation but from his experiences. There weren't many who witnessed these things, but his disciples and followers supported his claims. Among those who accepted him as authentic, the title Pāgal, or "madman," had deep meaning. It was a term of appreciation and love. For the others, it had another meaning—insanity.

Vijayakṛṣṇa Gosvāmī, from about the same period, had initially investigated many paths: Bāul, Sahajiyā, Kartā-bhajā, Brahmo Samāj. His yogic and *kuṇḍalinī* experiences led him to Vaiṣṇavism. His ecstatic paralysis, mad dancing, visions, and trances were initially seen as eccentricities, or even madness, but he was gradually accepted as a saint. I believe I mentioned him earlier—he's the one who performed the miracle of having events from the scriptures appear on his body.

Then, of course, there was Gaura Kiśora dāsa Bābājī, who was quite eccentric but clearly accepted by the Vaiṣṇava community as a passionate lover of Kṛṣṇa. He was properly initiated and belonged to an established lineage; so many accepted him as a *paramahaṁsa*, a devotee of the highest order. But no one understood his behavior. He wore his begging bowl on his head, did his worship in an outhouse, and beat with his umbrella anyone who praised him or wanted to take initiation from him. This may have been humility more than madness, or, according to some, it was simply a desire for privacy.

Gaura Kiśora was oblivious to the outside world, totally absorbed in Kṛṣṇa and Gaura *līlā*. Thus he was said to transcend physical laws, at times, and do miraculous things. In his *bhāvas*, distasteful and inedible foods became delicious to him and sustained him in a healthy condition. He would often eat raw rice or other grains soaked in water or Ganges mud. A respected local *paṇḍita*, Lalitā-dīdī of Rādhāramaṇabāgh, once witnessed a particular incident wherein Gaura Kiśora offered an unripe eggplant to his deity form of Caitanya, begging the image to accept his offering. As he prayed to Caitanya in this way, Gaura Kiśora's voice choked and his body began to swell, turning bright red. He began to weep so intensely that his face and chest became soaked with tears. This lasted for over an hour, and then he started to sing for his deity. Then he ate the raw eggplant as Caitanya's remnants, *prasāda*, and looked as if he were enjoying it—as if it were a delicacy.

He often fell into trances, madly calling upon the name of Kṛṣṇa. Once, he was seen chanting "Hā, Krsna Caitanya! Hā Kṛṣṇa Caitanya!" for many hours. His followers were afraid that his throat would get sore and bloody, so they started shouting various other names of God that might change his mood, or *bhāva*. Sometimes this worked. At other times, he would just go on chanting, at the top of his voice. Some say that he would chant like this for thirteen consecutive days, without stop. At times, he would sing and dance with Bhaktivinoda Ṭhākura, especially at the site of Caitanya's birth, where they both would exhibit the eight *sāttvika bhāvas* for all to see.

Many Gauḍīya saints showed—and continue to show—ecstatic behavior, which could be interpreted by an outsider as madness. Yet, in many cases, the religious components were strong enough to outweigh the secular notions of madness, and leaders of the tradition came to accept many of them as genuine devotees and visionaries. In addition, there were signposts to look for along the way, given by the Vaiṣṇava scriptures and the writings of the Gosvāmīs. For those who passed the test, their mad behavior was seen as spiritual ecstasy. Divine madness is not considered to be an aberration, as is ordinary madness—it expresses the highest religious goal in not only Gauḍīya Vaiṣṇava theology but also in certain mystical traditions associated with Judaism, Christianity, Islam, and Buddhism.

Rasa Theology: The Drama of Divine Love

Gerald Carney

Gerald T. Carney's Ph.D. dissertation (1979) focused on Kavi Karṇapūra's Caitanya-candrodaya-nāṭakam, a ten-act play about the life of Śrī Caitanya Mahāprabhu. He has since done research on the theological presentation of Caitanya's biography in this drama, on the rasa theory, on the work of Baba Premānanda Bhāratī, an early twentieth-century Vaiṣṇava missionary to the United States, and on issues relating to interreligious dialogue. He is currently Professor of Religion at Hampden-Sydney College, Virginia.

SR: The subject of *rasa* is vast. It delineates our basic relationship with God—it gives insight into who we really are, who we are in the spiritual world. Consequently, the subject, being the ultimate goal, is, in a sense, unlimited. Even the *Taittirīya Upaniṣad* includes the famous statement *raso vai saḥ*—"the ultimate reality is *rasa*, or spiritual/aesthetic experience; it is only this that gives the highest bliss."

After a few elusive references in the Vedic literature, however, the doctrine of *rasa* seems to get lost for a while, until it is picked up by Rūpa Gosvāmī. Perhaps you can talk about that, about how *rasa* became an important concept in Gauḍīya Vaiṣṇavism.

Dr. Carney: Well, the notion of *rasa* arose from the tradition of dramatic criticism. In this context, it denoted the response of one who had a refined aesthetic sensibility. In order to perceive the complex elements of a dramatic performance, one needed to "taste" *rasa*. This meant that one had to have the ability to "taste" the detailed and often hidden meanings of the performance, and also that one had to have "taste"—in the sense of "good taste."

SR: As Lee Siegel says, "The taster tastes the taste with taste."

Dr. Carney: [laughter] Exactly. But it goes further. Without proper *rasa* one would simply miss the essence of the drama. As Bharata said in his *Nāṭya-śāstra*, "Without taste or *rasa*, there is no significance in a work of art." So *rasa* is crucial. Bharata also indicated the elements of a work that can help a person become more sensitive to the emotional tone of the dramatic work. To quote Siegel, as you did, there are "literary spices, verbal herbs, poetic condiments"—all of these are meant to produce enjoyment or "juice" (a literal translation of *rasa*) so that one can appreciate the real meaning of a performance, and so develop the sensibility of a *rasika*, the sufficiently cultured individual, who is distinguished from one who merely enjoys raw emotion, a *bhāvika*.

SR: In dramatic theory, how is *rasa* distinguished from *bhāva*?

Dr. Carney: In dramatic theory (but not for Rūpa Gosvāmī and the Gauḍīya Vaiṣṇavas), *bhāva* is the particular and immediate emotion, the raw unrefined emotion that one feels as a reaction to a particular episode. *Rasa*, by contrast, is the refined emotion, generalized as a quality of human sensibility, transcending the individual personal experience. To take an example from Western drama, when we witness a performance of *Romeo and Juliet*, we see portrayed emotions that we would never want to experience in our own lives—the thwarted love, the despair and death of the young lovers—and yet we find the performance pleasurable, enjoyable, even uplifting. It is this distinctive ability of a drama to produce a heightened sentiment, a "taste," which is indicated by *rasa*.

This enjoyment of *rasa*, awakened by the drama, goes beyond everyday experience. All the factors of the dramatic performance intersect to awaken this heightened sensibility, the aesthetic sentiment called *rasa*, from the full spectrum of refined sentiments which is latent in human consciousness. This enriching of the *rasa*-enjoyer highlights the transcendent quality of *rasa*: it leads the individual beyond individual experience and raw emotion to an awakening, indeed an expansion, of the person's aesthetic sensibility. It was this transcendent quality of *rasa* that made *rasa* an ideal description of *mokṣa* for Abhinavagupta and for the transformative devotional experience which formed the basis of Rūpa Gosvāmī's theology.

These developments came later. First, Ānandavardhana, in the ninth century, extended the application of *rasa* from dramatic performance to become the model for all aesthetic enjoyment, as, for example, in the enjoyment of poetry and music, of works read as well as performed. Enjoyment of *rasa* and the aesthetic refinement of the enjoyer were considerably widened in this perspective.

SR: Now, Ānandavardhana flourished in the ninth century, and Abhinavagupta, I believe, came about two centuries later?

Dr. Carney: Correct. He flourished in the eleventh century and was one of the most important developers of the aesthetic theory. Edwin Gerow has written about this quite eloquently, and so did David Haberman. And, I think, Neal Delmonico, in his dissertation, deals with Abhinavagupta quite a bit.

Simply stated, Abhinavagupta made the important connection between aesthetic experience and religious transformation. Since the experience of *rasa* involves self-transcendence, an immersion in a higher reality beyond the individual self, Abhinava opined, this experience was a reflection of *mokṣa* or liberative release. Now, I already spoke about the transformative effect that occurs if one properly experiences a dramatic performance, and of the experience of *rasa.* You see, the point is this: *rasa* involves a measure of self-transcendence, a movement from particular and raw emotion to general, or universal, and refined sentiment. In the process of experiencing *rasa,* the sensibility of the spectator is refined as well. Emphasizing these transformative effects, Abhinavagupta compared *rasa* with a sort of spiritual liberation.

Another important contribution to *rasa* theory in that same century came from Bhoja, who emphasized the preeminence of the erotic *rasa, śṛṅgāra-rasa* or *madhura-rasa.* You can see, then, how this whole tradition of aesthetic and religious theory paved the way for Rūpa Gosvāmī, who, in the sixteenth century, developed this *rasa* theory into a theological system of devotion, a perspective that incorporated religious texts, Gauḍīya Vaiṣṇava devotional experience, and the aesthetics we have been discussing.

In Rūpa's devotional theology, the sufficiently refined individual of aesthetic theory, the ideal *rasika* or *sahṛdaya,* was replaced by the *rasika* devotee or *bhakta.* The love of Kṛṣṇa (*Kṛṣṇa-rati*) was understood as the dominant feeling (*sthāyi-bhāva*) of devotion, but this feeling constitutes a permanent relationship, rather than the transient feelings excited by a mundane performance. This *rasa* was awakened through a series of appropriate excitants (*vibhāvas*), manifestations (*anubhāvas*), and auxiliary feelings (*vyabhicāri-bhāvas*). When properly awakened, this *rasa* arouses bodily manifestations of devotional ecstasy (*sāttvika-bhāvas*), such as weeping and horripilation. In this devotional experience, the aesthetic cultivation of Sanskrit poetics, the traditional narratives of Kṛṣṇa's play with the *gopīs* in the *purāṇas* and with Rādhā in devotional poems, and devotional practices like the deeply emotional *kīrtana*, all of these combine, not only theoretically, but as the religious and emotional basis for exciting love of Kṛṣṇa in the devotee.

SR: Can you elaborate on the "excitants" and how they stir or inspire love for Kṛṣṇa?

Dr. Carney: Kṛṣṇa and the *gopīs* themselves are the essential excitants (*ālambana-vibhāva*)—they have this effect on each other. The sound of Kṛṣṇa's flute, the river Yamunā, and other audible and visible things that remind the lovers of each other act as enhancers of these excitants (*uddīpana-vibhāva*). The *anubhāvas* are such things as sidelong glances, bewitching smiles, and things of this nature. The taxonomy here is still based on *rasa-śāstra*, but it is modified quite a bit.

SR: So Rūpa Gosvāmī's religious meaning of *rasa* is clearly connected to earlier explanations of aesthetics?

Dr. Carney: Oh yes. Remember, Abhinavagupta saw the experience of *rasa*, the self-transcendence one undergoes while experiencing a dramatic performance, as a parallel to *mokṣa* or liberation. *Rasa* ultimately meant transcending ordinary experience and losing oneself in a deeper level of experience. Rūpa Gosvāmī and the Gauḍīya Vaiṣṇava tradition located this transformation, when it is experienced on the ultimate level, in Kṛṣṇa's play.

You know, the Gauḍīyas were quite fond of dramatic methods; plays written by Rūpa and Kavi Karṇapūra were important in expressing the theology as well as the experience of the movement. Even Caitanya himself took part in performances of Kṛṣṇa-*līlā*. In the *Caitanya-candrodaya* by Kavi Karṇapūra, Act III centers on a play in which Caitanya plays Rādhā, a perfectly appropriate role for him, and Śrīvāsa plays Nārada, acting out the role which he incarnates according to Gauḍīya theology.

This represents more than a play within a play here. Within the drama of Caitanya's *līlā*, Caitanya plays a role in Kṛṣṇa *līlā*. Now this play is the ultimate reality, not just a representation of it. This ultimate drama is the reality into which the audience is invited to enter and to play their roles, the play of Kṛṣṇa and Rādhā made manifest in the devotion of Caitanya and his followers, including the audience. This dramatic model of participation continues in the present-day *rāsa-līlā* plays of Vraja.

SR: Before we get ahead of ourselves, though, let's backtrack for a moment. You mentioned that Abhinavagupta saw a glimmer of *mokṣa*, a transformative experience, in watching a drama. . .

Dr. Carney: Oh yes, and it is interesting that while Abhinavagupta saw a glimmer of *mokṣa* in aesthetic experience, the Gosvāmīs and, ultimately, the Gauḍīyas, saw that the spiritual world *is* a drama: the drama of Rādhā and Kṛṣṇa, the eternal performance of the eternal world. What's more, *bhakti*, or love for Rādhā and Kṛṣṇa, according to Rūpa, was the only real drama, and certainly the only drama that can awaken *rasa* or *bhāva*, which he considered a permanent state of the devotee. For the practitioner, this is the drama in which all participate; these are the parts that we all ultimately play, roles discovered through self-realization: these are the devotees' true identities. All the rest is separation from relationship with Kṛṣṇa and thus an illusion.

This was the idea developed by Rūpa Gosvāmī. By using the concepts and terminology of the medieval aestheticians, he explained the ultimate drama in which all take part. Along with Jīva, he was the great theologian of the Gauḍīya *sampradāya*. They were not only theologians but they expounded the science of uncovering this relationship with Kṛṣṇa for devotees of their time and for the centuries that have followed. Rūpa, especially, guides us through this path step-by-step in his *Bhakti-rasāmṛta-sindhu* and *Ujjvala-nīlamaṇi*. In those books he works out the details of *bhakti-rasa*, the *rasa* theory as it applies to devotional love.

SR: Well, let's get into that a little bit. S.K. De, in the 1930s, wrote one of the few comprehensive pieces on *bhakti-rasa* in the English language. As you have mentioned, Gerow, Haberman, and Delmonico have made significant contributions as well. From the devotional point of view, Prabhupāda revealed quite a bit in his translation and commentary of *Caitanya-caritāmṛta* and also in the *Nectar of Devotion*, which is a summary of Rūpa Gosvāmī's *Bhakti-rasāmṛta-sindhu*. I wonder if we could break down the idea of *bhakti-rasa,* simplifying it a bit.

Dr. Carney: Well, that's a vast subject, and there are so many details! We might start with the idea that, for the Gauḍīyas, *rasa* became a matter of relationship with Kṛṣṇa, *Kṛṣṇa-rati. Rati* is the basic emotion that becomes love. This relation has many aspects, some transient, some that last. The kind of love that endures—that is what the Gauḍīyas are interested in. This *sthāyi-bhāva* is one's permanent relationship of love, one's eternal relationship with Kṛṣṇa.

SR: We might mention, too, that there is another aspect of *sthāyi-bhāva* that is brought to light by Gauḍīya commentators, and that is called *Bhāvollāsa-rati,* wherein one's eternal relationship is with Śrī Rādhā. This is also called *Rādhā-snehādhika,* or *Rādhā-dāsyam.* Now, there is also *Kṛṣṇa-snehādhika,* which you are talking about. And *sama-snehādhika,* wherein one is devoted to Rādhā and Kṛṣṇa equally.

Of course, in one sense, Śrī Rādhā's exaltation is dependent upon Kṛṣṇa's divinity. Rādhā is great, one might say, because she is Kṛṣṇa's consort. It assumes a prior assessment of Kṛṣṇa. So we can say that devotion to Rādhā and devotion to Kṛṣṇa are inextricably related. But I thought we should mention this *sthāyi-bhāva* that has Rādhārāṇī in the center, since this is distinctly Gauḍīya. . .

Dr. Carney: Yes, but that notion, as important as it is for the Gauḍīya tradition, is a later idea. In traditional aesthetics and poetics, there were eight *sthāyi-bhāvas,* primary or lasting emotions: love, laughter, sadness, anger, courage, fear, disgust, and wonder. These correspond to eight *rasas:* eros, humor, compassion, fury, heroics, horror, revulsion, and astonishment. Sometimes a ninth *rasa,* called *śāntī* or tranquillity, is added to this list; this corresponds to a ninth *sthāyi-bhāva* called *nirveda* or indifference. The exact relation between these *bhāvas* and *rasas* is disputed by scholars, but this is the basic list.

Rūpa made some modifications to this list. He relegated the comic, tragic, and horrific *rasas,* among others, to a secondary position, and he extolled the virtues of five particular forms of *bhakti,* which he described as the five primary *rasas: śānta-rasa,* the relationship of quiet and peace; *dāsya-rasa,* the relation of servant to master; *sakhya-rasa,* the relationship between friends; *vātsalya-rasa,* the parental relationship; and, of course, *śṛṅgāra* or *madhura-rasa,* the relation of erotic love. This last relation was rightly considered the most intimate, but also the paradigmatic form.

SR: Please, go on. Describe the various kinds of relationships that are mentioned by Rūpa Gosvāmī.

Dr. Carney: Well, as I said, at the very basic level there is *śānta-rasa,* a neutral, peaceful relationship with Kṛṣṇa or, rather, Viṣṇu. I say Viṣṇu because the devotee in *śānta-rasa* often feels awe and reverence before the majesty of God. It is sometimes called a neutral *rasa,* especially in relation to Kṛṣṇa, because it often involves passive adoration.

SR: Rūpa gives many examples of those who practice this kind of devotion, such as the four Kumāras. But sometimes, like in Mahāprabhu's dialogue with Rāmānanda Rāya, it seems that *śānta-rasa* is not really counted among the *rasas.* But Rūpa Gosvāmī says that even if this is true, it is still a starting point for devotional service and a genuine way to serve the Lord.

Dr. Carney: Right. And this relationship can foster a deeper love. So it is counted among the *rasas.* The next one is *dāsya-rasa:* the devotee as a perfect servant. This relationship is typical of some Vraja cowherds and others in Vṛndāvana and Dvārakā. Third, the relationship of friendship, *sakhya-rasa,* includes all those who have been friends to Kṛṣṇa, like the Pāṇḍavas; friendship may begin with a slightly distant reverence and develop into a deeper and more intimate form. Fourth, parental love, *vātsalya-rasa,* involves all who feel responsible for Kṛṣṇa and who exhibit protective feelings for him, in addition to Nanda, Yaśodā, Vasudeva, Devakī, and the elder cowherd men and women in Vraja.

One could make an endless list of these devotees, but the erotic sentiment, *madhura-rasa,* the relationship of erotic love, is the most intimate. This erotic love for Kṛṣṇa is distinguished from ordinary passion, ***kāma,*** which seeks its own satisfaction. *Premā,* this love for Kṛṣṇa, is selfless, for its whole focus is the pleasure of the Lord.

Vaiṣṇavas—especially the Gauḍīyas—developed this notion of erotic love still further, incorporating every aspect of erotic psychology and the rhetorical embellishments of the aesthetic tradition. All of the *rasas* reach a climax in *madhura-rasa* and the qualities of each prior relationship are incorporated and intensify as the relationship approaches the erotic. So the erotic love of Kṛṣṇa is the fullness and fulfillment of all of the other *rasas.*

SR: In addition to this, though, the tradition teaches that the *rasas* are absolute. That is to say that each *rasa* is satisfying for Kṛṣṇa and for the devotees who are engaged in their particular relationship with him. However, given this equitable view of *rasa* theology, it is true that *madhura-rasa* is the ultimate way of expressing love for Kṛṣṇa. Consequently, I think it would be a good idea for us to sort of dissect the gradual attainment of *madhura-rasa* and the different levels that lead to its perfection.

Dr. Carney: Well, Rūpa analyzes these things in painstaking detail. It all begins with *Kṛṣṇa-rati*—love that is pointed to Kṛṣṇa. When this intensifies, especially in the *madhura* mode, it is called *premā*. This love, too, develops through stages: *sneha, māna, praṇaya, rāga, anurāga,* and *bhāva*. Rūpa compares this process of development to the progressive steps in the refining of sugar, each form becoming more concentrated with greater sweetness. The ultimate end of this process is called *mahābhāva*.

These highest forms of love, in fact, lie beyond the sphere of ordinary human beings, and are limited to Rādhā and the inner circle of *gopīs*. Nevertheless, they remain the paradigm, the model, of love. The excellence of their love is characterized by two surprising facts. First, it is most often love experienced in the absence of the beloved (*viraha-bhakti*), also called love in separation (*vipralambha-bhāva*), rather than love in union (*sambhoga*). Just as ordinary lovers spend far more time suffering in the lover's absence than in the beloved's embrace, so the devotees of Kṛṣṇa possess a love which is purified through separation and yearning for a union which is not possessed. This quality of *premā* emphasizes the selfless character of such love, which is perfected in absence and not in union.

Second, these highest devotees of Kṛṣṇa are not lawful, "appropriate" love partners (*svakīyā*) in a union marked by exclusive commitment and marriage vows. Instead, Rādhā and the cowherd women (*gopīs*) fall into the two categories of *parakīyā*: unmarried women who violate society's standards of respectability and morality and married women who betray their husbands to become Kṛṣṇa's lovers. Such behavior would never be condoned in ordinary society, but the intensity of the selfless devotion, love of God in defiance of religious laws and social sanctions, renders this the highest love of all. Poets and playwrights delighted in describing all the stages and complications of this form of love. Together with the other forms of devotion that I have been describing, this highest form invites the devotee to become a player in the divine drama. Rūpa shifted the aesthetic norms to make enjoyment of feeling a goal (these *bhāvas*) and to emphasize that the actors themselves enjoy the *rasa* to the highest degree. The task of the devotee is to learn to play that role in the ultimate drama.

This is what *rāgānugā bhakti* is all about: learning or re-learning through spiritual discipline one's role in God's play, how to enter into that role in Kṛṣṇa *līlā* which is one's own original part. Individual life is a play with that ultimate framing drama. *Rasa* theology shows the Gauḍīya method for entering into that ultimate drama. So aesthetics and devotion converge to provide the integral developmental system.

SR: Is there anything else you would like to add?

Dr. Carney: Actually I am afraid that all of this talk of the highest stages of emotional and erotic devotion might seem terribly distant from ordinary experience and the everyday world. Traditional aesthetics was directed to a cultivated, but not extraordinary, person. Ordinary people experience the *rasa* of drama, music, dance, and poetry. The taste (or flavor) of Kṛṣṇa's love and the enjoyment of his love are destined for all: the everyday world of devoting oneself to God is the participation in divine play. Devotional activities (*kīrtana*, deity worship, *darśana* of Kṛṣṇa in *rāsa-līlā* plays and other performances, proper reverence toward teachers, observances of twice-monthly *ekādaśī* and *parikramā* and the seasonal festivals like Holī and Govardhana *pūjā*) and reverential identification with the land of Vraja through the *vana-yātrā* awaken and deepen an experience of participation in Kṛṣṇa's play. Thus *rasa*, which we have discussed from all of these perspectives of aesthetics, devotion and theology, returns to the experience of quite ordinary people and becomes the foundation for their religious lives.

Record puja & pilgrimage

Kṛṣṇa-līlā as Perceived in Meditation and Pilgrimage

David Haberman

David Haberman is Assistant Professor of Religion at Williams College. A revised version of his Ph.D. Dissertation was published under the title Acting as a Way of Salvation: A Study of Rāgānugā Bhakti Sādhana *(New York: Oxford University Press, 1988), and is now considered a preeminent work on the mystical side of the Gauḍīya tradition. He has since been called to write numerous articles for academic journals and has contributed to* Textual Sources for the Study of Hinduism, *edited by Wendy Doniger O'Flaherty (Chicago: University of Chicago Press, 1988). He is currently working on a book about pilgrimage in Vraja and a translation of Rūpa Gosvāmī's* Bhakti-rasāmṛta-sindhu.

SR: Your book on rāgānugā-bhakti-sādhana opened many doors for academics in regard to Vaiṣṇava mysticism. This went further, reaching a highpoint, I think, in your latest published work—in that textbook on Hinduism edited by Wendy O'Flaherty. There you translated Rūpa Gosvāmī's version of the *aṣṭa-kālīya-līlā*. This is important. In Kṛṣṇa's divine *līlā*, there are basically eight daily divisions, as you know, and this is meditated upon by the rāgānuga *bhaktas*. Perhaps we can talk about that for a moment. Is that okay?

Dr. Haberman: I would rather begin with where I am today with respect to all of that. In thinking about what I have been up to over the years, I realize that in many ways I am now balancing on a borderline. What I mean by this is that I'm now interested in more ambiguous voices within the tradition. Specifically, I'm interested in ambiguous voices concerning the Vaiṣṇava concept of *līlā*. On one hand, we see a concept of *līlā* as represented by the *līlā-smaraṇa* tradition, where the mind is withdrawn from the ordinary world and is completely concentrated on the divine *līlā*. This is reached only by meditation and in many ways this side of the tradition defines *līlā* as something otherworldly, where one needs to pierce the surface of life to get to some depth, to some core beyond the superficial reality of day-to-day life.

On the other hand, I've become more and more interested in another voice in the tradition, one which represents a more "this-worldly," if you will, aspect of the divine *līlā*. From this perspective the *līlā* experience is more characterized by pilgrimage activity in Vraja. This approach to understanding *līlā* can be found in the works of some of the early *ācāryas*. A figure that I've become very interested in is a Gauḍīya figure by the name of Nārāyaṇa Bhaṭṭa.

SR: I know very little about him, although I am aware that he was a contemporary of Rūpa-Sanātana, and that he had something to do with the development of Varṣānā.

Dr. Haberman: He has been greatly ignored by the tradition. It seems as though Kṛṣṇadāsa Kavirāja—in his decision as to who to include in the canon and who to exclude—was responsible for this. Nonetheless, Nārāyaṇa Bhaṭṭa has written amazing texts, both in terms of quality and quantity, and that really should put him on a par with the Six Gosvāmīs of Vṛndāvana. But he is not mentioned in that list. I think this is somewhat curious. I suspect there may have been some kind of competition between Nārāyaṇa Bhaṭṭa and the group in Vṛndāvana associated with Jīva Gosvāmī, or, more precisely, associated with Kṛṣṇadāsa Kavirāja.

SR: Is Nārāyaṇa Bhaṭṭa responsible for writing things that Kṛṣṇadāsa Kavirāja might have considered a little unconventional?

Dr. Haberman: No, I don't think so. I really don't think that was the problem. I suspect that it had more to do with politics and seeking patronage from the local courts of the time and those sorts of things.

SR: How does Nārāyaṇa Bhaṭṭa's work relate to your more recent interest in *līlā* as a pilgrimage experience?

Dr. Haberman: Well, his final words, for example, have become a *mahā-vākya*—a great saying—in Vraja. And they are now simply expressed as "Vraja is Kṛṣṇa and Kṛṣṇa is Vraja."

Now, this may seem like a simple enough saying, but it is actually quite profound. And in a lot of the pilgrimage activity, the implications of this aphorism are borne out. One can see the pilgrims worshipping the river—the Yamunā River—the trees, mountains, rocks, and specifically Govardhana mountain . . .

SR: As non-different from Kṛṣṇa?

Dr. Haberman: That's right. And Govardhana mountain is considered to be a *svarūpa* of Kṛṣṇa. One of his forms. So I'm interested in teasing out that side of the tradition, and that voice of the tradition, which seems to have an interest in surface over depth, in what is seen over that which is not seen.

This is the contrast that I was referring to. Instead of being something that's reached only through meditative discipline, ultimately understanding *līlā* as something removed from this world, it can also be seen on this very plane itself—as non-different from Kṛṣṇa. Activity in this world is another manifestation of *līlā*.

SR: Acting as a way of salvation?

Dr. Haberman: Right, but in that book, I was most interested in *līlā-smaraṇa*, because rāgānugā bhakti sādhana for the most part is understood as *līlā-smaraṇa*; it's pretty much defined that way by Rūpa Gosvāmī. Now I am interested in ordinary reality as *līlā*. It might be said that this is another side of the tradition, but it's really all over the place. Although one may not see it so much in the theological texts, one can definitely see it in pilgrimage activity, where it is a very concrete reality, so to speak.

Going back to Caitanya's own pilgrimage, at least as it is presented in the *Caitanya-caritāmṛta*, when Caitanya arrives at Govardhana mountain, for example, he actually embraces the mountain. That very mountain, that chunk of rock, is considered to be non-different from Kṛṣṇa. Now I've been very interested in that, and theologically expressed, if one wanted to think of how, say, a figure like Jīva Gosvāmī defined the world, the material world, in a work like the *Bhāgavata-sandharba*, he defines the world as a production of Māyā-śakti. This is found in his theory of the three *śaktis*.

In general, the term "*māyā*" is very ambiguous in Hindu traditions, and

I think that the ambiguity remains in the Gauḍīya tradition. On one hand, *māyā* is that which conceals ultimate reality from the *jīva*, from the soul, and in that sense, one needs to pierce maya to get to the *līlā*. This is clearly the perspective of the *līlā-smaraṇa* tradition. . .

SR: But there is Bhadrā and Subhadrā. My understanding is that there are two aspects. There is Mahā-māyā and Yoga-māyā.

Dr. Haberman: Okay, right. That's the other side. In Yoga-māyā, we see a very different notion of *māyā*. Yoga-māyā is responsible for spinning out the *līlā*. Once we begin to listen to that particular side of the tradition, we see that the *līlā* is not something reached only by rejecting the world; rather this very world *is* the *līlā*. And activity in this world, *if* it could be perceived correctly, is *līlā*.

SR: That's a big "if."

Dr. Haberman: That's a big "if." That's right. But that is still, I think, a different statement than that of those who claim that one needs to somehow reject the world to perceive the *līlā*.

SR: I think Rūpa Gosvāmī's idea of *yukta-vairāgya* is to use the things of this world in the service of the Supreme, and in that way transform them. This perhaps can account for the dual notion you are perceiving in the Vaiṣṇava tradition.

Dr. Haberman: That's right. But I think this ambiguity is represented in terms of Gauḍīya institutions, because one finds in the Gauḍīya tradition a split that one doesn't necessarily find in the other Vaiṣṇava traditions. This is the split between the ascetics, or the *sannyāsis*, and the householders. The ascetics seem to emphasize the *līlā-smaraṇa* tradition, while the householders, naturally, favor the pilgrimage tradition, seeing *līlā* in the here and now, in this world.

So this is my current interest—these two moves in the tradition. My earlier work, which culminated in *Acting as a Way of Salvation*, was more concerned with the concept of *līlā* as removed from the ordinary world; whereas the pilgrimage activity is showing me a different concept of *līlā*, one which intimately reconnects *līlā* with this very world. If, again, one could see things as they truly are.

SR: It's interesting that you are saying this because I've been thinking about these things quite a bit myself. I'm writing a book now on the lives of Narottama, Śrīnivāsa, and Śyāmānanda. And in studying Śrīnivāsa, especially, I've come upon this idea that you are alluding to. There are episodes in his life that underscore the importance of pilgrimage and how it plays a part in the nature of *līlā*.

For example, when Śrīnivāsa goes to see Gadādhara Paṇḍita to study the *Bhāgavatam*, he is sent by Gadādhara to Vṛndāvana to study under Rūpa and Sanātana. But instead of hurrying along, he takes his time because he wants to see the places of pilgrimage. It seems very odd that he procrastinates, and by the time he gets to Vṛndāvana, of course, both Rūpa and Sanātana have passed away. But he considered it *that* important, and he was warned that they may pass away due to separation from Mahāprabhu.

Śrīnivāsa stopped at Jāhnavā devī's house, and she said, "You'd better go quickly; they are about to leave this world." In spite of this, Śrīnivāsa insisted, "Alright, but I have to go to see this holy place and that holy place." So, I was thinking, this certainly speaks highly of the importance of pilgrimage as a type of *līlā* experience.

Dr. Haberman: And of the specific places he went to.

SR: That's right.

Dr. Haberman: I'm not sure which places he was visiting.

SR: He went to Śāntipura, Purī, he went to the house of Nityānanda, several places like that. And then in his later *līlā*—this is also interesting from the perspective of what you were just saying—in his *mānasa-sevā*, how he brings things from the spiritual world into tangible focus in this world. For example, Śrīnivāsa once meditated on Mahāprabhu giving him a garland in his *siddha-deha*, his perfected body in the spiritual world, and when his meditation broke in our earthly realm, he awakened to see that same transcendent garland on his material body. So it seems as though there is a tangible connection between his meditation in the spiritual realm and his physical manifestation here.

Dr. Haberman: That's an interesting connection, because there are many stories that tell of practitioners of *līlā-smaraṇa*, say, cooking something in the other world and burning their finger, and when they come back into this world, they discover that their finger is in fact burnt. This may be another connection point. You see, these two sides of the tradition certainly are not disconnected, but there is a real ambiguous voice in the tradition—it's just not that clearly defined.

SR: I wonder if it's an ambiguous voice or if the tradition offers various means to attain perfection: one is in renouncing the world and just becoming absorbed in that higher reality, and another is from within this world, say for the *gṛhastha,* the householder.

Dr. Haberman: I do think it is an ascetic/householder split. That's the way it is represented institutionally in the tradition. One can see those as separate paths, but in the end, I think the split is a bit more radical than that, because I think it really determines the way you live your life. I mean, an ascetic who is sitting off in a hut with his eyes closed to the world and thinking of the divine *līlā* is living a very different life than the one who accepts whatever comes, does whatever is to be done, and strives to really see *that* as *līlā.* I think that's where the real difference comes—it's in the kind of lifestyle that is produced from whichever viewpoint one seems to hold.

SR: My only hesitancy in accepting what you are saying is that I recall certain episodes in *Caitanya-caritāmṛta* where there is one householder devotee, for example, whose name is Kūrma, I believe. He comes to Caitanya Mahāprabhu and says, "I want to leave my family, renounce everything, and just travel with you." And Mahāprabhu says, "No. Stay with your family. Chant 'Hare Kṛṣṇa.' Tell people of these teachings. That is the highest duty one can perform." It seems as though there is not a real drive toward traditional renunciation. I mean, Mahāprabhu could have said to Kūrma, "Oh, of course. You want to give up your family and become a renunciate; that is best." That's one point. Moreover, there have been highly respected householder devotees in the Gauḍīya tradition who were not ridiculed because they did not give up their householder path. So it is not a definitive split. . .

Dr. Haberman: Right, even with some of the main leaders. . .

SR: Śrīnivāsa, also; he had two wives.

Dr. Haberman: Nityānanda as well.

SR: Nityānanda. So I see what you are saying, but I don't know if I can agree one hundred percent.

Dr. Haberman: I think you are referring to elements that begin to characterize the connection between these two interests for me, and it's something that I continue to think about. Because, as I said, this whole subject has led me to an interest in pilgrimage activity in Vraja, and study of the Vana-yātrā. This sort of pilgrimage experience is not some ethereal religion by any means, but it is quite substantial—pilgrims really get down in the dirt and mud.

SR: Literally. [laughter] As when they do *daṇḍavats* around Govardhana Hill.

Dr. Haberman: That dirt and mud is considered to be non-different from Kṛṣṇa.

SR: Right.

Dr. Haberman: And particularly in Vraja. That is the special place for the tradition and Vraja, or the soil of Vraja, is a Kṛṣṇa *svarūpa*. My point is this—if indeed that is a Kṛṣṇa *svarūpa*, then there is no need to close your eyes to it.

SR: Right.

Dr. Haberman: That's what I'm saying. Maybe they are two different paths, but it seems to me they are two different paths with a slightly different philosophical bent. Any tradition that calls itself by the philosophical name *acintya bhedābheda* is really setting one up to think about ambiguities in a particular way. It is not that they are ultimately opposing notions, but rather they are opposites that define one another and in some inconceivable way are non-different from one another.

SR: Unity in diversity.

Dr. Haberman: Or difference in non-difference.

SR: Let's move on for a second and talk about your translation of *aṣṭa-kālīya-līlā*. Maybe you could explain why it is such an important if also esoteric part of the tradition.

Dr. Haberman: *Aṣṭa-kālīya-līlā.* Are you referring to the practice? Or the concept of līlā? Or the poem? Which aspect are you referring to?

SR: First, I would like to discuss it conceptually. My understanding of *aṣṭa-kālīya-līlā* is that it is *aprakriṭa līlā*—the daily pastimes of Rādhā and Kṛṣṇa in the spiritual world. The *prakriṭa-līlā,* or the *līlā* that manifests in Gokula, in this world, is like a sampling of what goes on in the spiritual world. Is that correct?

Dr. Haberman: I think we need to talk about the literature that deals with this subject. I tie the *aṣṭa-kālīya-līlā,* conceptually, to the poem written by Rūpa Gosvāmī, which is called the *Aṣṭa-kālīya-līlā-smaraṇa-maṅgala-stotram.* I've translated this work both in my book, *Acting as a Way of Salvation,* and in the text edited by Wendy Doniger O'Flaherty, called *Textual Sources for the Study of Hinduism.* To my way of thinking, that poem is the real kernel of the Gauḍīya tradition, because it is the poem in which the eight time periods—and that's what *aṣṭa-kālīya* means ("the activity which is divided up into eight time periods")—is really first expressed for the Vaiṣṇava community. And the eight time periods go through a complete twenty-four hour cycle of the events in the *līlā* of Rādhā and Kṛṣṇa.

Rūpa Gosvāmī's esoteric poem is used in the context of a meditative technique called *smaraṇa,* which is a technique whereby one systematically withdraws the senses from this world so that one can ideally have, in the culmination of this technique, a *sākṣāt-darśana,* or a direct vision of the *līlā* of Rādhā and Kṛṣṇa. And the techniques that are used are continuous with the yogic techniques of contemplation which are spelled out in Patañjali's yogic system.

SR: The different types of *smaraṇa*—I think there are five or six?

Dr. Haberman: There are five different stages . . .

SR: Leading to *samādhi.*

Dr. Haberman: Right. And these were delineated by Jīva Gosvāmī in his *Bhakti Sandharba.* Jīva was really the first one to delineate the five stages of *līlā-smaraṇa* for the tradition.

SR: Did those verses by Jīva Gosvāmī come before those written by Kavi Karṇapūra in his *Kṛṣṇāhnika Kaumudī*? They certainly came after Rūpa Gosvāmī's poem, if chronology is at all important. . .

Dr. Haberman: I don't know the answer to that. Certainly in the theory of *līlā-smaraṇa*, Rūpa's poem is the most important because it then becomes embedded in Kṛṣṇadāsa Kavirāja's *Govinda-līlāmṛta*. And that more and more becomes the text that is used in the *līlā smaraṇa* meditation. Or some more contemporary versions of it.

SR: You mean, for instance, Viśvanātha Cakravartī's *Kṛṣṇa-bhāvanāmṛta*?

Dr. Haberman: Well, that's one, but I'm thinking of Siddha Kṛṣṇadāsa's. . .

SR: It's called Kutika, or something . . .?

Dr. Haberman: It is a *guṭikā*. . .a type of literature that really lays out the *līlā*.

SR: I read somewhere that all of these *aṣṭa-kālīya-līlā* pieces are based on the *Sanat-Kumāra Saṁhitā*. Did you ever hear that?

Dr. Haberman: No, I haven't.

SR: They trace it to two things. *Padma Purāṇa* and *Sanat-Kumāra Saṁhitā*. I noticed in your book you mentioned that it is probably an interpolation—placed in the *Padma Purāṇa* at a later time, or written by the Gosvāmīs.

Dr. Haberman: Oh, I see what you're saying. You're saying that they've come from *Padma Purāṇa*. My reading of that—and this was following the cue of other Bengali scholars—is that that section of the Padma Purāṇa post-dates Rūpa Gosvāmī and is an interpolation. This conclusion is reached by studying other texts that were dated after it and looking at *ślokas* that were quoted in other texts. This conclusion is reinforced by looking at the works of Rūpa Gosvāmī and seeing that he has not quoted from that section of the *Padma Purāṇa*, which is highly unusual. If that text is so close to what Rūpa is talking about, then it seems as though, if he were aware of it, if it were in existence during his time, he certainly would have quoted from it.

SR: Let's backtrack for a moment. You mentioned a later work, a *guṭika,* that elaborated on the *aṣṭa-kālīya-līlā* theme. . .

Dr. Haberman: Yes. The one that is most popular in Vraja today for the *līlā smaraṇa* meditation is the *Gaura-Govinda Līlāmṛta Guṭika* of Siddha Kṛṣṇadāsa Bābā. He lived at Govardhana.

SR: This *aṣṭa-kālīya-līlā*—you reminded me when you mentioned the *Gaura Govinda Līlāmṛta*—also exists for the eight times of the day in the līlā of Caitanya Mahāprabhu as well.

Dr. Haberman: But that was a later development. And that is a development that has occurred outside the region of Vraja—that was in Bengal. My primary focus has been, and I think continues to be, the Gauḍīya tradition in the region of Vraja. This specifically means the literature of the Six Gosvāmīs and other figures coming out of the sixteenth century such as Nārāyaṇa Bhaṭṭa. In their literature it is Rādhā-Kṛṣṇa that is the *viṣaya,* or the subject of the meditation itself. But it's true, later, and particularly in Bengali circles, the pattern that is expressed in the *aṣṭa-kālīya-līlā* literature is then replicated in terms of the life of Caitanya. This then relates to the whole notion of the *siddha-deha,* which is one's perfected body, literally, but which can perhaps be more generally understood as a meditative body that enables one to enter into the *nitya-līlā* or the eternal *līlā.* This is a body that, for most practitioners, is a *gopī* body.

SR: A mañjarī?

Dr. Haberman: Or the mañjarī *svarūpa,* yes. In the case of the *aṣṭa-kālīya* practices associated with Caitanya, the *siddha-deha* then becomes a *brāhmaṇa* boy. So one gets into the rather difficult situation of the existence of two *siddha-dehas,* or two spiritual bodies.

SR: Right.

Dr. Haberman: That's okay if you understand that the *siddha-deha* is really nothing more than a tool to enter the *līlā,* which is one understanding of it. But there is another understanding which says that it is your true form, your essential form, your *svarūpa,* and if that is the case, I think the issue becomes very complicated indeed.

SR: It does. And, in fact, Bhaktivinoda Ṭhākura has said—possibly basing his idea on Dhyānacandra's *Arcana-paddhati*—that Gauḍīya Vaiṣṇavas generally have two spiritual forms. One is a male in Caitanya *līlā*; the other is a female in Kṛṣṇa *līlā*.

Dr. Haberman: Well, that is the way it is expressed later on in the literature coming out of Bengal. But one does not find that in the early texts of the Vṛndāvana Gosvāmīs. Nor does one find it in the works of a figure like Narottama dāsa Ṭhākura, who is a very important figure.

SR: I'd like to talk about that. It's interesting—Narottama and how he developed mañjarī *sādhana*. We should explore his contribution to this meditative technique, especially in regard to *līlā-smaraṇa*.

Dr. Haberman: He was one of the key figures involved in developing the technique. Particularly in developing the notion of mañjarī *sādhana*. He did not so much write systematic texts as he did poems. It is really in his poems that one gets a sense of mañjarī *sādhana*. I think it was he who finally developed the understanding of rāgānugā-bhakti sādhana as mañjarī *sādhana*. He was one of the key figures. I've translated some of his poems. Do you want me to read you one?

SR: Absolutely.

Dr. Haberman: I think this gets at what we're talking about: "Hari. O Hari. When shall I attain such a state? When shall I, abandoning this male body, assume the body of a female and apply sandalwood paste to the bodies of the divine couple?"

That's an example of one of his poems. Expressed here is a desire to take on the *siddha-svarūpa*, the *gopī-svarūpa*, as a means of entering into the world of the *līlā*.

SR: He gets much more specific, though, doesn't he? He gets much more specific about services he will perform. . .

Dr. Haberman: That's right. I can read another one. "Having drawn up Your top-knotted hair, when shall I bind and encircle it with fresh *guñja* seeds, string various flowers and offer them to You as a necklace, assist the *sakhīs* in dressing Your body with yellow cloth and place betel nut in Your mouth?"

One finds those kinds of poems also. The whole concept of *sevā*, in the spirit of *līlā-smaraṇa*, is very evident in the works of Narottama dāsa.

SR: And then Narottama's disciple, not direct disciple, Viśvanātha Cakravartīpāda, who considered Narottama his life and soul—he also wrote about *aṣṭa-kālīya-līlā* and *rāgānugā* forms of worship.

Dr. Haberman: That's right.

SR: So a line sort of develops there, a line of thought.

Dr. Haberman: Exactly.

SR: Cakravartīpāda gave the last major formative statement on all of this with his *Kṛṣṇa-bhāvanāmṛta*.

Dr. Haberman: Correct. In many ways I think Viśvanātha Cakravartī was the cap on the tradition. He is the one most responsible for talking about the great difference between—well, one way I expressed it in the book—the difference between the models that are appropriate for the kind of meditative work that is to be done in rāgānugā bhakti sādhana. He is the one who insisted that the practitioner is to follow in the footsteps of the *gopīs*, or other of the Vraja-loka who serve as exemplary figures, only with the *siddha-deha*.

SR: It should probably be stressed that one is to follow the *gopīs*, for example, in one's meditative body, and not in one's external appearance. . .

Dr. Haberman: Well, a controversy arose. In my book I talk about a conflict that Viśvanātha was involved in with a figure named Rūpa Kavirāja. It seems that Rūpa Kavirāja was of the opinion that imitation of the *gopīs* could be done with *this* body, or with what he called the *sādhaka-deha*, which is not exactly this body, but rather the body transformed by an esoteric initiation. Viśvanātha Cakravartī, on the other hand, insisted that the models to be imitated with the *sādhaka-deha*, understood by him simply as the physical *deha*, were to be Rūpa and Sanātana Gosvāmī, etc. Only the *siddha* or mystical body, he insisted, could be like that of the *gopīs*. So Viśvanātha really is the one who devised the notion of dual models appropriate for each of the separate bodies of the *siddha-deha* and *sādhaka-deha.*

SR: Let me see if I understand what you are saying: this was a debate with regard to *prākṛta sahajiyās,* from what I understand.

Dr. Haberman: It's been labeled that, but I don't think Rūpa Kavirāja was really a sahajiyā, because in many of these sahajiyā practices the practitioner still keeps the male body. Much of the sahajiyā philosophy has it that a male is predominantly Kṛṣṇa, a female predominantly Rādhā, and that the sexual activity of the two could be spiritually beneficial. This, of course, is totally unacceptable in conventional Gauḍīya Vaiṣṇavism.

SR: Right.

Dr. Haberman: That's not the case with Rūpa Kavirāja. For him, I think, his trouble began because many used his theories to rationalize the practices of actually dressing up this very physical body as a *gopī.*

SR: But that's a type of sahajiyāism, too, isn't it?

Dr. Haberman: I wouldn't necessarily call it that. I would reserve that term for something else. It more appropriately applies to the practices that Edward Dimock laid out in his book, *Place of the Hidden Moon,* which are different kinds of practices. And one certainly can see in Vraja today male practitioners who dress themselves up as females. This can be seen among those in the Gauḍīya tradition and in other traditions as well, like the Rādhā-Vallabhīs and some other traditions. There have been some very famous cases of practitioners who have taken on this particular *sādhana.* And one sees them today, particularly around Varṣānā at the time of Rādhāṣṭami. I think it was this particular practice that Viśvanātha Cakravartī was trying to suppress.

SR: And I think the reason that he wanted to suppress it is that he viewed it as a type of sahajiyāism, at least that's what I've heard.

Dr. Haberman: Okay, but that term doesn't really appear in the debates themselves. It's simply labeled as a type of improper action. Anyway, to relate this to our initial discussion, Viśvanātha seems to be the one who put the final orthodox cap on the understanding of *līlā-smaraṇa* meditation.

SR: I agree. But where did it go from there? It developed further, didn't it? Of course, in one sense, the tradition didn't *develop* at all. It sees itself as absolute and eternally the same, an abiding truth that may be revealed progressively but that nonetheless exists as the same reality from the beginning. That's the way the tradition sees itself.

Dr. Haberman: As an historian of religions, of course, I cannot agree with what you are saying. I see change and development.

SR: But when you say that "Viśvanātha put the cap on it," you are obviously referring to the canonical texts—that's where it stood, I guess. Or did more texts develop after that? Did the process develop in any way with particular individuals *after* the time of Viśvanātha?

Dr. Haberman: It could be due to my own lack of understanding or researching the materials between the time of Viśvanātha Cakravartī and the present day, but I don't really see significant changes in texts that are written about the particular practice of mañjarī *sādhana* after the time of Viśvanātha. One of the best texts that lays out what *līlā-smaraṇa* meditation is today, in terms of the actual theory, is a text that was written by Kuñja-bihārī dāsa Bābājī, who is a resident of Rādhā-kuṇḍa. The text that he wrote is entitled *Mañjarī Svarūpa-nirūpaṇa.*

SR: Oh, I know that text. It has been partially translated from the Bengali by my friend Jan Brzezinski.

Dr. Haberman: I don't think one could find a better example of what mañjarī *sādhana*, rāgānugā bhakti, *līlā-smaraṇa*—whatever aspect—is really like today. Again, he focuses particularly on the practice as developed in Vraja, and the most important place for the practice of *līlā-smaraṇa* meditation or mañjarī *sādhana* meditation today is indeed Rādhā-kuṇḍa. In Radha-kunda. . .

SR: Before we discuss Rādhā-kuṇḍa, I wanted to ask you something. Your article brought this to my attention—the Rādhā-kuṇḍa of this world and the Rādhā-kuṇḍa that is seen by the mystics. I think it's Narottama who describes the sacred *kuṇḍa* in such an exalted way.

Dr. Haberman: Maybe this is an unpublished paper of mine that you saw called, "Shrines of the Mind"?

SR: No. I haven't seen that. Please send it to me.

Dr. Haberman: I should do that. You're talking about the work that was published in *Bengal Vaiṣṇavism, Orientalism, Society and the Arts*. . .

SR: No. This was a short article you wrote for a little booklet that was published in England by the School of Oriental and African Studies, affiliated with the University of London. The booklet was called *Re-Discovering Braj.*

Dr. Haberman: Right!

SR: That was excellent. I really enjoyed reading that. It developed the Rādhā-kuṇḍa concept to quite a degree, and I think it was based on something written by Narottama.

Dr. Haberman: That's right. That was actually part of the "Shrines of the Mind" paper.

SR: I see.

Dr. Haberman: I do much more with it there. What I do is take a poem by Narottama dāsa Ṭhākura by the name of *Kuñja-varaṇam* and translate and comment upon it—this is a text in which he describes the Rādhā-kuṇḍa pond complex. And this gets back to the balancing act, so to speak, that I'm interested in now—the relationship between the Rādhā-kuṇḍa that Narottama dāsa Ṭhākura describes in this text, which is a fantastic world, and the Rādhā-kuṇḍa that one can reach simply by hopping on a Uttar Pradesh bus. What is the relationship between these two? My previous work was more concerned with the Rādhā-kuṇḍa that is visualized in the mind and that is reached through *līlā-smaraṇa* meditation techniques. I have since become more interested in the pond that one reaches via a UP bus, because that pond is worshipped too. And that very pond is understood to be an aspect of Rādhā and Kṛṣṇa.

SR: It's really inconceivable.

Dr. Haberman: What's that?

SR: How that physical place, that pond, is considered non-different than the spiritual world. Especially when you go there and you see the turtles and the people and how small it is—the limited dimensions of the limitless spiritual world.

Dr. Haberman: Well, all those wonderful things, like *paṇḍas* bothering you and people trying to sell you tea—that's all part of it, ultimately, it's all part of the *līlā.* I enjoy Rādhā-kuṇḍa a great deal. Rādhā-kuṇḍa is the most important site in Vraja for the Gauḍīya tradition.

SR: That's what Rūpa Gosvāmī says in his *Upadeśāmṛta.*

Dr. Haberman: That's right. Many have said it. There are fascinating stories about the Rādhā-kuṇḍa pond that begin to make it all very clear.

SR: Can you tell some of them?

Dr. Haberman: Sure. I can tell you two. Here is one about how Rādhā-kuṇḍa came to be. I can tell you the way it came to be. Of course, I write about it in more detail in the book I'm working on now, but Rādhā-kuṇḍa is the site where Kṛṣṇa killed the bull demon, Ariṣṭa. After killing the bull demon, he was planning to meet Rādhā. He found Rādhā at their meeting place, and reached out to embrace her. Although he was very eager to do so, she stopped him. She said, "Oh, no, no, no, no, no. I heard that you killed a cow today, and you have thus committed a great sin—I do not want you to touch me until you have cleansed yourself of this sin." So Kṛṣṇa asked her, "All right. What do I need to do?" She said, "You will not be clean until you bathe in all the waters of all pilgrimage sites." Now Kṛṣṇa was so eager to embrace Rādhā that he couldn't imagine leaving her for a brief moment, let alone for the years and years and years that would be required to bathe in all the pilgrimage sites. So his response was to press his heel into the ground, making an indentation in the earth, into which he summoned the water from all pilgrimage sites. That became Rādhā-kuṇḍa.

So first the pond is sacred because it is understood to contain all water from all pilgrimage sites, which is amazing enough. But beyond that, there is another story which gives a good indication of what Rādhā-kuṇḍa is for the tradition, and this goes back to the *Aṣṭa-kālīya-līlā-smaraṇa-maṅgala-stotraṁ* of Rūpa Gosvāmī. It's in this text that Rādhā-kuṇḍa is revealed as the site of the mid-day love play. Radha, who is married to another, leaves her house under the pretense of the worship of the Sun, which ironically is done for the sake of the husband, and Kṛṣṇa, on the pretext of tending cows, leaves his house, and the two meet at Rādhā-kuṇḍa pond for their mid-day love play. So the water of Rādhā-kuṇḍa is also understood to be the liquid form of the *premā* that flows back and forth between Rādhā and Kṛṣṇa.

I think both those stories combined give one an indication of what Rādhā-kuṇḍa is for Gauḍīya practitioners. In the pilgrimage groups that I've travelled with, it was certainly a very, very important site.

SR: And that it was rediscovered by Mahāprabhu himself—this is significant.

Dr. Haberman: That is the story that is told in the *Caitanya-caritāmṛta*. However, in other texts, for example in the biography of Nārāyaṇa Bhaṭṭa, it is said that he is the one who discovered the pond.

SR: Nārāyaṇa Bhaṭṭa himself?

Dr. Haberman: Yes.

SR: Well, that in itself could be the reason why his literature is not accepted, or why he is downplayed by Kavirāja Gosvāmī.

Dr. Haberman: Maybe. There are definitely diverse views and even contradictions when one starts to look at texts in this way.

SR: That's a big issue. But it underscores the importance of *paramparā*, or the particular lineage in which one learns. Questions that are difficult to answer, in an empiric sense, must be humbly placed at the feet of the *guru*, with deference to his transcendent authority.

Dr. Haberman: This is what the tradition teaches, but in any case, I think for the Gauḍīya pilgrims who go on the Vana-yātrā in the Vraja area, especially those coming from Bengal, clearly, the site of Rādhā-kuṇḍa is associated with Caitanya's discovery. And also with the figure of Raghunātha dāsa Gosvāmī, because he was one of the key figures to develop the site. In fact, the most important, sacred site, sacred building, outside of the pond itself there, is unquestionably the *samādhi* of Raghunātha dāsa Gosvāmī.

SR: Which interestingly looks like a teepee. I was surprised to see it. It's different than other *samādhis* I've seen.

Dr. Haberman: But, tying it back into the *līlā-smaraṇa* meditation and practices, Rādhā-kuṇḍa is a site that is inhabited by many *bābās* who are engaged in this practice.

SR: It seems that there's great emphasis on Rādhā's position in the Gauḍīya *sampradāya*—a sense of Rādhā *dāsyam,* even more than worship of Kṛṣṇa. That's the thing that interests me, and mañjarī *sādhana* is a big part of this. The mañjarīs are Śrī Rādhā's attendants. Not even. They are the attendants of her attendants. In mañjarī *sādhana,* of course, a mañjarī is that *gopī* who is predisposed to Rādhā. So maybe we could talk about that a little bit—Rādhā's pre-eminent position in the Gauḍīya *sampradāya.*

Dr. Haberman: As you say, devotion to Rādhā is really considered to be higher than devotion to Kṛṣṇa, especially in terms of mañjarī theology.

SR: It seems like the perfect feminist theology. That the highest aspect of the Absolute is female. . .

Dr. Haberman: Perhaps, but if I had to talk about higher feminine theology, I would probably look at some of the independent goddesses.

SR: You mean like Śākta worship.

Dr. Haberman: Right. Such as Kālī, or Durgā, because their relationship is more one of independence. And Rādhā is never separate from Kṛṣṇa. She is the *śakti* and he is the *śaktiman,* and the two are non-different. The god or goddess of the Gauḍīya tradition is not Kṛṣṇa, nor is it Rādhā, but it is really Rādhā-Kṛṣṇa. This dual theology is important for the tradition. Especially in the personality of Caitanya. So, I guess I would qualify that statement in this way.

SR: It's more of an egalitarian theology than purely feminist or patriarchal, wouldn't you say? Both are there.

Dr. Haberman: That is the relationship between Rādhā and Kṛṣṇa. It's one of give and take, especially in the way that it is expressed in the sexuality of Rādhā-Kṛṣṇa. If you look at other goddesses, such as Sītā or

Lakṣmī, they are clearly dominated by the male. If you look at some of the goddesses such as Durgā or Kālī, they dominate the male. But if you look at the relationship of Rādhā and Kṛṣṇa, especially in texts such as *Gīta-govinda,* clearly they are equal; it is a situation of give and take. One does not dominate the other, or each temporarily dominates the other. The ideal is one of dynamic equality.

In terms of my own research, in my understanding of the tradition, mañjarī *bhāva* is considered to be a more intense *bhāva* than an independent approach to Kṛṣṇa, which is an option in the early texts. That is, one could become a *gopī* who is pursuing a direct relationship with Kṛṣṇa. Or one could pursue other relationships with Kṛṣṇa. The mañjarī relationship is quite distinct, however, and is focused on Rādhā.

SR: You are referring to *sambandhānuga*—you could be a parent, a servant, or a friend. . .

Dr. Haberman: That's right. But even in the *mādhurya bhāva,* where one is following the *gopī* role in the amorous mood, it is possible to have a direct relationship with Kṛṣṇa. That, however, was judged by the tradition to be inferior to the relationship which is defined as taking the role of a mañjarī who supports Rādhā. This can best be understood in the context of the *āśraya* theory, which I think is so central to these texts—the *āśraya* is the "container" of the emotions, so to speak.

Emotional experience is dependent upon the quality of the container. Rādhā, by definition, is the deepest container. Her container is defined as being infinitely deep. If one has an independent relationship with Kṛṣṇa, then one's emotional relationship will ultimately depend on the quality of one's own vessel. But if one is a mañjarī that is in communion with Rādhā, one shares *her* emotional experience. Since her emotional experience is infinite, in this way one can tap into that infinite experience. That's why Rādhā, in the mañjarī practice, is so important.

SR: That idea is expressed in *Govinda-līlāmṛta,* no doubt.

Dr. Haberman: Very much so. Yes.

SR: The idea of the mañjarī sharing in Śrī Rādhā's ecstasy and love for Kṛṣṇa—this is in *Govinda-līlāmṛita.*

Dr. Haberman: Right. It's there in the tradition in many ways. Again,

Kuñja-bihārī dāsa's text, I think, is very good at making that clear. I've written about this also in *Acting as a Way of Salvation*. But this is going off into a realm of abstraction. I'm now more fascinated with the pilgrimage side of the tradition. This relates to a different experience, because I think the goal of the pilgrimage is to have the experience of understanding that all life is *līlā*.

In my own work, I became very intrigued with the tremendous *tapas*, the tremendous difficulty, of the pilgrimage, and its relationship to the stated goal of the pilgrimage—*ānanda*, or bliss. This created an interesting dichotomy, a type of *acintya bhedābheda* in its own right. And it is basically these two divergent experiences—austerity and bliss—about which I would ask the pilgrims. Why undertake such a grueling pilgrimage? Why do it? I would hear a variety of answers to this question, but something I would hear again and again is that they were doing it to experience *ānanda*—joy or bliss. "*Ānanda*" is a technical term for the tradition, which transcends both happiness and unhappiness, and the experience of *ānanda* has a great deal to do with perceiving all life as *līlā*.

SR: So that's interesting. Even one's illusion is, in the ultimate analysis, a type of *līlā* that is meant to bring you out of illusion.

Dr. Haberman: Succinctly stated, yes. In some sense, illusion means only that we are missing the fact that all is *līlā*. If one can see that everything is *līlā*, then. . .illusion is not a bad thing, at least according to Vaiṣṇava theology. Mother Yaśodā, after all, when she lost her illusion, was no longer able to see Kṛṣṇa as her young son and was therefore unable to love him. In the *Bhagavad-gītā*, when Arjuna lost the illusion that Kṛṣṇa was his friend, or chariot driver, he was no longer able to have a close friendship with him. But it was only after that illusion was once again placed over the two of them that they were able to return to the kind of ultimate, expansive, and loving world we know of as the world of *bhakti*.

SR: But this, of course, needs to be stated in connection with what we were saying before: that there are actually two kinds of illusion. There's the kind that brings you closer to Kṛṣṇa and the kind that separates you from him.

Dr. Haberman: How do you mean?

SR: Well, for instance, the types of illusion you just described from the

Bhāgavata Purāṇa and the *Bhagavad-gītā* are the types that bring you closer to Kṛṣṇa. We identified that as Yoga-māyā. When they were in illusion they were brought closer to Kṛṣṇa.

However, conventional illusion—the kind that forges a fast bond to a life that is divorced from a sense of the spiritual—that is another thing altogether. That is called Mahā-māyā, and that takes us away from Kṛṣṇa, and it takes us away from seeing the ultimate *līlā* in everything.

Dr. Haberman: I see what you are saying. That's right. But I'm not sure what the relationship between these two is because they are both *śāktis* of Kṛṣṇa. It could be just a difference of perspective, not really a difference in the fabric of the universe. It could be that this world we live in is spun by Yoga-māyā, if we could only see it as *līlā*. But if we can only see it through the eyes of our separate, egoistic existence, then it is a world created by Mahā-māyā.

Rādhā: Beloved of Vraja

Eric Huberman

Eric A. Huberman's Ph.D. dissertation, entitled, **Language, Love, and Silence: Readings of Separation in the Sanskrit Epic, Poetic, and Purāṇic Traditions** *is a study in* **viraha-bhakti,** *or love of God in separation. This led him to extensively research the Gauḍīya tradition, which focuses on this phenomenon. Dr. Huberman is a Mellon Fellow in the Humanities at Columbia University, where he is teaching in the Department of Middle East Languages and Cultures.*

Radha in GV

Dr. Huberman: The interesting thing about Rādhā in terms of the Caitanya tradition, the Gauḍīya *sampradāya,* is that she is the apotheosis of spiritual attainment. She is the essence of *bhāva.* I'm going to explain how this is understood. Now, in doing this, I will bring in a few apparently disjointed subjects. Bear with it, though. It's all connected.

Now, *bhāva* is the distillation of pure feelings, and in later texts, the Gauḍīya tradition gets its lineage from Caitanya, right?

SR: Yes.

Dr. Huberman: So, the question is, what was Caitanya quoting, what were his main sources?

SR: The poets.

Dr. Huberman: Correct. Caitanya's sources, interestingly enough, were the poets.

SR: Like Caṇḍīdāsa, Vidyāpati . . .

Dr. Huberman: Right, Caṇḍīdāsa, Vidyāpati, and Jayadeva. You see. Jayadeva's *Gīta-govinda*, which is a twelfth-century text, is the first text we know that really delineates in detail what has become known as the pastimes of Rādhā and Kṛṣṇa as such. Now, where Jayadeva gets his information is quite mysterious. There are speculations of a folk tradition, and it is true that the name of Rādhā, and even the stories of the milkmaids and the cowherds goes way back. One could make an argument that it goes back to the Veda. But these stories are there and found in various inscriptions. Okay.

However, as you know, the scriptural basis of the Gauḍīya tradition is the *Bhāgavata Purāṇa*, and the *Bhāgavata Purāṇa* does not mention Rādhā. Well, at least not directly. The name "Rādhā" is not in the *Bhāgavata Purāṇa*. Be that as it may, the stories of Kṛṣṇa and the *gopīs* are in the *Bhāgavata Purāṇa*, and, once again, where they come from, as far as scholars are concerned, is up for grabs. Friedhelm Hardy has made a pretty good case of tracing them to South India.

Anyway, interestingly enough, what the *Bhāgavata* does—which is unprecedented, and it is in the first three verses of the *Bhāgavata* itself—is to combine the idea of the absolute Brahman from the Upaniṣads with the idea of *rasa*, from the *Alaṅkāra śāstras*, particularly the *Nāṭya śāstra*, which establishes the canon of Sanksrit aesthetics. And basically it makes the case that the absolute truth is approached, primarily, not through mental speculation, not through *yoga*, but through aesthetic experience. And that aesthetic experience is the tasting of *rasa*. Now *rasa* originally means "liquid," and it is related to the *soma*, the intoxicating ambrosia of the Vedas.

SR: That's interesting.

Dr. Huberman: And later, *rasa* is literally defined as the "mellow," or the "flavor," of the feeling that you get when you see a play or whatever. But the *Rasa śāstras* make the case very strongly that this flavor is transcendent—it is not mundane, but is, instead, a feeling that is beyond the mundane world. It is the abstraction of a pure feeling, which takes you out of space and time, and therefore is akin to the realization of Brahman. Okay?

SR: I think I follow you.

Dr. Huberman: So when the *Bhāgavata* appears, you have a very powerful aesthetic tradition, a very strong spiritual tradition, and the basic claim that the *Bhāgavata* makes, as you well know, is *kṛṣṇas tu bhagavān svayam*—that Kṛṣṇa is in fact the source of all *rasa*, that since Kṛṣṇa is the source of everything, Kṛṣṇa is the source of all feeling.

SR: Right. This is later articulated as *akhila-rasāmṛta-mūrtiḥ*—that Kṛṣṇa is the emporium of all *rasa*. The beginning, middle, and end of all relationships.

Dr. Huberman: Exactly. And so the proper place of this, as Clifford Hospital probably told you, can be understood in terms of any Purāṇa, which has ten different categories.

SR: But he didn't mention it in relation to this. Maybe you could elaborate.

Dr. Huberman: Well, these ten different categories are conventional for any Purāṇic work. They include things like creation, the secondary creation, welfare of all living beings, and things of this nature. There are two different lists, actually. And even in the *Bhāgavata Purāṇa*, there are two different lists. But in both cases, the last of the ten Purāṇic items is *āśraya*, the utlimate resting place, which is even beyond the concept of *mukti*, or liberation.

So the *Bhāgavata* presents Kṛṣṇa as this—the ultimate resting place. The first philosophical backdrop of the Gauḍīya school, then, is the *Bhāgavata Purāṇa*, which sees itself as *nigama-kalpa-taror galitaṁ phalaṁ*—as the fully ripened fruit from the desire tree of the sacred lore, which can be seen as the Vedas or could conceivably refer to tantric *śāstras* as well. So once you have the traditional backdrop, if you will, then the ultimate step will be the *rāsa līlā*, building upon these traditional texts, including the *Alaṅkāra śāstras*. Because the *rāsa līlā* starts: *Bhagavān api tā rātrīḥ*—"even though he is Bhagavān, even though he is the Supreme Lord, despite that fact. . ." Then, *śāradotphulla-mallikāḥ*—"seeing the beautiful flowers, the blooming things of autumn, he wanted to take refuge in it," not "refuge," he "resorted" to these things. Why? Because they are the contributing factors to *rasa*, or the aesthetic mood, according to the *Alaṅkāra śāstras*. In the *Bhāgavata*, this is envisioned as his *Yoga-māyā* potency, his playful energy, which is reflected as aesthetic beauty in the phenomenal world.

So you get the concept: beyond the *Māyā*, which is generally considered part of the *śakti*, the feminine principle, right?

SR: Right.

Dr. Huberman: Beyond the *Māyā* there is a higher form of *śakti*—*Yoga-māyā*, which is God's *līlā*, his play, which is inconceivable, beyond the conceptual world. Therefore it is beyond all considerations of self and non-self. Now the *Pūrṇa Māyā*, the complete, original *śakti*, would be Rādhikā, no? And that's what I'm getting to.

SR: Okay.

Dr. Huberman: The whole *līlā* of the *rāsa*, the circular dance, is conceived of and is part of the energy of *Yoga-māyā*. It is totally spiritual.

SR: Absolutely.

Dr. Huberman: Now, within this *rāsa*, within this *līlā*, there is mention of one principal *gopī* with whom Kṛṣṇa leaves the *rāsa* dance.

anayārādhito nūnaṁ
bhagavān harir īśvaraḥ
yan no vihāya govindaḥ
prīto yām anayad rahaḥ

"Certainly this particular *gopī* has perfectly worshiped the Personality of Godhead, Govinda, since he was so pleased with her that he abandoned the rest of us and brought her to a secluded place." (S.B. 10.30.28) That's the famous verse in which Rādhā is indirectly mentioned—an oblique reference.

SR: Yes, she is identified by the commentators, like Viśvanātha Cakravartī Ṭhākura. Śridhara Swami does not mention it, because it is said that he never took that which was implicit and made it explicit; that was not his method. Oh, and Jayadeva, too, in his *Gīta-govinda*, said, *Rādhām ādhāya hṛdaye tatyāja vrāja sundariḥ*—Rādhā is the one special *gopī*, superior to all the rest.

Dr. Huberman: Now, in the context of the *Bhāgavata,* this is concurrent with the disappearance of Kṛṣṇa from the *rāsa* dance. And the words they often use there are *antar-dhā*—he disappeared, but *antar-dhā,* where did he go? *Antara*—"within." He didn't go anywhere, not really. The text tells us that Kṛṣṇa is *tatraiva*—"right there." He's always right there. For him, space and time lose meaning.

SR: Just one comment in regard to Śrī Rādhā not being specifically mentioned in the *Bhāgavata.* The Gauḍīyas have a particular perspective on this. When I asked His Holiness Nārāyaṇa Mahārāja of Mathurā, he explained that Śukadeva Gosvāmī did not utter Rādhārāṇī's name because if he had, he would have gone into trance for six months. There's a verse explaining this in the *Brahma-vaivarta Purāṇa.* Śukadeva would have become filled with *aviṣṭa citta,* deep, deep ecstasy, and he would not have been able to speak. Remember, Mahārāja Parīkṣit did not have six months—he only had seven days to live. So, to avoid this ecstatic six-month detour, Śukadeva did not mention Rādhārāṇī's name.

Sanātana Gosvāmī explains in his *Bṛhad-bhāgavatāmṛtam* that Rādhikā is Śukadeva's *iṣṭadevī,* his worshipable deity. The *Bhāgavata* repeatedly says "*śrīyā śukadeva*" when Śukadeva Gosvāmī speaks, and Gauḍīyas take this to mean, in addition to its more conventional meaning, that Śukadeva is "the parrot of Rādhā," and in this way, too, Śrī Rādhā is found throughout the *Bhāgavata.* So the Gauḍīyas see Rādhārāṇī throughout. . .

Dr. Huberman: Yes. They have an uncanny knack for bringing Rādhārāṇī in whenever possible. When you love someone, that's what you do. Rādhā is the Goddess of the Gauḍīyas, and they see her everywhere. They have a basis for it though, so there's nothing whatever wrong with it.

But let's bring in some other ideas here. Let's move on. Now, in the Eleventh Canto of the *Bhāgavata,* you get the *Uddhava Gītā.* Krsna's *upadeśa*—the instructions given first to Uddhava, then through Uddhava. Here, Kṛṣṇa basically instructs Uddhava in the pre-eminence of the *gopīs* and the pre-eminence of *bhakti.* And Uddhava, when he goes to visit the women of Vraja, he realizes the power and the reality of their love. And he prays to be born as a blade of grass at their feet.

Now I have something subjective to say here: my particular opinion is that Uddhava is one of the most important characters in the Gauḍīya tradition because he mirrors the brother, he mirrors the friend, and he ultimately mirrors the highest relationship. You get Arjuna, or, let's say, Lakṣmaṇa, in the Rāmāyaṇa. There's always this character who is like a brother or a friend, who is closer to the hero, God, than anyone else. For example, in Rāmāyaṇa, it is not really the separation from Sītā that destroys Rāma. He can live with it. But he cannot live with separation from Lakṣmaṇa. If you study it closely, it's very interesting.

Now, even in the *Bhāgavata,* the last person Kṛṣṇa separates from is Uddhava, but, at that time, he shows Uddhava the pre-eminent position of the *gopīs.* So, in a sense, he is really up there—it's a parallel relationship. Kṛṣṇa's confidante. He's a very intimate associate and, I think, quite underestimated.

SR: Well, Uddhava appeared in Caitanya-*lila* as Paramānanda Purī, who was a *sannyāsī* and greatly revered by Śrī Caitanya. In the *Caitanya-bhāgavata* it is said that Mahāprabhu was living in this world "only because of the excellent behavior of Paramānanda Purī." So there is a case that this is an extremely important personality.

Dr. Huberman: Right. He was even important in Caitanya's *līlā.* That's interesting. But, for the Gauḍīyas, especially, everything can be traced to the *Bhāgavata.* To my mind, the *Bhāgavata* is the text, through its concentration on aesthetics, that was the first to create a real fusion of aethetics and religion—which the Gosvāmīs will then build upon and develop. . .

SR: Interesting.

Dr. Huberman: And the value of beauty, and henceforth feeling love, affection, *rasa,* you know, as opposed to knowledge. Much more so than the *Bhagavad-gītā.* The *Gītā* doesn't even touch it. The *Gītā* gives you the *mārgas* and that's it. That's why, number one, the Gauḍīyas will refer primarily to the *Bhāgavata Purāṇa* and not the *Bhagavad-gītā.* All right. That's one.

So then you get Uddhava, the pre-eminence of the *gopīs.* So that's basically where the *Bhāgavata* leaves you. It also leaves you with the sense that the best way to realize the mysteries of the Absolute is to enter into the loving mood of devotion. And the *Bhāgavata* presents paradigms of that mood of devotion. This is very important. The women of Vraja, the friends, like Uddhava, or Arjuna, the queens like Satyabhāmā and Rukmiṇī—they all eventually become paradigmatic figures whom you try to emulate, in a sense, and at one point you actually kind of become overtaken by their energy as part of your *sādhana.* That is *rāgānugā-bhajan.*

You see. And the highest of these figures we come to know as Rādhārāṇī. Not that we can ever become like her, not really, but we can seek to emulate her devotion.

Okay. Now, what the *Bhāgavata* gives you is this mood of frenzied, intense love in relationship to the Godhead. That is really not part of the established tradition, not until the *Bhāgavata*. Then you get the interpreters of the *Bhāgavata*, and for the Gauḍīyas, the living embodiment of the *Bhāgavata* is Caitanya, because he is seen by the Gauḍīyas, in particular, to be, not simply an incarnation of Kṛṣṇa, but Kṛṣṇa in the mood of Rādhā, in order to taste his own sweetness, and to share the essence of that *rasa*.

So I would say, for the Gauḍīyas, even more important than the scriptural tradition, is the event and the living embodiment of Caitanya. And particularly, the behavior of Caitanya, which goes deeper than that of a generic saint. He's more than even an incarnation in that he is kind of the living embodiment of Rādhā and Kṛṣṇa. And what does he do? Particularly according to the Gauḍīyas, because the *sahajiyās* and others would read this situation differently—they tend to emphasize more the union. But the emphasis on Caitanya will be on *viraha*—separation. So Caitanya embodies Rādhā worshipping Kṛṣṇa in separation, and this is the highest achievement of *rasa*.

Now let me just back up. You get the doctrinal Rādhā excerpted from the *Bhāgavata Purāṇa* and, let's say, the *Brahma-vaivarta Purāṇa*. And also *Gīta-govinda*. Because Caitanya, as you know, does not really write much. He doesn't write anything. Eight verses are attributed to him. But the Gosvāmīs of Vṛndāvana, especially Rūpa, Sanātana and Jīva, create this theological and scriptural basis of Gauḍīya Vaiṣṇavism, using as a foundation these other texts along with *Alaṅkāra śāstras* and what they have learned from Caitanya. The doctrinal Rādhā, then, becomes, in a sense, the creation of the Gosvāmīs. Or she is *revealed by them*, shall we say. This is particularly true for Jīva because Jīva is the theologian. Rūpa is more the poet; he writes these wonderful books on the *līlā* of the . . .

SR: Like his plays, *Lalita Mādhava*.

Dr. Huberman: Exactly. But Jīva establishes the scriptural basis.

SR: I'd like to mention here another important book by Prabodhānanda Sarasvatī, a contemporary of the Gosvāmīs, that was written around the same time. The book is called *Rādhā-rasa-sudhā-nidhi*, and it is all about the pre-eminent position of Rādhārāṇī. As far as the doctrinal Rādhā, it's probably one of the more important books for the Gauḍīyas. They say it's like Rādhikā's answer to *Kṛṣṇa-karṇāmṛta* and the *Bhāgavata Purāṇa*—what those are for Kṛṣṇa, this is for Rādhā. In fact, Bhaktivinoda Ṭhākura quoted quite a bit from this work in his book called *Bhajana-rahasya*. So it's a very important book for the Gauḍīyas.

Dr. Huberman: I am not personally familiar with it.

SR: Okay.

Dr. Huberman: But, in that period, the Gosvāmīs, Prabodhānanda Sarasvatī, Kavi Karṇapūra—the theology went through several important developments. Now, among other works, Rūpa writes the *Ujjvala-nīlamaṇi*. "The Jewel," or "the Shining Jewel," which, if you did not have any background in theology, you could easily mistake for a work of erotica. It's all about the intimate pastimes, intimate *līlās* of Rādhā and Kṛṣṇa. Now, in *Ujjvala-nīlamaṇi*, he refers to Rādhā as *tantre viśiṣṭhita*, as based on the *tantras*, which is very interesting. Rūpa explains *hlādinī śakti*, or the internal blissful energy of which Rādhā is the chief embodiment, on a tantric basis, and he cites seven tantric works.

Now, there is ample evidence of contact between the tantric and Vaiṣṇava schools before or during the time of Caitanya. And Bengal, in particular, has a strong tantric tradition and strong tradition of *śāktism*, or worship of the mother. In Sanātana Gosvāmī's *Bhāgavatāmṛta*, in Gopāla Bhaṭṭa's *Hari-bhakti-vilāsa*, there are a lot of references to tantric and *āgama* works. These are very esoteric *śāstras*, and they really deal with non-Vedic ritualistic systems which often exalt the *śakti*. So this is one of the scriptural foundations. The *Hari-bhakti-vilāsa* also cites this. There is found in the *Nārada-pañcarātra* references to the *śakti* in this sense. And, as you mentioned, the *Brahma-vaivarta Purāṇa*, which is a later text.

SR: Also *Nāradīya Purāṇa, Padma Purāṇa* . . .

Dr. Huberman: *Padma Purāṇa* has the story of Kṛṣṇa and the *gopīs*, as does the *Viṣṇu Purāṇa*. You also have references in the much earlier *Sumati Ratna Kośa*. The treasury of poems, the anthology that Ingalls has translated. So, in any case, you have a very strong goddess tradition in Bengal. You have the tantric influence which exalts the *śakti*, and from this Rādhā emerges. Not that she is not there all along. But from all of these sources she begins to jump out at you.

SR: This is in Bengal, and especially in the Gauḍīya tradition. But I think you would admit that, in general, the Vedic tradition is dominated by male divinities.

Dr. Huberman: Yes, in general. The Vedic culture is a very masculine, martial culture. The *Bhagavad-gītā* is a martial text. In the *Bhagavad-gītā* Kṛṣṇa is a prince. He's depicted like this in most of the Mahābhārata, except for the Harivaṁśa, which is tacked onto the Mahābhārata, and there you get the first discussion of the childhood and whole lineage of Kṛṣṇa.

So you get running streams of stories, or tradition, *smṛti*, that kind of incarnate in the personage of Caitanya. And in his lifetime, Caitanya is seen to be an *avatāra*. The different schools interpret this in different ways. But the Gauḍīya school, based on the works of the Gosvāmīs and, most important—although even the Gosvāmīs didn't want to accept it at first—is the *Caitanya-caritāmṛta* of Kṛṣṇadāsa Kavirāja. The reason they didn't want to accept it, of course, is because it's not written in Sanskrit. It's written in Bengali. And you know the apocryphal story: when Jīva Gosvāmī saw it, he took it and threw it in the Yamunā.

SR: Yeah, where is that story from?

Dr. Huberman: I don't know exactly where it's from. And the Yamunā delivered it back, so even he couldn't deny its value. So, Kṛṣṇadāsa Kavirāja, who is related to Raghunātha dāsa Gosvāmī, and the whole lineage, you know, talks about the mysteries of Caitanya. And the deepest mystery, which relates to the basic theological tradition of the Gauḍīya school, as you know, is that Rādhā is *hlādinī śakti* and that Kṛṣṇa descends to experience her ecstasy. This is Caitanya.

SR: Maybe you can elaborate on that a little bit.

Dr. Huberman: *Hlādinī śakti* is the essence, is the feeling essence, or the bliss essence of the absolute. And where, *samvit, sandhinī,* and *hlādinī,* three types of *śakti* that are . . . It's an interesting trinity—that divine energy. One of them creates the material universe and the world of form. The other is the source of the *jīva,* the *jīva śakti,* and the other is the potency of bliss. What it's related to in the Vedic literature, actually the Upaniṣadic, is *sat, cit,* and *ānanda.* The absolute is revealed or exists in three principle modalities—being, or *sat,* knowledge, or *cit,* and *ānanda,* or bliss. In addition, *sat cit ānanda* have their mundane aspects in this world—goodness, passion, and ignorance—but they have their absolute aspects in the absolute world. And Rādhā is the embodiment of *ānanda.* She is the *hlādinī,* the *śakti,* the bliss of the absolute.

SR: The other two would be Kṛṣṇa and Balarāma? *Samvit* and *sandhinī? Sat* and *cit?*

Dr. Huberman: I don't know for certain if they are necessarily personified in the same way. And I think you might go into different systems, because you get the *catur-vyūhas* in the Pañcarātras as well as. . . .Well, you get various types of divisions and other kinds of systems.

SR: So we can go on with Rādhā as *ānanda.*

Dr. Huberman: Yes, Rādhā is *ānanda,* and *ānanda* is the giving and receiving pleasure of the *svarūpa,* or Kṛṣṇa. So Rādhā, known as the *sāra,* the essence of the *hlādinī śakti,* which is also *premā.*

SR: S-Ā-R-A, long "a." *Rāsa.* The word "*rāsa*" inverted, huh?

Dr. Huberman: Yeṣ and no.

SR: How's that?

Dr. Huberman: Because *rasa,* the aesthetic mood, is spelled with a short "a"; it's different. Whereas *rāsa*—referring to the dance—is spelled with a long "a," and this long "a" has been grammatically interpreted as the *vṛddhi,* the expansion of the former: the aesthetic mood of *rasa* becomes full-blown in the *rāsa-līlā* of Rādhā-Kṛṣṇa.

So, to go on, the *sāra* of the *hlādinī śakti* is *premā.* And then, the essence of *premā* is *bhāva.* The *bhāva* is the ecstasy, which, being part of the absolute, the *jīva* shares in. And the essence of *bhāva* is *mahā-bhāva.* And the essence of *mahā-bhāva* is Rādhā. She is the embodiment of *mahā-bhāva.*

From the Gauḍīya point of view, the highest, eternal pleasure of the *jīvanmukta,* the realized, liberated soul, is not *sambhoga,* or love in union, but it is, rather, Rādhā in *viraha,* love in separation. This brings the most hankering, the most frenzied state. This enables one to appreciate union. The pleasure derived from that superior state is called *mahā-bhāva.* Most living beings who attain this level do not attain *mahā-bhāva* proper, for that is reserved for Rādhā and the inner circle, but they do achieve a facsimile.

So the whole concept, with its higher ramifications, is based on the *Caitanya-caritāmṛta,* and also the work of the Gosvāmīs, and in particular Jīva Gosvāmī. Jīva makes the point that separation is useless when talked about without union. That if there's no oneness, separation is meaningless, and vice versa. It wouldn't be separation. Therefore he says, *acintya bhedābheda tattva*—that the truth is inconceivably and simultaneously one and different. It's one, it's non-dual, but the *hlādinī* potency, the *ānanda* potency, creates two because they want to taste the sweetness of their *līlā.* So Kṛṣṇadāsa Kavirāja says that Rādhā and Kṛṣṇa are one, but that they become two in order to taste the bliss of the *līlā.*

SR: And then they become one again in the personality of Mahāprabhu.

Dr. Huberman: [laughter] Right. Right. But let's take it to the next step—the expansions of Rādhā. The next step in the Gauḍīya understanding—and this is where I'll go back to where I started, in the sense of Kṛṣṇa, back in the *Bhagavad-gītā,* saying, *mamaivāṁśo jīva loke,* right? *jīva-bhūtaḥ sanātanaḥ.* All the *jīvas,* souls, are *aṁśas* or parts of Kṛṣṇa. Now, since Rādhā and Kṛṣṇa are one, and they became two to taste the sweetness of their *līlā,* so, Kṛṣṇadāsa says, all of Kṛṣṇa's consorts, in other words, all the *gopīs* of the *Bhāgavata,* are *aṁśas* of Rādhā. They are fragments or aspects of Rādhā.

SR: Yes, this is clearly the tradition, and what you have, essentially, is a theology that shows how Rādhā and Kṛṣṇa are ultimately everything, in a sense. The impersonalists, of course, take this a bit too far. But, nonetheless, it is true that everything and everyone is, more or less, an expansion of Rādhā and Kṛṣṇa. Nothing is outside their jurisdiction. Everything comes from them.

Dr. Huberman: I think it's important that when you are dealing with Gauḍīya Vaiṣṇavism, you have to remember that there's the popular and the esoteric level. Now, the popular level tends to emphasize Rādhā and Kṛṣṇa as people. Which is true. But, also, from the esoteric level, Rādhā and Kṛṣṇa are *everything.* There's nothing, not one atom, where Rādhā and Kṛṣṇa are not present. The point being that the essence of this understanding is not an anthropomorphic projection of personality—Rādhā and Kṛṣṇa are the deepest mystery, indwelling all other mysteries and all other aspects of reality.

SR: It includes and transcends personality.

Dr. Huberman: Yes. That's a very good way of putting it. Includes and transcends personality. It includes and transcends conceptualization, okay? And it has all the *śakti*, and all the opulence, of the absolute. Yet it's imperceptible to those whose eyes are closed.

SR: And that's *acintya bhedābheda tattva*.

Dr. Huberman: Exactly. Now, I think the unique Gauḍīya perspective is *viraha*. Again, you have to go back to the example, if you will, in the hagiography of Caitanya, who at a certain point manifests symptoms of *viraha bhāva*, separation in the mood of Rādhā—he spends the last eighteen years of his life in Jagannātha Purī agonizing over this divine pain, if you will. And this, simultaneously, is considered to be the highest ecstasy. Again *acintya bhedābheda*—an inconceivable mystery. And the way you attain this ecstasy is by surrendering to and following in the footsteps of the servants of the servants of the servants of the *aṁśas* of Rādhā by entering into the mood of the *gopīs*. That's *bhakti*. That's the Gauḍīya vision.

SR: Right.

Dr. Huberman: I think one thing that's very important, which distinguishes perhaps the Gauḍīya *saṁpradāya* from *sahajiyā sādhana* is that the Gosvāmīs laid down, particularly in the *Bhakti-rasāmṛta-sindhu*, the specific mark of *bhakti sādhana*—that you start out as *vaidhī* and then it becomes *rāgānugā*. That this mystery of becoming a spiritual woman—which is essentially what the Gauḍīya *sādhana* is: you become a *gopī*—is not to be confused with a mundane mystery. It's not that Gauḍīyas should go around in *gopī* dress.

SR: That's important. I've just discussed this with David Haberman. There was a person named Rūpa Kavirāja (not to be confused with Rūpa Gosvāmī), just after the time of the Gosvāmīs, who stated that one's *sādhaka-deha*, or one's practitioner body—the body that one has in this world—should be dressed like a *gopī* and should engage in that kind of *sādhana*. Apparently, he based this on a text from Rūpa Gosvāmī's *Bhakti-rasāmṛta-sindhu* (1.2.295), which says that both the *sādhaka-deha* and the *siddha-deha,* or the perfected meditative body, should go through the transformations of becoming a *gopī,* or a *gopa,* etc., depending upon one's natural relationship with Rādhā and Kṛṣṇa. In other words, both one's external and internal bodies should follow the style of the inhabitants of Vraja.

Anyway, this was countered by Viśvanātha Cakravartī, who said that one's meditative body may be like that of the *gopīs,* or may simulate a personality of Vraja. But the *sādhaka-deha,* or the material body, may only follow in the footsteps of the Six Gosvāmīs and other devotees of *terrestrial Vraja.* After all, they, too, were inhabitants of Vraja, and so, according to Viśvanātha Cakravartīpāda, this was the real meaning of Rūpa Gosvāmī's text. Viśvanātha pointed out that Rūpa Gosvāmī himself kept his *sādhaka-deha* in renunciant form, never dressing like a *gopī.* But the *siddha-deha,* the meditative body, that's another matter. . . .In this way, Rūpa Kavirāja was defeated.

Dr. Huberman: Yes. There was a time in India—and there are still people who do this today—when people dressed up like women as a religious observance. They are basically transvestites. They dress up as women and say that they are doing Rādhā *sādhana.* At a certain point, this was actually quite popular, and it was threatening to become the accepted *sādhana* practice until there was the council convened by Viśvanātha Cakravartī, which you alluded to. There, the dictum was laid down that the *bhāva* is experienced within. It's not in the mundane sphere. So in the mundane sphere you follow your caste and your duties and your prescribed situation, as is given in the example of the Gosvāmīs of Vṛndāvana. This *gopī bhāva* was meant to be an internal meditation, under the guidance of one's *guru.* What else can you say?

SR: I have a nice section here written by B.B. Majumdar: "To a large number of devotees, Rādhā came to occupy a far more important position than even Kṛṣṇa."

Dr. Huberman: Right.

SR: It continues: "Rūpa Goswāmin considered himself as a female attendant of Rādhā named Rūpa Mañjarī. Raghunātha dāsa Gosvāmin expresses his exclusive attachment to Rādhā in his *Vilāpa Kusumāñjali:* he waits upon her as her maidservant and helps with her bath and other intimate services. The Rādhā-Vallabha sect founded by Hit Hari-vaṁśa in the sixteenth century accords the highest place to Rādhā as well. According to the tradition recorded in the old literature of the sect, Rādhā is said to be the founder. It was she who initiated Hit Hari-vaṁśa into spiritual life."

Dr. Huberman: They say that. Yes.

SR: Right. So that's an interesting thing. Rādhā-*dāsyam*. The pre-eminent position of Rādhikā.

Dr. Huberman: Okay, that's *Mañjarī-bhāva* . . .

SR: It seems to develop from the time of Śrīnivāsa, Narottama, and Śyāmānanda—this is where Mañjarī *sādhana* becomes prevalent. Meditating on Rādhā as the ultimate . . .*āśraya*? Would that be an appropriate word for Rādhā.

Dr. Huberman: Fine, the ultimate refuge. And there are two possibilities right? The *sakhīs* and the *mañjarīs*. You have either a direct relationship with Kṛṣṇa as a *gopī*, or you become one of the attendants, the attendant of the attendants of Rādhā—the mañjarīs.

SR: This is considered the highest position. But it is not generally discussed.

Dr. Huberman: That's right. And with good reason, I might add. I don't think it is possible to talk about it. I think, quite frankly, that there is a great danger in talking about it, which is why, in the Gauḍīya tradition, you don't talk about these things in public. Caitanya, in public, merely did *saṅkīrtana*, he did *Nāma bhajan*, he preached *Bhāgavata* and *Bhagavad-gītā*. But it was only with his most intimate devotees—Svarūpa Dāmodara, Rāmānanda Rāya, and few others that he really discussed the intimate nature of the Godhead.

SR: Right. This is an important point.

Dr. Huberman: And I think it's well founded. I think it's like Kṛṣṇadāsa Kavirāja always says, "This *kāma*, or lust, is like iron; *premā*, divine love, is like gold." And the great trap on this path is to mistake one for the other. So the Gauḍīya tradition generally teaches that as long as there is a shred of *kāma*, you cannot understand what Rādhā is, or what the *gopīs* are.

Now, there are ways to entice new practitioners, and it's not that they can't hear about more advanced subjects from time to time, to whet their appetites, but it should be done under the guidance of an experienced mentor. This is what the tradition teaches. Otherwise, the disciple may have serious misconceptions and the devotional creeper, the *bhakti-latā*, as they say, may be ruined.

SR: To conquer sex, sometimes, it is said that one should hear the *rāsa līlā*. Generally, one is asked to avoid such advanced subjects until proper spiritual maturity is reached. But *rāsa līlā* has a special potency; it can give its hearers the understanding that sensual pleasure—spiritual sensuality, the religio-erotic—is meant for Kṛṣṇa alone. It is for *his* pleasure, not ours. We are only the secondary enjoyers—when we bring him pleasure, we also enjoy.

Dr. Huberman: And, in fact, for many people, including Śrīdhara, the *Bhāgavata* commentator, and on through the whole tradition, the *rāsa līlā* itself is read as the ultimate encounter between *premā* and *kāma*. . . .I don't know if anyone has discussed this. . .

SR: No, I don't think so.

Dr. Huberman: It's a very popular and important aspect of the oral tradition surrounding the *Bhāgavata*. Shrivatsa Goswami shared this tradition with me in Vṛndāvana. Kāma, cupid, the god of mundane desire, or lust, in the tradition, has vanquished every other god: Śiva, for example, burned him. Śiva got angry. But no god can withstand the power of Kāma. And Śiva was defeated.

So here, in the *rāsa līlā*, we find the "showdown" between Kāma and Kṛṣṇa. Kāma has defeated all the rest, throughout the Vedic literature, or neo-Vedic literature. Now, can he defeat Kṛṣṇa? Kāma strikes the first blow. He creates the Spring and the jasmine flowers using all his power. Now he creates desire. Then he supplies all these beautiful young women. But Kṛṣṇa doesn't like it. Kṛṣṇa tells him to go home, to take back his creation. But this is not possible: he can't go home. So Kṛṣṇa engages Kāma's creation. But the minute that they feel a tinge of pride—the mundane comes in. It's described: Just when Kāma thinks he has won, "Now I've got him. He's dancing . . ."

SR: I don't recall this in the Tenth Canto.

Dr. Huberman: Well, this is elaborated on by later traditions. Kṛṣṇa is called the destroyer of Kāma. Just when Kāma thinks he has won . . . .Why or how does he think he has won? Because when Rādhā says to Kṛṣṇa, "Carry Me. I can't go by myself," Kṛṣṇa, at first, says, "Yes." But then he leaves her hanging on a tree and disappears. So this disappearance of Kṛṣṇa shows that he cannot be influenced by any feminine wiles, or by Kāma, desire, at all.

At that point, too, there is the *viraha.* So the *viraha* is the purifying factor, and it shows Kṛṣṇa's mastery over all relationships he's involved in. When Kṛṣṇa wants to, he simply goes away. He's able to be detached. In *Gīta-govinda,* by the end, Rādhārāṇī comes out supreme, exhibiting the same detachment. And Kṛṣṇa is mad after her love. But, in any case, it's important to note that when the love is purified through *viraha,* through this mystical separation, then that is how Kāma is transformed.

Then, when Kṛṣṇa reappears, the dance commences. The dance, the *rāsa līlā* does not begin until after Kṛṣṇa comes back, because it has to be done under pure *prema,* and therefore all the esoteric mysteries of God's sexuality, which is essentially what this is, make no sense at all unless, you know, *ceto-darpaṇa-marjanaṁ*—unless the mirror of the *citta,* the subconscious, is freed from all pre-conceived notions.

SR: Right. Only through such cleansing, through spiritual practices, can one realize the culmination of Kṛṣṇa consciousness. . .

Dr. Huberman: Which was expressed quite eloquently in the dialogue with Rāmānanda Rāya. That conversation, recorded in the *Caitanya-caritāmṛta,* plays an important role in describing Rādhā for the Gauḍīya tradition as a culmination of spiritual practice—her sort of devotion is the goal, if you will. Rāmānanda Rāya, step by step, has Caitanya take him through different gradations as to what is the highest attainment in life.

SR: I recall—*Madhya-līlā.* It's my favorite section in the *Caitanya-caritāmṛta.*

Dr. Huberman: What's interesting is that nothing is rejected. Rāmānanda Rāya suggests that the ultimate goal is fulfilling one's duty. Caitanya does not reject this; he merely asks Rāmānanda to take it further. Rāmānanda then offers several other conceptions as the highest aspect of truth, including doctrines such as working for the Lord, what is known as Karma-yoga, and the cultivation of knowledge, or Jñāna-yoga. Caitanya doesn't reject anything; he just keeps asking Rāmānanda to go a little further. And in doing this he is reframing the parameters of human possibility, seeing human life through a series of gradated perspectives—easing the frog out of the well. . .

SR: [laughter] Easing the frog out of the well?!

Dr. Huberman: Yes. This is a traditional Hindu metaphor for the state of the soul in the world. It's much like Plato's cave analogy. The frog in the well cannot conceive of the vastness of the ocean; his parameters do not permit him. Rāmānanda Rāya starts out within the bounded parameters of human convention, "the well," if you will, and this is a position from which one can never conceive of the absolute nature of Kṛṣṇa's loveplay. Caitanya slowly brings Rāmānanda out of the well, through human convention, and into divine vision.

SR: In this way everything is explained.

Dr. Huberman: Ultimately, Rāmānanda comes to pure *bhakti*, and Caitanya asks him to go still further, and he comes to the different levels . . . the idea of *rasa*, and the transcendental relationships with the Lord. And he still asks him to go further, right? Almost driving him mad. And finally he mentions totally unalloyed devotion, practiced in one's original relationship with God. Then, Caitanya is satisfied, and he allows Rāmānanda the vision of seeing his form as the combination of Rādhā and Kṛṣṇa.

SR: Mahāprabhu shows that he is Rasarāja Kṛṣṇa and Mahā-bhāva Śrī Rādhā.

Dr. Huberman: You know, of course, you are correct, the word *mahā-bhāva* is used in this text. And it's said that it is a *rasa-rāja* and *mahā-bhāva*, which are words that clearly elucidate the roles of Kṛṣṇa as the king of relationships, of feeling, of taste, and Rādhārāṇī as the personification of ecstatic love of God. She is the embodiment of the love with which Kṛṣṇa experiences relationship. So she is the highest form.

SR: That's right.

Dr. Huberman: So Rādhārāṇī is the highest, because she enables Kṛṣṇa to experience his highest pleasure, and he, in turn, brings Rādhā the highest pleasure. This is the great symbiotic mystery of the Gauḍīya *saṁpradāya*, and it's constantly growing, dynamically, emerging into deeper and deeper realities. This brings something to mind: when I first went to the Rādhā-ramaṇa temple, in Vṛndāvana, I just had to ask the question that naturally comes to mind: "Where is Rādhā?"

SR: Oh, right, because the deity of Kṛṣṇa in that temple is apparently alone, without Rādhā.

Dr. Huberman: You don't see Rādhā. All you see is her *mukuṭa*, her crown. And this is one point I would make, that the worship of Rādhā and Kṛṣṇa in Vṛndāvana is, in a sense, creative; it's a creative process—it's still evolving. Or let us at least say that it's constantly unfolding. That there are devotees who will come to the temple and spontaneously sing songs never heard before about the *līlā* of Rādhā and Kṛṣṇa.

Now, at one time, at the Rādhā-ramaṇa temple, there was a saint who came around to sing just about every night—I don't remember his name. But he had the revelation that, actually, in the image of Rādhā-ramaṇa, Rādhā is completely merged into the body of Kṛṣṇa. Aside from Rādhā's crown, one can only detect her presence in the Kṛṣṇa deity, right? So, in a sense, the great mystery of Rādhā-ramaṇa, he said, was that Rādhā-ramaṇa is the opposite of Caitanya.

SR: The opposite?

Dr. Huberman: The opposite in this respect: just as Caitanya is seen as Kṛṣṇa who assumed the mood of Rādhā, this devotee sings that Rādhā-ramaṇa is Rādhā, who has assumed the body and the complexion of Kṛṣṇa.

SR: I see. Yes.

Dr. Huberman: And in Rādhā-ramaṇa the general mood is *viraha*, which, again, is that very high separation feeling of Rādhā.

SR: Do they accept that, the people of Rādhā-ramaṇa, would you say?

Dr. Huberman: Well, some certainly do. In fact my source is Shrivatsa Goswami. Whereas you go to Rādhā Vallabha temple and most of the songs are about *sambhoga*—union—the different moods. Now, Rādhā Vallabha is not a Gauḍīya temple, so the different *saṁpradāyas* will kind of focus on different moods of *bhakti*. But as one studies the tradition, the texts, and the teachings of the greatest Vaiṣṇava saints, it becomes clear that Rādhā is the highest attainment, the embodiment of love for Kṛṣṇa. She represents, no, *embodies*, the highest truth, and it's known all over Vraja. So whatever the sectarian emphasis, it has to be understood that, ultimately, Rādhā rules in Vṛndāvana.

SR: Rādhā rules . . .

Dr. Huberman: Yes, Rādhā rules in Vṛndāvana. She is the beloved of Vraja.

SR: Jaya Rādhe!

Selected Key Word Index

Abhimanyu, 55, 57
Abhinavagupta, 297
Abyssinians, 170
ācārya, 134, 150, 278, 306
acintya bhedābheda, 5, 15, 139, 222, 240, 250, 253, 254, 258, 290, 311, 324, 337, 338
Acting as a Way of Salvation, 308, 312, 324
Acyutānanda Dāsa, 274
adhiṣṭhāna, 241
Adhyatma Rāmāyaṇa, 36
Ādi-līlā, 107
Advaita Vedānta, 45, 222, 242
Advaita, 12, 255
Advaitācārya, 256
Advaitin, 72, 140, 246
Advaitins, 241, 244
Afghans, 173
Āgamas, 265, 266
Agastya, 30
Agni, 265, 269
aiśvarya, 104, 114, 116, 186
Akbar, 173, 176, 197, 204
Akrūra, 281
akṣa-mālā, 275
Akṣobhya, 132
Ālālanātha, 181
Alaṅkāra śāstras, 124, 328, 329
Allahabad, 84
Almora, 164
Āḷvārs, 71, 91, 100
Amber, 257
American, 154
Āmṛta-ratnāvalī, 147
aṁśa, 113,117
ānanda, 324, 336
Ānanda-tīrtha, 134
Ānandavardhana, 297
Ananta-saṁhitā, 10
Antya-līlā, 110, 136
Aṇu-bhāṣya, 129
anubhāvas, 298
anukaraṇa, 86
Arabic, 4, 167
Arabs, 8
Aranya-kāṇḍa. 34
Āraṇyaka, 20
Arcana-paddhati, 315
Aring, 192
Ariṣṭa, 320
Ariṣṭāsura, 202
Aristotle, 255
Āriṭagrāma, 192
Arjuna, 55, 56, 59, 182, 324, 332
Arthaveda, 21
āśraya, 323, 340
aṣṭa-kālīya-līlā, 5, 289, 305, 312, 314, 316
āṣṭakas, 110
aśvamedha, 32
Aśvatthāman, 53, 56
At Play with Krishna, 77, 79
Atharva Veda, 20,21
Ativādī, 146
Āula, 146
Aurangzeb, 174, 201
Australia, 40
avatāra, 9, 68, 113, 116, 117, 335
Ayodhyā, 38, 138, 204
Ayurveda, 21

Back to Godhead, 47
Bāl Mahārāja, 162, 163, 164
Bala-kāṇḍa, 33
Balabhadra Bhaṭṭācārya, 190
Baladeva Vidyābhūṣaṇa, 12, 67, 130, 132, 139, 150
Baladeva, 186
Balarāma, 48, 336
Bangladesh, 175
Baron, Koeth, 159
Basham, A.L., 252
bastu, 147
Baudhāyana-Śrauta-sūtra, 22
Bāula, 146
Baurī-bandhu, 217
Beck, Guy, 5, 261
Beghines, 222
Benares, 204, 257
Bengal, 4, 7, 12, 82, 150, 181, 271, 321, 334
Bengali, 2, 11, 16, 47, 67, 93, 101, 106, 111, 112, 125, 142, 157, 169, 173, 177, 280, 313
Bhadrā, 69, 308

Bhagavad-gītā, 73, 127, 128, 154, 182, 264, 324, 325, 335
Bhagavān, 68
Bhāgavata Māhātmya, 161
Bhāgavata Purāṇa, 4, 10, 61, 62, 64, 65, 66, 71, 73, 87, 90, 96, 97, 122, 279, 325, 328
Bhāgavata Sandarbha, 118, 307
Bhāgavata, 329
Bhajana-rahasya, 334
Bhaktamāla, 81, 85
Bhaktikusuma Śramaṇa Mahārāja, 157
bhakti-latā, 341
bhakti-mārga, 8
Bhakti Pradip Tirtha Swami, 11
bhakti poetry, 97
Bhakti, 4, 9, 52, 58, 89, 91, 149, 230, 236, 299, 324, 345
bhakti-rasa, 121
Bhakti-rasāmṛta-sindhu, 16, 118, 120, 123, 233, 269, 284, 299
Bhakti-ratnākara, 10, 82, 121, 130, 250, 251, 253, 278
bhakti-śāstras, 82
Bhaktisiddhānta Sarasvatī, 13, 156, 201, 250, 268, 275
Bhaktivedanta Swami, 13, 141, 159, 160, 166 (see also Prabhupāda)
Bhaktivinoda Ṭhākura, 13, 98, 149, 150, 151, 172, 271, 275, 290, 315, 334
bhanitās, 94
Bhārata, 33, 96, 296
Bharatpur, 193
Bhartṛhari, 266
bhāva, 117, 296, 299, 323, 327,
bhāvas, 96
bhāvika, 296
Bhāvollāsa-rati, 300
bhedābheda, 72
Bhīma, 56
Bhiṣma, 53, 55
Bhūgarbha Gosvāmī, 189
Bible, 49
Bihar, 204
Bilvamaṅgala Ṭhākura, 85, 90
bindu, 271
biographers, 116
biographies, 98, 111, 115, 125
Bonaventure, 223, 224
Bon Mahārāja, 158, 159, 160
Bowtell, Mrs., 159
Brahmā, 8, 53
Brahma-kuṇḍa, 194
Brahmā-Madhva-saṁpradāya, 4
Brahma-saṁhitā, 71, 182, 243
Brahma-sūtra, 66, 72, 129, 132, 267
Brahma-vaivarta Purāṇa, 202, 331
Brahma-yāmala, 10
Brahman, 240, 241, 246
Brahmaputra, 202
brāhmaṇa, 20, 21, 154, 155, 156, 216, 257
Brahmaṇyatīrtha, 133
Brahmāṇḍa Purāṇa, 274
Brajbhāṣā, 81
Bṛhad-Bhāgavatāmṛtam, 291, 331
Bṛhaspati, 53
British, 214
Brook, Peter, 53, 54, 55, 56
Brooks, Charles, 4, 149
Bryant, Ken, 91
Brzezinski, Jan, 318
Buddha, 204
Buddhism, 142, 276
Buddhist, 142, 145
Buddhists, 276

C

Caitanya Cariter Upādān, 11
Caitanya līlā, 104
Caitanya Mahāprabhu, 13, 14, 17, 25, 101, 129, 134, 136, 137, 140, 141, 167, 168, 200, 233, 251,
Caitanya, 4, 8, 11, 12, 13, 14, 115, 117, 142, 149, 177, 179, 201, 204, 220, 230, 232, 280, 288, 322, 327
Caitanya-bhāgavata, 10, 101, 104, 106, 109, 114
Caitanya-candrāmṛta, 111
Caitanya-candrodaya-nāṭaka, 101, 105, 146, 298
Caitanya-carita Mahākāvya, 101
Caitanya-caritāmṛta, 10, 11, 14, 35, 48, 102, 105, 107, 112, 136, 152, 176, 180, 196, 251, 307, 310, 321, 335, 337, 342
Caitanya-maṅgala, 10, 103, 104, 105
Caitanya-tattva-pradīpa, 112
Caitanya-vilāsa, 10
Caitanyaite Vaiṣṇavism, 127
Caitanyaite, 7, 9, 12, 113, 118, 231, 250
Calcutta, 286
Caṇḍāluni, 217
Caṇḍī, 171
Caṇḍīdāsa, 90, 93, 172, 328
Cand Kazi, 174
Candrāvalī, 87
Carney, Gerald, 5, 295
Caryāpadas, 145
caste, 155
cāturmāsya, 185
cauliflower, 216
Ceylon, 40
chanda, 264
Chāndogya Upaniṣad, 23, 265
Chatterjee, A.N., 3, 7
Chaṇḍa, 21
China, 253
Christian, 139, 170, 214, 224, 230, 242
Christianity, 5, 219, 225, 230
Christians, 42, 216
coccyx, 41
Columbia University, 4, 5
Confucius, 253
Cotran, John C., 243
Cūḍa Dhārī, 146
Cūḍāmaṇi dāsa, 111

D

Dabīr Khāsa, 177
Dakṣiṇa-Tantra, 143
Dark Night of the Soul, 223
dāru-brahman, 210
Dasgupta, Surendranatha, 132
Davis, Richard, 4, 89
Dayānidhi, 132
Daśāvatāra, 91
De, S.K., 119, 131, 249, 250, 299
Deadwyler, William, 4, 127
Debnarayan Acharyya, 11
Delhi, 168
Delmonico, Neal, 121, 297
devadāsīs, 207, 212, 213
Dhanurveda, 21
Dhṛtarāṣṭra, 23
Dhruva, 64
dhvani, 262
Dhyānacandra, 315

Dibakāra Datta, 13
digvijaya, 183
Dimock, Jr., Edward C., 6, 101, 144, 146, 272, 280
disciplic succession, 137
Discovering Braj, 319
divine madness, 286
divyonmāda, 287
Diwali, 39
doha, 142
Dori Bazaar Road, 190
drama, 296, 299, 303
dramatic theory, 296, 299
Draupadī, 55, 56
Droṇa, 53
dualistic, 144
Durgā, 185, 322, 323
Duryodhana, 50, 55, 58
Dvādaśāditya-tilā, 196
Dvaita, 15
Dvārakā, 80, 138, 200, 213

E. Burnouf. 61
Eaton, Richard, 4, 167
eggplant, 216
eggs, 216
Eidlitz, Walther, 160
ekādaśī, 303
Elkman, Stuart, 129, 135
Emerson, 158
England, 159
English, 154, 157
Entwistle, Alan, 4, 189
Eschmann, Anncharlott, 215
Ethiopians, 170
Evans, Robert, 109

Father Camille Bulcke, 46
Fifth Veda, 52
fish, 216
Fox, Matthew, 242
France, 141
Franciscans, 224
French, 141, 154, 266
Freud, 200
Fruitful Journeys, 186

Gajapati, 114, 211, 215, 216
Gandharvaveda, 21
Gandhi, 14
Ganges, 31, 292
Gaṅgādāsa Paṇḍita, 102
garlic, 216
Garuḍa, 208
Gaura Kiśora dāsa Bābājī, 292
Gaura-candrikā, 86, 280
Gaura-carita-cintāmaṇī, 111
Gaura-gaṇoddeśa-dīpikā, 106, 108, 124, 130, 131, 211
Gaura-Govinda Lilāmṛta, 314
Gaura-līlāmṛta, 111
Gauragaṇa-svarūpa-tattva-candrikā, 130
Gaurāṅga-vijāya, 111
Gaurī, 205
Gautam, M.K., 4
Gautam, Mohan, 199
Gautamīya Tantra, 271
Gauḍīya Darśana, 268
Gauḍīya Maṭha, 13, 107, 151, 158, 160, 274
Gauḍīya Saṁpradāya, 130, 139, 205
Gauḍīya Vaiṣṇava, 4, 12, 94, 101, 116, 125, 138, 140, 142, 166, 246
Gauḍīya Vaiṣṇavism, 1, 4, 5, 13, 118, 317
Gauḍīya, 3, 4, 5, 8, 9, 10, 27, 36, 48, 49, 57, 62, 70, 84, 121
Gayā, 115, 204
gāyatrī, 264
Gaṇḍakī, 202
German, 154
Germany, 215, 222
Gerow, Edwin, 297
Gītā, 4, 14, 54, 58, 80, 245
Gīta-govinda, 90, 92, 94, 208, 323, 328, 330
God, 239
Godāvarī River, 181, 202
Goddess, 185
Gokarṇa, 191
Gokula, 195
Gold, Anne, 186
Goldman, Robert, 43
Goloka, 137
Gopāla Bhaṭṭa Gosvāmī, 25
Gopāla Tāpanī Upaniṣad, 273
Gopāla, 194
Gopāla-guru, 130
gopī, 58
gopīs, 10, 63, 74, 86, 90, 182, 200, 273, 281, 316, 332, 334, 337, 339
Goswami, Shrivatsa, 5, 77, 161, 249, 341, 344
Govardhana, 201
Govinda dāsa, 10, 17, 96, 109
Govinda Dāser Kaḍacā, 17
Govinda Singh, 37
Govinda, 58, 107, 109, 273
Govinda-bhāṣya, 130, 151
Govinda-līlāmṛta, 16, 121, 289, 313, 323
Govindadāsa, 176
Govindadeva, 196
gṛhastha, 310
guru, 236, 253, 289
guṭikā, 313, 314
Guṇarāja Khān, 172
Guṇḍicā, 213

Haberman, David, 5, 121, 235, 297, 305, 338
Hanumān, 29, 30, 35, 36, 39
Hardy, Friedhelm, 181, 328
Hari, 271
Hari-bhakti-vilāsa, 119, 272, 334
Haridāsa Ṭhākura, 277
Haridāsa, 14
Haridāsī, 277
Harivaṁśa, 58, 90, 96, 335
Harmonist, 139
Harris, Stella, 159
Hartshorne, Charles, 255
Harvard University, 3
Hawley, Jack, 90
Hawley, John Stratton, 4, 77
Hein, Norvin, 2, 77
Hiltebeitel, Alf, 4, 49
Himālayas, 142
Hindi, 81
Hindu, 7, 45, 80, 114, 204, 261, 276, 343
Hinduism Today, 34
Hinduism, 3, 5, 7, 8, 9, 157, 207, 214, 219, 266
Hindus, 13
Hit Harivaṁśa, 278
Holī, 303
Holtzmann, Adolf, 50
Holy Mother, 99
Hopkins, Edward W., 51
Hospital, Clifford, 4, 61, 329
Huberman, Eric, 5, 327
humanistic, 144
Husain Shah, 168, 171, 177

Ibrahim Sur, 174
Ilyas Shahi, 168
Imitation of Christ, The, 222
impersonalism, 242
India, 8, 67, 150, 158
Indra, 173, 265
Indradyumna, 209
Indus River, 7
International Society for Krishna Consciousness, 1, 4, 13, 150, 206, 259
Inversion View, 50
Islam, 170
Islamic Society and Culture, 173
Īśvara Purī, 133
Īśvāra dāsa, 10
Itihāsa, 23

Jagannātha Purī, 5, 338
Jagannātha, 5, 14, 151, 173, 185, 207, 216, 217
Jāhnavā-devī, 12, 82, 309
Jaipur, 174
Jaiva Dharma, 158, 290
Jalal al-Din Muhammad, 169
Janmabhūmi, 190
japa, 15, 180, 275, 276
Jarāsandha, 172
jāti, 155
Jayadeva Gosvāmī, 90, 172
Jayākhya-Saṁhitā, 275
Jayānanda, 10, 101, 103, 173
Jayatīrtha, 132
Jesus, 42, 220, 221, 226
Jews, 216
Jhārakhaṅda, 190
Jīva Gosvāmī, 9, 12, 67, 81, 82, 118, 205, 223, 240, 255, 267, 269, 307, 312, 313, 335, 337
jñāna-kāṇḍa, 8
Jñānasindhu, 132
Judaeo-Christian, 203, 220
Juergensmeyer, Mark, 82, 90
Jyotiṣa, 21

Kabīr, 98, 201
Kālī Santāraṇa Upaniṣad, 274
Kālī, 99, 205, 322, 323
Kali-yuga, 53, 57, 63, 75
Kalpa, 21
Kāma, 341
kāma, 301, 340
kāma-bīja, 272
Kapila, 64
Kapoor, O.B.L., 5, 11, 129, 135, 166, 239
Karma-kāṇḍa, 8
Kartā Bhajās, 146
kartālas, 154
Karṇānanda, 250
Katz, Ruth, 51
Kaurava, 50, 55
Kāverī, 202
Kavi Karṇapūra, 10, 11, 101, 105, 108, 118, 124, 125, 129, 131, 132, 134, 146, 211, 298
kāyastha, 155, 257
Kāzī, 114
Kaṭha Upaniṣad, 244
Kaṁsa, 80, 190, 200
Kaḍacā, 107, 108, 109, 110
Kennedy, Melville, 226
Keśava Bhāratī, 156, 281
Keśava, 191
Kheturīgrām, 155
kholes, 175
King Pratāparudra, 181
Kinsley, David, 4, 179
Kīrtana, 53, 152, 275, 276, 281, 303
Kiṣkindhā, 28
Kiṣkindhā-kāṇḍa, 35
Klostermaier, Klaus, 5, 219
Kṛṣṇa līlā, 4
Kṛṣṇa, 4, 5, 8, 14, 48, 51, 54, 57, 58, 68, 70, 78, 79, 83, 92, 95, 97, 100, 113, 115, 117, 120, 121, 136
Kṛṣṇa-bhāvanāmṛta, 121, 313, 316
Kṛṣṇadāsa Kavirāja, 11, 14, 101, 102, 105, 109, 116, 147, 182, 306, 335
Kṛṣṇāhnika-kaumudī, 121, 313
Kṛṣṇa-karṇāmṛta, 71, 90, 182, 334
Kṛṣṇa-rati, 300
Kṛṣṇa-yāmala, 10
Kulke, Hermann, 174, 215
Kumbhakarna, 44
Kuñja-bihārī dāsa Bābājī, 318
Kuñja-varaṇam, 319
Kūrma Purāṇa, 36
Kūrma, 181, 310
Kurukṣetra, 54, 182
Kusuma Sarovara, 193
kuṇḍalinī, 144, 292
Kuśa, 32

Lakṣmānasena, 145
Lakṣmaṇa, 31, 32, 33
Lakṣmī, 128, 186, 213, 323
Lakṣmīpati Tīrtha, 133
Lala Babu, 205
Lalitā, 87, 209
Lalita-mādhava, 121, 333
Laṅkā, 28, 35
Lava, 32
left-handed Tantrics, 143
leper, 181
līlā smaraṇa, 289, 291, 306, 309, 315, 317, 318, 319, 322
līlā, 62, 68, 73, 75, 78, 306, 307, 308, 310, 320, 324, 325
līlāvatāras, 117
Locana dāsa, 103
logic, 255
Lokanātha, 189
Lucknow, 163
Lutgendorf, Phil, 46

Madame Guyon, 223
Madana-Mohana, 196
Mādhava, 132
Mādhavendra Purī, 133, 134, 135, 136, 137, 194
Mādhavī-devī, 208
madhura-rasa, 86, 301
mādhurya, 70, 104, 113, 114, 116, 135, 186, 225
mādhurya-bhāva, 17, 118, 323
mādhurya-rasa, 16, 95, 138, 144, 198
Madhusūdhana, 95
Madhva, 8, 15, 118, 255, 270
Mādhva, 23, 132, 134, 135
Madhvācārya, 15, 220
Mādhvācārya, 129, 131, 135, 137
Madhya-līlā, 107, 342
madness, 287
Mahābhārata, 4, 10, 22, 37, 49, 51, 52, 59, 79, 200, 264
mahābhāva, 207, 284, 285, 302, 336, 343
Mahākāvya 105
mahā-mantra, 48, 271, 274
Mahā-māyā, 69, 308, 325
Mahānidhi, 132

Mahāprabhu, 10, 14, 15, 35, 90, 97, 103, 116, 117, 139
Mahārāja Parīkṣit, 57, 331
Mahā-rāsa, 87
Maharashtra, 24
mahāvākya, 67
Mahāyāna, 143
Maheśvara, 8
Majumdar, B.B., 11, 109, 130, 339
Mālādhara Vasu, 172
Man Siṅgh, 197
Mānasā, 171
mānasa-seva, 309
Mānasi-gaṅga, 194
mañjarī sādhana, 115
mañjarī, 123, 289, 290, 315, 318, 323, 340
Mañjarī-svarūpa-nirūpaṇa, 318
Mansel, Henry L., 246
mantra, 20, 48, 263, 264, 266, 270
mantra-patha, 24
Manu, 183
manvantarāvatāras, 117
Mao, 253
Maṅgala Mahārāja, 274
Maṅgala-kāvya, 171
Marglin, Frédérique, 5, 207
Mary Magdalene, 226
Mathurā, 80, 136, 166, 189, 200, 281, 331
māyā, 70, 307, 330
Māyā-Sītā, 36
Māyāpura, 167
māyāvāda, 183
Māyāvādī, 134
Māyāvādīs, 138
McDaniel, June, 5, 283
meat, 216
Mecca, 170
Medina, 170
Meister Eckhart, 222, 242
Mephistopheles, 223
Midnapura, 176
Miller, Barbara Stoler, 54
Mīmāṁsā, 183, 267, 268
Minhaj al-Din, 167
Mīrābāī, 81, 82, 90, 227
Miracle Plays of Mathurā, 77
Mishra, Purna Chandra, 216
Mithilā, 171
mleccha, 176
Moghuls, 114
mokṣa, 214, 297, 299
Mongols, 170
monistic, 144
Moses, 225
Mother Teresa, 13
Mother Yaśodā, 324
Mount Govardhana, 69, 193, 307
mṛdaṅgas, 154
Mughals, 176, 204
Muhammad Ghuri, 168
Mukerjee, Radhakamal, 97
Mukherjee, Prabhat, 131, 208
Mukundadeva, 173
mukuṭa, 344
Murāri Gupta, 10, 11, 35, 101, 102
Muslim, 4, 13, 14, 114, 173, 175, 177, 182, 194, 201
Muslims, 167, 169
Muṇḍaka Upaniṣad, 10
mysticism, 283
myth, 43

Nābhājī, 81
nāda, 265, 266, 271
nāda-sphoṭa, 268
Nadīyā, 167
nāgara saṅkīrtana, 115
Nāgārjuna, 242
Nāma-kirtana, 280
Nammāḷvār, 92, 98, 100
Nanak, 201
Nandagrāma, 194
Nārada Pañcarātra, 269
Nārada, 56, 193, 298
Nāradī, 193
Narahari Cakravartī, 111, 130, 278
Naraka-kuṇḍa, 201
Nārāyaṇa Bhaṭṭa, 197, 306, 314, 321
Nārāyaṇa Mahārāja, 166, 331
Nārāyaṇa, 74, 135
Narottama dāsa Ṭhākura, 12, 122, 279, 315, 319
Narottama, 12, 82, 98
Narottama-vilāsa, 250
Nāthjī, 194
Nava-nyāya, 171
Navadvīpa, 11, 107, 115, 167, 274, 281
Navadvīpa-dhāma-māhātmya, 172
Nāṭya-śāstra, 296, 328
Nectar of Devotion, 299
Nīla Mādhava, 209
Nimbārka, 220
Nimbārkācārya, 255
Nirukta, 21
nirviśeṣa, 240
Nityānanda Vaṁśa, 112
Nityānanda, 12, 13, 82, 104, 109, 134, 155, 256, 310
Nixon, Ronald, 163
Norway, 142
Nṛhari, 132
Nṛsiṁha, 114, 175

Objectivity, 252
Obscure Religious Cults, 143
O'Connell, Joseph T., 5, 146, 173, 229
O'Flaherty, Wendy, 305, 312
onion, 216
Orchha (Mahārāja of), 191
Orissa, 7, 12, 114, 131, 134
Oriya Vaiṣṇavism, 208

Padas, 111
Padāvalī, 232
Padāvalī-kīrtana, 86, 280
Padma Purāṇa, 128, 129, 161, 313
Padmanābha, 132
Pāgal Haranāth, 292
Pāla Dynasty, 145
Pañcarātra, 27, 269, 336
parakiyā, 144, 302
Paramānanda Purī, 332
Paramānanda Sena, 102
paramparā, 127, 128, 321
parikramā, 303
Parīkṣit, 65
Paris, 142
Pārvatī, 271
Patañjali, 183, 312
Patita-pāvana, 217
Paul, 170
Pāṇḍavas, 50
Persian, 4, 7, 167
personalism, 242, 244
Philokalia, 224
pilgrimage, 110
Place of the Hidden Moon, The, 6,

146, 317
Plato, 343
poetry, 89, 95
poets, 327
Pondicherry, 266
Portuguese, 109
Prabhupāda 1, 11, 45, 47, 62, 81, 97, 122, 135, 137, 154, 201, 206, 258, 274 (see also Bhaktivedanta Swami)
Prabodhānanda Sarasvatī, 10, 25, 111, 156, 256, 333
Prahlāda, 64
Prajāpati, 265
prajñā, 145
Prakaśānanda Sarasvatī, 205
Prakṛt, 22
Prākṛta-Sahajiyā, 146
Prameya-ratnāvali, 130
Prārthanā, 123
prasādam distribution, 13
Pratāparudradeva, 211
premā, 146, 301, 302, 321, 336, 340
Prema-vilāsa, 82, 250
Premānanda, 87,88
Purāṇas, 10, 67
Purī, 124, 151, 173, 180, 207, 214, 309
Purushottama Goswami, 78
Puruṣottama, 133
Puṣṭi-mārga, 129

Rādhā, 5, 16, 17, 82, 86, 93, 95, 123, 144, 145, 197, 200, 234, 271, 272, 284, 288, 300, 317, 320, 323, 327, 330, 334, 337, 344, 345
Rādhā-bhāva, 117
Rādhā-Dāmodara, 196
Rādhā-Gopīnātha, 196
Rādhā-kuṇḍa, 4, 192, 200, 201, 202, 206, 318, 319, 320, 322
Rādhā-Kṛṣṇa, 271, 281, 322
Rādhā-ramaṇa, 78, 162, 163, 165, 344
Rādhā-rasa-sudhā-nidhi, 333
Rādhā-Vallabha, 344
Radhakrishnan, 66, 67
Rādhārāṇī, 17, 136
Rādhāṣṭami, 317
Rādhāvallabha, 277
Radio City Music Hall, 32
rāgānugā bhakti, 16, 121, 136
rāgānugā, 143, 233, 234, 235, 236, 288, 303, 305, 307, 315, 316, 332, 338
rāgātmikā, 234
Raghavan, V., 37, 38
Raghunandana, 171
Raghunātha Bhaṭṭa Gosvāmī, 257
Raghunātha Bhaṭṭa, 119
Raghunātha dāsa Gosvāmī, 201, 321, 335
Raghunātha Dāsa, 11, 107, 108
Rāja Gaṇeśa, 169
Rājendra, 133
Rajshahi, 168
Rakṣasas, 41
Rāma kathā, 34
Rāma Pāda-Yātrā, 42
Rāma, 28, 29, 30, 32, 36, 42, 48
Rāma-carita-mānasa, 27, 45, 46, 47
Rāma-rāja, 28
Rāmacandra, 48
Ramakien, 37
Ramakrishna, 221
Rāmānanda Rāya, 14, 107, 146, 180, 181, 208, 256, 301, 340, 342, 343
Rāmānuja, 8, 15, 23, 24, 66, 71, 72, 221
Rāmānujācārya, 219
Ramanujan, A.K., 46
Rāmaprasāda Sen, 99, 100
Rāmāyaṇa, 4, 27, 28, 32, 33, 37, 38, 41, 44, 47, 65
Rāmnāvmi, 39
Rāmopākhyāna, 37
Ranchi University, 204
rāsa līlā, 80, 85, 86, 88, 186, 205, 213, 299, 329, 330, 341
Rasa, 5, 16, 96
rasa, 225, 226, 227, 295, 296, 297, 298, 300, 302, 303, 328, 329, 336, 343
rāsa, 336
rāsa-dhārīs, 88
rasa-kāvya, 137
rāsa-maṇḍala, 186
Rasarāja, 343
rasas, 59
rasika, 296
Rasikānanda, 12
Ratha-yātrā, 5, 208, 212, 214
Raval, 197
Rāvaṇa, 30, 40, 185
Ravenna, 40
Ravidāsa, 83
Reynolds, Frank, 46
Ṛg Veda, 20, 22, 263
Richmond, Paula, 46
rickshaw, 205
Rodanī, 103
Roman Catholics, 275
Romeo and Juliet, 296
Rudra, 56, 128
Rukmiṇī, 332
Rukn al-Din Barbak Shah, 172
Rūpa Gosvāmī, 16, 70, 81, 94, 118, 205, 226, 233, 269, 295, 297, 298, 301, 312, 320
Rūpa Kavirāja, 316, 317, 338
Rūpa Mañjarī, 123, 339
Russell, Bertrand, 255
Russian, 154

Śabaras, 209
Śabda brahman, 262
Sadānanda, 160
sādhaka-deha, 316, 338, 339
sādhana, 152, 229, 230, 231, 233, 288, 315, 332
sādhus, 156
sahaja, 147
Sahajayāna, 145
Sahajiyā, 4, 107, 142, 147, 235, 236, 317
Sahajiyāism, 143
Sahajiyās, 151
sahṛdaya, 297
Sāī Bābā, 221
Sailley, Robert, 4, 141
Sain, 146
Śaiva, 91
Śaivism, 207, 220
Śaivites, 9, 143
Sākara Mālik, 177
Sakhī Bekhī, 146
Śākta, 4, 185, 208, 215, 322
Śāktas, 143
śākti, 271
Śāktism, 152
Sāma Veda, 20
sambhoga, 17, 95, 285, 336
Sambidananda, 11
Saṁhitā, 20

Sāṁkhya, 64, 183
saṁpradāya, 9, 84, 88, 127, 140
Sanat-Kumāra Saṁhitā, 313
Sanātana Gosvāmī, 14, 196, 205
sanātana dharma, 8
Sāṇḍīlya Saṁhitā, 273
Śaṅkara, 15, 66, 156, 221, 222, 276,
Śaṅkarācārya, 183, 255, 267
Śaṅkara Digvijaya, 183
Śaṅkarites 140
saṅkīrtana, 53, 152, 232, 233, 261
Sannyal, 11
sannyāsa, 137, 156, 179
sannyāsīs, 134
Saptagrāma, 13
Sarvabhauma Bhaṭṭācārya, 179
Sanskrit, 2, 12, 16, 19, 22, 25, 43, 49, 62, 64, 80, 81, 95, 101, 106, 194, 262, 279
Śantipura, 309
Śatrughna, 33
Ṣat-sandarbha, 118
sāttvika bhāvas, 287, 288
Satya-yuga, 63, 113
Satyabāmā, 332
Sātyaki, 56
Satyarāja Khān, 172
saviśeṣa, 243
Schulze, Mr., 160
Sen, R.S. Dineshchandra, 47
Sen, Sukumar, 111
Śeṣaśāyī, 195
sex, 143, 144
Shams al-Din Muzaffar Shah, 171
Sharma, B.N.K., 132, 133, 135, 139
Sherbow, Paul, 268
Siddha Kṛṣṇadāsa Bābā, 314
siddha-deha, 122, 309, 314, 316, 339
siddhi, 144, 229
Siegel, Lee, 296
Śikhi Māhiti, 208
Śikṣa, 21
Singer, Milton, 204
Sītā, 29, 30, 32
Sītā-Rāma, 138, 271
Śiva, 8, 56, 220, 271, 276, 341
Śiva-kāñcī, 185
Six Gosvāmīs, 10, 12, 96, 105, 111, 119, 139, 149, 150, 186, 233, 256
smaraṇa, 312
smārta brāhmaṇas, 175
Smith, H. Daniel, 4,27
smṛti, 22, 23, 120, 335
Songs of the Saints of India, 90
sonic theology, 261
Sorbonne, 3,4
South India, 4, 11, 12, 109
Soviet Union, 160
sphoṭa, 265, 266, 267, 269, 274
sphoṭa-vāda, 270
Sphoṭa-vāda-vicara, 268
Śrī Caitanya Mahāprabhu, 3
Śrī Caitanya Prema Saṅsthāna, 5, 78
Śrī Caitanya, 10, 150, 207, 240, 250, 255
Śrī Kṛṣṇa Caitanya-caritāmṛta, 101
Śrī Kṛṣṇa Prema, 163, 164
Śrī Laṅkā, 40
Śrī Maṇḍira, 212, 213
Śrī Raṅgam, 185
Śrī Saṁpradāya, 128, 138
Śrī Vaiṣṇava, 219
Śrī Vaiṣṇavas, 24, 68
Śrīdhara Svāmī, 140
Śrīmad Bhāgavatam, 10, 57, 61, 150, 152
Śrīmatī Rādhārāṇī, 5, 16
Śrīnivāsa, 12, 82, 98, 309, 310
Śrīpāda Bābā, 165
Śrīvāsa, 298
śruti, 21
St. Dominic, 275
St. Francis, 181
St. John of the Cross, 227
St. John, 223
St. Teresa, 223
Stavāvalī, 110
Stewart, Tony K., 4, 101, 146
sthāyi-bhāvas, 300
stotras, 110
Subhadrā, 69, 186, 213, 308
subjectivity, 252
Śubhānanda dāsa, 259
Subodhinī, 129
Subuddhi Miśra, 103
Sufis, 143
Śukadeva Gosvāmī, 65, 331
Sukthankar, V.S., 51
Sultan Barbak Shah, 204
Sultan Sulaiman Karrani, 173
Sumati Ratna Kośa, 334
Sumatra, 40
Sūra-sāgara, 84, 85
Sūradāsa, 63, 78, 81, 83, 85, 90, 96, 98, 100
Sūta Gosvāmī, 279
sūtra, 106
svakīyā, 302
Svarūpa Dāmodara, 10, 107, 108, 118, 125, 208, 256, 340
Svayambhū, 191
Śvetāśvatara Upaniṣad, 10
Śyāma-kuṇḍa, 202
Śyāmānanda, 12, 82, 98
Sylhet, 175

Ṭabaqāt-i Nāṣirī, 167
tabula rasa, 244
Tagore, 98
Taittirīya Upaniṣad, 295
Taittirīya, 24
tantras, 10
Tantric, 142, 145, 334
Tāpana Miśra, 257
taste, 296, 303
Tattva Sandarbha, 267
Tattvavādī, 131
Teresa of Avila, 227
Thomas Aquinas, 223, 224
Thoreau, 158
Tibetan Buddhism, 141
tomatoes, 216
transpersonal, 239
Tretā-yuga, 75
Trinity, 225
Tripathi, Gaya Charan, 215
tulasī, 165
Tulasīdāsa, 27, 36, 39, 45
Turks, 167, 168, 177
turushka, 177

Uddhāraṇa Datta, 13
Uddhava, 76, 331, 332
Uddhava-gītā, 76, 331
Ugrasena, 200
Ujjvala-nīlamaṇi, 16, 118, 123, 233, 284, 334
University of Chicago, 204
University of Minnesota, 243
Upadeśāmṛta, 205, 320
Upaniṣad, 20, 231

Upaniṣads, 8, 23, 26
Upavedas, 21
upāya, 145
Uttar Vṛndāvana, 164
Uttara, 57
Uttara-kāṇḍa, 28, 29
Uttarādi Maṭha, 132

Vaidhī bhakti 121, 136
vaidhi, 143, 234
Vaikhānasa, 24, 25, 26
Vaikuṇṭha, 137, 138
Vaiṣṇava poets, 97
Vaiṣṇava, 4, 5, 8, 10, 13, 15, 23, 25, 52, 63, 113, 128
Vaiṣṇava-Sahajiyā, 144
Vaiṣṇavī, 82
Vaiṣṇavism, 5, 7, 8, 9, 12, 22, 23, 24, 99, 152, 181, 219, 268, 271
Vajrayāna, 142
Vāk, 263
Vakreśvara Paṇḍita, 130
Vallabha, 84, 87, 88, 128, 129, 194, 281
Vallabhācārya, 220, 278
Vallabhites, 83
Valmīki, 27, 28, 30, 31, 32, 33, 43, 47
Vāma-Tantra, 143
van Buitenen, J.A.B., 71
vana-yātrā, 303, 311, 321
Varāha Purāṇa, 202
Varāha-yuga, 63
Varṣānā, 194, 197, 306, 317
varṇa, 155, 262
Varṇāśrama, 14
Vāsudeva Vipra, 181
Vāsudeva, 74
Vaṁśi dāsa, 111
Veda, 20, 21, 24, 26
Vedānta Sūtra, 65, 139, 150
Vedānta, 45
Vedāṅgas, 21
Vedas, 8, 19, 22, 154, 263
Vedic, 3, 7, 8, 9, 10, 15, 19, 23, 24, 26, 231, 261, 279
via negativa, 242
via positiva, 242
Vidagdha-mādhava, 121
vidhi-bhakti, 16
Vidyādhirāja, 132
Vidyānidhi, 132
Vidyāpati, 90, 94, 172, 209, 328
Vijayakṛṣṇa Gosvāmī, 285, 292
Vikra, 220
Vikrāsura, 220
Vilāpa-kusumāñjali, 339
Vimalā, 213
Vincennes, 142
Vinodvāṇī Dāsī, 159, 160
Vipina-vihārī Gosvāmī, 152
vipralambha, 17, 285
Vīrabhadra, 12, 155
viraha, 95, 336, 342
Viraha-bhakti, 71, 223, 287
Viṣṇu dāsa, 109
Viṣṇu Purāṇa, 61, 63, 75
Viṣṇu Purī, 135
Viṣṇu Svāmī, 220
Viṣṇu, 8, 23, 24, 25, 48, 53, 64, 68, 72
Viṣṇu-sahasra-nāma, 48
Viṣṇupriyā, 159
Viṣṇusvāmī, 128, 129
Viśākhā, 182
viśeṣa, 241
viśiṣṭādvaita, 15
Viśrāma-ghāṭa, 190
Viśvakarmā, 210
Viśvanātha Cakravartī, 12, 107, 130, 313, 316, 317, 330
Viśvarūpa, 179
Viśvāvasu, 209
Viṭṭalnātha, 194
Vivarta-vilāsa, 147
Vopadeva, 70, 71
Vraja Academy, 203
Vraja Mohana dāsa, 112
Vraja, 2, 4, 16, 78, 85, 86, 93, 166, 180, 189, 192, 199, 200, 234, 281, 299, 306, 307, 311, 314, 332
Vraja-bhakti-vilāsa, 197
Vrindavan Research Institute, 203
Vṛndāvana dāsa, 10, 109
Vṛndāvana, 5, 11, 73, 78, 79, 80, 81, 88, 91, 104, 120, 124
vyākaraṇa, 21, 124
Vyāsa, 56, 65, 104, 255
Vyāsa-rāja Maṭha, 132
Vyāsadeva, 35, 36
Vyāsatīrtha, 133
vyavahāra, 252
Vyeṅkaṭa Bhaṭṭa, 139, 185

Walt Disney, 34
Westernization, 151
Whitehead, Alfred North, 255
Wilson, H.H., 61
Witzel, Michael, 3, 19
Wonder That Was India, The, 252
Wulff, Donna, 78, 80, 235
Wurlitzer, 32

Yadu, 92
Yajur Veda, 20, 24
Yajus, 20
Yale University, 3, 4
Yamunā, 78, 84, 183, 202, 307, 335
Yashoda Mai, 164
Yavana Haridāsa, 211
yavana, 176
Yoga-māyā, 69, 308, 325, 329
yoginis, 145
Young, Katherine, 2
Yuddha-kāṇḍa, 28, 29, 44
Yudhiṣṭhira, 55
Yugāvatāra, 113, 117

Zamindars, 175
Zukav, Gary, 242